Xcelsius® 2008 Dashboard Best Practices

Loren Abdulezer

800 East 96th Street
Indianapolis, Indiana 46240

Business Objects
an SAP® company
Press

XCELSIUS® 2008 DASHBOARD BEST PRACTICES

ISBN-13: 978-0-672-32995-1
ISBN-10: 0-672-32995-6

Library of Congress Cataloging-in-Publication Data

Abdulezer, Loren.
  Xcelsius 2008 dashboard best practices / Loren Abdulezer.
    p. cm.
  ISBN 978-0-672-32995-1
  1. Xcelsius (Computer file) 2. Dashboards (Management information systems)
3. Business—Computer programs. I. Title.
  HD30.213.A23 2009
  005.5'8—dc22

                              2008046377

Printed in the United States of America

Fourth Printing July2009

Trademarks

All terms mentioned in this book that are known to be trademarks or service marks have been appropriately capitalized. Sams Publishing cannot attest to the accuracy of this information. Use of a term in this book should not be regarded as affecting the validity of any trademark or service mark.

Warning and Disclaimer

Every effort has been made to make this book as complete and as accurate as possible, but no warranty or fitness is implied. The information provided is on an "as is" basis. The author and the publisher shall have neither liability nor responsibility to any person or entity with respect to any loss or damages arising from the information contained in this book.

Bulk Sales

Sams Publishing offers excellent discounts on this book when ordered in quantity for bulk purchases or special sales. For more information, please contact

U.S. Corporate and Government Sales

1-800-382-3419

corpsales@pearsontechgroup.com

For sales outside of the U.S., please contact

International Sales

international@pearson.com

CONTENTS

III   Advanced Features

FOREWORD

Have you ever experienced how data can change the world? How compelling presentations can get CEOs out of their seats? How a business dashboard can turn a regular business manager into an invaluable hero to a company? Or how a tool that simplifies data and makes information informative, useful, and actually fun can transform a career?

I have. It happened for me a couple years ago. My team at Business Objects was looking for a way to present a new business opportunity with key metrics, business drivers, and trends to our CEO. We had about an hour to present everything and help make a key business decision.

We had a lot of slides and spreadsheets and the usual information you'd expect. But then we summarized the entire business opportunity and how we wanted to look at the opportunity into a single dashboard. We combined all the key data that we were using to look at the business decision. Within a few hours, we turned mountains of tabular, virtually incomprehensible data into a powerful business tool. And we added the key element that every CEO wants: the power of "what-if." What if sales didn't meet expectations? What if we couldn't meet our cost-cutting objectives? And more importantly, what if it really worked!

As we were presenting, our CEO jumped out of his chair and started to "drive" the dashboard: He put his own experience and assumptions to the model. What we showed was that it was actually a bad idea to make the investment that many were asking for. The numbers didn't add up. By not making the decision, we saved the company potentially millions of dollars, countless resources, and a lot of churn trying to make something work that just didn't make sense to us or the CEO.

On the bright side, by taking advantage of the power of Xcelsius to build the dashboard, my team gained broad recognition for providing something that was simple enough, compelling enough, and actually fun enough to change the course of the business, and in the process, our careers. Having the right skills to build a business dashboard without overwhelming the audience made all the difference.

Sure, we could have shown some data in a spreadsheet, but the only reason CEOs get out of their chairs to look at a spreadsheet is because the font is too small to read. Put that data into Xcelsius and you will quickly change the way you see and monitor your business and completely change the decision-making experience.

Our challenge to you, the reader, is to go beyond the creation of a simple chart or graphic you've built in a presentation or spreadsheet tool to a real business dashboard that can have a major impact on your most important business aspects. Model your business. See how decisions impact the environment. See how pricing, promotions, and marketing impact consumer behavior. Liven up your dashboards by connecting your dashboard to real-time, live data from within your company or any web service to get up-to-the-second monitoring. Use your business data anywhere, and take your proposal from the shop floor all the way to the board room.

In my experience, the key elements that you need to effectively build business dashboards that will make a difference include the following:

- Designing a spreadsheet that clearly identifies the inputs and results for use by the dashboard. Of course, let the spreadsheet do the hard work of crunching the complex calculations!

- Mapping visual components on the dashboard to drive the inputs on the spreadsheet. You have a wealth of components to choose from—everything from sliders to dials and list boxes, and then some. You can also manage their properties so that they are truly interactive.

- Adding visual components to display spreadsheet results. Again, you have a wealth of components to choose from. Every dial, gauge, chart, map, and table can be imbued with complex properties and alerts.

- Building dashboard interactivity and managing visibility of the various components so that your dashboard keeps toe to toe with its embedded spreadsheet.

Loren's book shows how to take advantage of these features in Xcelsius 2008 to build astounding dashboards. Make sure you take some time to learn some best practices laid out in this book. Try out the samples to get you started. And make sure you share your great work with others.

Every day we see more great dashboards that are changing the world, one dashboard at a time. And remember, just as a good dashboard can improve you and your company's performance, bad data, poor layout, excessive use of unnecessary bells and whistles, and irrelevant data and information can have the opposite effect.

Good luck. Have fun. And don't be surprised when you get a welcome, yet unexpected, reaction when you share your dashboards. Done right, you've truly never seen a spreadsheet do this before!

James Thomas

Vice President, Product Management

Business Objects, an SAP company

PREFACE

A broad and growing community of professionals regularly prepares or needs to prepare dashboards and interactive visualizations and reports. Like many of those other professionals, I have used Excel to create useful reports and dashboards. The problem is that unless I incorporated extensive amounts of one-off code, Excel lacked some essential features that I was looking for:

- The ability to design a dashboard interface by dragging and dropping components on a canvas

- The ability to map visual components to a "live" spreadsheet built using my Excel models

- The ability to deploy simple, self-contained dashboards that are suited for visual data analysis by ordinary users

Those capabilities existed in Xcelsius 3.0. Two product generations later, Xcelsius 2008 has undergone a metamorphosis; Xcelsius now includes a well-honed and highly integrated spreadsheet and dashboard design environment, significantly greater spreadsheet functionality, more visual components and interface options, a revamped and expanded framework for data connectivity, and the ability to create entirely new custom-designed components on equal footing with built-in components.

This is great stuff. It sounds like everybody ought to be using Xcelsius 2008, for anything and everything. But Xcelsius 2008 isn't intended to be a jack-of-all-trades. First and foremost, Xcelsius 2008 is a serious tool for building interactive dashboards and intelligent visualizations. The secret to its power is how it is joined at the hip with spreadsheets.

Xcelsius 2008 is remarkably easy to use. From a dashboard layout perspective, everything is point and click. You don't need much in the way of spreadsheet prowess to start doing interesting and useful things with Xcelsius. This quick bang for the buck is like kindling wood in a furnace: It's enough to get a flame started, but it won't heat up the room. To get a roaring and self-sustaining fire, you need to take things to the next level.

So what is stopping you from building better dashboards? The biggest challenge holding most people back is lack of time. If you are busy worrying about monitoring and meeting production quotas, or allocating budgets among competing projects, you are probably not going to spend a lot of time improving on a dashboard design once you get it working. Maybe for an occasional dashboard, that's smart thinking. If your dashboard serves you well, you will no doubt use it to do more things. Who knows? Maybe you need to enable weekly or daily analysis in addition to monthly analysis.

Say that you want to add a second product line, monitored by a dashboard. You start with your already working dashboard design as your template and add more features. As you keep cloning, you are stepping up your maintenance responsibilities and possibly bloating your dashboard. At some point not far down the road, the dashboard capabilities plateau. It is not nearly agile enough to keep up with changing requirements or expectations. This is where best practices come into play. I know that time is premium for you. It is for every-one. To save you valuable time, I have worked out a wealth of best practices and techniques so that you don't need to reinvent the wheel.

In this book, I do a few other things:

- Introduce you to the features you need to know. I get you started with setting up your Xcelsius workspace. I introduce you to essential components and show you how to use them. I help you build up your spreadsheet skills in an Xcelsius-centric way.

- Show you how to use the new and important features of Xcelsius 2008 so that you can quickly transition to this newer technology.

- Cover the essential components you will regularly be using in dashboards, from charts to dials, gauges, sliders, and maps. I cover the standard features such as drill down and alerts.

- Show how to turbo-charge the various dashboard components so that they do things you wouldn't ordinarily expect. For instance, you'll learn how to use a single dial on a dashboard to set the values of dozens or hundreds of variables.

- Show how to design simple and effective dashboard interfaces. When these need to be scaled up to do complex things, the designs don't change, and they don't break down.

- Describe how the preparation and processing of data, including techniques for validat-ing and structuring of data, play a central role in dashboard best practices.

- Devote whole chapters to constructing spreadsheet formulas embedded in dashboards, statistical analysis, financial analysis, and working with less–than-optimal data.

- Show how to utilize features of Xcelsius 2008 for remote data connectivity, such as XML maps and Web Services.

- Explain how to construct custom components.

The undercurrent that runs through this book is empowerment. Every step of the way, I show how you can work smarter by using best practices.

Loren Abdulezer

December 2008

About the Author

Loren Abdulezer is CEO and president of Evolving Technologies Corporation, a New York–based technology consulting firm that specializes in visual data analysis. He has a long-standing record in the Xcelsius community and has been a staunch proponent of the technology since its early days.

Loren is the editor-in-chief of *Xcelsius Journal* (www.XcelsiusJournal.com), an online magazine dedicated to users in the Xcelsius user community. Loren also started the website Xcelsius Best Practices (www.XcelsiusBestPractices.com).

Loren is the author of *Excel Best Practices for Business* and *Escape from Excel Hell*. He served as the technical editor of *Crystal Xcelsius For Dummies*. He can be reached at dashboards@evolvingtech.com.

Dedication

To my wife, Susan, for inspiring me to achieve and exceed my expectations.

ACKNOWLEDGMENTS

In writing this book, I've been afforded extraordinary access to many talented people at Business Objects and early access to Xcelsius 2008 as it evolved. From the outset, Saskia Battersby and John McNaughton clearly perceived the need for an Xcelsius-centric book on dashboard best practices. They were tireless in opening up doors and making extensive resources available. You would not be reading this book were it not for their involvement. Andy Brathwaite and Matt Lloyd played a critical role in opening up key technical aspects of Xcelsius. They, too, saw the value in this book and worked closely with me to address all sorts of Xcelsius technical issues. They went above and beyond the call of duty. Their involvement helped me to produce a far better book.

Those of you who know me know that *Xcelsius 2008 Dashboard Best Practices* is a book of personal significance to me. The writing of a book on best practices can hardly be undertaken in a vacuum. In writing this book, I have drawn heavily on my discussions and interactions with countless individuals and companies, and I wish to acknowledge the benefits I have received, both direct and indirect.

Mike Alexander, a colleague whom I have had the good fortune of working closely with, has played an important role on this book and on *Xcelsius Journal*.

I also wish to thank the following individuals (in alphabetical order by first name): Andrew Bentnick, Ashton Holt, Bill Good, Blair Wheadon, Caryn Brannen, Charles Sampankanpanich, Chris McMahon, Chuck Vietrogoski, Claire Maytum, Connie Sevillo, Danny Ficetola, David Harper, David Lopez, Denise Baker, Dennis Blasius, Gerrit Neve, Howard Dammond, Jim Shields, John Picard, Jon Teopaco, Kalyan Verma, Katy Zarty, Kirk Cunningham, Mico Yuk, Nick Tenzing, Nicko Martadinata, Paul Clark, Philip Campbell, Ryan Goodman, Sean Bolte, Steve Newberg, Takin Babaei, and Yvonne Jones.

The team from Business Objects Press is an exceptional group to work with. I am grateful to my acquisitions and project editor, Michelle Newcomb, for doing an extraordinary job of shepherding this book from its inception. Todd Brakke, my development editor, and Kitty Wilson, my copy editor, have helped to turn my text into an enjoyable read. Betsy Harris, my project editor, added the finishing touches and turned this into a polished book. Javier Jimenez is a superb technical editor; his probing questions and feedback helped to keep my subject matter in sharp focus.

WE WANT TO HEAR FROM YOU!

As the reader of this book, *you* are our most important critic and commentator. We value your opinion and want to know what we're doing right, what we could do better, what areas you'd like to see us publish in, and any other words of wisdom you're willing to pass our way.

You can email or write me directly to let me know what you did or didn't like about this book—as well as what we can do to make our books stronger.

Please note that I cannot help you with technical problems related to the topic of this book, and that due to the high volume of mail I receive, I might not be able to reply to every message.

When you write, please be sure to include this book's title and author as well as your name and phone or email address. I will carefully review your comments and share them with the author and editors who worked on the book.

E-mail: feedback@samspublishing.com

Mail: Greg Wiegand
Associate Publisher
Sams Publishing
800 East 96th Street
Indianapolis, IN 46240 USA

READER SERVICES

Visit our website and register this book at informit.com/register for convenient access to any updates, downloads, or errata that might be available for this book.

INTRODUCTION

In this introduction

One of the first things that caught my attention about Xcelsius is that it is fundamentally a paradigm-shifting technology. Xcelsius intentionally blurs the distinction between spreadsheets and presentation-layer dashboards.

Back in 2005, when the product first started getting traction, it was ahead of its time. Most of all, Xcelsius needed to catch up to its own revolutionary ideas. Back then, the spreadsheet portion and the canvas lived in parallel but disjointed universes. They could be tethered by statically linking component properties to fixed cell coordinates. This was a great proof of concept and prototype but wasn't always practical.

From time to time, spreadsheet models do need to get updated. With early versions of Xcelsius, if you inserted or deleted a row or column, it sometimes completely derailed the Xcelsius component-to-spreadsheet-cell mapping. At the cost of increased spreadsheet design complexity, I developed a solution to this problem. This opened the floodgates so that I could redesign imported spreadsheets with impunity and not have to worry about upsetting the mapping between components and spreadsheets. In effect, it gave me a three-year head start in developing effective techniques and best practices that are applicable to Xcelsius 2008.

Xcelsius 2008 supports some new spreadsheet functions. One of them is an amazing and often-overlooked function called OFFSET. In earlier versions of Xcelsius, you could use INDEX to redirect data from any column or row of your choosing and pipe it into a chart or other visual component in your dashboards—a technique I call *context switching*. Thanks to OFFSET, this functionality can now be truly turbocharged using Xcelsius 2008.

Over the years I developed a wealth of techniques and best practices so that the data and computational side of the Xcelsius dashboards could be on par with the stunning visualizations so often associated with Xcelsius.

As Xcelsius 2008 moved past the drawing board, I reworked and substantially extended those techniques for the new Xcelsius. I often found myself more on the bleeding edge than cutting edge of this new technology.

After Service Pack 1 for Xcelsius 2008 solidified, the techniques, methodologies, and approaches to dashboard design with Xcelsius 2008 all fell into place rather naturally.

Xcelsius 2008 as a product and technology has caught up with its revolutionary ideas and is ready for primetime. That is half the battle. The task ahead of you is to use Xcelsius 2008 to catapult your dashboards and visualizations beyond toy demonstrations.

Using Xcelsius is easy when you understand the ins and outs of building and designing dashboards.

The first lesson you are going to learn in this book is that if you really want your Xcelsius dashboard to shine, you have to take responsibility for managing the data that feeds into your visualizations. This means you have to control the data, juggle it with formulas, and do what is necessary so that it is on rock-solid footing by the time it appears visually.

Why is all this really necessary? Dashboards are interactive, and Xcelsius dashboards perform live computations. The data in a dashboard is generally not static and is subject to ongoing updates and revisions. To complicate matters, the drivers and inputs in visualizations are subject to the whims of your dashboard users.

There are things you can do to keep your dashboards out of hot water. For example, say that you have three companies vying for market share—your company and two competitors. You know that 100% of the market share will never be exceeded. How can you build a dashboard to assess your competitive positioning, assign market share, and never have to worry about overallocating percentages? Best practices provide a structured methodology for dealing with issues of this kind and for taking what might be inefficient or unmanageable and keeping the process sane and contained.

NOTE

> You can find a dashboard of this kind in Chapter 2, "Showcase of Xcelsius 2008 Dashboards," and its implementation is covered in Chapter 12, "Smart Data and Alerts."

GETTING WHAT YOU NEED FROM THIS BOOK

My goal in this book is to help you quickly learn specific techniques and practices, provide information in a sensible order, and help you understand some practical matters about working with examples and your own files.

LOCATING SPECIFIC TECHNIQUES QUICKLY

 This book covers a broad range of topics in 16 chapters. The chapters are chock full of valuable techniques, tips, and strategies. The chapters are organized by subject matter rather than by best practice. To help you locate best practices, I've cataloged more than 100 best practice techniques and tips in Appendix C, "Xcelsius Best Practice Techniques and Hip Pocket Tips," which lists topics and where to find them in the book. To help you locate the details within the chapters, a best practices icon appears in the margin next to each best practice.

NOTE

> You can find the dashboard files that accompany this book on www.XcelsiusBestPractices. com.

HOW TO READ THIS BOOK

This book will be valuable to you whether you are new to Xcelsius or already have some experience under your belt. You may want to approach the text differently, depending on your familiarity with creating dashboards and using Xcelsius.

For New Xcelsius Users

If you are entirely new to Xcelsius, first skim Chapter 2, which quickly introduces you to various kinds of Xcelsius dashboards. Then read through Chapter 1, "Motivation for Using Xcelsius 2008," so that you have an idea of how your spreadsheets and dashboards work together in Xcelsius. Move on to Chapter 3, "Getting Familiar with Xcelsius 2008," to get a foundation for working with Xcelsius. Think of Chapter 3 as your first day of on-the-job training.

If you want, you can skim through Chapter 4, "Embedded Spreadsheets: The Secret Sauce of Xcelsius 2008," but you may be better off immediately jumping to Chapters 5, "Using Charts and Graphs to Represent Data," and 6, "Single Value Components: Dials, Gauges, Speedometers, and the Like." Don't worry about the details; concentrate on the basics. Now you can jump to pretty much any other chapter in the book. As you need, refer to Chapter 4 when the spreadsheet stuff gets too heady.

For Veteran Dashboard Designers with Prior Xcelsius Experience

If you are a veteran user of Crystal Xcelsius, you can initially concentrate on Chapter 3 to set up your Xcelsius 2008 environment. The Xcelsius 2008 workspace may take some getting used to, but you will definitely find the tight Xcelsius/Excel integration to be liberating.

Then spend some time reading through Chapter 4 but don't worry about reading it from beginning to end. Instead, pick a spreadsheet topic of interest to you—the text functions or date and time functions, for example. Read through that section thoroughly to learn how to set up and use those functions in a dashboard setting.

Make sure you go through Chapters 5 and 6, which describe valuable dashboard designs and constructions. They may give you ideas on how to redesign some of your own. From there on, feel free to read any of the chapters in any order you please.

Accessing Legacy Xcelsius Files

Xcelsius 2008 can read and convert Crystal Xcelsius files (that is, Xcelsius version 4.5). If you have files built with Xcelsius 4.0 or earlier, you will first need to open them by using Crystal Xcelsius and save them as Xcelsius 4.5 files. Then you may be able to open them by using Xcelsius 2008.

The process of converting legacy files to Xcelsius 2008 may not be so easy. Instead of trying to retrofit a legacy Xcelsius file, you may be better off building a new dashboard from scratch, using the best practices described in this book.

Best Practices Versus Shortcuts

Some quick solutions to vexing problems cut corners and work, and some are hacks. For example, the common practice of overlaying charts one on top of another can work and can be effective, and with the previous versions of Xcelsius, it may have been the only way to do certain things. I do not view such strategies as best practices, so I generally steer away from talking about practices of this kind. However, I do make some exceptions, discussing such techniques and explicitly citing them as not being best practices but being practical short-cuts. For example, Chapter 14, "Other Dashboard Techniques and Practices," discusses a filled radar chart with alerts. I point out in the chapter that this is not a best practice. I also list this as an item in Appendix C.

In summary, while I try to keep the discussions pure and focused on best practices, I balance this with practical techniques.

WHAT THIS BOOK COVERS

The purpose of Part I, "Xcelsius 2008 Fundamentals," is to color your impressions about Xcelsius 2008 and Xcelsius dashboards and lay a foundation for how to approach the use of Xcelsius 2008.

Chapter 1, "Motivation for Using Xcelsius 2008," gives you a backdrop for Xcelsius and spreadsheets and reveals how the two are heavily intertwined.

Chapter 2, "Showcase of Xcelsius 2008 Dashboards," is like a wine tasting party. You'll get a sampling of different kinds of dashboards and have a chance to think about what's important for you and what might be interesting to pursue when you start building dashboards. In this chapter, I point out where you can find more about specific dashboards or dashboard features. Additionally, I summarize the new and revised features introduced with Xcelsius 2008.

Chapter 3, "Getting Familiar with Xcelsius 2008," helps you set up your Xcelsius workspace so you can quickly begin to build rudimentary dashboards. It also sets the stage for building full-featured dashboards. It's important that you think clearly about using the features of the Designer environment and tapping into the unique dashboard capabilities for which Xcelsius is known.

The powerhouse behind Xcelsius is the underlying spreadsheet. If you want to do really powerful and astounding things with Xcelsius, you need to know how to use spreadsheet formulas and functions. Chapter 4, "Embedded Spreadsheets: The Secret Sauce of Xcelsius 2008," is a skill-building chapter that works from the ground up on how to construct spreadsheet formulas in Xcelsius. This chapter is a comprehensive reference guide that covers essential spreadsheet functions, replete with examples and pragmatic constructions, and identifies some important differences between Excel functions and their handling within Xcelsius.

Chapter 5, "Using Charts and Graphs to Represent Data," introduces you to charting components and how to use them. You'll learn about the major kinds of charts and how to work with them; you'll end up with a better understanding of practical matters such as chart scaling. You'll learn about some new kinds of components introduced in Xcelsius 2008, such as Tree Map components. I also show some techniques for handling known charting problems, such as displaying negative values in bubble charts.

Chapter 6, "Single Value Components: Dials, Gauges, Speedometers, and the Like," provides information on sliders, dials, and gauges. In this chapter, I cover Xcelsius themes to show how you can alter the appearance of your dashboards. A common criticism of dashboard dials and gauges is that they consume large swaths of screen space. I show a technique that allows you to share a single component, such as a dial, with a virtually limitless number of dashboard variables.

Part II, "Xcelsius 2008 Best Practices and Techniques," is a comprehensive guide to Xcelsius components and best practice techniques.

When you discover that you can pack a lot of punch in your dashboards with the wide array of components, you'll find your visualizations becoming quickly crowded. Chapter 7, "Using Multi-Layer Visibility in Your Dashboards and Visualizations," shows you how to avoid needless complexity by using best practice techniques for managing visibility.

Chapter 8, "Managing Interactivity," gives you more control in managing interactivity. You'll learn about putting to use drill down features and interacting with various kinds of interfaces.

Chapter 9, "Xcelsius and Statistics," is an Xcelsius-centric foray into statistics and statistical analysis. This chapter shows how to meaningfully integrate statistical techniques with Xcelsius. For example, histograms are commonplace, but is it commonplace to have a histogram where you can use a slider to set the boundaries between categories appearing in the histogram?

Chapter 10, "Financial Analysis," shows how you can use the power of an underlying spreadsheet to build dashboards for converting between accrual and cash accounting, Value at Risk dashboards, and ratio analysis.

Chapter 11, "Maps in Xcelsius," shows you best practices on using Xcelsius Map components for traditional and nontraditional applications, including augmented maps, colorized maps, multi-selection maps, international maps, and connected maps.

Chapter 12, "Smart Data and Alerts," shows you how to utilize alerts in Xcelsius and how to create smart data.

Chapter 13, "Working with Less-Than-Optimal Data," shows practical spreadsheet techniques for detecting the presence of transposed digits, dealing with raw and unclean data, working with rounding and truncation errors, fixing faulty formulas, and dealing with scaling issues.

Chapter 14, "Other Dashboard Techniques and Practices," addresses a variety of dashboard design solutions, including filled radar charts with alerts and avoiding occlusion with area charts. This chapter introduces a dashboard technique I call an "ABC" chart that flows two data sources into a combined chart. This chapter also addresses an interesting technique involving box plots.

Part III, "Advanced Features," introduces advanced features of Xcelsius 2008.

Chapter 15, "XML and Data Connectivity," explains how the Xcelsius Data Manager unifies data connectivity and outlines basic techniques for defining data connections and managing data refreshing. These principles are illustrated with XML Map components and Web Services.

Chapter 16, "Creating Custom Components for Fun and Profit," opens the door to doing something with Xcelsius not previously possible—constructing custom components. In this chapter, I spell out the essential setup needed for designing custom components, outline the workflow involved in building components, illustrate how to build a component, and outline important and expanded next steps.

This book includes three helpful appendixes.

Appendix A, "Supported Spreadsheet Functions in Xcelsius 2008," outlines the full range of Excel spreadsheet functions that are supported in Xcelsius 2008. This complements Chapter 4.

Appendix B, "Xcelsius Product Family Comparison," outlines the differences among the various editions of Xcelsius 2008: Xcelsius Present, Engage, Engage Server, and Enterprise. This appendix describes each edition's general features, built-in assistance, font support, data connectivity support, export and snapshot options, themes and styles, and back-end server support. I also run through a comprehensive list of component types, organized by Chart components, Contain components, Single Value components, Selector components, Map components, Art & Background components, Text components, Web Connectivity components, and Other components (such as the Interactive Calendar, Trend Analyzer, and other miscellaneous components).

Appendix C, "Xcelsius Best Practice Techniques and Hip Pocket Tips," is a guide that helps you immediately locate specific best practice techniques. It identifies valuable techniques and where to find each in the book.

CONVENTIONS USED IN THIS BOOK

This book uses several special elements:

TIP

> Tips provide advice or describe a different way of accomplishing a task.

NOTE

> Notes present extra information about a topic.

CAUTION

> Cautions pull out critical information about fixing or avoiding problems.

Code-continuation arrows are used when a line of code won't fit on one printed line. The code is wrapped to the next line and the continuation is preceded with a code-continuation arrow, like this:

```
-(B7*(EXP(B8*C12*(-1)))*(NORMDIST(((LN(B6/B7))+((B8+(B13*B13/2))*C12))/(B13
➥*(SQRT(C12)))-(B13*SQRT(C12)),0,1,TRUE)))
```

Xcelsius 2008 Fundamentals

MOTIVATION FOR USING XCELSIUS 2008

In this chapter

and the one immediately below it. For instance, the value 4 in cell B8 is computed using this spreadsheet formula:

=C8-C9

or this:

=30-26

Figure 1.1
Histogram chart in a typical spreadsheet.

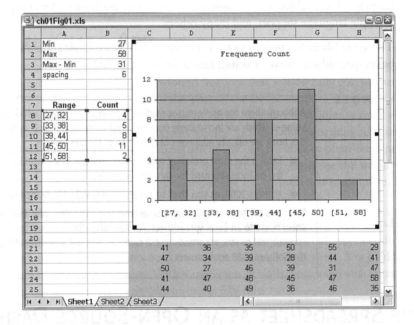

Figure 1.2
Hidden computations needed for the histogram in Figure 1.1.

	A	B	C	D	E	F	G	H
1	Min	27						
2	Max	58						
3	Max - Min	31						
4	spacing	6						
5								
6			Cumulative					
7	Range	Count	Count	from value				
8	[27, 32]	4	30	26				
9	[33, 38]	5	26	32				
10	[39, 44]	8	21	38				
11	[45, 50]	11	13	44				
12	[51, 58]	2	2	50				
13								
14								
15								
16								
17								
18								
19								
20								
21			41	36	35	50	55	29
22			47	34	39	28	44	41
23			50	27	46	39	31	47
24			41	47	48	45	47	58
25			44	40	49	36	46	35

Sheet1 / Sheet2 / Sheet3 /

I haven't even gotten to how the range labels in cells A8 through A12 are computed. Is your head spinning?

While many of the steps may seem arbitrary, I can assure you that all the steps are purposeful. Unless you are armed with advanced knowledge, or happen to know how I think, you may have a hard time figuring out what's going on, even if the steps are carefully and thoroughly documented.

This spreadsheet with the histogram in some ways qualifies as a dashboard. It may not be a dashboard connected to a practical application, but it is a dashboard nonetheless. If you start changing the numbers in the gray region, the histogram is automatically updated. The numbers in the gray region don't even have to be modified by hand. You could have formulas that use some kind of lookup to retrieve values from a table, based on any criteria you care to construct in a spreadsheet formula—even the time of day or whether the current year happens to be a leap year. There's more complexity here than meets the eye, and there could be more formulas than you care to know about or have any clear idea of what to do with.

This is a contrived example of a most rudimentary dashboard in a spreadsheet. By many people's criteria, it may not even qualify as a dashboard. The key, though, is to understand that if you want to create sophisticated and fancy dashboards in a spreadsheet, you could. Excel has plenty of graphical features. It provides spreadsheet functions and formulas galore. If you're an ace at VBA programming or have a budget to hire a dedicated programmer, or the luxury of the time to figure it out by yourself, then you may turn up a nice spreadsheet dashboard. Given the choice, however, you would probably opt to have quick turnaround time for dashboard preparation, while simultaneously lowering the skill threshold needed to crank out high-quality dashboards. Unfortunately, although you could use conventional spreadsheets to build dashboards, dashboards created that way will likely fall short of your goals, especially if you want to cost-effectively produce professional-quality dashboards.

The problem is that spreadsheets used to build dashboards are effectively open-source dashboards. The notion of open-source software can connote different things, depending on your perspective:

- On the positive side, your spreadsheet formulas are exposed for the world to see.
- On the negative side, your spreadsheet formulas are exposed for the world to see.

If you are preparing a dashboard, it may not be in your interest to have all the innards exposed. The chances are that the CEO of your company will not respond well to having all the formulas exposed. And that CEO will certainly not be happy if he or she accidentally clobbers a complicated formula. Even if users of a deployed dashboard respect the spreadsheet enough to avoid tinkering with its structure, there is the nagging issue of protecting intellectual property. A spreadsheet loaded with complicated formulas and conditional logic is just teeming with proprietary knowledge in its purest form. It would surely spell disaster if your dashboard based on an open-source spreadsheet got into the wrong hands. Giving away a sliver of your analyzed data is one thing, but giving away your analytical reasoning is entirely another.

To be fair, Excel does provide a basis for safeguarding deployed spreadsheets. You could make use of Microsoft's Information Rights Management, an enterprise-centric framework for establishing policies and roles that you can assign to all the employees of a company. As you might guess, this could entail a fair amount of IT infrastructure, staffing, and budget. Based on your company's needs, such an initiative might be warranted and cost justified. But it's a fair bet that this framework is not going to fit every company's needs. There are other Microsoft options, too, but that is not the focus of this book.

It sure would be nice to have some of the computational features of spreadsheets without the drawbacks cited in the past few pages. The good news is that Xcelsius makes this possible.

FROM EXCEL TO XCELSIUS

Pretend that there doesn't exist a product called Xcelsius. As product development director in a software company, you want to create some kind of a dashboard tool that confers the benefits of Excel to create dashboards without its drawbacks. What features do you think you would choose to incorporate?

Of course, before developing the product, you would do your market research to determine what paying customers want. You might ask them the following questions:

- Would you like to import any of your Excel spreadsheets into this dashboard creation tool to make use of its data?
- Would you like the ability to retain the spreadsheet formulas in the imported file so that the spreadsheet continues to work *inside* the dashboard?
- Would you like to overlay the internal spreadsheet with a visual interface or canvas composed of fully interactive components, such as dials, gauges, pick lists, sliders, and charts?
- Would you like to be able to map these components on the canvas so that they interact with the underlying spreadsheet?
- Would you like the ability to invent your own custom components if none of the available visual components suits your needs?
- As you refine your dashboard, would you like the ability to continue to make changes to your underlying spreadsheet, such as inserting rows or entering and revising formulas, and not have to re-import the spreadsheet?
- Would you like to be able to create a dashboard that you can run from your website by simply exporting it as a file?
- Would you like to be able to export your dashboard to alternative formats, such as a PowerPoint slide, PDF file, or Word document—or even post the dashboard to a web server?
- If you could export the dashboard to one of these alternative formats, would you want it to retain its full interactivity?

1

- If you want to run the dashboard in any of these alternative formats, would you like to eliminate the need to install any special software (including Excel) to run it?
- Would you like to be able to endow your dashboard with the ability to send and receive data to and from remote data sources, such as a database server?

I am guessing that the answer to each, or at least most, of these questions is a resounding yes. This scenario—being in charge of a software development group on a mission to develop a software application to meet these requirements—sounds like a tall order. Fortunately, it's already been created, and it's called Xcelsius 2008.

A WALK-THROUGH OF XCELSIUS

The purpose of this chapter is to familiarize you with some of the features of Xcelsius 2008. By the time you're done reading it, you should be conversant about some basic features and concepts, enough to be able to wrap your arms around the process of building Xcelsius dashboards.

Chapter 2, "Showcase of Xcelsius 2008 Dashboards," is a window into some of the kinds of dashboards you can create with Xcelsius 2008, both from the standpoint of dashboard interface ideas and the kind of applications you can build. Seeing what you like and what you don't can help you crystallize what you want to create for yourself.

When you have a sense of what's possible and how the possibilities apply to your goals, you'll have a meaningful context to think about building your own dashboards and visualizations in Xcelsius. Chapter 3, "Getting Familiar with Xcelsius 2008," gives you some hands-on experience using Xcelsius. So without further ado, let's begin.

GETTING STARTED WITH XCELSIUS 2008

To build dashboards using Xcelsius, you need two and a half software applications. That is not a typo. The fractional piece is Flash Player. Chances are, you already have Flash capabilities embedded in your browser, but if you don't, you need to install Adobe's Flash Player.

Besides Flash Player, you need Microsoft Excel (by itself or as part of the Office bundle) and Xcelsius 2008. In terms of an operating system, you need Windows 2000, XP, or Vista. If you want, you can run all the software on the Macintosh platform, using Apple's Boot Camp, VMWare Fusion, or Parallels Desktop for Mac.

TIP

> VMWare Fusion allows you to install an optional module called VMWare Tools—a set of keyboard, mouse, and device utilities that enhance device behavior. I highly recommend that you install the VMWare Tools onto the guest operating system. It allows your mouse and keyboard to work correctly with Xcelsius 2008.

The first software application you need to install is Microsoft Excel (or Microsoft Office). You can work with either Excel 2007 or Excel 2003. Xcelsius needs Excel, and Excel needs to already be installed on your computer before you install Xcelsius 2008.

If you don't already have Excel installed on your computer, you should do it now.

TIP

If you don't have either Excel or Xcelsius 2008, you can install trial versions of these packages. If you are installing the trial version of Excel, you need to activate it the very first time you run the program, or it will not function correctly.

The trialware versions of Excel and Xcelsius have a timeout period. If you are installing both trialware packages, pay attention to their timeout periods. For instance, if Excel has 60-day timeout and Xcelsius has a 30-day timeout, be sure to get Excel installed and working the way you need it to *before* installing Xcelsius. This way, you can maximize the time to use the trialware version of Xcelsius.

There's another good reason to ensure that Excel is installed and working the way you need it to first. The customized features of your Excel environment, such as toolbar icons that you can set, get carried over into the Xcelsius Designer environment. It doesn't make sense to fiddle with those while you're trying the trial version of Xcelsius with a timeout potentially looming.

When Excel is installed and working, you can go ahead and install Xcelsius 2008. There are different editions of Xcelsius 2008 which are outlined in Appendix B, "Xcelsius Product Family Comparison." This book principally covers the Engage product.

During the Xcelsius 2008 installation, the program may attempt to install Adobe's Flash Player. If you encounter difficulties, you might need to uninstall and reinstall Flash Player. If at a later point you need to install an updated version of Flash Player for your browser, be sure to install it on your Internet Explorer web browser. Xcelsius looks to your Internet Explorer configuration to determine where Flash is installed, even if you use Firefox or another application as your default web browser.

If all goes well, when you launch Xcelsius 2008, you should end up with a screen like the one shown in Figure 1.3. The environment where you create dashboards is known as the Xcelsius workspace. The first time you start using Xcelsius, you see a Quick Start pane on the right side of the *workspace*. The Quick Start pane is kind of like training wheels you might have with your first bicycle. If the Quick Start pane is closed, you can find it in the Xcelsius Help menu.

Notice that the top half of the screen is principally occupied by a blank canvas and the bottom half is occupied by what appears to be an Excel spreadsheet. When you create and export your dashboard, your users will only see and interact with the visual components on the canvas. Right now, no components have been placed on the canvas; it's blank. Eventually, you'll populate it with all sorts of goodies, such as menu components, corporate logos and artwork, fancy charts, and interactive maps.

Figure 1.3
The typical layout in the Xcelsius workspace.

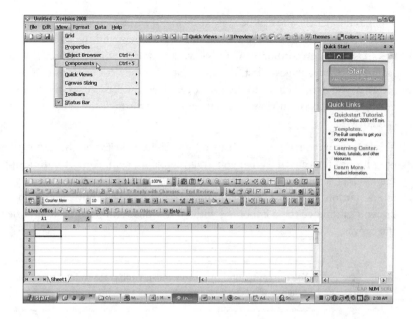

A FIRST LOOK AT THE CANVAS

Getting goodies onto the canvas is rather easy. As shown in Figure 1.3, you go to the Xcelsius View menu and select Components. The Components pane appears (see Figure 1.4).

Figure 1.4
The various visual components from the Components pane can be dragged onto the canvas.

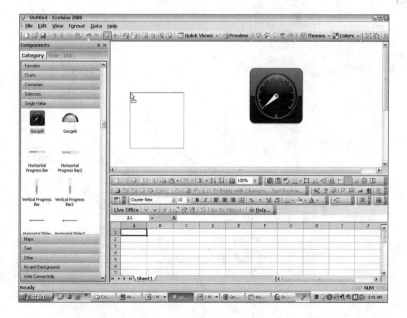

1

The Components pane can be viewed in any of three views: Accordion view (as shown on the left side of Figure 1.4), the hierarchical Tree view, and the alphabetically sorted List view. Using the Accordion view for viewing and depositing components onto the canvas has a number of advantages. First, the appearance of the various icons closely matches what you see after you drag them onto the canvas; in Tree and List views, the icons are far smaller. Second, the Accordion view makes it easy to sift through the catalog of components by category.

To place a component onto the canvas, you simply click it on the Components pane and drag it onto the canvas. When you drag the component, a ghost outline appears adjacent to the mouse (as shown on the left side of the canvas in Figure 1.4). When you release the mouse button, the ghost outline disappears and is replaced by the component. From there on, you can nudge the component with your mouse and position it anywhere you want on the canvas.

NOTE

You can resize most of the components you place on the canvas. Don't worry about the details at this stage.

If you are following along on your computer and have Xcelsius 2008 running, place a horizontal slider on the canvas, as shown in Figure 1.5. To find this slider, look in the `Single Value` category within your catalog of components.

Figure 1.5
As you position the components on the canvas, notice the resize handles on the selected component.

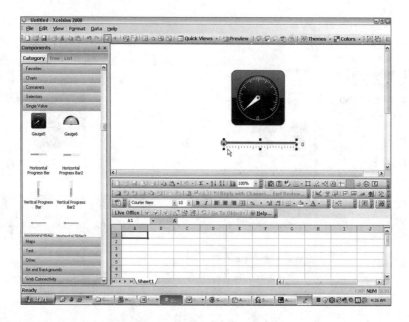

> Although the Accordion view is easy to use, it can be a maddening place to locate a specific type of component if you are not sure in which category to find it. If you switch to List view, you can see all the components in alphabetic order. Also, over time, the catalog of different types of components to choose from is only going to grow. Ultimately, List view may prove more practical to use than Accordion view, even though it is not as esthetically pleasing to view.

Laying out your components on a canvas and setting the overall look and feel is just one aspect of preparing a dashboard. Without a clear set of marching orders of where to find the dashboard data and how to interact with it, the visual components on the canvas will not be terribly useful. The key to invigorating your dashboard and bringing the components to life is to tap into a spreadsheet.

TAPPING INTO THE VIRTUAL SPREADSHEET

Now it's time to take a look at the virtual spreadsheet. In the spreadsheet portion of your Xcelsius workspace, you see the familiar grid of spreadsheet cells, the edit line for your formulas, and various toolbar icons. For all intents and purposes, your virtual spreadsheet looks and works according to the way you have Excel configured for your computer; it's just operating inside Xcelsius 2008.

Is the virtual spreadsheet real? To convince yourself, go ahead and enter the following values: cell B2 enter 25, in B3 enter 10, and in B4 enter the formula =B2+B3.

The behavior in the virtual spreadsheet is very much the same as it is when you run Excel on its own. The obvious difference with Xcelsius is that Excel is running live inside the Xcelsius environment. It is, however, a bit cramped.

TIP

> When you are designing dashboards, Xcelsius 2008 can display many things at one time. Sometimes the screen can get too crowded. Xcelsius gives you the ability to exclude everything but the portion of the dashboard you want to concentrate on. If, for instance, you want to see only the canvas, go to the Xcelsius application menu and select View, Quick Views, Canvas Only. At any time, you can revert to your original workspace from the Xcelsius application menu by selecting View, Quick Views, My Workspace.

To view the virtual spreadsheet by itself, you can select View, Quick Views, Spreadsheet Only.

There are some differences between the virtual spreadsheet and your standalone Excel environment:

- The virtual Excel environment inside Xcelsius is designed to support the use of a single spreadsheet or workbook. Your workbook can have as many worksheets as you need. The spreadsheet formulas in your virtual workbook cannot reference any remote workbooks or external data sources, such as a database server located halfway around the world. Because Xcelsius supports remote connectivity through alternative means, this should not be a show stopper.

- The traditional menu options that reside in your standalone Excel application are not generally available when you're running the virtual spreadsheet inside Xcelsius 2008.

- Not every Excel function is supported or fully supported in Xcelsius 2008. While Excel does have esoteric functions such as the BESSEL function, which is used for engineering applications, you shouldn't expect them all to be supported in Xcelsius 2008. Altogether, Xcelsius 2008 supports about 160 Excel functions. Many of the functions you use (such as SUM, AVERAGE, MIN, MAX, MEDIAN, SQRT, STANDEV, MID, VLOOKUP, and INDEX) are likely to be in this list of supported functions.

- Your VBA code and macros will not work in your deployed Xcelsius dashboards. However, while you are in the workspace, you can run your VBA code and macros. For example, you could have a macro that lets you interactively clean up data in a range of cells, such as removing multiple spaces separating the first and last name in a list of names. That macro could run in the virtual spreadsheet at design time, but that macro could not make its way into the dashboard as a runtime executable.

XCELSIUS: THE WHOLE IS GREATER THAN THE SUM OF ITS PARTS

So far, you have been designing with two halves of the Xcelsius dashboard. One of the halves is the canvas. It's the pretty face with which dashboard users will see and interact. The other half is the virtual spreadsheet, which allows you to construct formulas and do typical spreadsheet tasks, such as inserting rows and columns and copying, cutting, and pasting spreadsheet cells. It's time to connect the two halves together.

The concept is simple: The visual components in your dashboard need to be able to communicate with the underlying spreadsheet. By *communicating*, I mean that the visual components, such as the horizontal slider, need to be able to push a value onto one of the spreadsheet's cells, such as cell B2, and the results of computations (for example, cell B4, which has the formula =B2+B3) need to be read back to other components on the dashboard.

To see how this works, set up your Xcelsius environment as shown in Figure 1.6. Right-click the Horizontal Slider component on the dashboard to open up its Properties panel (see Figure 1.7).

The left vertical panel is the Properties panel, and it is currently labeled Horizontal Slider 1. It contains a variety of attributes, such as the component's title, data, and minimum and maximum limits.

TIP

There are a number of ways to open the Properties panel of a component. One way is to double-click the component. Another is to right-click it. Also, from the Xcelsius application menu, you can select View, Properties to open up the Properties panel. Alternatively, you can select the component in question and press Alt+Enter to view the component's properties.

Figure 1.6
Label your input and output cells in the underlying spreadsheet.

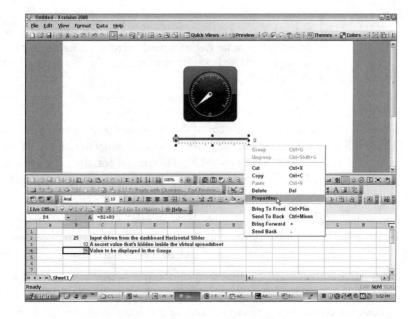

The Properties panel always displays the attributes of the component that has focus. In Figure 1.7, you can see that the horizontal slider has focus because the handle and sizing bars surround the component.

Figure 1.7
The Properties panel lets you bind component attributes to underlying spreadsheet cells.

TIP

> To shift the view of the Properties panel to a different component on the canvas, it is not necessary to close the Properties panel and reopen it. You can simply click the desired component, and the Properties panel automatically shifts its context to the component that has focus.

Immediately underneath the title bar of the Properties panel, you can see one or more tabs. There will always be a General tab in the Properties panel for any single selected component on the canvas. Depending on the kind of component, the Properties panel may also contain additional tabs, such as the Behavior tab, the Appearance tab, and the Alerts tab. You click the desired tab to display and set the appropriate attributes.

The Behavior tab allows you to set things such as when to make a particular component visible or invisible and to tell the component how to behave; for instance, you could tell a Column Chart component to ignore blank data cells when displaying data in graphical form.

With the Appearance tab, you can typically control factors such as text font style and size or color attributes of icons displayed in the component. For example, you could use the Appearance tab to change the appearance of the data points in a line chart.

The Alerts tab works much like conditional formatting in Excel. Say that you are displaying the production efficiency of various manufacturing plants. If some of the reported figures are dangerously low, you might want a visual alert, such as showing the specific data points in bold red so they stand out.

BINDING THE ATTRIBUTES OF COMPONENTS TO THE UNDERLYING SPREADSHEET

The Properties panel exposes the attributes of your components. For instance, in a horizontal slider, you might want to control settings such as the following:

- The title you want displayed next to the slider on your canvas (the `Title` text box)
- The value of the slider itself (the `Data` text box)
- The lowest and highest values allowed on the scale of your slider (`Minimum Limit` and `Maximum Limit` text boxes)

As shown in Figure 1.7, the minimum and maximum limits for the horizontal slider are `0` and `100`. You can change these values by simply typing in numbers of your choosing in the corresponding attribute input fields for the components. This gives lots of flexibility as you can pick pretty much any range you want.

With this slider, you want to set a value somewhere between the minimum and maximum limits and push that value onto one of the spreadsheet cells. Notice, as shown in Figure 1.7, that the `Data` text box is empty. To the immediate right of the `Data` text box is a small cell selector box with a red pointer. If you click this box, the `Select a Range` dialog box appears (see Figure 1.8), prompting you to specify a cell reference on your spreadsheet that maps back to the component. Sometimes you might want to map a single spreadsheet cell; other times you might need to specify a range of cells. In this particular case, it makes sense to associate a single cell with the slider's Data field; in this example, the cell would be B2.

Figure 1.8
Specify the cell range by clicking the respective cells in the underlying spreadsheet and then clicking the OK button on the Select a Range dialog box.

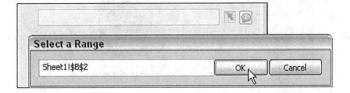

Typing in a cell range could be error prone. Fortunately, you don't have to. You can just click the cell you want, and the cell references are instantly populated in the empty field. You can then click the OK button on the Select a Range dialog box to complete the mapping.

If you click the Gauge component and map its data field to cell B4 of the spreadsheet, the gauge displays the value computed by adding cells B2 and B3. You can optionally map the Gauge component's title to the cell C4, as shown in Figure 1.9.

Figure 1.9
The Gauge component is set to read the calculation result in cell B4.

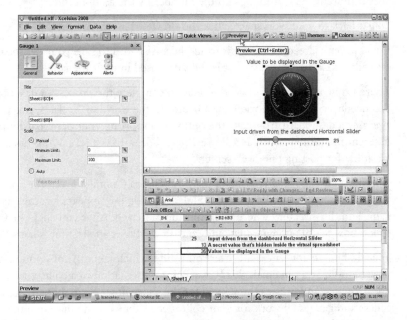

Now comes the moment of gratification. Running along the top of the Xcelsius workspace are a bunch of toolbar icons, buttons, and controls. Click the one labeled Preview. Your computer might pop up a brief message, saying that it is generating SWF (that is, an Adobe Flash file), and then your dashboard is alive and running (see Figure 1.10).

Figure 1.10
The live dashboard, where you can try moving the marker on the horizontal slider.

As you move the marker along the slider, the Gauge component keeps up with it. Not only does it move in sync, it bumps up the number by the amount in cell B3.

To get back to your workspace, click the Preview button once more.

If you haven't already done so, it would be a wise idea to save your dashboard file. Such files are called XLF files because that is the suffix used in their filenames.

There is one more step you need to take to complete the process of dashboard production: You need to create a deployable dashboard. In the world of Xcelsius, this process is called *exporting* a dashboard. You have the option of exporting your dashboard into a number of different file formats, such as a PowerPoint slide, a PDF file, a Word document, or even a Flash file for posting on a web server.

The steps for exporting a dashboard are ridiculously simple. From the application menu, you select File, Export, PowerPoint Slide. A dialog box appears, prompting you for a filename and the directory where you want the file saved. After you click the OK button in the dialog box, the file is generated, and your PowerPoint application is launched.

Your dashboard appears as a PowerPoint slide, which you can copy and paste into a full presentation. You can email this PowerPoint presentation to a colleague. When he or she opens the file and presses the F5 key for the slide show, the dashboard comes to life. The sliders and gauges all work for your colleague as they do on your computer. When you export an Xcelsius dashboard, there is no software installation required. Your colleague only needs to have his or her PowerPoint software and be Flash enabled. If you can view Flash-based videos on YouTube or see Flash animations in your browser as you surf the web, you're already Flash enabled.

WHERE TO GO FROM HERE

Think about what you've accomplished in this chapter. You created a dashboard by starting with a spreadsheet, added formulas to do some computation, dropped visual components onto a canvas, mapped the components so that you could push values onto the spreadsheet to drive the spreadsheet formulas, and displayed the results back onto the dashboard!

Before resting on your laurels, think about a couple more things that are related to getting more out of your dashboard. One of these relates to enhancing the look and feel of your dashboards and the other relates to getting more from your spreadsheets that power the dashboard.

WORKING THE XCELSIUS DASHBOARD

An important part of being successful in working with Xcelsius 2008 is to know how to work the tool. In this section, you'll go through the steps of enhancing the visual appearance of the dashboard you just created. In doing so, you'll learn how to approach making changes and enhancements to your Xcelsius dashboards.

The dashboard as displayed in Figure 1.10 works, but it's far from polished. First of all, look at the gauge. It displays a value under the needle, but the small font size makes it hard to read. In addition, the numeric value is not at all well positioned on the face of the gauge. You can easily remedy this by opening the Properties panel for the Gauge component and clicking its Appearance tab.

Notice that there are three subtabs: Layout, Text, and Color. Click the Text subtab and highlight Value (see Figure 1.11).

Figure 1.11
You can adjust the text appearance of the value displayed in the Gauge component.

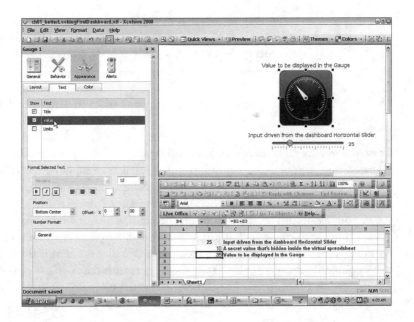

1

Try making the number boldface by clicking the B icon. This makes the text a little more readable, but you could do better. Instead of using a font size of 12 points, try something larger, like 18- or 24-point text. In picking a size, you need to think a little about what you expect your data to be like. You could also reposition the value on the face of the gauge by tweaking the X and Y offsets. After you make a few adjustments, the Gauge component is easier to read (see Figure 1.12).

Figure 1.12
The tweaked Gauge component is easier to read.

Value to be displayed in the Gauge

DASHBOARDS: MORE THAN SKIN DEEP

Now that your Gauge component is easier to read, how about improving the rest of the dashboard? There are a number of things you could do to give the dashboard a more professional appearance. Here are some quick and simple thoughts:

- You could improve the screen background.
- You could adjust the dashboard size so that it better frames the components.
- You could set up the gauge so that it alerts you when the gauge value enters a specific range of values or percentage of some target value.

> **TIP**
>
> Not only can you set up dynamic alerts for readout components such as a gauge, you can also set up alerts for input drivers, such as the horizontal slider.

- You could alter the appearance of the horizontal slider to better match that of the gauge.

These points may seem mundane, but consider the idea that you may want to incorporate a colorized alert in your slider, which is normally used as an input device. (For more on sliders, dials, and gauges, go to Chapters 3 and 6, "Single Value Components: Dials, Gauges, Speedometers, and the Like.") Why would you want to place an alert there? Presumably, you or your dashboard user fully controls the input, which is a value that is always known. There's nothing to compute. But just because the input (such as an amount to be invested) doesn't involve a computation, you shouldn't assume that the alert is fixed. The alert could be a dynamically changing value. If the slider represents the purchase price for a property you are investing in, you may be willing to invest the maximum amount or at least a large amount by pushing the slider close to its limit. The alert could signify that you've crossed the threshold for a mortgage you qualify for based on your income, prevailing interest rates, and a host of other factors.

In the case of the horizontal slider you've created, your input is serving a dual purpose as both an input device and an output device.

DASHBOARD FUNCTIONALITY ENHANCEMENTS

Further empowering your dashboard should be easy. Even with simple dashboards, there's a lot to think about, and many of the considerations carry over to complex dashboards. Let's look at one such example.

In the main dashboard example for this chapter, there is a "secret" number embedded in the spreadsheet in cell B3. Depending on what you are doing with your dashboard, you might want to keep this value hidden, or you might want to make it available for the user to manipulate. This value could be, for example, a numeric coefficient used in a calculation or a password. As far as Xcelsius is concerned, only two things can occupy a spreadsheet cell: a value such as a number or text or a formula.

NOTE

> If a spreadsheet cell contains a formula, you cannot use any component to directly set its computed value. The only way a computed value can change is through whatever is defined in the spreadsheet formula.

So you can see that it's important to develop a clear understanding of who your users are and how you want them interacting with your dashboards and visualizations.

WATCHING OUT FOR LIMITS

Dashboards have their equivalents of potholes. For example, you may have noticed that the limits on this chapter's dashboard slider and gauge are 1 to 100. If the value in cell B3 (the secret number you add to cell B2) is 10, then the gauge will be trying to display numbers between 10 and 110. The gauge dial will not be able to display numbers above 100 because that is presently a hardwired limit.

You need to think about how you want to handle situations of this kind. A number of strategies are available to you:

■ Do you want to dynamically shift the gauge limits so they match the minimum set of all possible calculation results? For example, do you want to make the limits 10 and 110 if cell B3 is fixed at 10? In this case, as long as the B3 cell is 10 or more, the dial will never extend into the single-digit range.

■ Regardless of the value of cell B3, would you want the gauge dial to start at 0 and go all the way up to 110? (This would be the maximum value of the slider plus the value of B3 =100+10.) This scenario would make sense if B3 were visible and could be manipulated by the dashboard user. Keep in mind that the angular sweep of the needle increasingly gets restricted as the value of B3 increases. Although the needle angle is an accurate representation of absolute value, the restriction of angular sweep is accompanied by a reduction of visual satisfaction associated with dashboard animation or perceived inter-activity.

■ You could leave the gauge dial limits as 0 and 100 and allow the gauge needle to "hit the wall" and stop moving when the numeric value exceeds the limit of 100. Because it is not always possible to predict the maximum or minimum computed value to be dis-played on a gauge, you need to think about this kind of scenario as a realistic possibility. You could, for example, create an alert to signal that the gauge dial is saturated. For now, I leave you to ponder how you might accomplish this. This topic is addressed in greater detail in Chapter 6.

IMPORTING SPREADSHEETS INTO XCELSIUS 2008

In the example presented in this chapter, the spreadsheet model with the single formula for adding B2 and B3 was created from scratch. As a practical matter, if you have a spreadsheet model you want to use for a dashboard, be it some net present value analysis of cash flows or presenting financial ratios, you are not going to be building the spreadsheet from scratch in Xcelsius 2008.

You can take your already built spreadsheets and *import* them into Xcelsius. From there, it's a very short step to drop components onto the canvas and map them to the underlying spreadsheet.

It is good to know that if you need to modify a formula or insert a few rows here or there, you can do so right from Xcelsius, without having to re-import the spreadsheet.

PUTTING SOME COMPUTATIONAL OOMPH INTO YOUR DASHBOARDS

The spreadsheet used in this chapter is just about as simple as a spreadsheet can be. However, you can use much more complicated formulas in your spreadsheets. If you care to dive into the deep end of the pool and dabble with options pricing, for example, you could specify parameters such as stock price, strike price, risk free rate of interest, time till expira-tion, and volatility in cells B6, B7, B8, C13, and B13, respectively, and then compute the option price with a formula like this:

```
=(B6*(NORMDIST(((LN(B6/B7))+((B8+(B13*B13/2))*C12))/(B13*(SQRT(C12))),0,1,TRUE)))
-(B7*(EXP(B8*C12*(-1)))*(NORMDIST(((LN(B6/B7))+((B8+(B13*B13/2))*C12))/(B13
➥*(SQRT(C12)))-(B13*SQRT(C12)),0,1,TRUE)))
```

All the parameters could be set using components such as Horizontal Slider components, Vertical Slider components, Grid components, Input Field components, and List Box com-ponents, just to name a few. You could display the results as a single number—in a table if you are doing a bunch of calculations, in a chart or graph, or whatever you choose.

This chapter is not the place to delve into complicated computations of this kind, but you should know that from a dashboard design point of view, there is very little you need to do differently to incorporate a powerful spreadsheet into an Xcelsius dashboard than you've already done in this chapter.

Figure 2.1
Matrix-style calculator.

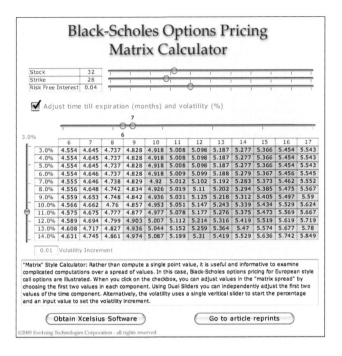

Figure 2.2
Setup of colorized alerts.

Figure 2.3
Smart sliders and
progress bars offer a
way to assess market
strategies.

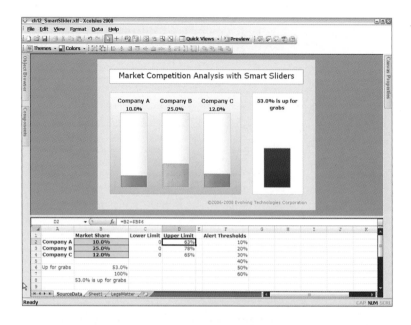

Figure 2.4
A connected map
dashboard that shows
worldwide downloads
of the Firefox browser
over a 24-hour period.

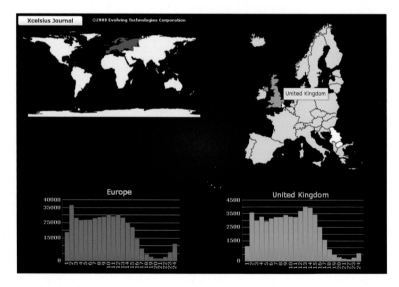

Figure 2.5
A tally map dashboard that lets the user paint the political landscape and conduct what-if analyses.

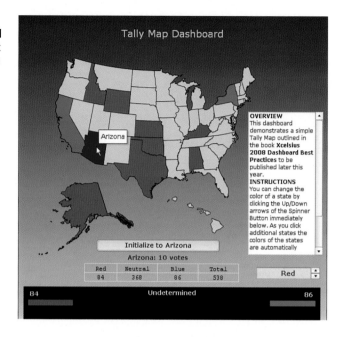

Figure 2.6
You can give individual components such as a dial a context to adjust several variables instead of just one.

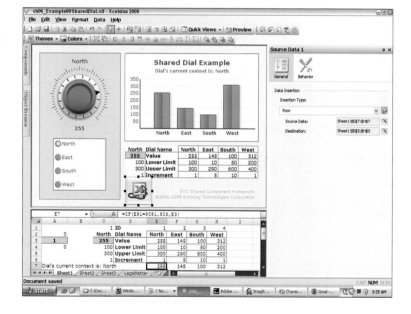

Figure 2.7
Snapshot of budget and actual figures across multiple geographic regions.

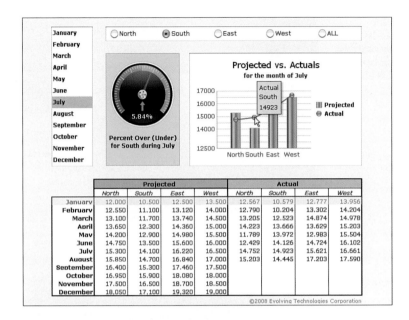

	Projected				Actual			
	North	South	East	West	North	South	East	West
January	12.000	10.500	12.500	13.500	12.567	10.579	12.777	13.956
February	12.550	11.100	13.120	14.000	12.790	10.204	13.302	14.204
March	13.100	11.700	13.740	14.500	13.205	12.523	14.874	14.978
April	13.650	12.300	14.360	15.000	14.223	13.666	13.629	15.203
May	14.200	12.900	14.980	15.500	11.789	13.972	12.983	15.504
June	14.750	13.500	15.600	16.000	12.429	14.126	14.724	16.102
July	15.300	14.100	16.220	16.500	14.752	14.923	15.621	16.661
August	15.850	14.700	16.840	17.000	15.203	14.445	17.203	17.590
September	16.400	15.300	17.460	17.500				
October	16.950	15.900	18.080	18.000				
November	17.500	16.500	18.700	18.500				
December	18.050	17.100	19.320	19.000				

©2008 Evolving Technologies Corporation

Figure 2.8
A timeline data viewer animates how you can move through time to visualize trends.

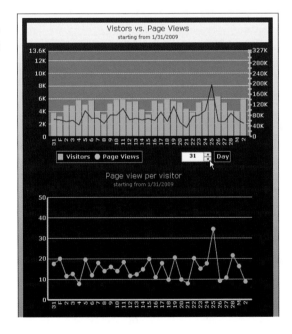

Figure 2.9
This desktop client portal dashboard lets you merge separate sources of accounting and currency exchange data on the spot.

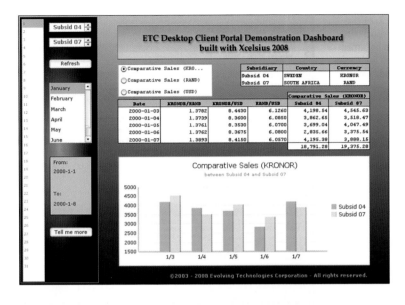

Figure 2.10
A speedometer-style array dashboard.

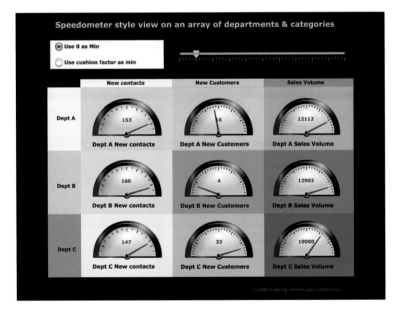

Figure 2.15
An abacus-inspired dashboard facilitates the visualization of financial projections when inputs are uncertain.

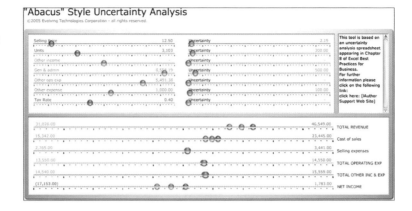

Figure 2.16
One of the new components in Xcelsius 2008 is the Tree Map component.

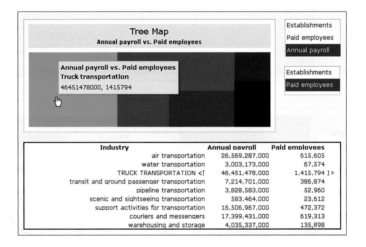

Industry	Annual payroll	Paid employees
air transportation	26,569,287,000	615,605
water transportation	3,003,173,000	67,574
TRUCK TRANSPORTATION <[	46,451,478,000	1,415,794]>
transit and ground passenger transportation	7,214,701,000	386,874
pipeline transportation	3,828,583,000	52,960
scenic and sightseeing transportation	583,464,000	23,612
support activities for transportation	16,506,967,000	472,372
couriers and messengers	17,399,431,000	619,313
warehousing and storage	4,035,337,000	135,898

CLOSING THOUGHTS

Dashboards are often associated with graphically intensive, highly interactive, and information-rich interfaces. But dashboards are more than skin deep. Getting data organized for easy consumption and comprehension requires a considerable amount of forethought and effort to prepare the data for the dashboard. Organizing predigested data simply doesn't cut it. Data is far too fluid to keep it rigid or unchanging. Even in cases in which data is unchanging and rigid, people's lines of inquiry and the types of analyses they want to subject their data to are not unchanging and rigid.

The needs imposed on a dashboard you might use or want to build could be open ended. You therefore need a facility that can structure data the way you need it prepared and presented.

A major thrust of Xcelsius 2008 as a dashboard technology is that it directly attempts to integrate on-the-fly data manipulation with the dashboard presentation facility. This just-in-time computational facility embedded within a portable dashboard is rather unique.

In this chapter, you have had a glimpse into the mechanics of meshing the presentation layer of a dashboard with a computational brain. It is rather remarkable that the metaphor chosen for handling the computational side is the spreadsheet and even more remarkable that its integration with Microsoft Excel is seamless.

In Chapter 2, you'll see a mini-gallery of Xcelsius dashboards. You'll start thinking about the kinds of things you could be doing with dashboards as well as the kinds of features you would want to use in your own.

SHOWCASE OF XCELSIUS 2008 DASHBOARDS

In this chapter

Before delving into the mechanics and strategies of building Xcelsius 2008 dashboards and visualizations, it is worth spending some time getting a feel for various kinds of dashboards. To help give you some perspective, this chapter provides a sampling of what's possible with Xcelsius 2008. In many instances, I point out where you can find further information.

All the examples in this chapter can be found as live working examples on the book's website, www.XcelsiusBestPractices.com.

With this chapter, you can sit back and try out some fun dashboards. Just think about the ideas. Don't worry about how to implement each dashboard. You'll learn the nuts and bolts in the next 14 chapters.

NOTE

> I decided early on in the process of writing this book that it was important for the figures in this chapter to be in color, so that you could get the best possible picture of what a variety of professionally done dashboards look like. With that in mind, the figures for this chapter have been placed together in the special color insert.

EMBEDDING SPREADSHEET SMARTS IN A DASHBOARD

Dashboards enjoy a reputation for being adept at representing information visually. Dashboards also make it easy to get at information through mechanisms such as drill down and various kinds of navigation aids. With the assistance of remote data sources such as databases, a dashboard can provide access to a staggering amount of data.

There's a difference between accessing data through queries and quantitatively analyzing information. In addition to retrieving data from remote sources, Xcelsius 2008 lets you perform a wide variety of computations—quite literally as if you had a whole spreadsheet embedded inside your dashboard. This opens up interesting capabilities that wouldn't be easily achievable if you didn't have a computation engine embedded within the dashboard.

 Figure 2.1 shows an example of a matrix-style calculator involving the Black-Scholes Options Pricing model. The spreadsheet formula that powers this dashboard is actually shown at the end of Chapter 1, "Motivation for Using Xcelsius 2008." Rather than compute the result for a single cell, it calculates the results across an array of input values. The basic technique of setting up a matrix-style calculator is described in Chapter 13, "Working with Less-Than-Optimal Data." I don't want you to get the idea that complicated formulas are required. I just want to make the point that Xcelsius 2008 won't stand in your way if and when you need your dashboards to get mathematical.

One of the interesting features of the visualization shown in Figure 2.1 is the use of colorized alerts. In this particular case, the dashboard values are split into colorized bands, based on their numeric values.

Colorized alerts are straightforward to set up in Xcelsius 2008. Figure 2.2 shows the behind-the-scenes setup of colorized alerts for another dashboard. In this example, the color of the vertical bars in a column chart can be red, yellow, or green, and the color is based on the bar height. The color threshold is actually tunable: Adjusting the vertical slider changes the color threshold value. This is an interesting concept. Not only can you construct a dashboard with meaningful alerts, you can, if you wish, empower dashboard users to set the colorization thresholds. You'll find out more about colorized alerts in Chapter 12, "Smart Data and Alerts."

THINKING CREATIVELY WITH COLORS AND VISUAL COMPONENTS

Colorized alerts offer a great way to convey numeric information. Imagine three competitors vying for market share in a very limited market. As any one competitor increases its share, what's up for grabs shrinks. You need a way to show not only what is available but also how close each company is to what it can ultimately obtain. Figure 2.3 shows one way of addressing this. In this dashboard, you can click each of the three vertical progress bars that vaguely resemble grain bins and adjust their height. As you resize any of the bars, three things happen:

- Based on the percentage of market share, the color of the bar changes
- The proportion of market share is adjusted immediately
- The height of the vertical bars for the competitors is adjusted

This last behavior is revealing. As available market share dries up, what remains for the taking relative to what has been taken is automatically adjusted. You'll find out more about this type of dashboard in Chapter 12.

PUTTING YOUR DATA ON THE MAP

The business environment today is not only fast paced, it spans a broad geographic range. In many cases, you can learn a lot by monitoring activities geographically. Figure 2.4 shows a connected map dashboard. This dashboard provides a 24-hour snapshot of worldwide downloads of the Firefox web browser on a continent-by-continent and country-by-country basis. Click a continent, and you simultaneously see the total downloads by the hour for the continent and a corresponding map that highlights the countries in that continent. Clicking any country reveals a 24-hour timeline of downloads for just that country.

The framework for setting up a connected map dashboard is provided in Chapter 11, "Maps in Xcelsius."

In the example shown in Figure 2.4, the Map component is relegated to serving as a readout or navigation aid. That is, clicking a map gives you access to additional information. But you can also use Map components as input devices. Doing so requires the ability to click more than one map region at a time. Out of the box, Map components do not directly support the selection of multiple regions. However, Xcelsius 2008 does permit the construction of multi-selection maps. Figure 2.5 shows one such implementation, called a tally map, that allows dashboard users to classify states into colors and tally values associated with those states. In this example, the states can be classified into red, neutral, or blue states, and the value for each state is the number of electoral votes.

The tally map shown in Figure 2.5 works by allowing you to switch from red to neutral to blue, using a text-based spinner button. (Text-based spinners are described in Chapter 12.) You can click on a succession of states. Each one takes on the color associated with the spinner button at the time the state is clicked. As you click the states, a tally or count is made for the red states and the blue states. This is displayed in a pair of colorized horizontal bars immediately below the map. Once either side achieves more than half the number of electoral votes, the winner is announced. At any time after a state is colorized, you can change the color, so the tally map is a great tool for what-if analysis.

RETHINKING DASHBOARD INTERFACE DESIGN

Dashboard components such as dials and gauges have a reputation for consuming valuable screen space. If you used a separate dial for each variable you could tweak, you would quickly run out of space. Fortunately, through the Shared Component Framework, Xcelsius 2008 gives you the ability to structure your interfaces so that an individual component such as a dial can be used to adjust as many variables as you require. For example, in Figure 2.6, you can click the radio button to dynamically remap the dial to adjust values for any of the designated regions. In this example, you can use one dial to set the values for four geographic regions.

This framework is applicable to any kind of component, not just dials. You are not restricted to using radio buttons to set the context. You can use just about any component—list boxes, combo boxes, check boxes, label-based menus, or text input fields. Basically, if you can define it, you can use it. There is no fixed limit on how many variables you can adjust from a single component. You could manage several dozen or even hundreds of variables from a single component. You will find out more about the Shared Component Framework in Chapter 6, "Single Value Components: Dials, Gauges, Speedometers, and the Like."

CHOOSING THE DATA YOU WANT TO VIEW

One of the nice features of Xcelsius 2008 dashboards is that they enable you to easily specify what data you want to graphically view. Figure 2.7 shows a graphical viewer that displays budget versus actual values across multiple geographic regions for any month. You can find the details of how to set up this type of dashboard in Chapter 6.

Sometimes the data you want to view stretches across an extended timeline. You may be looking at daily data over the course of a whole month but want to advance forward or backward in time over the course of several years. Figure 2.8 shows a timeline viewer that lets you advance forward or go backward in time by clicking a spinner button. This has the advantage of creating an animation effect. Chapter 5, "Using Charts and Graphs to Represent Data," describes how to set up a timeline viewer.

DESKTOP CLIENT PORTALS

Sometimes the data you want to analyze requires an on-the-spot merge of data from several sources. Xcelsius 2008 Engage lets you create dashboards that can connect to remote data sources and retrieve XML data. Server-based portals can retrieve data from multiple sources. A "desktop client portal" can do the same, running entirely from a dashboard on your computer (see Figure 2.9).

Consider retrieving financial data for various subsidiaries of a company, with each subsidiary located in a different country, each of which has a different currency. If you want to compare revenue for any two subsidiaries over a timeline, you have to incorporate some currency conversion. And when you merge the revenue from subsidiaries in multiple countries, you need to consider the fact that the spot exchange rate varies daily. Fortunately, Xcelsius 2008 Engage lets you connect to several remote data sources with a single click and harness the computational facilities of a spreadsheet to dynamically merge the data. You'll find out more about client portals and remote connectivity in Chapter 15, "XML and Data Connectivity."

VIEWING MULTIPLE SOURCES OF INFORMATION IN A SINGLE VIEW

The term *dashboard* conjures an image of an instrument panel that at a glance gives a picture of what's happening across multiple departments and initiatives.

Consider a company that identifies potential customers. That company is able to turn these new contacts into customers. It would be helpful to track across departments the progression from new contacts to new customers and the sales from these customers. Figure 2.10 shows one such design.

The objective of this kind of dashboard is to display an across-the-board, all-in-one view of information. Because the treatment of information by department is uniform, a tabular layout serves the purpose of representing information, even though the indicators are in the form of visual components.

MANAGING THE VISIBILITY OF COMPONENTS IN YOUR DASHBOARDS

Xcelsius 2008 allows you to control the visibility of individual dashboard components on demand. An alert message can automatically appear when some combination of dashboard data or variables falls out of bounds from what is expected. The criteria can literally be any spreadsheet formula you care to create. This gives you an awful lot of freedom to control the behavior and visual appearance of your dashboards.

The freedom Xcelsius 2008 gives you to design arbitrarily complex interfaces and behaviors is not completely free: You are responsible for managing all those components.

Fortunately, a number of frameworks allow you to manage the visibility of components without creating maintenance bottlenecks. Figure 2.11 shows one such approach. In this framework, the visibility logic of components is decoupled from the components. This framework lets you quickly and effortlessly remap component behavior. Creating sophisticated and complex dashboards or scorecards need not be accompanied by a hefty amount of overhead or design complexity. Chapter 7, "Using Multi-Layer Visibility in Your Dashboards and Visualizations," is devoted to the topic of managing the visibility of components.

EMBEDDING VISUAL ANALYTICS IN A DASHBOARD

Because Xcelsius dashboards incorporate spreadsheet capabilities, you can use computational facilities to gain a tangible feel of the quantitative and mathematical relationships. It is not uncommon to speak about normal or Gaussian curves. But when someone speaks about a curve whose mean value has doubled and standard deviation has decreased by 32%, will you have an intuitive feel for how the curve compares to a standard normal distribution? Even if you are comfortable thinking mathematically, having a dashboard like the kind shown in Figure 2.12 helps to make the quantitative relationships intuitive. You can find out more about this dashboard and using statistical techniques and reasoning in Xcelsius in Chapter 9, "Xcelsius and Statistics."

You can get fairly sophisticated and employ mathematical techniques in sensitivity analysis in your mathematical models. Figure 2.13 shows the use of tornado and spider charts, both sensitivity analysis tools, within Xcelsius. You can find information about these tools in Article 17 of *Xcelsius Journal* (www.XcelsiusJournal.com).

INTERESTING APPROACHES TO FINANCIAL ANALYSIS IN XCELSIUS

With Xcelsius 2008, you are free to invent your own kind of visualizations. Let's look at two examples.

Ratio analysis is regularly used in analyzing financial statements. Instead of simply publishing ratios by themselves, you can show the underlying numbers that contribute to the numerator and denominator of a ratio. Figure 2.14 shows a ratio analyzer dashboard on which the dashboard user clicks an accounting period and a ratio. In this example, return on assets (ROA) is selected. ROA is defined as net income divided by total assets. The ratio analyzer dashboard addresses questions such as, "What makes up net income?" and "What makes up total assets?" You'll learn more about this type of dashboard in Chapter 10, "Financial Analysis."

You can use Xcelsius dashboards for financial projections. You can do more than simply project a point estimate; you can even incorporate "fuzzy" reasoning. For example, your car dealership might expect to sell 3,100 hybrid automobiles at the wonderfully low price of $12,500 each. In reality, you can't be certain how many units will be sold until the season comes to pass. For all you know, you may exceed your expectations and sell 3,400 units, or you may fall short and sell only 2,800 units. Each scenario is equally likely. In addition, customers can purchase cars with more options or trim down the options to a bare minimum. Operating expenses can also vary. When you take into account the range of different factors that can vary independently of one another, it becomes a complicated affair to arrive at an objective estimate—unless you use specific techniques for reasoning with uncertainty. One such technique that has been adapted for spreadsheets is called adding in quadrature (described in my book *Excel Best Practices for Business*, ISBN 076454120X), and you can easily use this technique in an Xcelsius dashboard.

For example, the dashboard shown in Figure 2.15 is divided into three main panels. The top-left panel is for all the inputs of the pro forma income statement projection. The top-right panel is for the uncertainty in each of these inputs. The bottom panel displays the financial projection. The input variables include quantities such as the number of units sold, their selling price, general and administrative expenses, other operating expenses, and other sundry items. You can adjust these inputs by moving horizontal sliders. As they are varied, the relevant items for the financial projection (such as total revenue, cost of sales, selling expenses, and net income) are presented in the bottom panel. Notice that these estimates appear as a set of horizontal sliders but are flanked on the left and right by green and red markers to indicate uncertainty in each of these estimates. This type of tool makes it very easy to incorporate uncertainty in visual data models and dashboards.

NEW FEATURES IN XCELSIUS 2008

Crystal Xcelsius has been characterized by some as a groundbreaking technology. As good as Crystal Xcelsius was, its successor Xcelsius 2008 provides even greater advances in dashboard design and technology.

ENHANCED SPREADSHEET SUPPORT

The integration of Xcelsius 2008 and Excel is virtually seamless. Without ever having to leave Xcelsius 2008, you can build very full-featured spreadsheets, map visual components to them, and export dashboards with made-to-order spreadsheets tucked neatly inside.

Xcelsius 2008 has brought in support for eight additional spreadsheet functions, including OFFSET and ISERROR. Chapter 4, "Embedded Spreadsheets: The Secret Sauce of Xcelsius 2008," provides more information about Excel-supported spreadsheet functions.

IMPROVED SUPPORT IN EXISTING COMPONENTS

In addition to enhancing integration of spreadsheet design within the workspace, Xcelsius 2008 has enhanced many of its existing components. Many chart types support the use of dual axes. You can find information about this in Chapter 5. Many components, such as list boxes, enable inline alerts. In-depth coverage of alerts is provided in Chapter 12.

Nice touches have been added to existing components in Xcelsius. In the Interactive Calendar component, you can now easily navigate to any of the calendar dates in a month by using your keyboard's arrow keys. You'll be pleased to find that you can now include Alaska and Hawaii in a map of the United States. You now have a choice of two U.S. map components—one that has the complete map of all 50 states and the District of Columbia and one that shows the continental United States (without Alaska and Hawaii).

Xcelsius 2008 greatly enhances text representation within your dashboards. Specifically, Xcelsius dashboards now support the use of multiple fonts. Label and Input Text Area components now support the use of HTML formatting.

Xcelsius 2008 improves visualization of your dashboards. In addition to supporting JPG and SWF file formats, the Image component can support BMP, GIF, and PNG files. The Rectangle component, which has been greatly enhanced, lets you create a wide range of gradient fills (see Chapter 8, "Managing Interactivity"). Another nice touch is the ability to print in high resolution directly from the dashboard and avoid pixelization from screen dumps. In addition, Xcelsius 2008 has expanded the array of themes and colors.

Xcelsius 2008 Engage has a variety of new features worth noting:

- The Add-on Manager enables you to incorporate custom-built components.
- You can deploy dashboards to Adobe Air.
- A unified data manager provides a universal framework for accessing remote data. (The Professional Edition of Crystal Xcelsius had no support for remote data connectivity.)

NEW COMPONENTS IN XCELSIUS 2008

Xcelsius 2008 provides a number of new components. For example, Figure 2.16 shows a Tree Map component. (You'll learn more about tree maps in Chapter 5.)

Here is a brief list of some of the other new components in Xcelsius 2008 that are worth exploring:

- Panel Container and Tab Set (see Chapter 7)
- half gauge
- Ticker (not found in Crystal Xcelsius Professional)

- Europe maps
- Asia-Pacific maps
- Canada by Province
- History
- Trend Analyzer
- Print Button
- Reset Button

WEB CONNECTIVITY IN XCELSIUS 2008

The range of web connectivity features previously found in the Workgroup version of Crystal Xcelsius is now bundled in the Xcelsius 2008 Engage product. Chapter 15 gives you the lowdown on how to tap into remote data sources.

CLOSING THOUGHTS

There is a tendency when working with many software applications to create files that all look the same. A PowerPoint presentation (that is, one that doesn't incorporate Xcelsius dashboards) can be spotted from a million miles away. The same is true of many other types of visualization and data analysis tools. Products created from a single application typically look like clones of one another.

In stark contrast, all the Xcelsius dashboard examples in this chapter are fundamentally different from one another. The software doesn't fight you when you want to think outside the box and invent an entirely new kind of visualization. It is indeed liberating to build a dashboard using little more than pointing and clicking with your mouse and incorporating a spreadsheet behind the scenes.

Creating marvelous dashboards and visualizations does require some forethought, ingenuity, and discipline. This book introduces you to the basic and advanced techniques and practices of dashboard design with Xcelsius.

Best practices entail more than simply useful techniques. If you are going to be regularly building dashboards, you want to carry your experiences from one project to the next. It would be nice if you could manage visibility of components in your deployed dashboards so that your users won't have to face a cluttered screen. Less clutter translates to simpler and more elegant layouts, with shorter design time. If you can reuse a visual chart component for multiple kinds of data (using a technique called *context switching*), you will have an easier time maintaining dashboards.

 This book describes more than 100 best practice techniques, indicated with the best practices icon. They are summarized in Appendix C, "Xcelsius Best Practice Techniques and Hip Pocket Tips."

Chapter 3, "Getting Familiar with Xcelsius 2008," gets you started with Xcelsius 2008, and Chapter 4 addresses how to incorporate spreadsheet formulas in your Xcelsius dashboards. When you master this material, you will be able to incorporate all sorts of computations in your dashboards. Chapters 5 and 6 address charts and selectors, giving you a basic grounding in Xcelsius 2008. The rest of the book, which can largely be read in any order, will elevate your skill beyond the intermediate level.

CHAPTER 3

GETTING FAMILIAR WITH XCELSIUS 2008

In this chapter

As with many other technologies and products, a demonstration of building an Xcelsius dashboard makes it look like child's play. There's a wonderful sense of simplicity when you can just import a spreadsheet, drop visual components onto a canvas, map them to actual spreadsheet formulas and data, and click a button to export the dashboard to a fully interactive Flash or PowerPoint slide.

My goal in this chapter is to quickly get you familiar with the things you need to know when working with Xcelsius and to arm you with practical information to help you put oomph into your dashboards and visualizations.

The emphasis of this chapter is on Xcelsius 2008 features. Chapter 4, "Embedded Spreadsheets: The Secret Sauce of Xcelsius 2008," focuses on the underlying spreadsheet.

LEARNING TO BUILD DASHBOARDS

There are two things that separate me from you: I have textbook knowledge of Xcelsius, which is something that anyone should be able to pick up by simply reading the product documentation, and I have years of experience designing Xcelsius dashboards and know what works and doesn't work.

I could easily write an encyclopedic chapter, systematically detailing the broad array of Xcelsius product features. It would get you familiar with the product, but I'm not convinced that such an approach would give you a clear sense of what to do when faced with building dashboards on your own. Instead, in this book, I show you how to go about building dashboards, and in the process, I cover the many product features I might have covered using the encyclopedic approach.

Starting with this chapter, I want you to be hands-on. By hands-on, I don't simply mean opening a file on your computer and passively looking at ready-made file samples as you read. I want you to be working with the files and examples as you would in the workplace and tackle the same kinds of challenges you would face when working with Xcelsius for real. Think of this chapter as your first day of on-the-job training with Xcelsius 2008. Along the way in this and later chapters, you'll gradually fill in the gaps in the product features and capabilities.

To begin, imagine that you need to analyze and present both historical sales and projected sales for four regional divisions in your company (see Figure 3.1)

Your objective is to turn this into a dashboard that outlines corporate sales both nationally and regionally. You can open the sample spreadsheet file `ch03_01SampleSpreadsheet.xls` in either Excel 2003 or Excel 2007.

When you launch Xcelsius 2008 for the first time, it may look similar to Figure 3.2. It may look somewhat different from Figure 3.2, depending on which edition of Xcelsius you have and how you have configured your Xcelsius workspace.

Figure 3.1
Sample spreadsheet data.

XCELSIUS 2008 DASHBOARD BEST PRACTICES
Sample Data for Use with Xcelsius
for projected vs. actual monthly data

	Projected				Actual			
	North	South	East	West	North	South	East	West
Jan	12,000	10,500	12,500	13,500	12,567	9,579	12,777	13,956
Feb	12,550	11,100	13,120	14,000	12,790	10,204	13,302	14,204
Mar	13,100	11,700	13,740	14,500	13,205	10,523	13,874	14,978
Apr	13,650	12,300	14,360	15,000	13,223	10,666	14,629	15,203
May	14,200	12,900	14,980	15,500	13,789	11,972	14,983	15,504
Jun	14,750	13,500	15,600	16,000	14,429	12,126	15,724	16,102
Jul	15,300	14,100	16,220	16,500	14,752	13,923	16,621	16,661
Aug	15,850	14,700	16,840	17,000	15,203	14,445	17,203	17,590
Sep	16,400	15,300	17,460	17,500				
Oct	16,950	15,900	18,080	18,000				
Nov	17,500	16,500	18,700	18,500				
Dec	18,050	17,100	19,320	19,000				

SampleData / Sheet2 / Sheet3 / LegalMatter

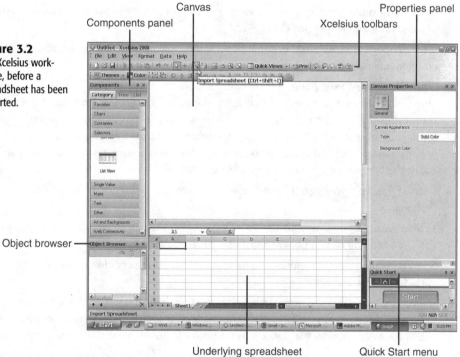

Figure 3.2
The Xcelsius workspace, before a spreadsheet has been imported.

You don't want to be distracted by your software configuration, setup, and layout when you need to put to use your creative and analytical skills. So before diving into the dashboard design, let's digress a bit and customize the workspace.

ORGANIZING THE XCELSIUS WORKSPACE

As you can see, even without any file open, the Xcelsius screen is pretty busy. When you start opening files, it will get even busier and more cluttered. Fortunately, you can customize your workspace to suit your needs.

ELEMENTS OF THE WORKSPACE

Your workspace environment is composed of the following:

- **The canvas**: The canvas is the visual representation of the dashboard that your users see. On the canvas, you can place various components. Users can interact with the components, such as clicking a button, typing in a phrase, or moving a slider. The components, in turn, interact with an underlying spreadsheet, and through the spreadsheet, indirectly interact with one another.

- **The Components pane**: This is a virtual catalog or gallery of available components you can drag and drop onto the canvas.

- **The Properties panel**: You use this panel for displaying and setting the attributes of components placed on the canvas.

- **The Object Browser pane**: As you add components to the canvas, it quickly becomes cluttered. You need some way of managing them, and the Object Browser is the tool for this purpose. This pane contains a list of named components that match exactly what's on the canvas. From the Object Browser, you can make the components you want hidden, or you can lock them into place after carefully positioning them. Also, you can adjust the "depth" of a component within the canvas.

- **Underlying spreadsheet**: This is the spreadsheet that you work with to create your dashboards.

  While you are designing your dashboard, Xcelsius closely watches all your formulas, data, and binding of component attributes to spreadsheet cells.

  Simultaneously, Xcelsius builds a virtual spreadsheet that very closely mimics the spreadsheet you are working on.

  When Xcelsius generates your dashboard file, it embeds the virtual worksheet into the dashboard file so it can run alongside the dashboard visual components. Because the virtual spreadsheet runs in Flash, there is no need for the dashboard user to install Excel.

- **Toolbars**: Similarly to applications such as Microsoft Office, Xcelsius provides an assortment of toolbars to facilitate dashboard building. From a toolbar, for instance, you can specify themes and color combinations for your dashboard.

- **Quick Start pane**: This pane provides some information that may be useful the very first time you try using Xcelsius. It gives you a quick tour of Xcelsius, and when you're done with this tour, you'll no longer need this pane. You can close it to free up some screen space in your workspace.

CUSTOMIZING YOUR WORKSPACE LAYOUT

Xcelsius provides a number of different options for customizing your workspace layout. I explain here some of the options and choices, but in truth, there is no single best way to customize your workspace. You need to choose what works for you.

For those of you used to Crystal Xcelsius, the Components pane is typically positioned along the upper-left edge of the screen, and the Object Browser is underneath it. Xcelsius 2008 allows you to customize the default locations and behaviors of these panes.

THE COMPONENTS PANE

The Components pane displays a gallery or catalog of available components for your dashboard. You can view components in any of three views (see Figure 3.3).

Figure 3.3
The Components pane has an Accordion view, a Tree view, and a List view.

3

It is easy to sift through the components by using the Accordion view. The icons showing each component are easy to view. You can also jump to a specific category. The Tree view offers much the same functionality as the Accordion view, using a tree folder interface. The component icons in Tree view are smaller than the icons in Accordion view. The List view provides an alphabetic list of all available components, without regard to category.

Although the Accordion view of components may be aesthetically pleasing, the number of components directly visible and selectable at a glance is comparatively small. In addition, with Accordion view, if you are looking for a specific component, you need to know which component category to click on to find it. It's not obvious that a Dual Slider component would be grouped with Single Value components, even though it adjusts two values. There is nothing really wrong with the classification; it's just that when you are using the Accordion view, you may need to tax your memory more than if you use the alphabetic List view.

So which of these views—Accordion, Tree, or List—is the best to work with? Fortunately, you don't have to choose. You can switch from one to another by clicking the appropriate tab. Personally, I find it most expedient to work in the List view: I get what I want right away, and there is no guesswork to figure out if there's a component that matches my needs.

THE CANVAS

The canvas frames your dashboard and visualizations. It is the place where components are positioned. There are a number of intriguing parallels between a canvas for an oil painting and the Xcelsius canvas. Paint on an oil painting is deposited in layers, and objects painted in the background are obscured by those in the foreground. Similarly, components placed on the Xcelsius canvas are arranged in layers. Those in the foreground obscure those that are behind. Unlike with an oil painting, however, with the Xcelsius canvas, the order of components can be rearranged. You do this with the aid of the Object Browser.

You can set the canvas size a number of ways. First, from the File menu, you can select Document Properties and set the width and height. You can use one of the preset options or use any pixel width and height of your choosing.

TIP

While you are not locked into a specific size for the canvas, it is generally good practice to standardize on a fixed size for your dashboards and visualizations. It is far easier to reuse previously prepared dashboards or dashboard components if they are uniformly sized.

Another way to set the canvas size is to have the canvas hug your components by using the Fit Canvas to Components button. This works well if your outermost component happens to be a rectangle or one of the other Art and Background components. In addition, you can incrementally expand or decrease the canvas size by using the toolbar buttons Increase Canvas and Decrease Canvas. In this way, you can create an invisible border to frame your components.

NOTE

The canvas is normally a generic white background. You can change the background to a solid colorized background or a gradient-filled colorized background, or you can embed an image file that is any of the following file types: JPG, PNG, GIF, BMP, or SWF.

Technically speaking, the canvas is not a layer in your dashboard, and as such, it is not accessible within the Object Browser, which I talk about next.

THE OBJECT BROWSER

The Object Browser allows you to manage the components placed on the canvas. You can do things like select them; hide and show them; lock them in place; cut, copy, and paste them; and give them descriptive names.

As you drop or place components onto the canvas foreground, new component items are added to the bottom of the list in the Object Browser (see Figure 3.4). The foremost component on the canvas is a combination chart, which corresponds to the item at the bottom of the Object Browser pane.

Figure 3.4
Components in the
canvas and items in
the Object Browser
correspond to one
another.

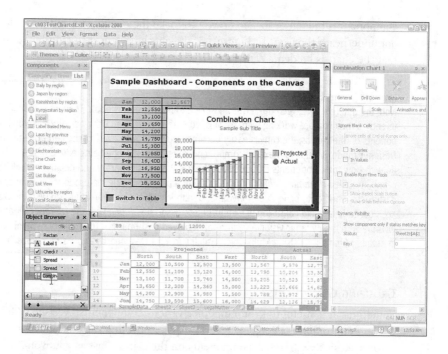

Notice that when a component on the canvas is selected, the corresponding object is highlighted in the Object Browser.

Note that double-clicking the title bar of the Object Browser, Components pane, or properties panel pops out the panel into a free-floating window that can be resized and moved about on the screen (see Figure 3.5). Double-clicking the title bar of the free-floating window parks the window back to its original location and size.

Figure 3.5
The Object Browser
as a free-floating
window.

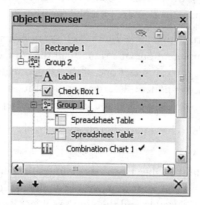

Notice near the upper-right corner (see Figure 3.5) of the Object Browser that there are two icons and a corresponding column of dots under each of the icons. One of these icons is an eye, and the other is a padlock. A checkmark under these icons signifies that the component is hidden or locked down. To make the component hidden or locked, click the dot underneath the icon. In Figure 3.5, the checkmark next to Combination Chart 1 means that the chart is hidden.

Invisible Versus Hidden

Note the difference between the terms *invisible* and *hidden* in this book. They appear similar but are used differently. When you are working with Xcelsius, you are said to be in Designer mode. If you have a lot of components on the canvas, the canvas easily becomes cluttered with overlapping components. While you are in Designer mode, it helps to make all components other than the one being edited *hidden*. This has nothing to do with how the components appear when the dashboard is exported and deployed. Xcelsius also supports a capability called *dynamic visibility*. This is more of a programmable feature to tell a component in a deployed dashboard whether to be *visible* or *invisible*. Dynamic visibility has nothing to do with the Designer mode of Xcelsius. To help avoid confusion, it's important to associate *hidden* with the Designer mode of Xcelsius and *invisible* with the dynamic visibility feature of deployed dashboards. (The topic of dynamic visibility is covered in detail in Chapter 7, "Using Multi-Layer Visibility in Your Dashboards and Visualizations.")

GROUPING COMPONENTS

Sometimes it is useful to group together various components. Xcelsius 2008 supports grouping and ungrouping. There are several ways of selecting the components you want. One way is to successively Ctrl+click components on the canvas, just as you would when selecting multiple nonconsecutive files in the Windows file browser. You can also select multiple elements with Ctrl+click within the Object Browser.

When the components you want are selected, you can group them together by pressing Ctrl+G; you can ungroup them by pressing Shift+Ctrl+G. There are also toolbar equivalents for grouping and ungrouping.

Grouping serves a number of purposes. It may be easier and less error prone to position a group of components in the center of the canvas or somewhere off to the side. In addition, you can hide or unhide all the components that are grouped together.

When you are designing a dashboard with a large number of components, it may be inefficient to click on each and every component one at a time. If all the components are next to one another on the Object Browser, you can select one of the components and, in the Object Browser, Shift+click another component. Every component in the Object Browser that falls in the intervening range becomes selected and eligible for grouping.

As shown in Figure 3.5, it is possible to have nested groupings (that is, a group within a group).

Changing the order of items listed in the Object Browser changes the depth of the corresponding component on the canvas. If you want to move a component closer to the foreground, you select the component in question and then in the Object Browser, click the + key. You can click and drag the item in the Object Browser to reposition it in the list of items. To make a selected component recede toward the back (in terms of the layer depth), you click the - key in the Object Browser. Clicking and dragging items (including grouped items) on the Object Browser list accomplishes the same thing as clicking the + and – keys.

POSITIONING THE COMPONENTS PANE, OBJECT BROWSER, AND PROPERTIES PANEL

Customizing the layout of your workspace can get a little complex. You have a variety of options available to you, and they are not necessarily evident.

When you have a free-floating panel, you can "park" it at the left, right, top, or bottom edges of your application. You do this by clicking the title bar of the panel and dragging it toward one of the sides. As you move the panel, a compass-like icon appears (see Figure 3.6).

Figure 3.6
Parking the Object Browser to the left edge and directly underneath the Components pane.

Notice that on each of the four sides is a tiny rectangle. When your mouse moves over a rectangle, a larger shaded region appears, outlining where the panel will be parked. In the case of Figure 3.6, the Object Browser is going to be positioned on the left side, directly under the Components pane.

Xcelsius 2008 incorporates an interesting and useful space-saving feature. You can turn parked panels into sliding drawers so that they remain tidy when not in use. To take advantage of this feature, you park your panel to one of the sides, as previously illustrated. Then you click the pushpin icon (see Figure 3.7). This collapses the panel so that it is neatly tucked to the edge. Notice in Figure 3.7 that the Components pane has already been collapsed in this fashion.

The sliding drawer interface frees up a lot of space on your screen, but it takes a little getting used to.

At this point, I leave you to consult the Xcelsius product documentation for more information and experiment on your own to determine what kind of layout works best for you.

Figure 3.7
Clicking the pushpin icon changes the panel to a sliding drawer.

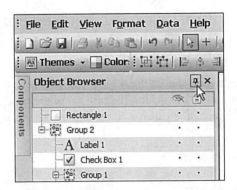

USING THE DASHBOARD DESIGN FACILITIES OF XCELSIUS

Perhaps the best way to get acquainted with Xcelsius 2008 is to explore and tinker with it. So fire up Xcelsius and, from the download set (available on www.XcelsiusBestPractices.com), import the ch03_01SampleSpreadsheet.xls file. The data in this spreadsheet depicts monthly projected and historical sales for four regional divisions in a company (refer to Figure 3.1).

NOTE

As of the time of this writing, Xcelsius 2008 supports Excel 2007 files in Compatibility Mode. That is, although you can save a spreadsheet as an .XLSX file, Xcelsius treats it as if its features are restricted to Excel 2003. When preparing spreadsheet files that are going to be imported into Xcelsius 2008, be sure to save them using Excel 2003 Compatibility Mode.

Note that the Xcelsius 2008 designer environment actually runs an instance of Excel in the background. The instance of Excel, if it is Excel 2003, retains whatever toolbars you have open when Excel normally launches. If you want certain toolbars to show, you need to configure this in Excel and then quit Excel. Thereafter, Xcelsius 2008 retains these characteristics in the embedded Excel.

Regardless, from this default view you can transform this dashboard in a wide variety of ways. Rather than charging you with a narrowly focused mission, this book explores various ways you can go about constructing dashboards. The goal at this point is not to be comprehensive but to give you a flavor for how to use various components.

TIP

If you are using Excel 2007, you might want to set the Excel Ribbon in minimized mode and then quit Excel 2007. This will cause Xcelsius 2008 to automatically display the Ribbon in the embedded spreadsheet in minimized mode.

Regardless of the kinds of dashboards you tend to build, you'll likely have common elements, such as identifying information, charts and/or tabular information, and possibly some navigational controls (for example, menus, list boxes, and other selectors).

TEXT-BASED COMPONENTS

Xcelsius 2008 has various text-related components, including labels, text areas, and input text. You'll be using labels all over the place, and I want to explain a few things about this. If you're used to using Crystal Xcelsius, you're going to be in for a few surprises. ☺

A label can be a static piece of text, such as the title of a report or the name of a company. There's nothing very exciting about that. What if you could extract text from the underlying spreadsheet? What if that text were the result of some spreadsheet formula? For instance, in the spreadsheet example, there's a bunch of sales-related information. Say that you want your text to display the total projected sales for the North region, which is the sum of cells B9 through B20. In your spreadsheet, place the following formula in cell B24:

```
=SUM(B9:B20)
```

Next, try dragging a Label component onto the canvas. Link it to cell B24 (see Figure 3.8).

Figure 3.8
Linking a text label to a spreadsheet cell that contains a formula.

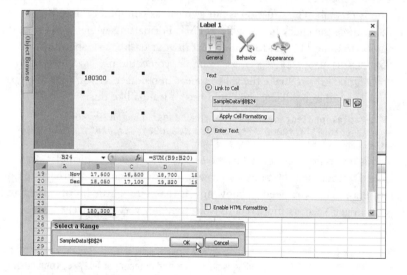

 As the numbers in the underlying spreadsheet change, so does the computed sum, and this gets picked up by the Label component. This is good, but an isolated number by itself is not very informative. This column of numbers refers to the total projected sales for the North region. So why not try stuffing this information into the formula? The word "North" is contained in cell B8. Revise cell B24 to the following formula:

```
="The total projected sales for the "&B8&" region is "&SUM(B9:B20)
```

Now the label says "`The total projected sales for the North region is 180300.`" This is definitely more informative, but you could improve on readability. Inserting a comma to separate the thousands would aid in clarity. It might help to include a currency symbol as well. Conveniently, Excel has a function called `TEXT` that does just this. Instead of using `SUM(B9:B20)`, you could use `TEXT(SUM(B9:B20),"$#,###")`. The formula then looks like this:

```
="The total projected sales for the "&B8&" region is "&TEXT(SUM(B9:B20),"$#,###")
```

Now the label says "`The total projected sales for the North region is $180,300.`" (If you feel lost when it comes to spreadsheet formulas, don't worry; I cover them in Chapter 4.)

Notice how I approach building components in the dashboard using successive baby steps. This technique of incrementally enhancing your dashboard components is instrumental to the overall dashboard construction process and constitutes a best practice. If nothing else, pick up this skill of incremental refinement.

How far can you carry the incremental improvement approach? Suppose the projected sales for the region of $180,300 is below the required sales quota of $250,000. It might be helpful to alert the dashboard user; maybe you could display the message in red. If you are used to using Crystal Xcelsius, you might know that the Label component doesn't support alerts. In Xcelsius 2008, the Label component has General, Behavior, and Appearance tabs, but there is no Alerts tab. The situation is not as bleak as you might think. If you look back at Figure 3.8, you see the check box Enable HTML Formatting. When you select this check box, you can incorporate HTML-formatted text in your dashboard labels. Instead of using `TEXT(SUM(B9:B20),"$#,###")`, for example, you could use `"&TEXT(SUM(B9:B20),` `"$#,###")&"` to make the value appear in boldface. If you want the text to be both the color red and in boldface, you could use a formula like this:

```
="The total projected sales for the "&B8&" region is <b>
➥<font color=""#ff0000"">"&TEXT(SUM(B9:B20),"$#,###")
➥&"</font></b>"
```

At this point, don't get mired in the details of spreadsheet formulas. In Chapter 4—and, indeed, throughout the book—I provide a more systematic approach to building spreadsheet formulas. What you need to know now is that with a little bit of insight and elbow grease, you can get Xcelsius and Excel to work together very effectively.

NOTE HTML formatting is also supported in the Input Text Area component.

CHART-BASED COMPONENTS

Xcelsius 2008 charts are in many ways similar to Excel charts, but there are some differences. One facility worth noting is the ability of Xcelsius charts to recognize mouse events and drill down. In this section, we'll look at how to set up a chart like a pie chart and drill down to a column chart.

Pie charts are good for providing broad summary information (such as sales totals by each of four regions) but not highly granular detail. The finer detail (such as month-by-month sales) might be better left for a column chart or line chart.

You should begin this example with exactly the same dataset used throughout this chapter. Somewhere below the bottom of the data, tabulate the total sales for the 12 months for each of the regions. You could place the totals in cells B24 through E24.

Drop a Pie Chart component on the canvas and map it to the region totals (see Figure 3.9).

Figure 3.9
Pie chart is linked to the North, South, East, and West totals.

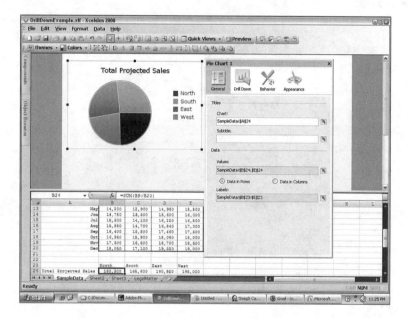

Next, you need to enable drill down. In the properties panel for the pie chart, select the Drill Down tab and click the Enable Drill Down check box. When drill down is enabled, you can specify how you want the drill down to work. Five different ways, or insertion types, are available:

- Position
- Value
- Row
- Column
- Status list

While your pie chart data stretches across a row (B24:E24), the monthly detail for each region runs down individual columns. That is, the monthly data for the North region is located in column B. The monthly data for the South region is located in column C.

Columns D and E hold the East and West sales data, respectively. If you want to drill down to the monthly detail for a given region, you need to look for the data in columns. For the insertion type, select Column (see Figure 3.10). The source data that's needed for the monthly estimates has to come from columns B, C, D, and E, spanning rows 9 through 20, or cell coordinates B9:E20.

Figure 3.10
Drill down settings within a pie chart.

The objective here is that when the user clicks or moves the mouse over a specific region in the pie chart, an event should be triggered that retrieves one of the columns in the source data and pushes the selected column of data onto a destination. When the needed data has arrived at a destination, it can be used by other charts, such as a column or line chart.

The destination can be a range of cells elsewhere on the spreadsheet. In order for the pie chart drill down feature to work correctly, it needs to be told where the destination is. For the time being, you can designate cells B27 through B38—basically one cell for each of the 12 months.

The next step is to drop a Column Chart component onto the canvas, perhaps placing it immediately to the right of the pie chart. This chart doesn't need to do any fancy footwork. The pie chart has done all the hard work setting up the drill down information. The column chart only needs to read the contents straight off the destination cells (B27:B38).

There are just a couple problems here. You have the numeric data for a particular region in the destination cells. How do you know which region the data refers to? All that has been transferred are the 12 monthly sales estimates. It certainly would be nice to have the region name displayed in the column chart. Was column the correct insertion type?

It turns out that more than one kind of insertion type can work (for instance, in this example, position could also be used). However, column is a perfectly appropriate choice. It's just that we didn't do a good enough job of specifying the source data and destination.

Part of the information needed is the region name. The source of this resides on row 8. So, really, the source data should start from row 8 instead of 9 and continue through row 20. (The source data cells should be B8:E20, and the destination cells should be B26:B38.)

When pushing the data, there is no reason not to combine non-numeric and numeric data. However, when they are read, they need to be read separately.

Now you can create a completed dashboard with drill down (see Figure 3.11). The monthly data is picked up in the column chart. The chart subtitle is linked to cell B26 so it correctly reads the region name. Still, there's something possibly wrong with this chart. Can you guess what it is?

Figure 3.11
Drill down is working, but something is wrong. Can you guess what it is?

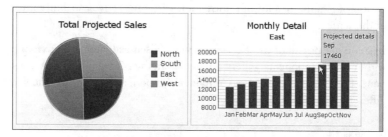

Although the chart is not super polished, there's nothing that outwardly appears out of alignment. It would be nice to have commas in the numbers. And the months running along the X-axis are a bit scrunched up, but so what? There is something else that weighs in much more heavily. Look at the vertical bars in the chart. Is it reasonable that in every successive month, the monthly sales is *always* greater than in the prior month?

The data graphed in the dashboard only reflects the projected sales. It is possible that the person who prepared the projection was overly zealous. Look carefully at *all* the data in the spreadsheet. There is historical sales data as well. The historical data also has the same anomaly. It turns out that the data you have been looking at is cumulative sales data. Calculating how much cumulative sales jump from one month to the next reveals the correct level of sales and is what you should be using in your dashboards.

There's an important lesson to be learned from this: The data provided in this example happens to be cumulative sales but is, nonetheless, valid. The dashboard for the drill down is correctly set up to take monthly data, aggregate it for a pie chart, and interactively drill down to the appropriate monthly detail. There is nothing fundamentally wrong with the dashboard design or, for that matter, the data collected and generated. What's wrong is that that there is a grand disconnect between the world in which the data gets captured and assembled and the world where the data is presented and relied on by interested parties (for example, the CEO, investors, whoever uses the dashboard).

CONTAINER COMPONENTS

Container components, as the name suggests, are used to hold things. Xcelsius containers include Panel Container, Panel Container 2, and Tab Set components. I elaborate on each of these types in the following sections.

PANEL CONTAINER COMPONENTS

A Panel Container component is kind of a mini-canvas with a surrounding border and place to designate the Panel Container component's title. You can drop components into the interior of the Panel Container component. As you are designing your dashboard and position a Panel Container component, its interior components move with it. In a way, it is like having grouped components inside a window.

There is one reason to consider using a Panel Container component: If the components inside it are larger than the Panel Container component, it auto-scrolls. This affords the option of cramming a lot of information with interactive capability into a restricted portion of the screen.

In some but not all of the Xcelsius themes (discussed later in this chapter), you see listed within the Components gallery a Panel Container 2 component. A Panel Container 2 component is the same as a Panel Container component, except that the surrounding border has different artwork.

NOTE

> If you use a Panel Container 2 component within a dashboard and later decide to change the theme to one that does not have a Panel Container 2 component, your component will be converted to a Panel Container component, and this process is irreversible.

TAB SET COMPONENTS

The Tab Set component is a welcome addition to Xcelsius 2008. It allows you to click through the "tabs" and interact with different sets of components. It is relatively easy to use a Tab Set component. First, you drag a Tab Set component onto your canvas. Notice in Figure 3.12 that there are + and - icons at the top of the component. You click the + icon to add an additional tab to your set. As you add each one, you are prompted for a tab label.

You can rearrange the tab order by using the Object Browser (see Figure 3.13). Each tab of the Tab Set component has a mini-canvas within the Object Browser. You select the one you're interested in and reposition it in the Object Browser. Within the Object Browser, you can select one of the tabs in your Tab Set and use the + and - keys on your keyboard to rearrange the order of the tab within the Tab Set. Pressing the + key shifts the tab to the right and pressing the - key shifts it to the left.

Figure 3.12
You click the + icon to add a tab.

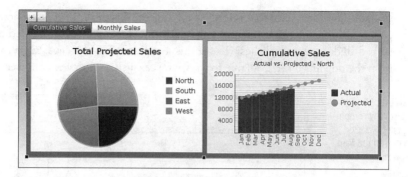

Figure 3.13
Tab order can be reassigned in the Object Browser.

SELECTORS

Xcelsius 2008 has a broad array of selectors, including Accordion Menu, Check Box, Combo Box, Filter, Horizontal Fisheye Menu, Horizontal Sliding Menu, Icon, Label Menu, List Box, List View, List Builder, Radio Button, Ticker, Toggle Button, Spreadsheet Table, and Play. You'll use many of these throughout the book, so I don't go into great detail about them here. The ones you might want to learn about first are Accordion Menu, Check Box, Label Menu, List Box, Radio Button, Toggle Button, and Spreadsheet Table. They are easy to learn and you'll find common uses for these.

Incidentally, the Spreadsheet Table component in Xcelsius 2008 is the same thing as the Table component in Crystal Xcelsius. Spreadsheet Table component and List view are similar to one another, except that List view permits sorting and allows the user to adjust column width. Like many of the other list- and table-based components in Xcelsius, List view is interactive and can respond to your mouse clicks or movements.

I need to explain something that may not be self-evident, especially among selectors. While you may not find a drill down feature for a given component, you may still be able to accomplish the equivalent. Selectors allow you to pick an item from many members or a list. Once you've chosen an item, you can place its row, position, value, label, or whatever is available and then place that reference on a spreadsheet cell. From that point on, other components can retrieve that reference and perform a lookup or other needed task. Isn't that what drill down accomplishes? To see this in action, open the `ch03_ListViewMap.xlf` file from the download set, available from www.XcelsiusBestPractices.com (see Figure 3.14).

Figure 3.14
The List View component punts selected data over to the Map component.

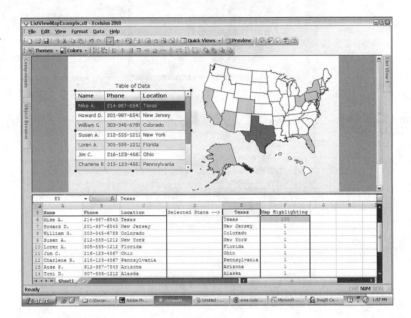

When previewing or exporting the dashboard, you can click on any person in the list. Instantly, the state corresponding to the selected list item is highlighted in a different color. Also note that all the states associated with any member in the list are also highlighted.

You can simplify much of your work with dashboards if you can get the various components in your visualizations to tag team. Not only will this make it easier for you to design and build dashboards, it will reduce the degree to which dashboards are perceived as disconnected.

SINGLE VALUE COMPONENTS

A Single Value component generally targets a single cell of the underlying spreadsheet. Oddly, a Dual Slider is treated as a Single Value component, but let's look at what you can do with it. In the `ch03_DualSliderExample.xlf` file, a Dual Slider is used to control the range of values plotted on a line chart (see Figure 3.15).

The slider is allowed to vary between the range of 0 and 3600 (see Figure 3.16), but the high and low values of the slider are read from cells B2 and B3.

What is happening in this dashboard is that the minimum and maximum X values in the plot are being set by the user via the Dual Slider. When the extremes are updated, the increment size between successive plot points is recalculated, and all the plot points are regenerated.

Dials and gauges are discussed in Chapter 6, "Single Value Components: Dials, Gauges, Speedometers, and the Like."

Figure 3.15
A Dual Slider controls
a plot.

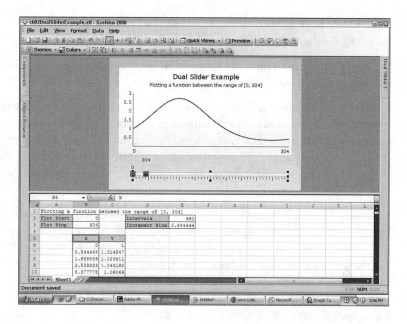

Figure 3.16
Slider values control
the plot parameters.

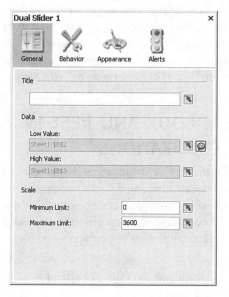

MAPS

As shown earlier in this chapter, Xcelsius 2008 supports the use of maps. For more information about maps, see Chapter 11, "Maps in Xcelsius."

ART AND BACKGROUND COMPONENTS

Aside from the overall approach of varying the color fills and gradients in various components, Xcelsius 2008 provides a number of specially-designed components to build the backdrop for your dashboards and visualizations. The components include the Background, Image, Rectangle, Ellipse, Horizontal Line, and Vertical Line components.

Horizontal and vertical lines can be useful to serve as visual separators, making it easier to read what might otherwise be a dense and noisy visualization.

The Rectangle component is also very useful in conjunction with other components. Some components, like the Line Chart component, offer online basic colorization features. For instance, you can set the plot area to a solid color, but you can't apply a gradient fill rotated at, say, a 45-degree angle. What you can do is turn off the Line Chart component's background so it is transparent and then place a Rectangle component immediately behind it and apply the fancy colorization in the Rectangle component.

Some new features in Xcelsius 2008 are cause for celebration. In addition to the previously supported JPG and SWF file formats, the Image component also supports BMP, GIF, and PNG file formats. If you are new to Xcelsius, you might think "So what?" Well, lack of support for those file formats has been a thorn in the side for many who have built dashboards and visualizations with Crystal Xcelsius.

WEB CONNECTIVITY AND OTHER COMPONENTS

An important change in Xcelsius 2008 Engage (whose predecessor is Crystal Xcelsius Professional) is that web and remote data connectivity are now built in to the product, and the licensing restrictions have been significantly relaxed. If you want to seamlessly connect your dashboards to back-end data sources, you can now do so. Look in Chapter 15, "XML and Data Connectivity," for detailed information on web and remote data connectivity.

ACHIEVING A UNIFORM LOOK AND FEEL IN DASHBOARDS AND VISUALIZATIONS

An important feature for any visualization or dashboard is the visual clarity with which information is conveyed. As has been demonstrated in the various dashboards in this book, you can fine-tune the appearance of just about any component placed on the canvas. As your dashboards get more elaborate, they are bound to have more components. This means you could be spending more time repetitively fine-tuning components, even if they all have the same kind of branding.

There are some strategies for achieving uniform look and feel while reducing the "electronic pencil pushing" nature of dashboard construction.

SIMPLE REPLICATION AT THE COMPONENT LEVEL

The simplest step you can take, if you have multiple components, is to build a base component the way you want and then copy and paste it. The advantage of this approach is that there is zero skill involved. But it also has some clear disadvantages: You may still end up doing a lot of replicating, and if you need to uniformly tweak the appearance of components of a similar type, you must hand edit each and every one of them.

This is not a good solution, but you'll learn about a design approach called *context switching*. There are numerous examples of this throughout the book. In a nutshell, the idea is that you may set up a chart or other component that reads data from a designated range of cells in your spreadsheet. For example, it could be quarterly sales in cells B3 through E3. The chart title could be read from cell A3.

You pour a lot of effort into creating this awesome looking chart. Your font selection and chart color choices and shading effects are superb. Now that you've gone through designing this chart, it would be great if you could repurpose it, on the spot, for other quarterly data. To extend this example, let's say the other data you are interested in are the quarterly cost of goods sold, which are located in row 4, and gross profit, which is in row 5.

Here is the crux: Create a set of conduit cells, perhaps cells A2 through E2. Set these conduit cells to retrieve the values of the spreadsheet data in row 3 when you want sales info, row 4 when you want cost of goods sold, and row 5 when you want the gross profit information. Instead of mapping your chart to the cells in row 3, map them to the conduit cells in row 2.

Your next step is to place a value into a context cell (maybe use cell A1 for this). The conduit cells in the second row watch the value of the context cell A1. You can use components like a List Box or Radio Button to monitor the value of the context cell. So by clicking an item inside a list box, you can instantly have a chart change the data it displays.

The spreadsheet functions for picking up the data based on the context are discussed in Chapter 4 (in particular, the OFFSET function serves this purpose well).

In this example, I speak about context switching for three different sets of data—sales, cost of goods sold, and gross profit. In principle, you could just as easily set up context switching for many hundreds of sets of data. This certainly seems like a good strategy to inhibit the proliferation of almost identical visual components.

For now, focus on the concept of context switching. The formulas come later. There are plenty of examples throughout the book that use context switching.

PASTING COMPONENTS BETWEEN XLF FILES

Xcelsius 2008 allows you to copy and paste components between dashboard files. This was not possible with Crystal Xcelsius.

In order to copy and paste components across multiple XLF files, you need to launch a second instance of Xcelsius 2008. Whenever you're running more than one instance of Xcelsius, be prepared for your computer to consume a lot of memory.

When you copy and paste across dashboards (as opposed to within a dashboard), the links to the underlying spreadsheet are erased.

XCELSIUS 2008 TEMPLATES

Xcelsius supports templates, which consist of saved XLF files and saved SWF files. A template offers the ability to organize starter files that are easy for you to build on. You might, for instance, have a standard set of corporate logos, confidentiality notices, or label-based menus. You can place all these in a template, and the template will save you some time and help establish a uniform appearance for your dashboards.

Assuming that your files are on the C: drive, you can create a template by saving your XLF file to C:\Program Files\Business Objects\Xcelsius 2008\assets\template. You also need to save your dashboards as SWF files to the same directory.

Optionally, you can create categories of templates by creating new directories inside the template directory and saving your files in them. The next time you want to start with a template file, you select File, Templates from the Xcelsius application menu, and the dialog box shown in Figure 3.17 appears.

Figure 3.17
You can easily preview custom templates.

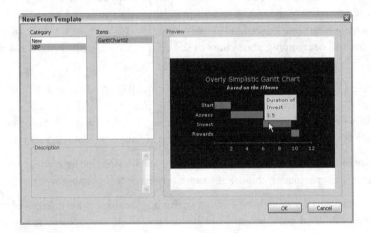

XCELSIUS 2008 THEMES

Similarly to templates, themes give you another way to control the look and feel of your dashboards. There are two ways to preview and select Themes. One of them is through the application Format menu, and the other is through the Xcelsius toolbars. Notice in the preview in Figure 3.18 that the currently selected theme is highlighted.

I recommend that you use the toolbar to preview the themes for two reasons. First, you get to compare them all in a single view. When previewing themes from the menu, you are forced to cycle through the themes one at a time. Second, you will notice that with each theme in the toolbar-based preview, there is a horizontal swatch of colors. This corresponds to the coloring scheme for the theme. When you preview themes by navigating through the application menu, the swatch of colors is totally absent.

Try experimenting with different themes to see what you like. There are two key factors to keep in mind with themes. One of them relates to data protection of open dashboards. The other relates to a strategy for choosing some themes over others.

Figure 3.18
You can easily
preview themes.

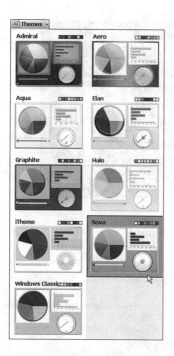

CAUTION

If you have a dashboard open and, while it is open, change the theme, the coloration settings and many of the components' attributes will be irrevocably altered. Unless you previously saved your dashboard, you will not be able to restore any of your custom settings. Going back to the original theme will force your dashboard to use the default settings. Any custom settings you made will be lost.

One practical issue may influence your choosing of one theme over another. You may have noticed that bar charts and column charts use shading to give an embossed look. This makes a chart look fancy but sometimes can get in the way. For example, suppose you want to create a Gantt chart, a graphical representation for tracking the timeline of various tasks that is typically used as a project management tool. While Xcelsius doesn't have a Gantt chart component, it is not difficult to construct such a chart (see Figure 3.19). The key is to use a Stacked Bar Chart component and make one of the data series the same color as the background. This allows the second series to appear as if it is floating.

This Stacked Bar Chart component has two data series. The first one pertains to the start time of a task. It is colored black, the same as the background. Unfortunately, bar charts in most of the themes do not use solid-color bars. Thankfully, the theme called iTheme does have solid-color bars.

Figure 3.19
A simple Gantt chart based on a camou-flaged data series.

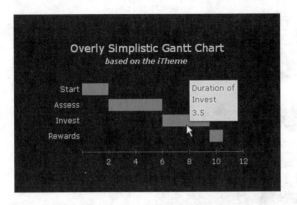

FONTS IN XCELSIUS

With Xcelsius 2008, you can pick and choose from a wide variety of fonts in a dashboard. As you can see in Figure 3.20, you can specify multiple fonts, even within a single component.

Figure 3.20
Using multiple fonts in an Xcelsius component.

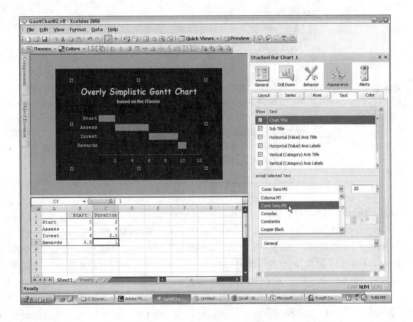

By default, Xcelsius makes use of device fonts, and your exported dashboards rely on Flash Player to render device fonts. As long as the computer on which you are running a dashboard has the matching TrueType font, it will render correctly. If the font is missing, Flash Player will substitute the closest available font. Before you start having conniptions about missing fonts and ugly font substitutions, you should realize that the situation is really no different than when font substitution is done with a word processing document. When was the last time you received a word processing file that was rendered unusable because of a font substitution? You have two options to guard against this happening:

- You can use fonts that are common in usage, such as Verdana, Times New Roman, and Courier New.
- You can use an embedded font.

Embedded fonts travel with exported dashboard, thus increasing the file size. Because of the large number of characters, Asian character sets are not supported with embedded fonts.

Don't worry about how to configure for device fonts. Xcelsius 2008 is already configured to take advantage of device fonts, so you generally don't need to bother finagling with device versus embedded fonts.

CLOSING THOUGHTS

This chapter, almost more than any other, is written with two audiences in mind: those entirely new to Xcelsius and those who have experience working with its predecessor product, Crystal Xcelsius. Regardless of which of these two camps you associate yourself with, the basic premise of giving a spreadsheet a dashboard interface is a simple concept to grasp. To make effective use of this framework, you have to figure out how to make things work the way you want in Xcelsius 2008.

This chapter is basically a first-day on-the-job training. While the chapter exposes you to many Xcelsius 2008 features, emphasis is given to skill acquisition so that you know components can be made to work together. The practice of building dashboards and visualizations with successive refinements is strongly encouraged. One of the chapter examples illustrates how easy it is to get ensnared if you don't consciously connect data preparation and analysis with the dashboard or visual presentation.

The skills of knowing how to work with data and moving it to the dashboard realm are just as essential as composing an aesthetically pleasing and functional dashboard layout.

This chapter is focused on getting you comfortable and familiar enough with Xcelsius 2008 that you can begin using the tool productively. To really put to use the empowering features of Xcelsius, you need to be armed with specific knowledge and techniques about how to incorporate spreadsheets in Xcelsius 2008, and that is the subject of Chapter 4.

EMBEDDED SPREADSHEETS: THE SECRET SAUCE OF XCELSIUS 2008

In this chapter

It doesn't take much to realize that Xcelsius 2008 is distinctive. First, there's the ability to deploy dashboards to a variety of formats, such as PowerPoint, Word, or PDF, while retaining full interactivity. But while important, this alone is not enough to distinguish the software. Xcelsius 2008 uses scalable vector graphics to render text, shapes, backgrounds, and charts. This ability to avoid pixilation is another nice feature, but again, this is not what makes Xcelsius so remarkable. What really makes the software so distinctive is that it embeds spreadsheets within the Xcelsius environment, both during design and deployment.

This chapter is about how Excel partners with Xcelsius 2008 and how you can empower your dashboards and visualizations with Excel. Chiefly, this chapter serves the needs of two audiences:

- Those who consider themselves relatively new to Excel and the mechanics of handling spreadsheets
- Those who consider themselves seasoned spreadsheet users and are looking for new approaches and techniques to enhance their Xcelsius dashboards

Even if you are fluent with spreadsheets, don't be too hasty in reading through the spreadsheet fundamentals section of this chapter; there may be an insight or two you have yet to absorb that are worth knowing. In addition to spreadsheet fundamentals, this chapter covers specific spreadsheet techniques that are sure to energize your dashboards. An example of this is the ability to use named ranges in your formulas, whose boundaries are determined by dashboard inputs rather than being set at design time.

SPREADSHEET FUNDAMENTALS

Spreadsheets offer a wide range of capabilities, with everything from formulas to macros, charting, conditional formatting, data validation, worksheet protection, and remote data access. Principally, when working with Excel in Xcelsius 2008, you only need to be concerned about two Excel-specific things: the spreadsheet formulas and, to some extent, the formatting of cells that are linked to the Xcelsius canvas.

Many of the features of Excel already exist or can be implemented in Xcelsius:

- Xcelsius 2008 has its own charting capabilities, so you don't have to rely on the ones built in Excel.
- You can incorporate data validation facilities. Later in the chapter, I show some techniques you can use.
- Conditional alerts, discussed throughout this book, are also available.
- Spreadsheet formulas and content are automatically protected. All that is exposed is what you allow to show in the canvas.
- Xcelsius 2008 Engage, Engage Server, and BusinessObjects Xcelsius Enterprise provide built-in support for accessing remote data, so you don't have to rely on Excel-based facilities for this.

However, several functions are missing from an Excel spreadsheet embedded in Xcelsius:

- Approximately 160 Excel functions are supported in Xcelsius 2008. Some of the most important functions are outlined in this chapter. For a complete list of Excel-supported functions, see Appendix A, "Supported Spreadsheet Functions in Xcelsius 2008."

- You do not have access to the Excel application menus (although I show some workarounds that enable you to regain much of this functionality).

- Only a single Excel workbook can be embedded in an Xcelsius dashboard. In addition, you cannot deploy dashboards that incorporate references to remote workbooks.

FORMULA FUNDAMENTALS

Spreadsheet formulas can be quite elaborate. It pays to start off by keeping things simple and gently and progressively layer in more sophistication.

BUILDING ON SIMPLE FORMULAS

 Even if you are not comfortable with spreadsheet formulas, you shouldn't have difficulty figuring out what would result from the following spreadsheet formula:

```
=AVERAGE(30,40,50)
```

This is the average of the numbers 30, 40, and 50. Of course, the average of these three numbers is `(30+40+50)/3 = 40`.

Notice the structure of an Excel formula: It starts off with an equal symbol (=) and is followed by some algebraic expression, which typically results in a number, text, or a true/false value. There are other possible results, such as an expression that returns an error. But for now, apply the KISS principle: "Keep it simple, stupid."

> **NOTE**
>
> If you need a refresher on spreadsheets, feel free to consult my book *Escape from Excel Hell* (0471773182). (In particular, Chapter 2 provides a good review of Excel functions.) If you are in need of a comprehensive reference on Excel, look at *Special Edition Using Microsoft Office Excel 2007* (078973611X) or *Special Edition Using Microsoft Office Excel 2003* (0789729539).

In Excel, you could get the same result by using a formula like this:

```
=(30+40+50)/3
```

So far, all this amounts to is that Excel can be used as a glorified calculator. To get beyond the mindless calculation stage, you can incorporate spreadsheet cell references and more complicated expressions in your formulas. Let's work through an example.

Launch Xcelsius 2008 and enter the number 30 in cell A1 (that is, the cell in row 1 and column A) and 40 in cell A2. In cell B1, enter the following formula:

```
=(A1+A2+50)/3
```

4

Because A1 is `30` and A2 is `40`, the spreadsheet computes the expression in cell B2 as `(30+40+50)/3`, which once again results in `40`. By now, you should be tiring of this example, but let's stay with it a few moments longer. In your Xcelsius 2008 environment, try placing a slider on the canvas and link its Data value to cell A1. Also place a gauge on the canvas and link it to the result in cell B1. For good measure, you can throw in a Spreadsheet Table component and link its display to cells A1 though B3 (see Figure 4.1).

Figure 4.1
Cell A1 can be set from the dashboard.

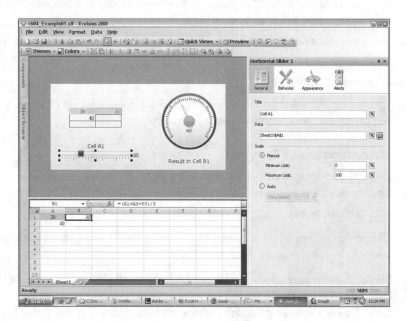

As a rule, you should highlight all *input cells* that can be driven by the Xcelsius dashboard from the canvas. The common practice is to shade such spreadsheet cells with a noticeable but easy-to-read color, such as bright yellow. These cells might be easier to read if you also give their text a boldface appearance and apply a centered justification, as is done for cell A1 in Figure 4.1.

FORMULA CHAINING IN SPREADSHEETS

Let's extend what can be done with spreadsheet formulas. Suppose that you give cell A2 the following formula:

`=(A1-150)*A1/50`

What happens to cell B2? Cell B2 is `(A1+A2+50)/3`, but A2 is `(A1-150)*A1/50`. Fortunately, Excel knows how to *chain* these formulas so that everything gets computed automatically.

Formula chaining lets you easily build sophisticated mathematical models and incorporate them into your Xcelsius dashboards.

BUILDING SPREADSHEET MODELS IN XCELSIUS 2008

One of the advantages of working with Xcelsius 2008 is that you can build your spreadsheet and dashboard in tandem. There is no requirement to have a complete spreadsheet before you begin the dashboard design.

Of course, it is advantageous to have a readymade spreadsheet with absolutely no changes required. All you would have to do is import the spreadsheet into Xcelsius, throw the needed components onto the canvas, link them to the underlying spreadsheets, set some of the properties in the components, and export a polished dashboard. The only time it works this way, though, is in a sales demonstration.

The motivating factor is that you should be able to take a preexisting spreadsheet that was built without any knowledge that it could eventually be used with Xcelsius and directly incorporate into an Xcelsius dashboard or visualization. This, too, is a wonderful thought, but the chances are that some spreadsheet modifications will be necessary to make it well suited for use with Xcelsius 2008.

The great advantage with Xcelsius 2008 is that you can make changes directly in the imported spreadsheet as you are building your dashboards and visualizations. As you make changes, you can test and validate that they work the way you expect them to. The changes can include things like inserting rows and columns, as well as revising formulas.

SPREADSHEET CELL REFERENCES

There are four ways to reference spreadsheet cells: using relative references, absolute references, hybrid references, and named references.

The first three of these methods are related to the physical cell coordinates of column letter and row number. The distinction between relative, absolute, and hybrid references has to do with how cell references get adjusted when a cell formula is copied and pasted to other cells.

For example, within the spreadsheet for a dashboard, you may have some quantity (say, in column A) that is increased by a surcharge factor. The final amount could be computed in column C (see Figure 4.2).

Figure 4.2
Cell referencing affects how formulas get cloned.

	C2	f_x =A2*(100%+B2)		
	A	B	C	D
1	Base Amount	Surcharge factor	Total Amount	Formula used in column C
2	100	11%	111	=A2*(100%+B2)
3	125	11%	138.75	=A3*(100%+B3)
4	193		214.23	=A4*(100%+$B$2)
5	225		249.75	=A5*(100%+$B$2)
6	255		283.05	=A6*(100%+$B$2)
7				
8				
9				
10				

Sheet1

For your convenience, Figure 4.2 shows the formulas used in Column C. As you can see, this is the formula in cell C2:

`=A2*(100%+B2)`

If you copy and paste this formula into cell C3, this is the resulting formula:

`=A3*(100%+B3)`

If you were to paste this formula into, say, cell C47, this would be the resulting formula:

`=A47*(100%+B47)`

This formula is logical enough. It requires that you supply a value for the amount and surcharge factor in every row where you are computing the total amount. But what if you have a single surcharge you would like to apply across the board? You could replicate that surcharge in column B for every row. That would be inefficient and potentially prone to error. Every time you needed to update the surcharge, you would have to replicate it into each and every instance where it occurs. It would be simpler to lock the cell reference of the surcharge to a single cell. In this manner, when you replicate the spreadsheet formula for total cost, there would be a single master surcharge rate. This buys you simplicity of design and peace of mind. You won't have to worry about your formulas going awry.

Locking in a cell reference does come at a slight cost, however: You have to identify what is being locked when you replicate your formulas. This is done by prepending a dollar ($) symbol to either or both the column letter and row number of the cell reference. If you want to lock both the column letter and the row number, so that the cell reference is absolute, you would therefore have to use the dollar symbol twice—once in front of the column letter and once in front of the row number. In the current example, you might designate the "master" surcharge rate to be located in cell B2. This could be the formula for the total result in cell C4:

`=A4*(100%+$B$2)`

Notice that there is no need to populate a surcharge factor in cell B4 because the reference is locked to cell B2. If you replicate the formula in cell C4 to C5, the formula becomes the following:

`=A5*(100%+$B$2)`

What was A4 is now A5 because it is a relative reference. The surcharge factor is locked in column B and row 2 because the absolute reference, $B$2, is used in the formula.

All this may seem like an undue amount of complication just to replicate a handful of formulas. But when you're working with a spreadsheet that has dozens or hundreds of formulas, you'll appreciate that you can lock cell reference with a high degree of control.

So far, you've seen relative references and absolute references. What if you want to lock in the column but not the row, or lock the row but not the column? These are known as *hybrid cell references*. Sometimes a formula can involve both kinds of hybrid cell references—where one of the terms locks the row and not the column and the other locks the column and not the row. You will typically encounter this when you try building a table in a spreadsheet (see Figure 4.3).

Figure 4.3
A spreadsheet table driven by two cells (A3 and B2).

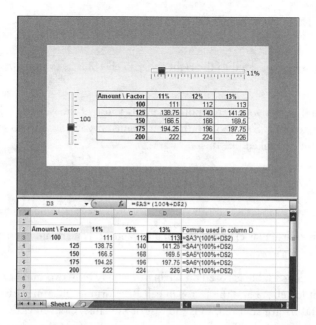

The contents of the spreadsheet table are computed by using the amount that is in column A and the surcharge rate, which is in row 2. You could have a formula like the following in cell B3:

```
=A3*(100%+B2)
```

If you try copying and pasting this formula across the table, the formula will not replicate correctly. You need to lock the column so the amount is always associated with column A. In this case, you would change A3 to $A3. You also need to lock the surcharge rate to row 2, so you would change B2 to B$2. This would be the resulting formula for cell B3:

```
=$A3*(100%+B$2)
```

TIP

> There is a very easy way to cycle through the various permutations of relative, absolute, and hybrid cell references in your spreadsheet formulas. While you are entering or editing a formula, you highlight the portion of the formula you want to change and then repeatedly press the F4 key. Each time you do so, the locking $ symbols will be inserted and/or deleted, thus allowing you to cycle through the various reference modes.

To make the Spreadsheet Table component on the canvas a little more useful, I have placed two sliders, one vertical and one horizontal (refer to Figure 4.3). The vertical slider is bound or linked to cell A3.

In cell A4 I have the following formula:

```
=A3+25
```

Because this is a relative reference, I can replicate the formula down to cell A7.

This is the surcharge factor in cell C2:

`=B2+1%`

This formula can be replicated to the right so that cell D2 is as follows:

`=C2+1%`

There are several things you should notice here. Because of the way the cells are arranged, it is not necessary to insert $ symbols in the expressions. If you chose to do so, however, your formulas would have looked like this:

`=$A3+25`

and this:

`=B$2+1%`

Both ways in this particular example are equally valid, so you should choose the set of formulas that's easier to read.

The idea of building a table is based on having to supply only two numbers—in this example, the amount in cell A3 and the factor in cell B2. Formula chaining drives the whole table, so that as A3 and B2 are adjusted, so is the rest of the table. Conveniently, the vertical and horizontal sliders on the dashboard canvas can be used to affect the values of the two input cells A3 and B2.

Notice also that Excel allows you to embed percentage symbols in a formula, as in the following example:

`=B2+1%`

Alternatively, you could use a decimal representation, such as the following:

`=B2+0.01`

While either way is valid, I recommend that you generally opt for the decimal representation. Suppose you need to add the value `1234.073` to cell B2 and you used percentages. You would have a formula like this:

`=B2+123407.3%`

Very large and very small percentages tend to be difficult to read. I suggest that you use percentages only when you are formatting a cell (that is, for presentation purposes) and avoid the use of percentage representation in actual spreadsheet formulas.

 In addition, generally speaking, you should avoid using hardwired values in your spreadsheet formulas. As an example, you could place the `0.01` (or `1%`) value in cell B1 and then use a formula like this:

`=B2+$B$1`

There are several very good reasons to isolate hardwired values:

- If a hardwired value is embedded inside a formula, it is impossible to change it without hand editing your formula.

- If you need to update a hardwired value in a formula, you might have a difficult time finding all your needles in the haystack. For example, say that you have several formulas in your spreadsheet that incorporate the sales tax rate for New York City. Say that the rate changes, and you change it in 12 places, but you miss an unlucky 13th place. Such potential spreadsheet errors are avoidable.

- When you have an isolated hardwired value, it can be used as an input cell in your Xcelsius dashboard.

NAMED RANGES

Xcelsius 2008 allows the use of named ranges in spreadsheet formulas. However, there are some strict limitations regarding their usage. In Xcelsius 2008, named ranges must either point to single cells or use functions that return single values over the range of cells.

If you are familiar with Excel, you may recall that you can associate a name of your choosing, such as `NYC_SalesTaxRate`, with a single spreadsheet cell or range of cells. After you make such a definition, you can use the defined name instead of physical cell coordinates within your spreadsheet formulas. For instance, you could define `NYC_SalesTaxRate` to be the contents of cell B1. After you make this definition, you could write a formula like this:

`=B2+NYC_SalesTaxRate`

Computationally, this formula would return exactly the same result as the following:

`=B2+$B$1`

Named ranges can make formulas easier to read. But can you use them in Xcelsius 2008? The answer is, in a limited manner, yes. It turns out that named ranges work inside Xcelsius in two situations:

- A defined name range can apply to only a single cell. For instance, `NYC_SalesTaxRate` can be defined or associated with only one spreadsheet cell and not a group of cells.

- A group of cells can be associated with a named range, but the only valid usage of the named range involves returning a single result from the group of cells. For example, you can have a named range such as `MonthlySales` that is composed of 12 numbers in a row or column, 1 for each month. In this case, you could incorporate functions that return a single value from the group of cells that make up the defined named range. For instance, you could use formulas like these:

```
=SUM(MonthlySales)
=AVERAGE(MonthlySales)
=MAX(MonthlySales)-MIN(MonthlySales)
=STDEV(MonthlySales)
=SUM(MonthlySales)-SUM(MonthlyExpenses)
```

But you should not incorporate expressions like this:

```
=MonthlySales-MonthlyExpenses
```

unless both `MonthlySales` and `MonthlyExpenses` point to single cell references and not to a group of cells. For instance, if `MonthlySales` is defined as cell A1 having a value of 243000, and `MonthlyExpenses` is defined as cell A2 having a value of `203000`, then Xcelsius 2008 would compute the value of `MonthlySales-MonthlyExpenses` as `40000`.

To define a named range in the underlying spreadsheet, you can press Ctrl+F3. Within Excel 2003, a Define dialog window appears, asking you to identify a name and range of cells. If you are using Excel 2007, pressing Ctrl+F3 opens the Name Manager window (see Figure 4.4).

Figure 4.4
Pressing Ctrl+F3 in Excel 2007 opens the Name Manager, and clicking New allows you to define a new name.

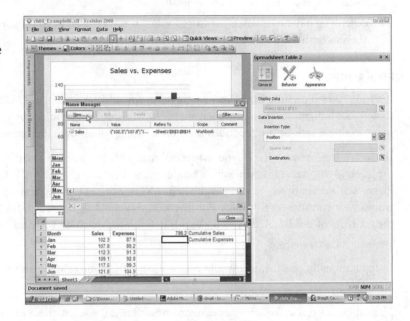

You click the New button to open the New Name window (see Figure 4.5), which is very much like the Define Name window in Excel 2003.

Figure 4.5
Identifying the name and cell reference for a named range.

TIP

If you run Xcelsius 2008 on a Macintosh using VMWare, Parallels, or Bootcamp to run Windows or Vista, you will need to adjust the keyboard preferences so that Ctrl+F3 doesn't move focus to the Dock. You can find this setting in the Keyboard Shortcuts section of the OS X Keyboard & Mouse System Preferences tab.

Within Xcelsius 2008, if you want to use a named range that occupies more than a single cell, you must apply a function that returns a single value. For instance, if Expenses is associated with cells C3 through C14, you can use a formula like the following for your dashboard:

```
=SUM(Expenses)
```

If you want to retrieve individual values (such as the expenses for the month of March) from a named range, you have to use a function like OFFSET, which is described later in this chapter.

USING EXCEL FUNCTIONS IN XCELSIUS 2008

You can use a variety of Excel functions and formula constructs in Xcelsius 2008; it supports roughly 160 Excel functions. This section introduces you to some of the salient features of functions that you might want to know.

Functions can be grouped into a variety of categories:

- Mathematical and statistical functions are useful for numeric computations.
- Text-related functions allow you to control what is displayed in your dashboards. Interestingly, text-related functions can tag team nicely with other spreadsheet computations, such as dynamic lookups.
- Your spreadsheet formulas will be further enhanced as you incorporate conditional logic and Boolean functions, which are invaluable for controlling dynamic visibility of your dashboard components.
- It is not uncommon for dashboards to present data that is date or time specific. There are a number of date and time specific functions you can use in Xcelsius.
- There is a category of Excel functions that I like to refer to as selectors, similar to the concept of selectors in Xcelsius. These spreadsheet functions allow you to pick the data that you want. If you are already familiar with Crystal Xcelsius or are a spreadsheet veteran, you may have already come across functions such as VLOOKUP and INDEX. This chapter covers these functions, as well as some other selector-style functions you should know about, such as OFFSET.

UNDERSTANDING THE ROLE OF SPREADSHEET FUNCTIONS AND OPERATORS IN XCELSIUS 2008

In order to precisely nail down how things get computed in Xcelsius, it's important to delineate what kinds of entities an Xcelsius spreadsheet uses and how things fit together. It really boils down to evaluation of expressions. This section is a little bit technical, so feel free to skim through it on a first read.

EVALUATING SPREADSHEET CELLS

If a spreadsheet cell is not blank, it must be occupied by a either a literal value or a formula. A literal is something that does not require any calculation. A literal is its own value. Literals include TRUE, FALSE, special constants such as #N/A, numbers, strings of text, and any expression whose first character is a single apostrophe.

All computations in any spreadsheet cell must be in the form of a formula, which starts with an equal symbol followed by an expression that gets evaluated by the spreadsheet engine.

An expression can be a combination of operators, literals, references (such as a range of cells), and Excel functions (which start with a function name followed by an opening parenthesis, followed immediately by a closing parenthesis, or an expression immediately followed by a closing parenthesis).

OPERATORS IN XCELSIUS SPREADSHEETS

Spreadsheet formulas in Xcelsius can evaluate compound expressions. A compound expression could be something like this:

```
=SQRT(3*3+4*4)
```

The SQRT function, which returns the square root of an expression returns the value 5 in this example. The Xcelsius 2008 spreadsheet environment makes use of various mathematical operators, including the colon operator, the comma operator, negation, percentage, exponentiation, multiplication, division, addition, subtraction, concatenation, and comparison operations (including =, <, >, <=, >=, and <>). At this time, Xcelsius 2008 does not support the Excel intersection operation (denoted by a space).

The colon operator specifies a range of cells and can be incorporated in an expression used by a function. For example, this:

```
=AVERAGE(A1:A5)
```

is the equivalent of this:

```
=AVERAGE(A1,A2,A3,A4,A5)
```

which is computed as follows:

```
=(A1+A2+A3+A4+A5)/5
```

A range doesn't necessarily need to be a single row or column of cells, as illustrated in the following formula:

```
=SUM(B2:C4)
```

which is the equivalent of the following:

```
=B2+B3+B4+C2+C3+C4
```

The comma is referred to as the "union" operator. It effectively unites cell ranges when you're evaluating expressions supplied to a function. For instance, the following:

```
=SUM(D3,A1:A4,C1:C3)
```

is the same as this:

```
=D3+A1+A2+A3+A4+C1+C2+C3
```

Understanding Operator Precedence

Spreadsheets allow you to create all sorts of complicated algebraic formulas by using operators. There are different kinds of operators. *Infix operators*, like those for addition and multiplication, are sandwiched between two expressions. The following is a good example of this:

    3+4

The numeric computation of 3+4 is easy to evaluate because there is no ambiguity.

A *postfix operator* appears immediately after the value it operates on. An example of this is the percentage operator. When a spreadsheet encounters 20% inside a formula, it converts this to the decimal value 0.2.

A *prefix operator* immediately precedes the value it acts on. The negation operator is a good example of this. You could have a formula like this:

    =-3

Sometimes, there can be ambiguity. Suppose you have the following formula:

    =-3^2

There are two ways of interpreting this formula. Should the -3 be squared? Or should the 3 squared be multiplied by -1? Without any precedence rules, you wouldn't know what Excel would do and how your spreadsheet formulas would behave inside Xcelsius 2008. It turns out that the negation operator has the higher precedence and is called into action before the exponentiation operator gets computed. So the preceding formula is computed as if it were written like this:

    =(-3)^2

and returns the value 9 (because a negative number times a negative number is a positive number).

When formulas involving operators are evaluated and have competing operators that are vying for the same expression, operator precedence determines who gets first dibs. The hierarchy is as follows:

1. **Reference operators:** Examples include the Colon operator, such as A1:A12, and the Comma operator, such as SUMPRODUCT(A1:A2,B1:B12).

2. **Negation:** An example would be -24.

3. **Percentage:** An example would be 25%.

4. **Exponentiation:** 2^3 is 2 raised to the third power, which would result in the value 8.

5. **Multiplication and division:** Examples include 8*1.2345678 which results in the value 9.8765432, and 9/4 which results in 2.25.

6. **Addition and subtraction:** Examples include 92+3, which results in 95, and 18-32, which results in -14.

7. **Concatenation:** For example, for "Xcelsius "&(1998+10), the resulting expression is "Xcelsius 2008".

8. **Comparison operations:** Examples include the following:

    0=1 results in a FALSE value

    4>2 results in a TRUE value

    4<2 results in a FALSE value

    4<=2*2 results in a TRUE value

    4>=2*2 results in a TRUE value

    0<>1 results in a TRUE value (because zero is not equal to one)

When operators on the same level of precedence (such as addition and subtraction) are acting on the same expression, the order of evaluation is from left to right.

4

MATHEMATICAL AND STATISTICAL FUNCTIONS IN XCELSIUS 2008

Xcelsius 2008 supports a great many mathematical and statistical functions. They are classified into three principal groups: aggregation and statistical functions, financial functions, and math functions.

NOTE

> To help make examples concrete, I tend to use explicit values rather than ranges of spreadsheet cells. If I tell you that the following:
>
> =MAX(A1:A6)   returns 13
>
> it may not be clear what the function MAX is doing. There will be more clarity if I state the following:
>
> =MAX(1,2,3,13,7,9)   returns 13
>
> There are times when it's appropriate to use cell references by themselves or cell references combined with explicit values. A good example of this is as follows:
>
> =MAX(0,A1:A100)
>
> A formula of this kind ensures that no negative value will be returned, because 0 is always greater than any negative value.

AGGREGATION AND STATISTICAL FUNCTIONS

There are many functions that aggregate or summarize information in terms of single measures, such as average values. The most common of these are detailed in the following sections.

MAX, MIN, AVERAGE, AVERAGEA, MEDIAN, AND MODE

```
MAX(number1,number2,...)
MIN(number1,number2,...)
AVERAGE(number1,number2,...)
AVERAGEA(Value1,Value2,...)
MEDIAN(number1,number2,...)
MODE(number1,number2,...)
```

MAX returns the largest value found in a list of numbers or ranges of cells.

MIN returns the lowest value found in a list of numbers or ranges of cells. It is important to note that negative values are always lower than any positive value, no matter how small they are. Positive values are always greater than any negative value.

Here are some sample calculations:

```
=MAX(10,20,45)                                                  returns 45
=MAX(10,20,SQRT(10000))                                         returns 100
=MIN(-986,0.002,1200,0)                                         returns -986
=MIN(986,-0.002,1200,0)                                         returns -0.002
```

AVERAGE returns the statistical mean or average value over a set of numbers or range of cells. Here is a sample calculation:

```
=AVERAGE(240, 180)                                    returns 210
```

There are some important subtleties to keep in mind when using AVERAGE and the similar function AVERAGEA. AVERAGE tries to be intelligent about how values are computed. Suppose you are tracking average monthly sales for the year. You just finished the month of July and have seven months of data in cells A1:A7. Of course, you can use a formula like this:

```
=AVERAGE(A1:A7)
```

It would be time-consuming and error prone if you rewrote this formula every time an additional month's worth of data were added. It would be a whole lot simpler if you could write a formula that accommodates all 12 months in a year and intelligently ignores the blank cells or cells with text labels. Fortunately, AVERAGE does precisely that. For example, the following formula:

```
=AVERAGE(A1:A12)
```

sensibly computes averages based on the non-blank cells. There are times when you want to take into account the blank cells in a range.

The function AVERAGEA is a little more literal in its computation of averages. It treats empty cells, cells with text labels, and cells with a FALSE value as if they are zero values. It treats TRUE values as if they are the value 1, and it treats numeric values as whatever the numeric value happens to be.

Understanding the MEDIAN function is fairly straightforward. For a dataset, it arranges the data points from lowest to highest. Then it removes both the highest and lowest data points. Your dataset shrinks a bit. The function repeats this process of removing the highest and lowest data points until there is only one member or data point left standing. That member is the value returned by MEDIAN. If there is an even number of data points, MEDIAN returns an appropriate interpolated value. The order of the data members doesn't change the outcome of the computed median. The following is an example:

```
MEDIAN(15,12,13) = MEDIAN(12,13,15).
```

The following are sample calculations:

```
=MEDIAN(1,9,5,6,8)                                    returns 6
=MEDIAN(1,3,99,2,3)                                   returns 3
=MEDIAN(1,2,976,977,978)                              returns 976
=MEDIAN(1,3,11,11)                                    returns 7
```

MODE returns the most common value in a dataset. MODE tends to be most useful for coarse-grained classification. Chapter 9, "Xcelsius and Statistics," addresses some practical issues to keep in mind when working with MODE.

```
=MODE(1,2,3,3,3,2,1,2,3)                              returns 3
```

COUNT, COUNTA, AND COUNTIF

```
COUNT(value1,value2,...)
COUNTA(value1,value2,...)
COUNTIF(range,criteria)
```

COUNT returns the number of cells that contain numbers and also numbers within a list of arguments.

COUNTA indicates how many values are in a list of arguments.

COUNTIF counts the number of cells that meet the criteria specified in the argument.

COUNT tallies the number of numeric entries found in the arguments supplied to COUNT.

For example, if there are 13 cells populated with numeric values, and the cell D29 contains the value 1.239, then the following results would be returned:

```
=COUNT(A1:B3,G1:K4)                    returns 13
=COUNT(A1:B3,D29,G1:K4)                returns 14
=COUNT(A1:B3,D29,G1:K4)+2+78-65        returns 15
```

COUNTA is similar to COUNT except that non-blank cells are also counted. With COUNTA, non-blank cells can be text, numeric, or any kind of formula.

For example, open a new spreadsheet and enter the following in cells A1, A2, and A3:

```
99                                       (cell B1)
=IF(B1<23,"B1 is smaller than 23","")    (cell B2)
B3 has text in it                        (cell B3)
```

Leave the cell B4 blank, and you will find the following:

```
=COUNTA(B1:B4)                         returns 3
=COUNT(B1:B4)                          returns 1
```

COUNTIF tells you how many cells match a specific criterion for a range of cells that's identified. For example, you may want to see how many of your 40 sales reps have reached their quota of $50,000. If you have this data in cells A1:A40, then your count of how many achieved their target would be computed using this formula:

```
=COUNTIF(A1:A40,">=50000")
```

This formula works but it is a bit restrictive because it is hardwired to the threshold of $50,000. That may be the target for this month, but next month, you might want to up it to $53,000. A better construction would be to remove the hardwired dependency by placing the threshold in a separate cell, such as B1. Your formula could then look like this:

```
=COUNTIF(A1:A40,">="&B1)
```

If you define a named range for the threshold (cell B1) as SalesQuota and your sales data (cells A1:A40) as SalesTeamData, you could write your formula as follows:

```
=COUNTIF(SalesTeamData,">="&SalesQuota)
```

This formula is a lot easier to understand than the first COUNTIF example given a few lines earlier. It is also more flexible because you can control the formula's behavior externally. For example, because the threshold is isolated to a single cell, you could set the threshold value from a slider or dial on the Xcelsius canvas.

If you want to start getting creative at the spreadsheet level, you can come up with all sorts of interesting metrics or measures for your dashboards. For example, you could find the number of sales reps who performed above average by using either of the following formulas:

```
=COUNTIF(A1:A40,">="&AVERAGE(A1:A40))
=COUNTIF(SalesTeamData,">="&AVERAGE(SalesTeamData))
```

SUM, SUMIF, SUMPRODUCT, AND SUMSQ

```
SUM(number1,number2,...)
SUMIF(range,criteria[,sum_range])
SUMPRODUCT(array1,array2,array3,...)
SUMSQ(number1,number2,...)
```

If you are accustomed to working with Excel, you are already familiar with SUM. SUM can accept a range of cells as its "arguments." You can have formulas like these:

```
=SUM(A1:B12)
=SUM($A$1:C19)
```

SUM can also accept multiple arguments separated by commas:

```
=SUM(DailyExpensesForJanuary,DailyExpensesForFebruary)
```

Like essentially all other Xcelsius-supported Excel functions, SUM evaluates its arguments before passing them to the function. Therefore, if you encounter a formula like this:

```
=SUM(3.14,12,1+2+3)
```

1+2+3 is evaluated and converted to 6 so that the formula is effectively treated as SUM(3.14,12,6).

CAUTION

There are some differences between the way Xcelsius computes with SUM and the way Excel computes with SUM. In Excel, SUM treats text that resembles a number as a number. In Xcelsius 2008, SUM blissfully ignores text that resembles numbers. The same holds true for true/false values and also for dates that appear as text. The following Xcelsius 2008 examples make this clear:

```
=SUM(50,25,"35")            returns 75
=SUM(3.14,TRUE)             returns 3.14
=SUM(3.14,6=3*2)            returns 3.14
=SUM("12/31/2009")          returns 0
```

If you were to compute these in Excel, the results would be 110, 4.14, 4.14, and 40178, respectively.

One of the reasons the spreadsheet metaphor is popular is because it is easy to work with numeric data in rows and columns. It is easy to think about multiplying all the numbers in one column (such as price) by the corresponding numbers (such as units sold) in a second column, to arrive at a combined quantity in a third column (such as sales). While you can get all this detail on a line-by-line basis, sometimes all you need is the total result. The

SUMPRODUCT function exists for such circumstances. If you didn't have a third column, you could write a formula like either of the following:

```
=SUMPRODUCT(A1:A99,B1:B99)
=SUMPRODUCT(Price,Units)
```

In one fell swoop, you could calculate the aggregate sales. This is a powerful method for directly and efficiently computing numbers you may need. You can make SUMPRODUCT even more versatile, as shown in the following example.

Assume that you are tracking the changes in price and quantity sold for a single product over time. For the sake of simplicity, consider only 12 lines of such data, 1 for each month of the year. The formula SUMPRODUCT(Price,Units) results in a single number for the whole year. What if you want to calculate cumulative sales as of any month and graph only the relevant data? Say that a reportable period includes all months on or before some point in time of interest, as set by clicking a visual control on a dashboard. It might be convenient to tag these in a third column, alongside price and units (as in column H in Figure 4.6).

Figure 4.6
SUMPRODUCT of price, units, and reportable period calculates cumulative sales.

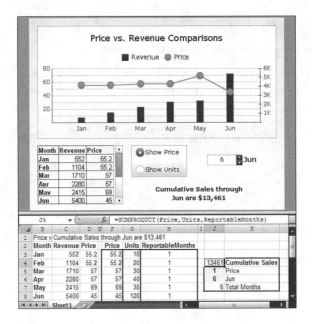

The month number (input cell J6) is set by a Spinner component on the canvas. In column H, the cells are set to either 1 or 0, depending on whether the month number in column A is less than or equal to the value in cell J6. The following formula appears in cell H3:

```
=IF($A3<>$J$6,1,0)
```

J6 is an absolute reference, so its cell coordinate won't change as you replicate the formula. A3 is referenced as $A3, so only the column is fixed. This way, you can freely replicate the formula down the column. If you want to replicate the formula to other columns, you want the formula to reference column A. That's why you see the $ symbol in front of the column letter.

If you define `Price` as cells F3:F14, `Units` as cells G3:G14, and `ReportableMonths` as cells H3:H14, you can compute the cumulative sales with this formula:

```
=SUMPRODUCT(Price,Units,ReportableMonths)
```

Needless to say, there are plenty of other ways to calculate the cumulative sales, but this is one idea of how you can use SUMPRODUCT.

There is one thing you must keep in mind with SUMPRODUCT: All the arguments supplied to it have to be identically sized. For example, if `Price` is 12 cells stacked up in a vertical column, `Units` and `ReportableMonths` must also each be 12 cells stacked up in a vertical column. You cannot combine different-sized cell ranges in SUMPRODUCT. The following formula, for example, *will not* work:

```
=SUMPRODUCT(1.5,A1:A12,B1:B12)
```

Because 1.5 is a single number, you can pull it out of the function and apply it correctly by using this formula:

```
=1.5*SUMPRODUCT(A1:A12,B1:B12)
```

NOTE

In Figure 4.6 and the `ch04_ContextSwitchingExample.xlf` file, the Radio Button component allows you to switch between displaying price and units. Effectively, this gives you two views from a single chart. I call this *context switching*. I explain context switching in detail in Chapter 5, "Using Charts and Graphs to Represent Data."

4

SUMIF is a very useful facility for gathering certain kinds of information. SUMIF works a little like COUNTIF, except that it performs a sum of the range that matches a criterion rather than counting the number of times a match is found. You could have a list of numbers in, say, cells A1:A100. These numbers could be insurance claims. Perhaps there might be some deductible, possibly $500. If you want to find the sum of these claims for which there would be no reimbursement, you could use a formula like this:

```
=SUMIF(A1:A100,"<=500")
```

Of course, it would be better to remove the hardwired reference to the $500 deductible and park it in another cell, such as B1. Your formula would then look like this:

```
=SUMIF(A1:A100,"<="&B1)
```

Notice that the range (cells A1:A100) is the same cells used for the testing and the summation. There may be circumstances in which the test for inclusion in the conditional sum doesn't directly involve the value being summed. For such situations, there is a second form of SUMIF that incorporates three arguments: a range of cells for testing against some criteria, the test criteria, and a corresponding set of cells that would be summed when matches are found. A formula for estimating potential exposure if customers having a lower credit rating than a given threshold default on their loans could be something like this:

```
=SUMIF(CustomerCreditRating,"<="&CreditThreshold,OutstandingLoans)
```

Figure 4.7 shows how this might be applied in a dashboard. The SUMIF formula is now incorporated into a more full-featured formula, as you can see here:

```
="Potential exposure is
➥"&DOLLAR(SUMIF(CustRating,"<"&(Alert_Threshold_Pct*(MAX(CustRating)
➥-MIN(CustRating))+MIN(CustRating)),LoanAmt),0)
```

Notice in the dashboard shown in Figure 4.7 that the radio button controls context switching and that conditional formatting is applied by using the vertical slider.

Figure 4.7

SUMIF is used to compute potential exposure of outstanding loans to customers.

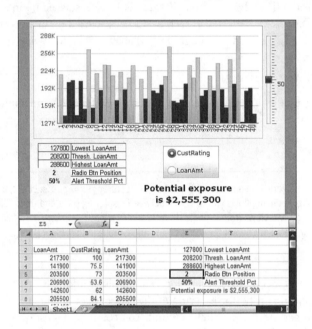

SUMSQ returns the sum of the squares of a series or range of numbers. It looks like an esoteric function that would be used infrequently. Actually, it is very practical. The concept is simple: The square of a number, whether positive or negative, always results in a positive value, and you can use this to your advantage. You may be populating a range of cells with some values. How can you determine whether the range is non-empty? You could try a formula like this:

```
=IF(SUM(C3:L3)<>0,"The cells are non-empty","The cells are empty")
```

The <> is a "Not Equals" comparison operator. The formula almost works, but it is not guaranteed to always work correctly. Suppose there are precisely five values of +1 and five values of -1? The sum would result in the value zero, and the formula would fail. The following would be a better formula:

```
=IF(SUMSQ(C3:L3)>0,"The cells are non-empty","The cells are empty")
```

LARGE, SMALL, AND RANK

LARGE(*array*,*k*)
SMALL(*array*,*k*)
RANK(*number*,*ref*,*order*)

LARGE returns the *k*th largest value in a dataset.

SMALL returns the *k*th smallest value in a dataset.

RANK returns the rank of a number in a list of numbers.

Displaying information in a horizontal bar chart can quickly become dizzying if you don't organize the sequence of data for the chart. You could, of course, sort the data from largest to smallest or vice versa. Hand sorting doesn't work very well, though, because you would have to manually sort the data every time it changes. There is a way you can actually sort the data, sort of. The technique doesn't really involve sorting the data but rather picking items from an array of cells, by largest to smallest or smallest to largest, one at a time.

You could have a series of formulas in a column of cells like the following:

```
=LARGE($A$1:$A$10,1)
=LARGE($A$1:$A$10,2)
=LARGE($A$1:$A$10,3)
...
=LARGE($A$1:$A$10,10)
```

For all intents and purposes, this list of cells is automatically sorted, even as the values of the chart data (cells A1:A10) change. Plotting this sorted data on a bar chart works well, but there is one minor detail: Bar charts stack their data in reverse order of the way it appears on the spreadsheet. Consequently, instead of having a chart resembling a tornado (with the largest items appearing at the top and the smallest at the bottom), you would get a chart resembling a pyramid. There's an easy way around this problem. Instead of ordering your sequence from largest to smallest, you do it the other way around:

```
=LARGE($A$1:$A$10,10)
=LARGE($A$1:$A$10,9)
=LARGE($A$1:$A$10,8)
...
=LARGE($A$1:$A$10,1)
```

Figure 4.8 shows an illustration of this. As in previous examples in this chapter, you can switch the data series by using context switching.

Alternatively, you could use the SMALL function and reverse the lookup index to achieve the same effect as you get with LARGE.

RANK is kind of complementary to SMALL and LARGE. Instead of plucking out values from a range of cells, it lets you know how high up the food chain the value of a specific cell is.

NOTE

> Duplicate items in a range of cells are given exactly the same rank. This can cause some complications if you need to uniquely distinguish each and every item on a list (that is, keep track of all the individual duplicates).

Figure 4.8
Auto-sorted tornado-style bar charts can be created using *LARGE(*ChartData, ReverseRank Index*)*.

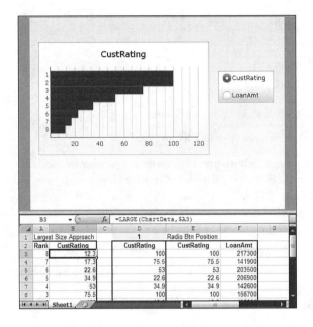

STDEV AND VAR

STDEV(*number1,number2,...*)
VAR(*number1,number2,...*)

STDEV estimates standard deviation based on a sample, ignoring text and logical values.

VAR estimates variance based on a sample, ignoring logical values and text.

Data can be voluminous. You might be collecting data for, say, insurance claim amounts, the real cost of installing fiber-optic cable on a property-by-property basis, or profit on product sales. If you want to analyze the overall import of such data to your business, it would make sense to aggregate these quantities and compute total expenses or whatever item you are measuring.

There are times, however, when it is more appropriate to characterize a statistical profile in terms of individual transactions or events. At its most rudimentary level, the AVERAGE function gives you this kind of measure. It may not be informative enough. To help prove the point, let's look at some specifics. Supposed you have the following sales data for six transactions:

120, 75, 86, 128, 92, 102

The average sale here is 100.5. You can verify this by entering values in your spreadsheet and using the AVERAGE function. It may be that for the next 100 or so transactions, you'll really average just a tad over $100 per transaction. Assuming that the data you have is representative of future transactions, what would you guess the seventh transaction would be? Lacking any additional information, your probable best guess would be $100.50. How certain are you that you will get the value correct? If all the numbers in your sample were pretty close to the average, you'd be more certain than if they were all over the place.

Consider another dataset:

```
98, 110, 97, 102, 95, 101
```

Here, the average sale is also 100.5. If you are projecting the seventh transaction, you could use the same $100.50 estimate. Assuming that this data is representative of future transactions, how far off do you think your estimate would be? There is a measure known as standard deviation that gives you a handle on this:

```
=STDEV(120, 75, 86, 128, 92, 102)          returns approx 20.3
=STDEV(98, 110, 97, 102, 95, 101)          returns approx 5.3
```

Notice in the first dataset that four of the six transactions fall between 100.5-20.3 and 100.5+20.3. In the second dataset, four of the six transactions fall between 100.5-5.3 and 100.5+5.3. Perhaps standard deviation could be a good measure to characterize your historical data in quantitative terms. It turns out that as your sample size grows, the reliability of standard deviation as a way to characterize your data increases.

As a rule of thumb, roughly two-thirds of your data will fall between your average plus or minus the standard deviation, and close to 95 percent of your data will fall between your average plus or minus two times the standard deviation.

Variance and standard deviation are closely related measures. The choice between the usage of one metric and the other is largely a matter of industry practice and convenience. In the world of risk management and the actuarial sciences, variance is more popular than standard deviation:

```
=VAR(120, 75, 86, 128, 92, 102)            returns approx 414.3
=VAR(98, 110, 97, 102, 95, 101)            returns approx 28.3
```

NOTE

> The variance is approximately the square of the standard deviation.

RAND, NORMINV, AND NORMDIST

```
RAND()
NORMDIST(x,mean,standard_dev,cumulative)
NORMINV(probability[,mean=0,standard_dev=1])
```

RAND is a pseudo-random number generator. It returns a decimal number between 0 and 1. Every time the RAND function is recalculated, it is virtually guaranteed to return a different number between 0 and 1. What that number will be is as good as anybody's guess, and this is what makes RAND suitable for simple probability analysis.

One of the characteristics of the RAND function is that the values it returns are pretty much uniformly distributed between 0 and 1. This kind of probability distribution, called a uniform distribution, has some precise mathematical properties. Statistical and probability analysis in Xcelsius is covered in detail in Chapter 9, so I don't cover this in detail here. However, I do want to provide two techniques here that relate to generating other kinds of distributions.

One of the Excel functions (found in the Excel Analysis ToolPak) that is nice to have but is not supported in Xcelsius 2008 is RANDBETWEEN, which takes two arguments: a minimum integer and a maximum integer. It returns a whole number in that range. If I say to you: "Pick a number, any number, between 1 and 10," you could use the following formula to provide such a number:

```
=RANDBETWEEN(1,10)
```

Although Xcelsius 2008 doesn't have such a function, you can effectively simulate it by using RAND. Here is an example:

```
=ROUND(RAND()*(10-1),0)+1
```

A more generalized form would be as follows:

```
=ROUND(RAND()*(TopValue-BottomValue),0)+BottomValue
```

Basically, this formula simulates a discrete uniform distribution.

Uniform distributions are not the only kind of probability distribution you might want to simulate. Another commonly encountered distribution is the normal distribution, sometimes referred to as a bell-shaped curve. You can simulate values in a normal distribution by using the NORMINV function in conjunction with RAND. For example, if you want to simulate a distribution with an average value of 100 and a standard deviation of 15, you would use this formula:

```
=NORMINV(RAND(),100,15)
```

In general, this would be the formula:

```
=NORMINV(RAND(),MeanValue,StandardDeviationValue)
```

While we're on the topic of the normal distribution, there's a function called NORMDIST that tells you the probability of some event occurring if you know the expected value and standard deviation. For example, if you are projecting sales of $6,500,000 next quarter and the standard deviation is $750,000, you could calculate the probability of actually achieving sales in excess of $7,500,000 by using the following formula:

```
=1-NORMDIST(7500000,6500000,750000,TRUE)
```

This would be about a 9.1% chance. Hopefully, you'll beat the odds!

FINANCIALLY ORIENTED FUNCTIONS

Xcelsius supports a number of financially oriented functions relating to depreciations, interest type calculations, return on investment, and the like.

DB, DDB, SLN, SYD, AND VDB

```
DB(cost,salvage,life,period,month)
DDB(cost,salvage,life,period,factor)
SLN(cost,salvage,life)
SYD(cost,salvage,life,period)
VDB(cost,salvage,life,start_period,end_period,factor,no_switch)
```

Depreciation is a way to allocate the use of an asset over its lifetime. There are different methods of depreciation, which take into account things like the cost of an asset, its lifespan, and a salvage value at the end of its useful life.

The best way to gain familiarity with the wide diversity of depreciation methods and their calculations is to use them interactively so that you can examine their behavior "in the wild" and, more importantly, learn how to construct a spreadsheet and dashboard that puts their features to use. Open the file ch04_Depreciation.xlf (see Figure 4.9) and try out combinations of parameters.

Figure 4.9
A depreciation exploratorium for comparing a variety of methods, options, and values.

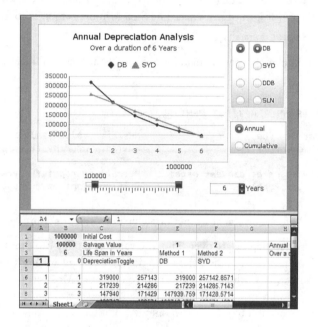

NOTE

Chapter 5 discusses the graphical features and enhancements of spreadsheet construction.

This dashboard allows you to choose two depreciation methods from any of a number of different possible methods; the four that are used here are declining balance, sum of the year's digits, double declining balance, and straight-line depreciation. To accomplish this, you use context switching. To spice things up a bit, you can add an additional construction—the ability to display depreciation expense, year by year, or to show the cumulative depreciation.

Here is how it works. You don't bother creating a calculation for year-by-year expense and then another one for cumulative expenses. Instead, you can use a multiplication factor (cell B4), which is either going to be a 0 or a 1, depending on whether the data to be charted is yearly or cumulative. If it is yearly, B4 is set to 0, and if it is cumulative, B4 is set to 1.

You just add the current year's depreciation expense, B4, multiplied by whatever was reported in the prior year. So if the depreciation toggle is set to 1, the tally is automatically cumulative. The following is the simplified version of the formula for cell C6:

```
=E6+$B$4*C5
```

where the current year's depreciation expense relevant to the data series in column C is in column E.

To make the calculation results a little easier to handle, you do some rounding. To make this formula a bit more robust, you can turn off the formula by sensing when the current year is beyond the maximum lifespan of the asset. The final formula is then as follows:

```
=IF($B6="","",ROUND(E6+$B$4*C5,0))
```

All sorts of visual refinements can be made to this dashboard, as you'll learn in later chapters.

FV, IPMT, IRR, MIRR, NPER, NPV, PMT, PPMT, PV, AND RATE

```
FV(rate,nper,pmt,pv,type)                    NPV(rate,value1,value2,...)
IPMT(rate,per,nper,pv,fv,type)               PMT(rate,nper,pv,fv,type)
IRR(values,guess)                            PPMT(rate,per,nper,pv,fv,type)
MIRR(values,finance_rate,reinvest_rate)      PV(rate,nper,pmt,fv,type)
NPER(rate,pmt,pv,fv,type)                    RATE(nper,pmt,pv,fv,type,guess)
```

In this section, we'll focus on the NPV function, which deals with net present value.

Like physical assets that depreciate over time, the value of money can diminish over time. Given the choice of having a hundred thousand dollars today or waiting 10 years to receive a hundred thousand dollars, which option would you choose? Most people would correctly choose to have the money now. There are several good reasons for this. In 10 years from now, you may not be around to enjoy the money. Also, inflation is likely to kick in during the intervening time, so a hundred thousand dollars will buy you less wealth then than it can today. Most importantly, you can invest that money today and generate greater wealth over the next 10 years.

Any way you look at it, there's a time value of money that tends to deflate at a certain rate if you do nothing with it. In effect, net present value analysis answers the question, "What is my investment paid out today really worth if I get an income stream down the road?" The "really worth" is not only dependent on future cash flows but also the rate at which money changes value over time.

You can easily set up net present value calculations on a spreadsheet in Xcelsius 2008. The NPV function basically has two arguments: a rate and a range of cells to tabulate the cash flow. Figure 4.10 shows how this might be set up.

The essential idea is that cash flows are represented on a timeline. In Figure 4.10, the cash flow can be found on row 7. The rate at which the value of money dissipates over time is set in the input cell A4 and can be controlled using a horizontal slider.

Figure 4.10
Net present value analysis lends itself to interactive visualization.

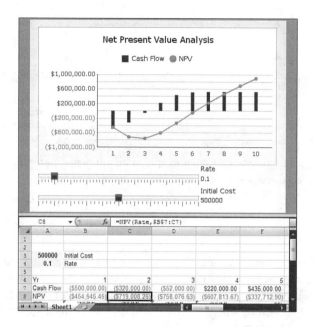

In addition, the initial investment or cost (input cell A3) is set by using a second slider on the canvas. Notice that the initial cost or investment (cell A3) is automatically converted into a negative number in the cash flow.

Net present value is computed on row 8, using the following formula in cell C8:

```
=NPV(Rate,$B$7:C7)
```

Notice that B7 is an absolute or fixed location, but C7 is a relative reference. As the formula is replicated to the right, the number of cells evaluated for the net present value increases.

On the combination chart shown in Figure 4.10, the cash flow is displayed as a column chart, and the net present value is rendered in the form of a line chart.

NOTE

It is easy to visually find the internal rate of return. You simply adjust the rate on the dashboard slider so that the NPV at the end of the projected timeline is 0. When the net present value reaches 0 at the end of the timeline, the rate shown on the slider will match the internal rate of return.

MATHEMATICAL FUNCTIONS IN XCELSIUS 2008

There are, of course, numerous mathematical functions in Xcelsius 2008. Some of them are relatively common, and others are used less frequently, but you'll be glad you have them here for ready reference.

ABS AND SIGN

ABS(*number*)
SIGN(*number*)

SIGN returns 1 for positive numbers, 0 if the number is 0, and -1 if the number is negative:

=SIGN(-10.793)	returns -1
=SIGN(250)	returns 1
=SIGN(0)	returns 0
=SIGN(2*3-100)	returns -1

The idea of an absolute number is rather simple. The following examples make it easy to understand what ABS does:

=ABS(-10.793)	returns 10.793
=ABS(250)	returns 250
=ABS(0)	returns 0
=ABS(2*3-100)	returns 94

Functions like these, although simple, can be powerful when combined with other functions. The following example shows a practical example of ABS. The problem is simple: You have an XY chart for which you want to designate a particular point of data to be the very center of the chart, and you want the chart to be scaled appropriately to frame all the data points. Oh, and you want to have the option of choosing which point is to be designated the "center" data point (see Figure 4.11 and the file ch04_MovableChart.xlf).

Figure 4.11
Absolute value computations aid in positioning a designated point at the center of the chart.

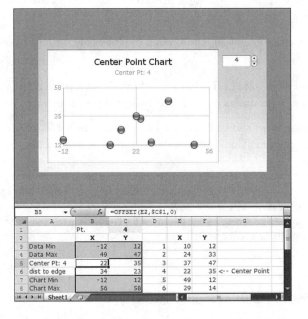

The logic is simple: Start by selecting any data point in the chart. For the sake of illustration, let's use the fourth data point, whose x and y values are (22, 35). Right now, just think about the X-axis. You want the X position of 22 to be smack in the middle of the X-axis. If you look at all the X values, you will find that the minimum X value is -12. This means the farthest-away data point to the left of 22 is 34 units to the left (=ABS(22-(-12))). The distance along the X-axis from the maximum X value of 49 to the midpoint of 22 happens to be ABS(34-49)=15. If you really want 22 to be the midpoint of the chart along the X-axis, it would be necessary to extend the right edge of the chart by another 19 units, so that the midpoint of 22 is equally centered between the left edge and right edge of the chart. The computation of distance to the edge for cell B6 is as follows:

```
=MAX(ABS(B5-B4),ABS(B5-B4))
=MAX(ABS(xCenterValue-xDataMin), ABS(xCenterValue-xDataMax))
```

After this value is computed, simply add this maximum absolute distance to the X midpoint to get the X position of the right edge and subtract it from the midpoint to obtain the distance to the left edge.

Performing these steps for the Y-axis is basically the same.

TRIGONOMETRY FUNCTIONS: SIN, COS, TAN, ACOS, ASIN, ATAN, RADIANS, DEGREES, AND PI

```
SIN(number)            ATAN(number)
COS(number)            RADIANS(angle)
TAN(number)            DEGREES(angle)
ACOS(number)           PI()
ASIN(number)
```

You may have noticed that Xcelsius supports a variety of trigonometry functions, such as SIN and COS. And I'll bet you thought trig would never be useful for your dashboards, that all this trig stuff is a bit too abstract and would only be of value for an engineer or a scientist. If you believe this to be true, part of your thinking is right, but part of it is dead wrong.

There is a level of abstraction involved in things like trigonometric functions. Because you may not have reason to use such things everyday, they can be difficult to understand and even more difficult to commit to memory. Fortunately, you don't have to struggle with complicated formulas. You can just put them in your dashboards, validate their correctness, and use them.

Suppose you have a dashboard that provides the distance between city pairs of any two cities, from a long list of cities. The list could include major cities such as New York, Chicago, and San Diego. It could also include locations of the manufacturing plants and supplies for your business operations. The list of locations could be on the order of hundreds or more. If you were to create a table of every possible combination of distance between city pairs, it would quickly become far too voluminous to handle in a dashboard. A simple way around this could be to use a formula that calculates an approximate distance based on longitude and latitude. Here is one such formula that calculates the greatest circle between two pairs of longitude and latitude:

```
=3963*ACOS(SIN(RADIANS(Lat1))*SIN(RADIANS(Lat2))
➥+COS(RADIANS(Lat1))*COS(RADIANS(Lat2))*COS(RADIANS(Lon2-Lon1)))
```

How, exactly, could you put this to use in a dashboard? The ch04_TrigLonLat.xlf file (see Figure 4.12) shows how this could be done.

Figure 4.12
Using trigonometry to calculate distance between city pairs selected from a list of cities.

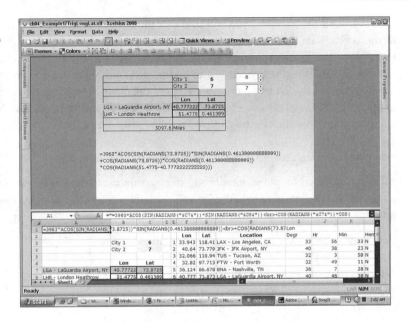

It's a simple matter of performing a lookup of cities and their longitudes and latitudes. To make explicit what is happening, Figure 4.12 displays the actual formula populated with the input values.

Now that you have a formula that does things that are tangible, it might be worth knowing a few things about these trig functions.

There are a variety of trigonometric functions. The principal ones are sine, cosine, and tangent. In your spreadsheet, these functions are called SIN, COS, and TAN, and each of them operates on an angle. The angular measure needs to be in terms of radians. If you are used to measuring angles in terms of degrees, you will need to convert it to radians. To convert a number from degrees to radians, you have to multiply it by pi and then divide the result by 180. For example, you could convert 45 degrees to radians by using this formula:

`=45*PI()/180`

PI is a function that returns the value 3.14159265358979.

All this seems rather messy. Thankfully, there is a function called RADIANS that does all this work for you. This is the formula for computing 45 degrees in radians:

`=RADIANS(45)`

You may have noticed in the formula for computing the distance between cities that there is a function called ACOS. It's not a typo. ACOS refers to arc cosine, or the inverse cosine function. If the cosine of some angle is 0.5, what is the angle that would produce it? Here's the formula to determine this:

`=ACOS(0.5)`

The angle returned would be in radians, which is great for computing things such as distances between cities. To make the result more palpable, though, it would be nice to be able to convert the radians into degrees. Conveniently, there's a DEGREES function for this. You could write the formula as follows:

```
=DEGREES(ACOS(0.5))                                    returns 60
```

Finally, the ATAN2 function is similar to the ATAN function. It returns the angle that would be made if you were to make a triangle with width x and height y. Its form would be as follows:

```
=ATAN2(x_num,y_num)
```

ATAN2 returns the angle in radians. To get the value in degrees, you would use this:

```
=DEGREES(ATAN2(x_num,y_num))
```

PRECISION: ROUND, ROUNDDOWN, ROUNDUP, CEILING, FLOOR, EVEN, INT, TRUNC, AND DOLLAR

```
ROUND(number,num_digits)            EVEN(number)
ROUNDDOWN(number,num_digits)        INT(number)
ROUNDUP(number,num_digits)          TRUNC(number,num_digits)
CEILING(number,significance)        DOLLAR(number,decimals)
FLOOR(number,significance)
```

Dashboards allow people to acquire lots of information visually, without contracting a case of "digit-itis." An appealing chart is much easier to read when size, color, and position of graphical elements meaningfully convey information. Dashboard components also convey numeric information, be it in the hover text of a chart, the chart legend, text labels, the Grid component, the List component, the Spreadsheet Table component...the list goes on and on.

It is quite possible for full numeric precision to "leak" through onto the visual display and make a dashboard or visualization feel like a spreadsheet that's dense with numbers. There are ways to combat this tendency. One approach is to format numbers so the visual information is dumbed down, while the underlying precision is retained. This is an attempt to have the best of both worlds, to show numbers that are easy to read. Instead of displaying the numbers like this:

```
 99987.65
 93472.16
 79234.81
103399.78
107339.26
 95353.22
 97349.67
107384.63
217477.25
```

You could keep the internal precision but display them in thousands, like this:

```
100,000
 93,000
 79,000
103,000
107.000
```

```
 95,000
 97,000
107,000
217,000
```

Clearly, the second list is a lot easier to read. There's just one problem: When you add up these displayed numbers, they total 998,000, but the true total is 1,000,998.43. If you round the true total to the nearest thousand, it would be 1,001,000.

You need to be aware that if the precision of numbers in your dashboard display doesn't match the underlying precision, you may have to account for the discrepancies.

ROUND adjusts a number to a specified number of digits to the left (-) or right (+) of the decimal point:

```
=ROUND(5146.283,2)                    returns 5146.28
=ROUND(5146.283,1)                    returns 5146.3
=ROUND(5146.283,0)                    returns 5146
=ROUND(5146.283,-1)                   returns 5150
=ROUND(5146.283,-2)                   returns 5100
=ROUND(5146.283,-3)                   returns 5000
=ROUND(5146.283,-4)                   returns 10000
```

ROUNDDOWN rounds a number toward 0 to a specified number of digits to the left (-) or right (+) of the decimal point.

ROUNDUP rounds a number away from 0 to a specified number of digits to the left (-) or right (+) of the decimal point.

CEILING rounds a number (away from zero) to the nearest multiple of significance.

FLOOR rounds a number down toward 0 to the nearest multiple of significance. Here are some examples of CEILING and FLOOR:

```
=CEILING(942,15)                      returns 945
=CEILING(945,15)                      returns 945
=CEILING(948,15)                      returns 960
=FLOOR(942,15)                        returns 930
=FLOOR (945,15)                       returns 945
=FLOOR (948,15)                       returns 945
```

EVEN rounds a number to the nearest even integer. Xcelsius does not support a matching ODD function. However, the following computation returns what the ODD function would return in Excel:

```
=EVEN(number)-1
```

INT simply chops off the decimal portion of a number for positive numbers, but it doesn't quite work the same for negative numbers:

```
=INT(50.01)                           returns 50
=INT(50)                              returns 50
=INT(50.9999999)                      returns 50
=INT(-50.01)                          returns -51
=INT(-50)                             returns -50
=INT(-50.9999999)                     returns -51
```

CAUTION

> Using INT on negative values may work differently than you expect. For negative numbers, it returns the next lower number. For example, INT(-1.9) returns -2, not -1.

TRUNC truncates a number to specified precision by removing the fractional part of the number:

```
=TRUNC(1.9,0)                                    returns 1
=TRUNC(-1.9,0)                                   returns -1
```

DOLLAR converts a number to text, using currency format. This function works well with the Xcelsius Label component.

MOD AND QUOTIENT

```
MOD(number,divisor)
QUOTIENT(numerator,denominator)
```

MOD returns the remainder from division, with the result having the same sign as the divisor.

QUOTIENT returns the integer portion of a division. Computationally, QUOTIENT is identical to ROUNDDOWN taken to zero decimal places. Here are some examples:

```
=QUOTIENT(6.5,3)                                 returns 2
=QUOTIENT(-6.5,3)                                returns -2
=ROUNDDOWN(6.5/3,0)                              returns 2
=ROUNDDOWN(-6.5/3,0)                             returns -2
```

Modulo is something that harkens back to my days in elementary school, where we were taught to think about clocks in 12- and 24-hour cycles. Back in those days, there were no such things as digital clocks. The clock faces were all analog dials, which made the modulo, or MOD, function easy to understand. If you start at midnight and allow a clock to advance 34 hours, the clock face would be showing 10 AM. Although the concept was easy to grasp, the range of practical applications presented by my school teachers were limited. It seemed that we were forever trapped in intervals of 12 or 24 hours. If you can't vary the interval, you are not going to find many practical applications.

Figure 4.13 shows an interesting example.

Here is the basic setup: You have a start date, which can be pretty much any date you want. You can adjust this data forward or backward by using the Spinner component. Or you can pick a date by using the Calendar component. Wouldn't it be nice if relative to your start date, you could be given a reminder, say, every fourth day? This is where the MOD function steps in. If your start date is in cell A1, the selected date in the calendar sets A2, and the reminder interval in A3, you could construct the following formula:

```
=MOD(A2-A1,A3)
```

If you define named ranges, your formula might look like this:

```
=MOD(MySelectedCalendarDate-MyStartDate,ReminderInterval)
```

Whenever this MOD function returns the value 0, a reminder note appears. Because you can set both the start date and the reminder interval, you have a lot of flexibility.

Figure 4.13
Setting up a flexible reminder tool with the MOD function and Calendar and Spinner components.

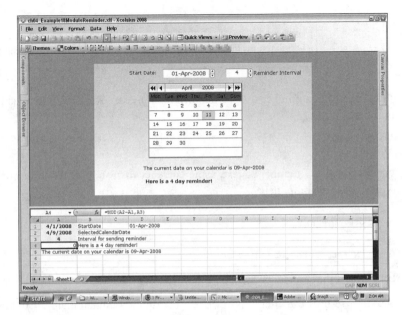

EXP, LN, LOG, AND LOG10

```
EXP(number)
LN(number)
LOG(number,base)
LOG10(number)
POWER(number,power)
```

Xcelsius supports a variety of functions related to exponents and logarithms. Before getting into concepts about these, I want to illustrate some examples of the POWER function and the ^ exponentiation operator.

Here are three ways to calculate 2 raised to the third power:

```
=2*2*2                                                        returns 8
=POWER(2,3)                                                   returns 8
=2^3                                                          returns 8
```

It is easy to understand exponents involving whole numbers, but what about exponents involving factional or decimal quantities? For instance, what is POWER(36,0.5)? Try it:

```
=POWER(36,0.5)                                                returns 6
=36^0.5                                                       returns 6
=36^(1/2)                                                     returns 6
=SQRT(36)                                                     returns 6
```

A logarithm sounds complicated, but it's really not. Logarithms are the exponent parts of a number raised to a power. Here is an example:

```
POWER(10,2) is 100
POWER(10,3) is 1000
=LOG(100)                                                     returns 2
=LOG(1000)                                                    returns 3
```

What's the benefit of all this? The logarithm of 100000 is as follows:

```
=LOG(100000)                                            returns 5
```

100000 is 100*1000, and in logarithmic form this is the following:

```
=LOG(100*1000)                                          returns 5
```

But it is also the following:

```
=LOG(100)+LOG(1000)                                     which is 2+3
```

So if C=A*B, then LOG(C)=LOG(A)+LOG(B). In effect, logarithms turn multiplication into addition.

Whether explicit or implicit, all logarithmic functions are calculated using a "base" much as with arithmetic in base 10. Several versions of logarithms are supported in the Xcelsius spreadsheet environment. The LOG function normally has two arguments, a number and its base:

```
=LOG(3,9)                                               returns 0.5
=LOG(9,9)                                               returns 1
=LOG(27,9)                                              returns 1.5
=LOG(16,2)                                              returns 4
=LOG(22.62472,2)                                        returns 4.5
=LOG(32,2)                                              returns 5
=LOG(100,10)                                            returns 2
=LOG(100)                                               returns 2
```

The LOG10 function works like LOG with no base supplied. There is a natural logarithm function called LN, which is premised on the base of the logarithm being 2.71828182845905. The use of natural logarithms and the inverse function EXP often simplify mathematical and statistical equations in science and finance.

Logarithms and exponents arise naturally in business and finance applications and dashboards, as in the example shown in Figure 4.14. Many industrial operations, such as in manufacturing, improve over time and with experience. This incremental improvement can be mathematically projected by using a *learning curve*.

Mathematically, the cost per unit for producing a specific number of units can be computed by using an equation like this:

```
=CostOfInitialProductinRun*NumberOfUnits^(-1*LOG10(1-ImprovementFactor)
➥/LOG10(ExpansionFactor))
```

For example, if your production run costs go down by 5% when you double your product output and the initial cost is 100, this would be your cost equation:

```
=100*NumberOfUnits^(-1*LOG10(1-0.05)/LOG10(2))
```

or approximately this:

```
=100*NumberOfUnits^(-0.07)
```

4

Figure 4.14
A dashboard that uses logarithms to project a learning curve.

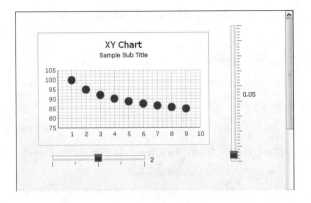

FORECAST AND INTERCEPT

FORECAST(*x,known_y's,known_x's*)
INTERCEPT(*known_y's,known_x's*)

When you plot X and Y data on a chart, the data might be representative of a continuous trend. If the trend is linear (that is, if it forms a fairly straight line), it can be projected using the FORECAST function (see Figure 4.15).

Figure 4.15
Forecasting a Y value, given a hypothetical X value and known Y values and X values.

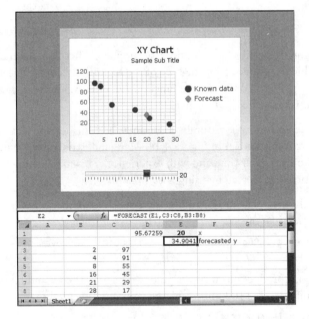

In this example, the horizontal slider sets some hypothetical X value. The corresponding forecasted Y value is projected based on X value and the known Y values as well as known X values. This would be the formula:

=FORECAST(HypotheticalXValue,KnownYValues,KnownXValues)

If `HypotheticalXValue` is in cell E1, `KnownYValues` are in cells C3:C8, and `KnownXValues` are in cells B3:B8, the formula would be as follows:

```
=FORECAST(E1,C3:C8,B3:B8)
```

In this case, the projected curve would intersect the Y-axis at the following:

```
=INTERCEPT(C3:C8,B3:B8)
```

FORECAST is a wonderful function for projecting curves when they are linear or straight lines. It is not designed to work with nonlinear curves. Often, you can "linearize" your data by using logarithms of your X and/or Y values instead of the actual X and Y values.

N, VALUE, AND PRODUCT

```
N(value)
VALUE(text)
PRODUCT(number1,number2,...)
```

VALUE converts a string of text into its numbered equivalent:

`=VALUE("2"&"3")`	returns 23
`=VALUE("2"&"3")+4`	returns 27
`=VALUE("12/31/2009")`	returns the serial number 40178

VALUE does not operate on TRUE or FALSE values.

N is a function that returns the numeric representation of its argument. Here are some examples:

`=N("2"&"3")`	returns 0
`=N("23")`	returns 0
`=N(23)`	returns 23
`=N("12/31/2009")`	returns 0

If you use the Xcelsius Calendar component to set a date in cell A1 to, say, December 31, 2009, then you get the following:

`=N(A1)`	returns the serial number 40178
`=N(TRUE())`	returns 1
`=N(TRUE)`	returns 1
`=N(2=1+1)`	returns 1

Incidentally, you can coerce a TRUE/FALSE value into numeric representation by using a -- trick:

`=--(TRUE)`	returns 1
`=--(2=2)`	returns 1
`=--(FALSE)`	returns 0

PRODUCT simply multiplies up to 30 or so cell ranges together:

`=PRODUCT(1,2,3,4)`	returns 24
`=PRODUCT(13,A1:C1)`	returns 13*A1*B1*C1

4

USING CONDITIONAL LOGIC AND BOOLEAN FUNCTIONS

One of the objectives in using Xcelsius 2008 to build dashboards and visualizations is to give them some sophisticated ability. For instance, say that you're creating a pricing calculator that is smart enough to detect weekends and holidays from selected data in a Calendar component and automatically use the appropriate pricing table. Constructing such a dashboard requires the use of conditional logic and date arithmetic (discussed later in this chapter).

TRUE and FALSE

```
FALSE()
TRUE()
```

The Xcelsius spreadsheet environment has two functions for generating TRUE and FALSE values. The functions have basically the same names as their values:

```
=TRUE()                                                    returns TRUE
=FALSE()                                                   returns FALSE
```

Excel also has TRUE and FALSE functions.

In general, there is no real need to use a TRUE() or FALSE() function, as you can just use the TRUE and FALSE values and not waste a computing cycle to compute TRUE() or FALSE().

TRUE and FALSE are not quite the same as 1 and 0. If you want the number 1 instead of a TRUE value (or 0 instead of a FALSE value), you can just shroud it with the function N:

```
=N(TRUE)                                                   returns 1
=N(6=3+2+1)                                                returns 1
=N(SUMSQ(A1:A100)+1>0)                                     returns 1
=N(FALSE)                                                  returns 0
```

The first formula here should be obvious. In the second formula, 3+2+1 does add up to 6, so the propositional expression 6=3+2+1 evaluates to TRUE. In the third formula, the sum of the squares of any range of cells should return a non-negative result (that is, zero or larger). Because 1 is being added to something non-negative, the total must necessarily be greater than zero. Hence, this relationship evaluates to TRUE (and N(TRUE) returns the value 1). The fourth formula should be obvious.

CONDITIONAL OPERATORS   You can use the following conditional operators in spreadsheet formulas:

```
>
<
>=
<=
<>
=
```

Unless the cells you are comparing have errors, such as a formula that attempts to divide a number by zero, the result of the operation will either be a TRUE or a FALSE value.

The operator <> stands for "not equal."

Notice that there are no =>, =<, or >< operators, as these are meaningless.

LOGIC COMBINERS: AND AND OR

```
AND(logical1,logical2,...)
OR(logical1,logical2,...)
```

The AND function returns TRUE if every logical test it is fed returns TRUE, as in these examples:

```
=AND(2+3>1,10=5+5,MID("Xcelsius",1,4)="Xcel")          returns TRUE
=AND(2+3>1,10=5+59,MID("Xcelsius",1,4)="Xcel")         returns FALSE
```

The OR function returns TRUE if at least one of the tests results in TRUE, as in these examples:

```
=OR(10=5+5,MID("Xcelsius",1,4)="Xc")                   returns TRUE
=OR(10<>5+5,MID("Xcelsius",1,4)="Xc")                  returns FALSE
```

LOGIC SWITCHES: NOT

```
NOT(expression)
```

Excel has a NOT function that reverses the conditional logic of the expression it evaluates. If an expression would normally result in a TRUE value, NOT(*expression*) returns a FALSE value and vice versa. Here are some examples:

```
=NOT(TRUE)                                             returns FALSE
=NOT(10=5+5)                                           returns FALSE
```

IF-THEN-ELSE LOGIC   Having an expression that evaluates to TRUE or FALSE is the starting point for conditional logic. For example, the following is classic if-then-else logic: If requested loan amount plus outstanding loans exceeds maximum borrowing power, then deny loan application; otherwise, continue processing loan application. The spreadsheet environment readily accommodates this kind of logic with the IF function. You might have a formula that calculates the size of the loan approved, like this:

```
=IF(LoanAmt+OutstandingLoans>CreditLimit,0,LoanAmt)
```

The general form of an IF function is as follows:

```
=IF(logical_test,value_if_true,value_if_false)
```

logical_test is an expression that evaluates to either TRUE or FALSE. The logical test could be something like A1-A2>0 or Assets=Liabilities+OwnersEquity. Incidentally, if the logical test results in a number instead of a TRUE or FALSE value, your IF function will treat the numeric value as FALSE if the value equals zero; otherwise, it will treat it as TRUE. This is the case even if the value is a negative number:

```
=IF(99,21,3)                                           returns 21
=IF(0,21,3)                                            returns 3
=IF(-99,21,3)                                          returns 21
```

OTHER CONDITIONAL FORMULAS   There are three more conditional formulas to think about here. They apply to single cells and not cell ranges.

ISBLANK(*Value*) returns TRUE if the referenced cell value is blank. Sometimes a spreadsheet cell can appear empty, but it is not. The cell may have a non-visible space or a formula like this:

```
=" "
```

If cell A1 has such non-visible but non-empty contents, then you could prove it is non-blank with the following:

```
=ISBLANK(A1)                                                  returns FALSE
```

Another function that could prove useful is ISNA. This function returns TRUE if the value is the #N/A error value. This can arise from formulas involving lookups where no value is found. In situations where this occurs, you might want to split the computations into two or more cells.

For example, let cell A1 be an input cell that is set by user input from the dashboard; a user could be prompted to enter something like his or her age. Let cell A2 be the following:

```
=VLOOKUP(A1,Table1,2,FALSE)
```

If nothing is found in Table1, the #N/A value is returned. You might have an alternate table called Table2. Then you could have a formula like this:

```
=IF(ISNA(A2),VLOOKUP(A1,Table2,2,FALSE),A2)
```

ISNUMBER is similar to ISBLANK and ISNA. It returns TRUE if the value is a number.

NEW EXCEL FUNCTIONS SUPPORTED IN XCELSIUS 2008

```
ISERR(value)
ISERROR(value)
ISEVEN(value)
ISLOGICAL(value)
ISNONTEXT(value)
ISSODD(value)
ISTEXT(value)
TYPE(value)
```

Service Pack 1 of Xcelsius introduces support for several Excel functions.

ISERR(value)

ISERR returns TRUE if evaluating value returns an error other than the #N/A error.

```
=ISERR(3/0)                                                  returns TRUE
```

If VLOOKUP(A1,B1:C10,2,FALSE) fails to find a value it returns a #N/A value. ISERR doesn't acknowledge this kind of error, as is shown in the following example:

```
=ISERR(VLOOKUP(A1,B1:C10,2,FALSE))                          returns FALSE
```

ISERROR(value)

ISERROR returns TRUE if evaluating value returns any kind of error including #N/A, #VALUE!, #REF!, #DIV/0!, #NUM!, #NAME?, or #NULL!.

```
=ISERR(3/(2-2*1))                                           returns TRUE
=ISERROR(LOG10(-91))                                        returns TRUE
=ISERROR(VLOOKUP(A1,B1:C10,2,FALSE))                        returns TRUE
```

ISEVEN(*value*)

ISEVEN returns TRUE if value is a whole number divisible by 2 having no remainders.

`=ISEVEN(2)`	returns TRUE
`=ISEVEN(3)`	returns FALSE

On the functions ISEVEN and ISODD, be very careful if value is not an exact whole number, as the following indicates:

`=ISEVEN(2.00001)`	returns TRUE
`=ISEVEN(1.99998)`	returns FALSE

ISLOGICAL(*value*)

ISLOGICAL returns TRUE if value is a TRUE or FALSE value.

`=ISLOGICAL(2>300-1097.23)`	returns TRUE
`=ISLOGICAL(2<300-1097.23)`	returns TRUE
`=ISLOGICAL(2)`	returns FALSE

ISNONTEXT(*value*)

ISNONTEXT returns TRUE if value is any item that is not text. ISNONTEXT returns TRUE when a cell is blank, but if a cell equates to an empty string, it returns FALSE.

`=ISNONTEXT(3.14159)`	returns TRUE
`=ISNONTEXT("Pi is "&3.14159)`	returns TRUE
`=ISNONTEXT(IF(2>0,"",0.5)`	returns FALSE

ISODD(*value*)

ISODD returns FALSE if value is a whole number divisible by 2 having no remainders.

`=ISODD(3)`	returns TRUE

ISTEXT(*value*)

ISTEXT returns TRUE if the value is the form of text.

`=ISTEXT("Hello")`	returns TRUE

TYPE(*value*)

TYPE returns a numeric value that corresponds to the data type of value. The specific values returned are as follows:

Data Type	Example Value	Returns
Number	23+5	1
Text	"Pi is approximately "&3.14159	2
Logical value	2>3	4
Error value	2/0	16
Array	{1,2,3}	64

4

MAKING DASHBOARDS DATE AND TIME AWARE

Much of the information you work with involves dates and time. This presents an interesting challenge to spreadsheet software and data analysis in a spreadsheet environment. A date such as December 31, 2009, appears as text, yet it's fundamentally numeric information. The solution developed and used in spreadsheets is to keep the visual representation of the date as text but to "serialize" it under the hood so it can be treated numerically. The chief benefit of this approach is that it enables "calendar arithmetic." This section presents a brief overview of the date and time functions that Xcelsius 2008 supports.

NOW AND TODAY

```
NOW()
TODAY()
```

NOW returns the date/time serial number of the current date and time.

TODAY returns the date/time serial number of today's date.

Say that the current date and time is 4/8/2009 5:13:26 PM:

=N(NOW())	returns 39911.7176620370
=N(TODAY())	returns 39911

CONSTRUCTING DATES

DATE

DATE(*year*,*month*,*day*)

DATE returns the serial number that represents a particular date. The following are examples:

=DATE(2009,7,4)	returns 7/4/2009 in the display internally represented as 39998
=N(DATE(2009,7,4))	returns 39998

DATEVALUE

DATEVALUE(*date_text*)

DATEVALUE converts a date text form to a date serial number:

=DATEVALUE("7/4/2009")	returns 39998

TIME

TIME(*hour*,*minute*,*second*)

TIME generates, in decimal form, the time serial number for a particular time based on the number of hours, minutes, and seconds:

=TIME(17,13,26)	returns 0.717662037037037

TIMEVALUE

TIMEVALUE(*time_text*)

TIMEVALUE converts a time represented as narrative text to the decimal portion of a date/time serial number:

TIMEVALUE("5:13:26 PM")   returns 0.717662037037037

PARSING DATES AND TIME: YEAR, MONTH, DAY, HOUR, MINUTE, AND SECOND

YEAR(*serial_number*)   HOUR(*serial_number*)
MONTH(*serial_number*)   MINUTE(*serial_number*)
DAY(*serial_number*)   SECOND(*serial_number*)

YEAR converts a date/time serial number to a year.

MONTH converts a date/time serial number to a month number.

DAY converts a date/time serial number to the day of a month.

HOUR converts a date/time serial number to an hour.

MINUTE converts a date/time serial number to a minute.

SECOND converts a date/time serial number to a second.

Say that the date and time displayed in cell A1 is 4/8/2009 5:13:26 PM:

```
=YEAR(A1)                                   returns 2009
=YEAR(39911.7176620370)                     returns 2009
=MONTH(A1)                                  returns 4
=MONTH(39911.7176620370)                    returns 4
=DAY(A1)                                    returns 8
=DAY(39911.7176620370)                      returns 8
=HOUR(A1)                                   returns 17
=HOUR(39911.7176620370)                     returns 17
=MINUTE(A1)                                 returns 13
=MINUTE(39911.7176620370)                   returns 13
=SECOND(A1)                                 returns 26
=SECOND(39911.7176620370)                   returns 26
```

KEEPING TRACK OF YOUR DAYS AT WORK: NETWORKDAYS

NETWORKDAYS(*start_date,end_date,holidays*)

If you have a project with a fixed end date, you may need to figure out how many workdays (excluding weekends and holidays) you have available to complete your task. The NETWORKDAYS function addresses this question.

NETWORKDAYS returns the number of whole working days between two dates, excluding specified holidays and other specifically identified dates.

Holidays can be any designation of dates. For instance, 11/26/2009 is a federal holiday (Thanksgiving, and it falls on a Thursday). You may also elect to give your employees the day off on the following day, which is also a weekday. If cell B1 is set to 11/20/2009, cell B2 is set to 12/1/2009, cell C10 is set to 11/26/2009, and cell C11 is set to 11/27/2009, then the net number of working days from 11/20/2009 to 12/1/2009 would be calculated as follows:

`=NETWORKDAYS(B1,B2,C10:C11)`   returns 6 (days)

The flip side of that question: Given a set number of days available to complete a project or task, when will it get done if you exclude weekends and holidays?

Assuming that the project start date in cell B1 is set to 11/20/2009, the duration is 6 days, and C10:C11 contain the exclusion dates (cell C10 is set to 11/26/2009, and cell C11 is set to 11/27/2009), then the formula is as follows:

`=WORKDAY(B1,6,C10:C11)`   returns 40149

This is the serial number for the completion date. You can convert this to a more readable form by using the following:

`=TEXT(WORKDAY(B1,6,C10:C11),"m/d/yyyy")`   returns 12/2/2009

OTHER DATE FUNCTIONS

In addition to the date and time functions discussed so far, a number of other useful date and time functions are supported in Xcelsius 2008. The following are brief descriptions of some of them.

DAYS360

DAYS360(*start_date*,*end_date*)

Some accounting systems and financial calculations, such as interest calculations involving daily compounding, are based on a 360-day year with 12 equal months of 30 days. DAYS360 calculates the number of days between two dates, using a specified 30-day month, 360-day year method.

EDATE

EDATE(*start_date*,*months*)

EDATE returns the date/time serial number of the date that is the indicated number of months before or after the specified number of months from *start_date*.

EOMONTH

EOMONTH(*start_date*,*months*)

EOMONTH returns the date/time serial number of the last day of the month before or after a specified number of months from *start_date*:

`=N(DATE(2009,1,1))`   returns 39814

The end of the month of 1/1/2009 should be 39914+30 = 39844:

`=EOMONTH(DATE(2009,1,1),0)`   returns 39844

WEEKDAY

WEEKDAY(*serial_number*)

WEEKDAY converts a date/time serial number to the number of the day of the week.

WEEKNUM

WEEKNUM(*serial_num*)

WEEKNUM returns the week number in the year.

YEARFRAC

YEARFRAC(*start_date*,*end_date*,*basis*)

YEARFRAC returns the difference between *start_date* and *end_date*, expressed as a number of years, including the decimal fraction of a year.

USING CALENDAR ARITHMETIC

In order to make effective use of calendar arithmetic, you need to think about it at two levels: managing formulas on the spreadsheet and integrating those formulas with the visual components on the dashboard.

SETTING UP CALENDAR ARITHMETIC ON A SPREADSHEET

This section poses an interesting problem and its solution. Instead of focusing on the problem itself, we focus on how the problem is structured in a spreadsheet setting.

Think about how many days there are between today and New Year's Day. The problem is not difficult to set up on a spreadsheet when you know you can specify dates (and their serial numbers) for both the present day and the upcoming New Year's Day. If you specify the problem correctly, you can write a formula that doesn't hardwire the year the question is being asked.

If the current day is 2/21/2008, the subsequent New Year's Day is 1/1/2009. If the current day is 2/21/2009, the subsequent New Year's Day is 1/1/2010. At first glance, it would appear that the number of days for both these scenarios would be identical, but they're not because 2008 is a leap year. You could take into account calculations with leap years, but that's not really putting calendar arithmetic to use.

To begin looking at the problem, determine the date of today, which you can get with this function:

```
=TODAY()
```

Determine the date of the upcoming New Year's Day, which is on the first day of January of next year. Next year can be calculated using the following:

```
=YEAR(TODAY())+1
```

So the date for New Year's Day for next year is found as follows:

```
=DATE(YEAR(TODAY())+1,1,1)
```

All you need to do is subtract the day number of the "today" date from the upcoming New Year's Day date, and you're done! Here is a formula that gives it to you:

```
=N(DATE(YEAR(TODAY())+1,1,1)-TODAY())
```

Alternatively, you could split this out into two formulas:

```
=N(DATE(YEAR(A1)+1,1,1)-A1)
```

where A1 has this formula:

```
=TODAY()
```

Splitting up complicated formulas is a good practice for the following reasons:

- The shorter formulas are easier to follow and less prone to accidental errors when you're typing in the formulas.

- You can potentially eliminate otherwise repeated computations. Notice in the original formula that TODAY has to be computed twice. When it is split from the original formula, the computation is done only once.

- The split-out portions are accessible to formulas in other spreadsheet cells.

CALENDAR ARITHMETIC AT THE DASHBOARD LEVEL

To get a better handle on calendar arithmetic at the dashboard level, think about how you get a dashboard and a spreadsheet to mesh with one another.

Here's an interesting problem: Say that you're running a call center or help desk operation, and you're creating a dashboard with a Calendar component that provides a specific phone number, based on whether the day is a weekday, weekend, or holiday. If it is a holiday, you could assign a specific phone number to each of the holidays (see Figure 4.16).

Figure 4.16
Conditional matching of dates with the Calendar component.

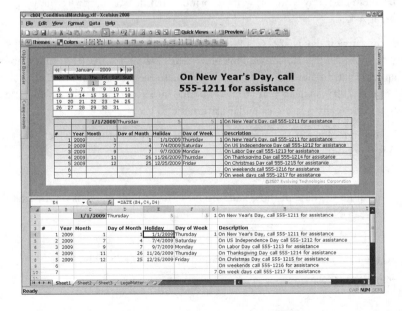

In the file ch04_ConditionalMatching.xlf, the Spreadsheet Table component shows the underlying computations while the dashboard is running live. When you select a date in the Calendar component with your mouse or arrow keys, the corresponding message is displayed to the right of the calendar. As you select a date from the Calendar component, the date is placed onto the input cell C1.

The date in cell C1 can match with one or more of seven possible scenarios (five are holidays, and the remaining two are weekdays or weekends). If there is a match, the corresponding scenario number appears in column G. The formula (starting with cell G4 through G8) used for this matching is as follows:

```
=IF(E4=$C$1,A4,"")
```

Effectively, the formula says the following:

```
=IF(HolidayDateInColE=SelectedCalendarDate,ScenarioNumber,"")
```

The formulas for scenarios six and seven are slightly different. They determine whether the date in the Calendar components is a weekday or weekend. Notice that 1/1/2009 is both a holiday (New Year's Day) and a weekday, so two conditions simultaneously match. Assuming that holidays are given greater priority, you can take advantage of the scenario numbers for holidays being smaller than the numbers for a weekday or weekend. Cell G1 identifies the appropriate scenario number, using the following formula:

```
=MIN(G4:G10)
```

When you have identified the scenario number, you can retrieve the appropriate text message for display. This is done in cell H1, using the following formula:

```
=OFFSET(H3,G1,0)
```

The OFFSET function is discussed later in this chapter. Other functions, such as INDEX, could also perform this lookup.

The contents of cell H1 are displayed in the Label component on the dashboard.

NOTE

> So far, I have not concentrated on the aesthetics of the dashboard design; that is left for later chapters. I haven't placed an emphasis on the details of the spreadsheet formulas. Instead, I've focused on the overall setup.

In columns B, C, and D, you place numeric values for the year, month, and date, and you construct a date in column E from these values. You could have hardwired the dates in column E and omitted the information in B4:D8. By hardwiring the dates, though, you would lose the advantage of being able to dynamically set the date at runtime. This could be set from either a formula or by a user interaction with a visual component on the canvas.

You are also taking advantage of positional arrangements so that if more then one match is detected, the one with the highest priority prevails.

MANIPULATING TEXT IN SPREADSHEET FORMULAS

Within a dashboard, it is important to stay on message. This means that you must have the ability to control the content of your text labels, titles, and legends. We'll quickly review the functions available to manage text at the spreadsheet level. Some of these functions adjust how text appears when it is displayed. Others involve surgery on text—literally cleaving, changing, and gluing strings of text.

MAKING TEXT CONFORM TO A SPECIFIC APPEARANCE

Text, especially if it is coming from a remote source, such as a database, or a hand-typed entry from an input component on the canvas, may be not be well behaved. To keep the appearance of text in check, you can make use of a number of functions, such as LOWER, UPPER, and TEXT.

LOWER AND UPPER

```
LOWER(text)
UPPER(text)
```

LOWER and UPPER adjust the capitalization of text. Here are a couple of examples:

```
=LOWER("Xcelsius Engage")                          returns xcelsius engage
=UPPER("Xcelsius Engage")                          returns XCELSIUS ENGAGE
```

Adjusting capitalization is important because it can aid in doing things like searches and matching.

TEXT

```
TEXT(value,format_text)
```

TEXT is a rather dexterous and versatile function. Here are some examples of using TEXT for formatting dates.

You have flexibility in choosing your format. Here are some examples (with A1 set to the date 7/4/2009):

```
=TEXT(A1,"m/d/yy")                                 returns 7/4/09
=TEXT(A1,"m/d/yyyy")                               returns 7/4/2009
=TEXT(A1,"mm/md/yyyy")                             returns 07/04/2009
=TEXT(A1,"dd-mmm-yyyy")                            returns 04-Jul-2009
=TEXT(A1,"ddd")                                    returns Sat
=TEXT(A1,"dddd")                                   returns Saturday
=TEXT(A1,"m")                                      returns 7
=TEXT(A1,"mm")                                     returns 07
=TEXT(A1,"mmm")                                    returns Jul
=TEXT(A1,"mmmm")                                   returns July
=TEXT(A1,"mmmmm")                                  returns J
```

Note that all these are returned as text, including the 7 and 07.

Don't get the impression that TEXT is restricted to formatting date and time. You can also use it to adjust text to conform to specific patterns for numbers (specifying decimal places and

1000 separators), currency symbols, accounting, and percentage, to name a few. Here's an example to give you a taste:

`=TEXT(0.0375,"0.00%")`	returns 3.75%

In addition, if cell A1 has the value as either of the following:

```
_($* #,##0.00_);_($* (#,##0.00);_($* "-"??_);_(@_)
="_($* #,##0.00_);_($* (#,##0.00);_($* ""-""??_);_(@_)"
```

then this occurs:

`=TEXT(-123456,A1)`	returns $(1,234.56)

Why are there two ways of setting the value in cell A1? The first is a literal value that can be set by the end user of the dashboard with components such as drop-down menus, list boxes, and the like. The second version is a formula that could be modified so that the format pattern is set by a computation. That computation could be anything you want it to be, including some kind of a lookup formula, the time of day, or the day of week. You get the picture.

You can experiment to see how best to use the TEXT function.

SPLICING AND RESTRUCTURING TEXT

It is often necessary to modify text by pulling it apart or gluing it together. The following functions help with such procedures.

LEFT

LEFT(*text*,*num_chars*)

LEFT returns the leftmost characters from a text value. The following formula returns the text string "535.25", which is not a number:

`=LEFT("535.25¦639¦123",6)`	returns 535.25 as a string of text

If cell A1 is set to this value:

535.25¦639¦123

then you can search for a delimiter and excise the remainder of the text in cell A1:

`=LEFT(A1,FIND("¦",A1)-1)`	returns 535.25 as a string of text

To turn this into the number 535.25, you could use the following:

`=VALUE(LEFT(A1,FIND("¦",A1)-1))`	returns 535.25

The RIGHT function is identical to LEFT, except that it keeps the specified number of characters and cleaves the leftmost characters.

MID

MID(*text*,*start_num*,*num_chars*)

MID returns a specific number of characters from a string, starting at a specified position:

=MID("Xcelsius Engage Server",10,6)   returns Engage

REPLACE

REPLACE(*old_text*,*start_num*,*num_chars*,*new_text*)

REPLACE replaces characters within text. Here's an example of how it can be used:

=REPLACE("1/1/YEAR",5,4,"2009")   returns 1/1/2009

A better construction would be to place 1/1/YEAR in cell A1 and 2009 in cell A2 and use the following formula:

=REPLACE(A1,5,4,A2)   returns 1/1/2009

Incidentally, either the value 2009 or the string "2009" can be used.

You can use a FIND function to locate where YEAR begins and incorporate it in the REPLACE formula:

=REPLACE(A1,FIND("YEAR",A1),4,A2)   returns 1/1/2009

You can convert this to an actual date value by using the following:

=DATEVALUE(REPLACE(A1,FIND("YEAR",A1),4,A2))   returns 49814

Keep in mind that there is no overriding need to write your formulas by using compound expressions. You can chain them across multiple cells.

FIND

FIND(*find_text*,*within_text*[,*start_num*])

As just shown, FIND allows you to locate a string of text within another. Keep in mind that FIND is case-sensitive. If you are worried about case-sensitivity, then combine FIND with the UPPER or LOWER function, as in the following:

=FIND("YEAR",UPPER("1/1/Year"))   returns 5

REPT

REPT(*text*,*number_times*)

REPT allows you to repeat a string of text. This can be effective if you need to indent a label, as in the following example:

=REPT("*",4)&"Text Title"   returns ****Text Title

LEN

LEN(*text*)

LEN returns the number of characters in a text string.

On occasion, whether set by formulas or modified by components on the canvas, the contents of a cell (for example, cell A1) may be set to an empty string. A formula might be set to this value:

```
=""
```

When you run the function ISBLANK on cell A1, you get a FALSE value returned. You can test to see whether it is an empty string by using either of these two formulas:

```
=IF(A1="","Empty","Not Empty")
=IF(LEN(A1)=0, "Empty","Not Empty")
```

EXACT

EXACT(*text1*,*text2*)

EXACT checks whether two text values are identical:

```
=EXACT("United States","UNITED STATES")          returns FALSE
="United States"="UNITED STATES"                 returns TRUE
```

CONCATENATE

CONCATENATE(*text1*,*text2*,...)

The CONCATENATE function and the & operator join strings of text together. Here are a couple examples:

```
="Xcelsius "&2008                    returns 'Xcelsius 2008'
=CONCATENATE("Xcelsius ",2008)       returns 'Xcelsius 2008'
```

4

USING SELECTOR-STYLE SPREADSHEET FUNCTIONS

One of the powerful features of Xcelsius 2008 is the ability to reference or retrieve specific pieces of information that could reside pretty much anywhere on the underlying spreadsheet. While the visual components possess capabilities of this kind, so do a number of spreadsheet functions. This section covers them.

OFFSET

Entirely new to Xcelsius 2008 is a function called OFFSET. If you are already used to using its cousin, the INDEX function, you may feel right at home with OFFSET. There are clear distinctions between OFFSET and INDEX. The main one is that OFFSET returns a reference to a single cell or a range of cells.

RETRIEVING A SINGLE CELL WITH OFFSET

OFFSET(*reference*,*rows*,*cols*)

To retrieve a single cell, OFFSET needs three arguments: an initial cell location, a row offset, and a column offset.

For example, if you want the cell that's four rows below cell A1 and one column to the right, it would be cell B5. To perform this in a spreadsheet cell, you could use a formula like this:

```
=OFFSET(A1,4,1)          returns the cell reference to B5
```

If you want a formula that's the equivalent of B5+1, you could use this:

```
=OFFSET(A1,4,1)+1
```

So why not simply use the following:

```
=B5+1
```

Both of these two formulas perform exactly the same computation (returning the value of B5+1), but the second formula is already hardwired to cell B5. Think a moment about what is being said: The second formula is hardwired to a cell reference. When you create your Xcelsius dashboard and export it to a SWF file, a PowerPoint slide, or whatever format is appropriate, there will be no ability to change the hardwired B5 cell reference in the exported file.

In this example, the offsets of 4 and 1 are static values, but they don't have to be. You could construct a formula like this:

```
=OFFSET(A1,WEEKDAY(TODAY()),B1)
```

Cell B1 could be set by using a drop-down menu on the dashboard. This sets the column offset. The row offset is determined by the day of the week. Each of the cells that OFFSET may reference could have an entirely different kind of formula or value. Obviously, this is a contrived example, but it points to the fact that OFFSET can fundamentally change the way a spreadsheet behaves.

RETRIEVING A RANGE OF CELLS WITH OFFSET

```
OFFSET(reference,rows,cols,height,width)
```

OFFSET is not limited to returning a reference to a single cell. It can also return a reference to a range of cells. Suppose you have data stretching across a row, say, starting from cell B7. If this were data such as sales for each month, a year's worth of sales would take you out through column M. If you wanted cumulative sales for the first six months of data, you could construct a formula like this:

```
=SUM(OFFSET(A7,0,1,1,6))
```

Basically, this formula is saying "Starting from cell B7, draw a box occupying just one row but six cells wide, and give me the sum of what's inside the box."

If the data stretched over multiple years and you want cumulative sales spanning two years, you'd use this formula:

```
=SUM(OFFSET(A7,0,1,1,24))
```

Hardwiring the number 24 in the formula is not a good practice. You could park that value in another cell, such as A1, and use a formula like this:

```
=SUM(OFFSET(A7,0,1,1,D2))
```

The advantage of this approach is that D2 could be set using a dashboard component on the canvas.

You could make such a dashboard more dynamic. Imagine that cells B7:M37 contains daily transaction data. All the sales data for the first day of the month are placed on row 7. Sales for the second day of the month are placed on row 8, and so forth. Column B could hold January's data, column C could hold February's data, and so forth (see Figure 4.17 or the file ch04_DynamicRangedSums.xlf).

Figure 4.17
Using OFFSET to perform computations on a dynamically chosen range.

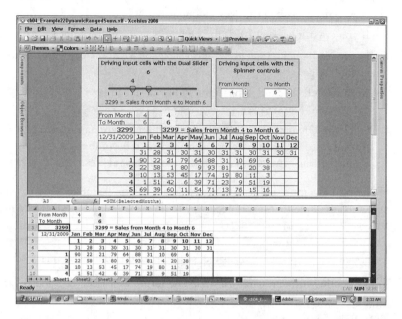

You compute the cumulative sales for the first six months with this formula:

```
=SUM(OFFSET(A7,0,1,31,6))                                      returns 6600
```

What if you want cumulative sales for just the second quarter? One easy but computationally inefficient way to do this is to subtract the first quarter's sales from the first six months of sales:

```
=SUM(OFFSET(A7,0,1,31,6))-SUM(OFFSET(A7,0,1,31,))             returns 3299
```

A better way would be to combine the formula elements into a single expression:

```
=SUM(OFFSET(A7,0,4,31,3))                                      returns 3299
```

Because you have the OFFSET locked down, it would be nice to compute the second quarter MAX, AVERAGE, and MIN:

```
=MAX(OFFSET(A7,0,4,31,3))                                      returns 96
=AVERAGE(OFFSET(A7,0,4,31,3))                                  returns 36.25 (approx)
=MIN(OFFSET(A7,0,4,31,3))                                      returns 0
```

Rather than marring a formula with a complicated OFFSET expression, it would be nice to have a named range, such as SelectedRange, that is determined from the visual components on a dashboard and just ask Xcelsius to compute something like this:

```
=STDEV(SelectedRange)                                          returns 27.79 (2nd Qtr)
```

Basically, you can do this. You can create a dynamically defined named range as follows:

1. Press Ctrl+F3.

   If you are using Excel 2007, this opens the Name Manager window, where you click the New button to open the New Name window.

   If you are using Excel 2003, the Define Name window appears.

2. In the Name field, type in `SelectedRange` or whatever name you want to give to the named range.

3. In the Refers To field, type in the following formula:

   ```
   =OFFSET($A$7,0,$B$1,31,1+$B$2-$B$1)
   ```

   Click the OK button. The worksheet references are automatically inserted, so the formula associated with `SelectedRange` would become this:

   ```
   =OFFSET(Sheet1!$A$7,0,Sheet1!$B$1,31,1+Sheet1!$B$2-Sheet1!$B$1)
   ```

There are a few more points I want to add about this example. You may have noticed in the hardwired example that it was necessary to do some mental jockeying to get from `OFFSET(A7,0,1,31,6)` to `OFFSET(A7,0,4,31,3)`. When you have the formula, you can just read the From Month and To Month values in cells B1 and B2, respectively. With a little setup, you can keep your spreadsheet structure and formulas simple.

Notice another little preparatory step. The formulas for cells B1 and B2 are as follows:

```
=MIN($D$1:$D$2)
=MAX($D$1:$D$2)
```

Cells D1 and D2 are input cells set from the dashboard. There's a reason for this kind of design. If you were to make cells B1 and B2 the input cells, there would be no provision to ensure that the values placed into cell B2 would never be less than the value in cell B1. If what is supposed to be the maximum of two ranges turns out to be less than the minimum, your formulas could get awfully confused. This extra layer of formulas is really a safety feature.

Notice that this dashboard example makes use of a Dual Slider component, which is excellent for applications where lower and higher values for a variable can be chosen.

INDEX

```
INDEX(RangeOneColumnWide,RowPosition)
INDEX(Range,RowPosition,ColumnPosition)
```

`INDEX` is similar to `OFFSET` in that it can pluck a value from a vertical list of cells or from a row-and-column position in a rectangular array of cells.

In Xcelsius 2008, if you want to retrieve the value of a specific cell residing in a single row, you cannot use a construction like this:

```
=INDEX(B1:G1,5)                                    returns an error
```

Although this construction is well behaved in Excel, it does not work in Xcelsius 2008. You must use a construction that specifies the row, even though it is the only row:

```
=INDEX(B1:G1,1,5)                              returns contents of cell F1
```

There are some distinguishing features when comparing INDEX and OFFSET:

- INDEX requires that you prespecify an array (think of it as a bounded box). If you try to use an INDEX lookup beyond the edges of the "bounded box," you get an error. Because OFFSET requires only the starting point, there is no need to worry about searching beyond a fixed-size array.

- You cannot search above or to the left of the range of cells specified in INDEX. With OFFSET, you can search above and/or to the left of the reference cell. You just need to use negative-value offsets to reverse the direction, and you need to make sure you are not trying to retrieve a cell above row 1 or to the left of column A.

- INDEX returns the contents of only a single cell and cannot return a reference to a range of cells, such as SUM(SelectedRange).

- INDEX computes positions starting with the value 1, whereas OFFSET starts counting from 0.

Admittedly, the syntax of INDEX is easier to understand, but the versatility of OFFSET easily outstrips that of INDEX. Use whichever function serves your purpose.

CHOOSE AND MATCH

```
CHOOSE(index_num,value1,value2,...)
MATCH(lookup_value,lookup_array)
```

Say that somewhere in a spreadsheet or database, you have a set of projects that is assigned numeric ratings. If the project's rating is 90 or higher, it is deemed safe. If the rating is 60 or higher but less than 90, it is deemed to be of moderate risk. If the rating is 0 or higher but less than 60, it is considered very risky.

Here is how you can set up a way to look up the ratings, based on a numeric score in cell A1. Assume that cells B1, B2, and B3 contain the threshold values 0, 60, and 90. In cell C1, type the word Risky, in cell C2, type the word Moderate, and in cell C3 type the word Safe. You could use a formula construction like this:

```
=CHOOSE(MATCH(A1,0,60,90),"Risky","Moderate","Safe")
```

or this:

```
=CHOOSE(MATCH(A1,$B$1:$B$3),$C$1,$C$2,$C$3)
```

In some ways, the combination of CHOOSE and MATCH works much like the VLOOKUP function.

VLOOKUP AND HLOOKUP

```
HLOOKUP(lookup_value,table_array,row_index_num[,range_lookup])
VLOOKUP(lookup_value,table_array,col_index_num[,range_lookup])
```

VLOOKUP searches for a lookup value in the first column of a table array. When it finds the closest match, it retrieves the item from a specific column of that data range.

To construct the equivalent formula that was developed in the CHOOSE/MATCH example of the previous section, you could write this:

```
=VLOOKUP(A1,$B$1:$C$3,2)
```

In the cell range $B$1:$C$3, the terms you want to retrieve (Risky, Moderate, and Safer) all reside in the second column. Notice that the table range $B$1:$C$3 is specified using absolute cell reference coordinates. This is done on purpose because there is a reasonably good chance you would want to copy and paste the VLOOKUP formula to other cells. (You might, for instance, be rating several projects at one time.) When you paste the formula, you don't want the table array to change.

VLOOKUP is a little more versatile than the CHOOSE/MATCH combination. You might want to augment the original table with some supplementary data. Instead of limiting yourself to only two columns, you could make use of dozens or, in principle, well over 100 columns. Of course, you have to take into account the sheer volume of data and its organization, as well as computation performance.

There are several other things you may need to factor in; one of these relates to Excel, and the others are specific to Xcelsius.

If the first column in your table array is unordered, you need to add a FALSE parameter to the formula to tell VLOOKUP that the data is unordered. In this regard, VLOOKUP works identically in Excel and Xcelsius 2008:

```
=VLOOKUP(A1,$B$1:$C$3,2,FALSE)
```

In Xcelsius 2008, the values in the index column (in the current example, cells B1:B3) are frozen when the dashboard is loaded, and they are never refreshed. In Excel 2003 and Excel 2007, the index column does get refreshed.

In addition, in Xcelsius 2008, VLOOKUP returns a value based on the first match found. In Excel, VLOOKUP returns a value based on the last match found. For example, if you set cell B1 to 0 and cell B2 to 60 but change B3 to 60 and keep the rest of the table array unchanged (cell C1 is set to the word Risky, cell C2 is set to the word Moderate, and C3 is set to the word Safe), then your Xcelsius 2008 dashboard does the following:

```
=VLOOKUP(60,$B$1:$C$3,2)        returns Moderate (in Xcelsius 2008)
=VLOOKUP(60,$B$1:$C$3,2)        returns Safe (in Excel)
```

You need to be aware of how VLOOKUP behaves.

HLOOKUP is similar to VLOOKUP. Instead of searching in a downward direction along the leftmost column and then returning the item in the column number, however, HLOOKUP searches the topmost row in a left-to-right direction. When the match is found, HLOOKUP returns the value of the cell in the same column of the match but on the nth row of the table array.

Say that cells B1, C1, and D1 are `0`, `60`, and `90`, and cells B2, C2, and D2 are `Risky`, `Moderate`, and `Safe`:

```
=HLOOKUP(90,B1:D2,2)                                    returns Safe
```

In searching along the top row (B1:D1), a match is found in column D. Within column D, the cell in the second row of the lookup table is cell D2, which has the value Safe. This is what `HLOOKUP` returns.

CLOSING THOUGHTS

It's no secret that the "secret" sauce behind Xcelsius 2008 is how it embeds spreadsheet capabilities. Much of the emphasis of this chapter has been to reveal the flavor of how spreadsheet formulas empower the dashboard.

This chapter covers spreadsheet fundamentals from the simplest baby steps all the way through esoteric topics such as dynamic name ranges. All the while, the focus is on how you go about constructing and building formulas.

When you realize that you can control the input cells from the dashboard, you can approach spreadsheet design in a whole new light. If this is not immediately clear, it will be by the time you finish reading the next chapter.

Sprinkled throughout the chapter are examples of how formula chaining makes the process of building complicated spreadsheets much more manageable.

As you build dashboards and visualizations, you can make changes to, test, validate, and tweak your spreadsheet in tandem with the visual dashboard design. This is a whole new experience that's not really present in Crystal Xcelsius.

Although the experience of building spreadsheets in Xcelsius 2008 works quite the same way as it does in Excel by itself, we needed to go through the various features and Excel functions to explain how to work the spreadsheet side of Xcelsius.

This chapter covers the broad classes of functions you will need to know about. It shows you some of the potential pitfalls and outlines best practices in the construction of spreadsheet formulas. It also introduces examples of how to apply context switching, a technique you'll repeatedly see in later chapters.

Now that you've seen the spreadsheet side of things, in Chapter 5, you'll see the flip side: the visual components.

4

USING CHARTS AND GRAPHS TO REPRESENT DATA

In this chapter

One of the reasons dashboards are popular and successful is that they help you show information and relationships that would otherwise be difficult to see. It should come as no surprise that charts and graphs play a key—or even central—role in the preparation of dashboards.

The goal of this chapter is to introduce you to using charting components in Xcelsius 2008. While many of the features of charting or graphing components are outlined, the emphasis is on how to use charting and graphing components to better convey information. Sometimes, important information is buried in the rows and columns of data. Visualizing data the right way can help to reveal insights.

CHOOSING THE RIGHT COMPONENTS FOR A DASHBOARD

Every dashboard has a story to tell. As you create a dashboard, your choice of components and the way you set your chart attributes can either bring out that story or bury it.

Say that you want to incorporate the following snippet of data, which represents the number of daily visitors to a website, in your dashboard:

Date	Visitors	Date	Visitors
1/1/2009	4667	1/12/2009	4648
1/2/2009	4349	1/13/2009	5154
1/3/2009	3678	1/14/2009	5281
1/4/2009	3094	1/15/2009	5088
1/5/2009	4326	1/16/2009	4709
1/6/2009	4627	1/17/2009	3477
1/7/2009	4615	1/18/2009	3078
1/8/2009	4743	1/19/2009	4617
1/9/2009	4888	1/20/2009	5357
1/10/2009	3321	1/21/2009	5421
1/11/2009	2955	1/22/2009	4902

What is printed here is just a snippet. The full data can easily span a year or more. You can find the full spreadsheet for this example in the file ch05_SampleData.xls.

Your first hurdle is to determine how much data you want to display. Figure 5.1 shows two alternative views of the data. The top-left graph represents a 22-day snippet of data. The lower-right graph represents data over the full range of dates, roughly spanning a full year.

A quick glance reveals an increasing progression in the data over time, but there is a lot of variation throughout the course of a week. It would be nice to be able to choose an arbitrary point in the timeline and show all the data over, say, a 30-day period. You can do this by using the OFFSET function (see Figure 5.2 or the ch05_SampleDataEnhanced.xls file).

Figure 5.1
Two ways to represent the data on a dashboard.

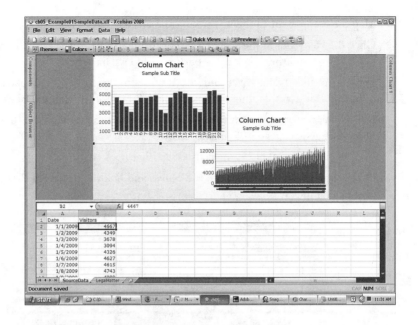

Figure 5.2
OFFSET allows you to choose data from any point in the timeline.

	A	B	C	D	E	F	G	H	I
1	XCELSIUS 2008 DASHBOARD BEST PRACTICES					Day		10	
2	Source Data								
3	with the ability to retrieve data from a point in the timeline								
4									
5									
6	Date	Visitors					Date	Visitors	
7	1/1/2009	4667				1	1/10/2009	3321	=OFFSET(B$6,$H$1+$F7-1,0)
8	1/2/2009	4349				2	1/11/2009	2955	
9	1/3/2009	3678				3	1/12/2009	4648	
10	1/4/2009	3094				4	1/13/2009	5154	
11	1/5/2009	4326				5	1/14/2009	5281	
12	1/6/2009	4627				6	1/15/2009	5088	
13	1/7/2009	4615				7	1/16/2009	4709	
14	1/8/2009	4743				8	1/17/2009	3477	
15	1/9/2009	4888				9	1/18/2009	3078	
16	1/10/2009	3321				10	1/19/2009	4617	
17	1/11/2009	2955				11	1/20/2009	5357	
18	1/12/2009	4648				12	1/21/2009	5421	
19	1/13/2009	5154				13	1/22/2009	4902	
20	1/14/2009	5281				14	1/23/2009	5415	
21	1/15/2009	5088				15	1/24/2009	3610	
22	1/16/2009	4709				16	1/25/2009	3265	
23	1/17/2009	3477				17	1/26/2009	4740	
24	1/18/2009	3078				18	1/27/2009	5169	
25	1/19/2009	4617				19	1/28/2009	5142	
26	1/20/2009	5357				20	1/29/2009	5241	
27	1/21/2009	5421				21	1/30/2009	5053	
28	1/22/2009	4902				22	1/31/2009	3793	
29	1/23/2009	5415				23	2/1/2009	3230	
30	1/24/2009	3610				24	2/2/2009	4962	
31	1/25/2009	3265				25	2/3/2009	4900	

SourceData / LegalMatter

It's not difficult to turn this into a rudimentary dashboard (see Figure 5.3).

Here are some quick steps to take:

1. Launch Xcelsius 2008 and import the ch05_SampleDataEnhanced.xlf file.

2. Drag a Column Chart component onto the canvas. If you prefer, you can instead use a Line Chart component or a Combination Chart component.

3. Map the component to the underlying spreadsheet data.

Click the chart and in the General tab of the chart's properties panel, click the By Series radio button and then click the + button to add a data series.

Within the added data series, link the Y values to the data to be displayed. If you are following this example, this would be cells H7:H37 of the SourceData worksheet.

If for some reason you want the Y-axis to appear on the right side of the chart, choose Secondary Axis instead of Primary Axis.

Link the category labels to the cells G7:G37.

4. Drag a Spinner component onto the canvas and link the data field to the day number (in this example, it is cell H1).

Figure 5.3
A very basic timeline dashboard.

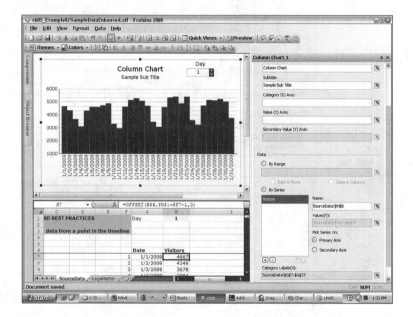

When you open the dashboard in preview mode or export the dashboard, you should be able to move along the timeline by clicking the up and down arrows in the Spinner control or jump to a day number by typing in the number.

There are a number of things you need to fix in the dashboard you've created so far. As you use the Spinner control to advance in the timeline, the column chart is a bit jittery between clicks. This is because the data animation feature of the Column Chart component is enabled. In general, data animation is a good thing; however, when you are trying to incrementally advance along a timeline, this feature becomes distracting.

In your Xcelsius workspace, select the Column Chart component. In the Behaviors tab of its properties panel, click the Animations and Effects tab and deselect Enable Data Animation (see Figure 5.4).

Figure 5.4
Turning off data animation can remove the "jitters" from a chart.

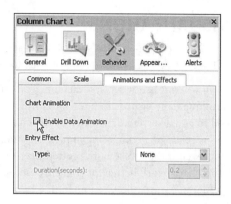

Eliminating the jitters is easy enough. Unfortunately, the Spinner component still doesn't behave exactly as you need it to because you haven't given it minimum and maximum limits. Unless you specify otherwise, the Spinner component automatically defaults to a minimum of 0 and a maximum of 100. In this example, you should set the minimum to 1 instead of 0. The maximum limit should be a number well above 100. You have a choice of typing your own value or linking to some value on the underlying spreadsheet.

The Column Chart component in Figure 5.4 is set to display 31 vertical bars. They appear a little cramped. You can improve the appearance by setting the marker size for the data series to a value smaller than its default of 17 (see Figure 5.5).

Figure 5.5
Adjusting the vertical bar width in a column chart.

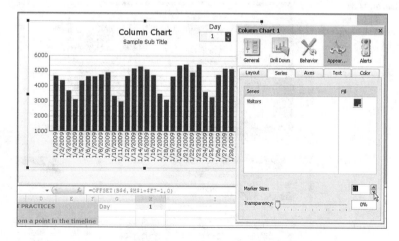

NOTE

Xcelsius 2008 allows you to specify a theme such as Nova, Halo, Elan, or Microsoft Classic. If you plan on trying out different Xcelsius themes on your dashboard, I strongly recommend that you do so *before* making custom formatting changes to your canvas components.

BUILDING ON YOUR VISUALIZATIONS

The Spinner component is not the only component that's suitable for setting a point in a timeline. You could instead use Slider, Dial, or Calendar components, to name a few.

The data becomes more interesting when it is not set in a vacuum. You might, for instance, want to compare the number of unique daily visitors to a website to the number of page views. To do this, you would need to add a second data series to the chart. Because comparing unique visitors and page views is really like comparing apples and oranges, a column or bar chart is not suited for this task, even if they were both plotted over the same range of dates. Line charts and combination charts work better for this purpose. As long as you don't need to make use of the Xcelsius Alerts feature, the Combination Chart component is the best choice in this situation.

PUTTING YOUR DATA ONTO A TIMELINE

Figure 5.6 shows how a combination chart can be used to present two data series: The vertical bars represent visitor count, and the line graph represents page views. Because visitor count and page views are not exactly the same kind of quantity, you need to make use of a dual-axis facility.

Figure 5.6
A combination chart is well suited for simultaneously displaying different kinds of information along a common axis.

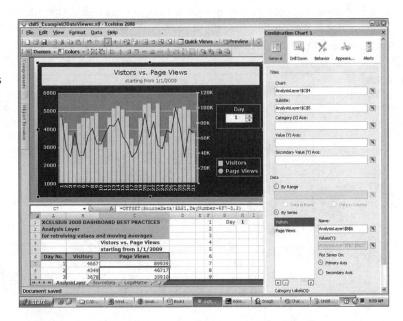

The following are important design features of this combination chart:

- You can make the chart title and/or subtitle dependent on the underlying spreadsheet content. In this example, the subtitle is pegged to cell C5, which changes every time the day number in the Spinner control is changed.

- The Spinner control title and rectangular background are purposely similar in appearance to the Combination Chart legend. This allows the dashboard user to perceive the Spinner control as an actual part of the combination chart.

- The plot area of the chart is a distinctly different color or shading than the area immediately behind the chart. This helps the visual data to stand out. The horizontal gridlines are visible, but they don't compete for attention with the chart data. In particular, only the major gridlines are enabled. If minor gridlines were enabled, the chart might be a little too busy.

- The labels along the axes and in the legend appear in boldface, making the chart easier to read. Using contrasting colors or shades between the chart labels and their background also helps the readability.

There are some hidden wrinkles that you need to be aware of related to combination charts. Figure 5.6 shows one of them. The primary axis ranges from a value of 1000 (a nonzero number) to 6000. The secondary axis ranges from a value of 0 to 120K. As you cycle through the days, as shown in Figure 5.7, notice that the scaling is not exactly proportional.

Figure 5.7
The scaling in this chart is not always proportional.

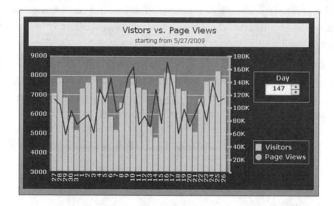

On day 147, the maximum value of both axes jumps up 50% (from 6000 to 9000 and from 120K to 180K), but the minimum values do not change uniformly. The primary axis originally starts at 1000, and on day 147, it grows to 3000. The secondary axis originally starts at 0, and it remains unchanged when the timeline advances to day 147. Clearly, the scales do not remain proportional as you advance the timeline.

You can force these scales to be proportional, but to do so, you must have complete control over the scaling, and you may not always be happy with the chart appearance. You can experiment with the file ch05_DataViewer.xlf, which provides a solution.

You may need to be aware of a couple other things. Dual-axis charts are generally supported in Xcelsius 2008. If you plan on displaying three or more data series in a chart, at least two of the series will have to share either the primary axis or the secondary axis. If your data series contains similarly valued items (such as percentage of efficiency or market penetration), this would not be a problem. If the values between data series vary significantly, this could be problematic. Consider the example of unique visitor counts and total page views. If you want to plot the ratio of page views per visitor, you might find numbers typically varying between 10 and 25. When you try including these as an additional data series in the combination chart, the data becomes flatlined, as the numbers are too small for either of the primary or secondary scales. To cope with this issue, you have several strategies available.

- You could put the page views on the same axis as the visitors and place the page views per visitor on the other axis. Unless the data series sharing a common axis have similar values, this is not going to be a very effective solution. In this particular case, the page views dominate. The visitor count is visible but too small, resulting in loss of meaningful information.

  A common technique for dealing with quantities that are vastly different in order of magnitude is to apply logarithmic scaling instead of linear scaling.

- You could apply context switching so that only one data series is displayed at any time, but the user would have complete freedom to choose which two data series you want to view.

- You could overlay a line chart on top of the combination chart. The line chart would need to be precisely positioned. Its background would have to be disabled so it is fully transparent. You would not display the line chart axis labels. The line chart axes could be hidden as well.

- Instead of overlaying a chart, you could make a separate chart that is pegged to the same timeline as the main chart. If you are going to follow this strategy, and the timeline shifts the displayed data to the left or right, you should place the separate chart directly below or above the main chart, not to its left or right (see Figure 5.8).

Figure 5.8
A possible layout for two charts on the same timeline.

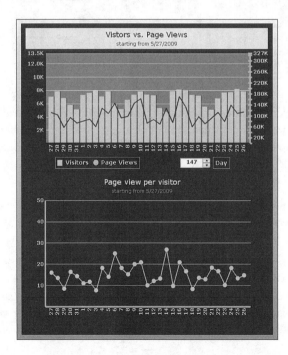

T I P

> In order to create a unified appearance when displaying more than one chart in a dashboard, you can enclose the charts in a single rectangular shaded region, as is done in Figure 5.8.

VIEWING GROUPED DATA WITH STACKED CHARTS

Stacked charts—whether column, bar, or area charts—have features similar to their unstacked counterparts. An obvious difference is that the data displayed in a stacked chart is shown cumulatively.

With stacked charts, you can set the transparency of the data series. The transparency slider shown in Figure 5.9 applies to all the data series. The series cannot be individually set.

Figure 5.9
Adjusting the transparency for your data series.

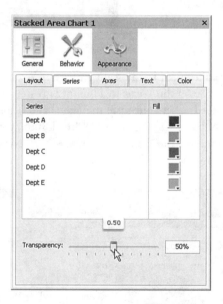

Transparency plays a more important role with a regular area chart than it does with a stacked chart because valuable data can be easily obscured with a regular area chart (see the lower-left corner of Figure 5.10).

Xcelsius 2008 has the Stacked Area Chart component, but there is no option to automatically represent data based on its relative contribution, as shown in the top-right corner of Figure 5.10. To do this, you need to prepare your spreadsheet data so that the data is represented in terms of its relative contribution. Mathematically, this is straightforward. In the current example, you simply divide each of the values for the department by the total quantity for the quarter. Because the quantities for the quarters add up to 100%, the maximum limit for all the quarters is the fixed value 1. This is what gives this kind of stacked area chart a horizontal plateau.

Figure 5.10
Various ways to represent data by using the Area Chart and Stacked Area Chart components.

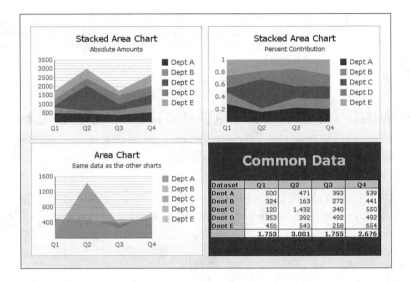

You still need to make a further adjustment to the scaling for your Y-axis. Use of auto-scaling will push the maximum value on the Y-axis to a number greater than 1, to something like 1.2. To regain control, you need to set your scale to manual and peg the minimum and maximum values to 0 and 1, respectively (see Figure 5.11). In addition, you have the choice of setting the number of divisions along the Y-axis or the size of the division. Both of these approaches are equally suited because your scale is fixed.

Figure 5.11
Setting the chart scaling for displaying relative contribution.

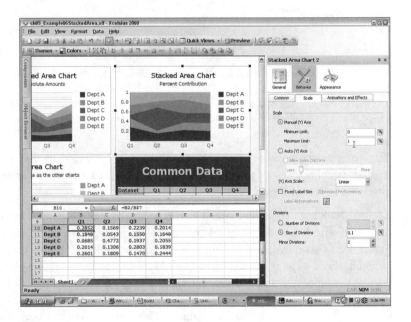

AVOIDING NEEDLESS DATA SERIES CONGESTION

One of the challenges of presenting information in a dashboard setting is that graphical displays can easily get overcrowded with data. The List Builder component allows a dashboard user to cope with this situation by enabling him or her to select which data series to display and in which order.

The Stacked Area Chart component is useful, but it is even more useful when combined with other components, such as the List Builder component (see Figure 5.12).

Figure 5.12
A List Builder component lets you choose which data series to plot on a display.

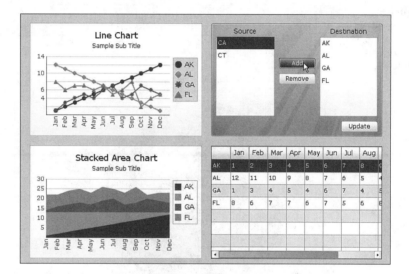

In the bottom-right corner of Figure 5.12, the data is displayed in tabular form, using the List View component. List View components have several benefits:

- They are scrollable.
- The column widths are individually adjustable.
- You can sort the data on any column by clicking the appropriate column header. You can toggle between sorting in ascending order and sorting in descending order.

List Builder components are great for when you want to cherry-pick certain pieces of information. Say, for instance, that you want to compare the sales performance of two managers.

CAUTION

There is one thing you need to consider if you are thinking about using a List Builder component. This component works by copying values, so the values displayed in the destination cells are "frozen" when the List Builder component update button is pressed.

There are circumstances in which you may want to see the totality of all the data but want to lump the smaller data values into one big group. You might, for example, be analyzing sales and want to see the detail for your four or five biggest customers and also see the combined total of all the remaining customers. Having a slider to magically set the dividing line between showing details and grouping the remainder would be very convenient.

Dynamically grouping or lumping data is especially important when it comes to Pie Chart components. Figure 5.13 shows an example of this.

Figure 5.13
Dynamic data grouping lets you control how much detail you want to see.

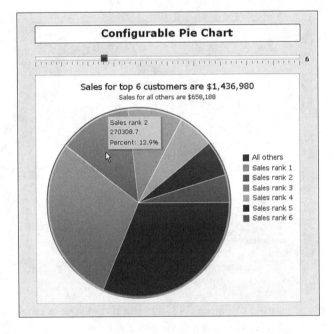

The framework for implementing dynamic data grouping is straightforward. In your underlying spreadsheet, start by having your data sorted from largest to smallest (see column C in Figure 5.14).

Place an input cell (see cell C4 in Figure 5.14) whose value is set by a slider or some other selector-style component, such as a Dial or Spinner control.

Calculate the total amount of sales or whatever you are displaying for the top-tier customers or items displayed in your Pie Chart component (see cell C2 in Figure 5.14). This is based on the value in the input cell, as set by your slider- or selector-style component. In this example, subtract the top-tier sales from the total sales to get the sales for "all others."

Populate a portion of the spreadsheet (such as columns F and G) with information needed for the Pie Chart component. You can use a formula like this:

```
=IF(A10<=$C$4,C10,"")
```

where cell C4 is the location of the input cell that is set by the slider.

Figure 5.14
Populate columns F and G with only the data needed based on the input cell.

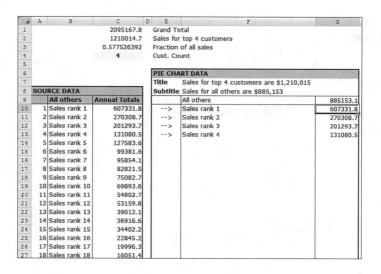

	A	B	C	D	E	F	G
1			2095167.8		Grand Total		
2			1210014.7		Sales for top 4 customers		
3			0.577526392		Fraction of all sales		
4			4		Cust. Count		
5							
6					PIE CHART DATA		
7					Title Sales for top 4 customers are $1,210,015		
8		SOURCE DATA			Subtitle Sales for all others are $885,153		
9		All others	Annual Totals		All others		885153.1
10	1	Sales rank 1	607331.8		--> Sales rank 1		607331.8
11	2	Sales rank 2	270308.7		--> Sales rank 2		270308.7
12	3	Sales rank 3	201293.7		--> Sales rank 3		201293.7
13	4	Sales rank 4	131080.5		--> Sales rank 4		131080.5
14	5	Sales rank 5	127583.6				
15	6	Sales rank 6	99381.6				
16	7	Sales rank 7	95854.1				
17	8	Sales rank 8	82821.5				
18	9	Sales rank 9	75082.7				
19	10	Sales rank 10	69893.6				
20	11	Sales rank 11	54802.7				
21	12	Sales rank 12	53159.8				
22	13	Sales rank 13	39012.1				
23	14	Sales rank 14	36916.6				
24	15	Sales rank 15	34402.2				
25	16	Sales rank 16	22845.2				
26	17	Sales rank 17	19996.3				
27	18	Sales rank 18	16051.4				

NOTE

Remember to set your Pie Chart component's behavior properties to ignore blank values.

DRILLING DOWN WITH PIE CHARTS

What good is having lots of data if you can't get to the underlying details? The quantity of sales in the previous example may be annual sales, which is composed of monthly data. It would be convenient to examine the breakdown of sales on a month-by-month basis. This is accomplished using the drill down feature that is built into many of the Xcelsius 2008 visual components.

In your Pie Chart component's properties panel, go to the Drill Down subtab of the Behaviors tab. Click the Enable Drill Down check box (see Figure 5.15). You need to specify whether you want to drill down based on position, value, row, column, or status list. You need to specify a destination range and, depending on the type of drill down, a source range. For this example, you want to choose the position—that is, which slice of the pie you want to examine—so it is not necessary to specify the source range.

You also need to tell Xcelsius whether you want to drill down whenever the mouse passes over a slice in the Pie Chart component or when the slice is clicked.

Because you only need to find out which slice is selected for drill down, the destination range is a single cell, namely the position. It would be a good idea to set the location for this nearby the input cell set by the slider (in this example, cell C5).

To get the drill down data, it's just a matter of extracting the particular row from the monthly data based on the input cell (C5 in this example). You could display the retrieved data on a Bar Chart component.

5

Figure 5.15
Setting drill down
options.

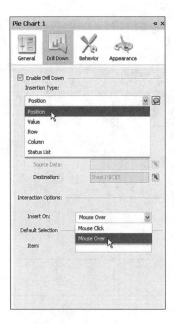

There's just one problem: If your tabular data follows a left-to-right chronologic sequence (such as January, February, March, and so on), the bar chart displays the most recent month at the top. The result is a sequence of dates that reads downward as December, November, October, and so on. To have the bar chart show a January, February, March, and so on sequence, you need to reverse the retrieved data (see Figure 5.16).

Figure 5.16
Notice that the
extracted data needs
to go from right
to left.

J4		fx	=OFFSET($J$8,$C$5,J$2-1)							
	I	J	K	L	M	N	O	P	Q	R	S
1	Drill Down Data										
2		12	11	10	9	8	7	6	5	4	3
3		Dec	Nov	Oct	Sep	Aug	Jul	Jun	May	Apr	Mar
4	All others	139812.1	134399.1	135302.8	127727.9	131539.9	129377	127898.8	118556.6	115357.9	112587.9
5											
6											
7											
8		Jan	Feb	Mar	Apr	May	Jun	Jul	Aug	Sep	Oct
9		107061.9	108214.1	112587.9	115357.9	118556.6	127898.8	129377	131539.9	127727.9	135302.8
10		34675	39262.1	42977.8	39932.4	41167.2	44151.7	46351.3	54434.4	56459.3	65054.9
11		15954.5	15771.6	17146.9	16737.6	20771.3	23953	24159	26222.6	25948.9	27136.4
12		9598.7	12169.5	14135.9	16310	18008.2	18941.5	19568.6	18691.6	18600.1	16966.3
13		10440	8463.1	9909	12057.3	11478.7	12615.1	11529.3	11404.8	9676.5	11803.3

When this is corrected, the dashboard renders as expected (see Figure 5.17).

As a little extra added touch, you can create a miniature isolated slice, as shown in the upper-right inset of the bar chart in Figure 5.18. This helps provide feedback on what slice of the pie chart is being revealed in detail within the bar chart.

Figure 5.17
A Pie Chart compo-
nent with drill down
to the monthly data.

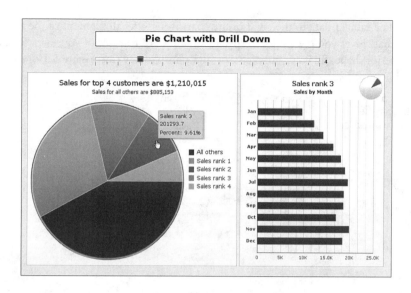

WORKING WITH XY AND BUBBLE CHARTS

Bar charts, column charts, combination charts, line charts, and a few other variants are charts that are continuous on one axis and discrete on the other. This is fine for histograms and the like, but it offers little benefit when you need both the horizontal and vertical axes to be continuous. Xcelsius 2008 provides two kinds of continuous charts: XY and bubble charts.

Each data series in an XY chart houses data for a range of values along the X-axis and a corresponding range of values along the Y-axis. This affords a lot of interesting possibilities.

WORKING WITH XY CHARTS

Suppose you have some raw data on individuals' years of education and age (see Figure 5.18).

Figure 5.18
XY charts displaying
representative demo-
graphic data.

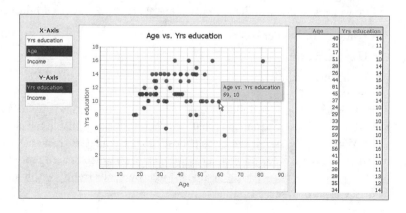

The tabular data to the right of the chart is just a small segment of the full dataset. An XY chart gives you the ability to specify a number of features of your data series, including the series shape, fill color, marker size, and transparency (see Figure 5.19).

Figure 5.19
Customizing the data series appearance in an XY chart.

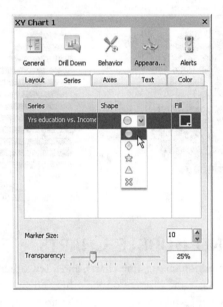

NOTE

If you are displaying more than one data series, you cannot individually set the marker size and transparency for each series.

XY charts can display only two sets of values at any time—one on the X-axis and the other on the Y-axis. However, you might have a multitude of factors from which to select. It would be great to start from a list of parameters—such as age, income, and education—and choose which two go onto the XY chart. There are three ways to do this:

- Using a List Builder component
- Using naive lists
- Using intelligent lists

At first glance, using List Builder would appear to be the natural way to do this. You may have 10 or 20 kinds of parameters that you want to make available for plotting on an XY chart. With List Builder, it is easy to choose more parameters than an XY chart can accommodate (see Figure 5.20). In such a case, the extra parameters are ignored. One thing you don't want to do is to surprise a dashboard user by inadvertently withholding information he or she expects to see.

Figure 5.20
List Builder doesn't stop you if you select more than two parameters.

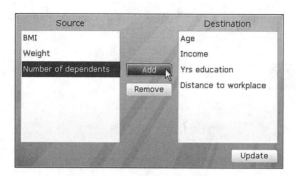

There are a couple other reasons to avoid using List Builder to create an XY chart. List Builder copies data to a location. If the original data changes, the changes are not reflected in the chart until the List Builder is updated. In addition, any time the user wants to switch which items appear in a chart, he or she must go back to the List Builder chart and reconstruct the list. List Builder may be indispensable for constructing reports, but it does not always provide the fluid interactivity needed for dashboards.

Another approach would be to supply for each axis a list-like selector such as a List Box or Radio Button component and, based on the parameter selected, look up the respective dataset. This technique overcomes the primary challenges of using List Builder: It is not possible to oversaturate the XY chart with too many parameters, and there is no wait time; as soon as an item is selected from the list, the data appears on the plot. There is one wrinkle with using a List Box or Radio Button component, though: It is possible to select the same item in each of the independent lists. For instance, it is possible to plot income on both the X-axis and Y-axis. Although this is not problematic, it isn't very elegant.

You can use a strategy that automatically eliminates the item chosen from the list (see Figure 5.21). This strategy involves what I call *correlated lists*. There is a list for the X-axis and one for the Y-axis. Notice in Figure 5.21 that the X-axis list box has three items, and the Y-axis list box has two items. Also notice that the item selected in the X-axis box is conspicuously absent from the Y-axis box. This is by design. No matter which item is chosen in the X-axis box, it is automatically eliminated from the Y-axis box.

Figure 5.21
You can select parameters in the XY chart by using correlated list boxes.

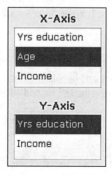

Let's look at some implementation details. Your List Box component should be based on inserting values, not position (see Figure 5.22).

Figure 5.22
List box properties for the X-axis.

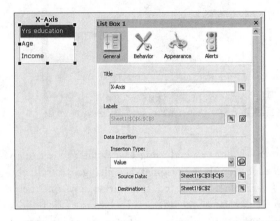

In cells C3, C4, and C5, you need to place the value 1, 2, and 3 (see Figure 5.23). In cells C6, C7, and C8, you need to place the labels Yrs education, Age, and Income.

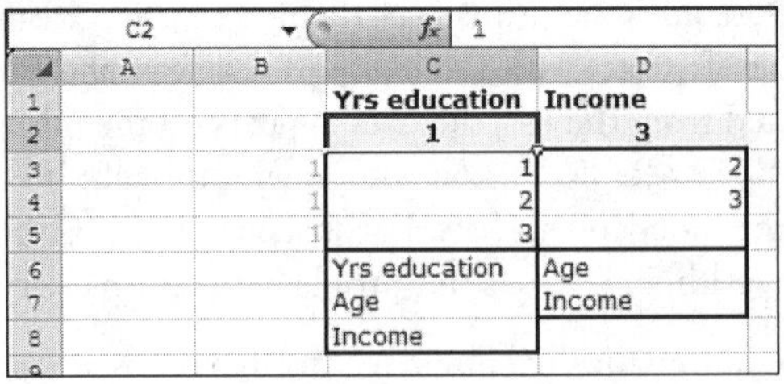

Figure 5.23
Spreadsheet setup for correlated list boxes.

Your list boxes for the X-axis and Y-axis should be reading the labels from your underlying spreadsheet (cells C6:C8 and D6:D7).

The formulas for cells D3 through D7 get a little complicated. I leave you to explore these on your own in the file ch05_XYChart.xlf. Essentially, the logic behind them is that if an item was already selected for the X-axis omit this item for the Y-axis and go to the next item in the list.

NOTE

> Depending on the quantity of data, XY charts and bubble charts can consume a fair amount of time and CPU resources in opening the XLF file and adding data to the components.

To complete the picture, the datasets that are chosen (the shaded cells on the right side of Figure 5.24) are retrieved for display in the XY chart (the left side of Figure 5.24).

Figure 5.24
Datasets are chosen for graphical display.

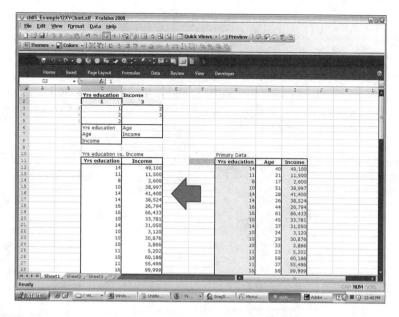

In this example, you can choose any 2 of 3 data sets. There is nothing to stop you from setting up your dashboard to select from, say, 20 possible datasets. Unlike using the List Builder approach, with this method, the retrieved data is still live. Changes to source data for the values plotted are instantly reflected in the chart.

EXTENDING GRAPHICAL PRESENTATION WITH BUBBLE CHARTS

The bubble chart can be regarded as the sibling of the XY chart. The essential differences between the two are that in a bubble chart, the marker size is variable, based on the value of some data, and the marker shape is round. Bubble charts offer a convenient way to pack more information into a chart. Rather than being forced to choose two of three parameters, you can simultaneously display all three in a single chart. With a bubble chart, you need to decide which parameter is associated with the X-axis, which parameter is associated with the Y-axis, and the bubble size (see Figure 5.25).

5

Figure 5.25
You can choose bubble chart parameters from the list boxes.

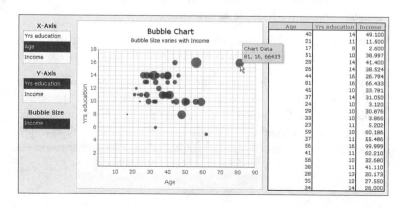

Bubble charts use size to represent a quantity. So how would you represent a negative quantity with size? Does a circle implode in on itself and invert its color? Xcelsius 2008 does not provide a particularly elegant solution for negative values. Basically, it shrugs its shoulders and gives you a little dot that is non-changing in size.

Fortunately, there's a workaround that allows for a relatively clean implementation. The setup is quite simple. You position your data to display your X coordinates, Y coordinates, and bubble size (see columns B, C, and D in Figure 5.26).

Figure 5.26
Setting up a bubble chart to support negative values.

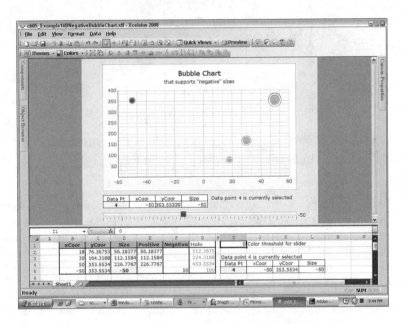

The next step is to separate positive and negative sizes (columns E and F of Figure 5.26). The respective formulas in columns E and F could be something like this:

```
=IF(D2>=0,D2,"")        positive values in column E
=IF(D2<0,D2,"")         negative values in column F
```

Next, create a data series for the positive and negative values (see Figure 5.27). (You'll learn the details behind the halo sensors shortly.)

In the Appearance tab, set the color of the positive data series to something like green and set negative values to red. Choose whatever colors suit your needs.

In this particular example, all the data is static except for a single data point, whose size can be adjusted with a slider to both positive and negative values. The X and Y coordinates for this data point use formulas that incorporate the size. Consequently, the data point moves as you adjust the slider, and the chart automatically rescales. This example is a little contrived, but it helps to make the essential concepts and their implementation clear.

Figure 5.27
Properties of the data series detailing negative values.

Displaying Values of Individual Data Points

At this time, Xcelsius 2008 does not natively support the display of negative sizes. Negative values for bubble size are rendered as tiny dots that never change size. In the preceding section, you used a little trick to fool Xcelsius into treating negative size bubbles as if they are positive and at the same time, change their colors. This size/color combination renders correctly, but Xcelsius still thinks the bubble size is a positive value. When your mouse hovers over the "negative" size bubble, the hover text displays the correct X and Y coordinates, but the negative value for size shows up as a positive number.

Rather than deliver a broken dashboard, it is better to turn off the mouse over text. But don't despair. I know another useful trick. By using the drill down capability of the bubble chart, it is easy to extract which point the mouse is positioned over and push relevant data about the point, including the negative bubble size, to a table that's suitable for displaying the data. I call this technique the *halo sensor*. With this method, you surround each data point with a thin ring, or "halo," that is capable of sensing when the mouse is positioned over it. It uses the drill down feature of the chart to identify which data point has focus. When the data point is identified, its related information can be easily retrieved.

The halo is set up as a separate data series. It visually appears behind the positive and "negative" size circles. If a halo were smaller than or the same size as these positive or negative circles, it would be eclipsed. Consequently, the halo needs to be a larger size than the circle size for the data points. Doubling the size seems to work well.

When you enable drill down, you may want to set the interaction options to mouse over instead of mouse click. Incidentally, you can drill down with each of the series as long the insertion points do not overlap.

5

WORKING WITH TREE MAPS

New to Xcelsius 2008 is the Tree Map component. Tree Map components simultaneously use color and size to represent data pairs, such as median income level and employee turnover. A Tree Map component is a collection of non-overlapping colored tiles that completely fill up a large rectangle (see Figure 5.28).

Figure 5.28
Tree Map components display data by size and color and support drill down.

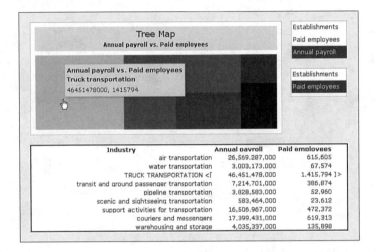

Each tile represents a row of data. Its size corresponds to the relative contribution of a specific measure, such as sales volume. The color of each rectangle can represent a different kind of measure, such as profitability.

A Tree Map component automatically arranges the tiles based on size and then by color or shading.

Tree maps are pretty, but unless you can easily connect them to data they use, their benefits are limited. In a world where there are lots of different kinds of data to examine, it would be nice to be able to choose datasets as easily as you can with the XY chart examples outlined a few pages ago.

Figure 5.29 shows the spreadsheet used to create the dashboard shown in Figure 5.28. The dataset in column C determines the tile size on the tree map. The dataset in column C is used to set the shading of colors for each of the tiles. When you start thinking about placing your data in two columns, one of which shows up as tile size and the other as tile color, the setup of a tree map becomes particularly easy to envision. The greater complexity comes about by shuttling data so that it is conveniently easy for a tree map to use.

Rather than reinvent the wheel, it makes sense to reuse spreadsheet designs already developed and vetted. You can use one of the spreadsheets already prepared in this chapter (refer to Figure 5.23) for the tree map.

Figure 5.29
The spreadsheet
setup for a tree map.

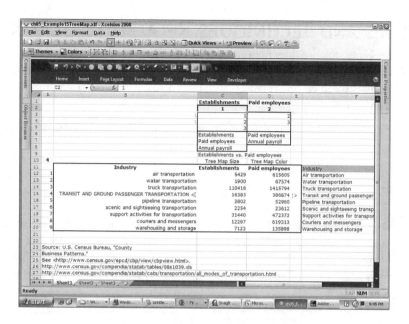

In fact, the spreadsheet of Figure 5.25 was actually used to build this dashboard. Basically, the data was swapped, and a few formulas were tweaked. There is also a little extra work involved in drilling down to detailed information based on the selected tile.

Before we leave the topic of tree maps, I need to mention a few things about them:

- The hover text in a tree map typically consumes a fair amount of screen space. It can easily obscure other relevant data. For this reason, the drill down data is placed below the tree map and not to the right of it.

- When selecting colors for high and low values, try to stay in the same color family and vary the brightness.

- Each data series in a tree map consists of a pair of correlated datasets—one column for the size and the other for color. If you want to add a second series, place the data immediately to the right of the first data series.

- The tile area, and not the tile length or width, is proportional to its underlying data. If sales increased by a factor of 9, the relative length and width of the tile would increase by a factor of 3. This is both a good and bad thing. Because the total area for the whole tree map remains conserved, the other tile sizes get scaled down by a lesser amount. Small values don't get diminished so quickly. It is also more difficult to interpret because we are used to linear proportionality, but in a tree map, tile size is proportional to the square root of its underlying data.

While a tree map may be pretty to look at, it doesn't do anything that an XY chart doesn't. Actually, an XY chart can be easier to interpret than a tree map. If you stop and think about it, the data points in an XY chart are, by definition, already sorted.

ISSUES AND TECHNIQUES RELATED TO SCALING

Xcelsius 2008 provides for auto-scaling of charts. This relieves you of the burden and drudgery of manually setting a chart scale. Most of the time, auto-scaling works well, but if your living is based on presentations and dashboards, you might want more fine-tuned control than auto-scaling allows.

Consider the following data regarding estimates of manufacturing efficiency:

```
day        production efficiency
7          59%
14         88%
21         91%
28         99%
```

Depending on real-world circumstances, the data scale that auto-scaling chooses may or may not be appropriate (see Figure 5.30). In this example, the scale reaches 120%. In terms of manufacturing efficiency, 120% is a physically meaningless quantity. Except for reporting or rounding errors and incorrectly calculated estimates, manufacturing efficiency would not exceed 100%.

Figure 5.30
Auto-scaling can go well beyond the data extremes.

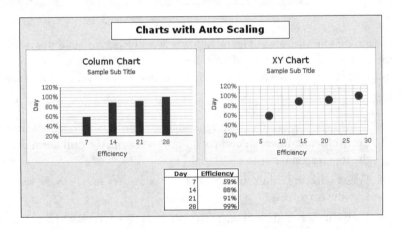

The point here is that there will be times you will want to take charge of how Xcelsius scales the data in your charts. With the aid of spreadsheet formulas you can design, you may be able to create the scaling behavior you are looking for.

EXPLORING THE SCALING LABORATORY

Rather than try to explain the intricacies of the various permutations and combinations of scaling settings, in this section I provide you with a scaling laboratory dashboard (see Figure 5.31 or have a go at it with ch05_ScalingLab.xlf).

In the scaling lab dashboard, you have the option of specifying how minimum and maximum scales are handled.

Figure 5.31
Chart scaling dashboard for which you can adjust the data extremes.

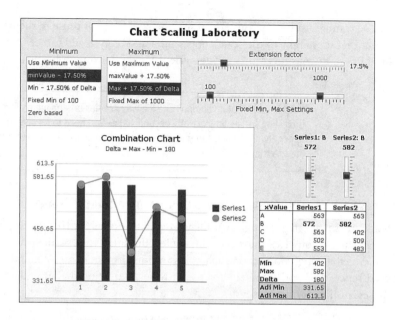

This dashboard has two data series, which are displayed in a combination chart. The data used for the chart is displayed in a table (on the right side of Figure 5.31). Notice that two of the data points in this table are shaded. You can adjust the values for the two data points by using the vertical sliders immediately above the data table. The vertical sliders allow you to dynamically adjust values plotted on the chart, so you can see what happens based on the prevailing scaling behavior.

You set the scaling behavior by clicking the various options in the two list boxes near the upper-left portion of the dashboard.

Here is a brief description of the various terms in the Minimum list box:

- **Use Minimum Value:** This is the minimum value of all the data points displayed in the data table. It includes the values from both series.

- **minValue - x%:** This is the minimum value reduced by an extension factor. You can adjust this extension factor by using the horizontal slider labeled Extension Factor near the top-right side of the dashboard.

- **Min - x% of Delta:** This takes the minimum value of all data points and sets the lower limit of the scale to be a set percentage of the difference between the maximum and minimum values of both data series. If all your data is concentrated over a narrow range of values, this type of scaling would be appropriate.

- **Fixed Min of x:** This hardwires the lower limit of the scale to a fixed number. You have the option of setting this value by using a slider. Once you set it, the value is unchanging until you decide to manually revise it.

- **Zero based:** This option hardwires the scale's lower limit to 0.

The Maximum list box options are largely the equivalent of those in the Minimum list box, except that they apply to the scale's upper limit and tend to add rather than subtract values. In addition, there is no zero-based equivalent for the Maximum list box.

NOTE

Keep in mind that if you don't like the way Xcelsius is handling scaling—for example, if it is creating scaling limits clearly beyond 100%—you need to be able to handle *both* the upper and lower limits of the scale. You can't get away with addressing only one side of the spectrum.

DEALING WITH VASTLY DIFFERENT VALUES ON THE SAME CHART

Sometimes you can get caught with having quantities such as 10, 100, and 60,000 in the same chart. If you place these on a linear plot, the small values will virtually disappear. If you are tabulating information such as loss or impairment of an asset and frequency of occurrence, then you definitely don't want to forgo treating the infrequent but very expensive events in your data analysis.

Figure 5.32 shows government-published data on number of oil pipeline accidents versus barrels lost in the United States during 2006. There is a remarkable level of linearity on the upper limit for the number of accidents.

Figure 5.32
A LogLog scale (that is, logarithmic scaling on both the X- and Y-axes) reveals structured relationship over many orders of magnitude.

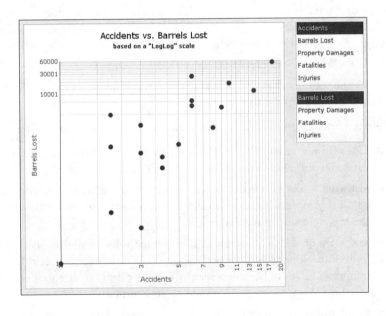

Setting up logarithmic scaling is rather straightforward. You simply open the Scale subtab of the chart's Behavior tab and select Logarithmic for both Horizontal and Vertical Axis Scale (see Figure 5.33). You can also experiment with applying logarithmic scaling for only one of the axes.

Figure 5.33
Specifying logarithmic scaling on an XY chart.

What happens if you keep both axes linear? The details for the smaller values are almost completely lost because they are too small to be seen (see Figure 5.34).

Figure 5.34
The smaller values for barrels lost are too small to discern in linear scaling.

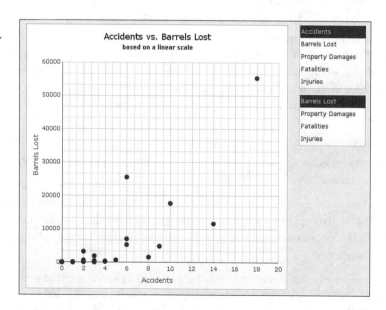

5

PUTTING VISUAL DATA ANALYSIS INTO FOCUS

Before leaving this chapter on charting, I want to address a key point that has been nagging at me ever since I started doing work with visual data analysis and dashboards. Many people who work on dashboard design are literally consumed with cramming as much as they can onto a single screen. They revel in the aesthetics of interface design and are quick to criticize a dashboard layout without offering alternatives or workarounds.

Understandably, it is very easy to get consumed with the visual interface and its aesthetics. One of the major premises of the dashboard is that an executive or a decision maker who uses it may have a limited opportunity to closely examine details, so the dashboard has to bring together all the information in one place. The information has to be easy to consume.

Focusing on the interface design without taking into account the mechanics, tasks, and practical challenges of building the visual interface is like coming up with a requirements document: It is a starting point but not a solution.

One of the alluring features of Xcelsius is that you can use it to harness a spreadsheet engine to intelligently and dynamically feed the dashboard visual display with appropriate information when and where it is needed. When information moves in such a fluid fashion, you can begin relaxing the all-consuming need to cram data onto a single screen. This, in turn, helps you sensibly design your dashboards and visualizations with greater simplicity and clarity.

CLOSING THOUGHTS

The goal of visual data analysis is to make obvious implicit and otherwise difficult-to-discern relationships. I started out this chapter by saying that every dashboard should have a story to tell. Sometimes, it's the dashboard designer who knows exactly what has to be said and is in need of a way to masterfully present the message. Other times, the dashboard lets the data speak for itself, by making it easy for the end user to examine and explore the data with ease and turn over stones that would otherwise be left untouched. I refer to the latter as "planned serendipity."

This chapter presents key issues, possible strategies, useful techniques, and hidden gotchas that tend to come up when presenting data visually. Along the way, many of the principles and techniques are shown in action.

The best place to begin is to ask, which components do I use? Then you can tackle, how do I tame the data? One answer is to put the data on a timeline. In this manner, you can see trends but not be overwhelmed by a dizzying array of distracting information competing for your attention.

In some cases a dashboard may be otherwise well designed, but the cosmetics get in the way. Xcelsius automatically enables data animation, which gives the dashboard a certain coolness and is designed to "wow" the audience. Unfortunately, when you are trying to analyze patterns and trends, the jittery behavior of this feature can be downright distracting!

As you get more sophisticated in your dashboard skills, you are bound to combine several components so they work as one. People often forget to make components visually blend together as if they are one larger component. Sometimes all it takes to glue them together is a single visual background. Sometimes it makes sense to stack data together so you can see all the data together at one time. Stacked data and its components become further empowered when you can drill down to get at the underlying details.

A common perceived limitation of pie charts is that they are only well suited to situations in which the various slices of the pie are roughly similar in size, and there are not too many of them. However, by dynamically grouping the smallest slices, you can use pie charts in many other situations as well.

Many of the Xcelsius charting components, such as column charts, are designed to handle histogram-like data where one of the axes is continuous, and the other varies in discrete measures or categories. There are times when it is necessary to get more quantitative and display two or more measures. This is where XY charts, bubble charts, and tree maps come into play. Standing behind these charts can be a variety of different kinds of datasets, waiting to be visually mixed and matched. I introduce a technique of using correlated list boxes to seamlessly select the datasets to be displayed. This technique takes context switching to an extreme.

In this chapter, you saw a solution for rendering bubble charts when the bubble sizes have negative values. You also learned how to set up tree maps. In addition, you learned about chart scaling because it is important to be able to fully control a dashboard's visual elements.

The theme of visual elements continues into Chapter 6, "Single Value Components: Dials, Gauges, Speedometers, and the Like."

5

SINGLE VALUE COMPONENTS: DIALS, GAUGES, SPEEDOMETERS, AND THE LIKE

In this chapter

Some of the favorite Xcelsius features among many dashboard users are gauges and dials. There is also a community of dashboard users who look at the very same gauges and dials with disdain because they quickly gobble up valuable screen real estate. It is true that they can consume a significant portion of your screen, but there is no need for this to be problematic. There are things you can do from an interface design perspective to ameliorate such concerns. This chapter explores a number of strategies. Before embarking on this mission, though, I want to introduce you to the feature sets of these components.

UNDERSTANDING THE SINGLE VALUE COMPONENTS

One of the key features of Xcelsius is the ability to tap into and control an underlying spreadsheet by using visual components on the canvas. One of the categories of components is referred to as Single Value components. Interestingly, Dual Sliders are lumped together with Single Value components, even though they drive two values on the spreadsheet, not just one.

In the Xcelsius Nova theme, there are eight visually distinct kinds of dials and gauges. There are also horizontal, vertical, and dual sliders (see Figure 6.1). Not all Xcelsius themes have this variety of components. Table 6.1 shows the number of Single Value components, by type, for each of the various themes.

Figure 6.1
Single Value components in the Xcelsius 2008 Nova theme.

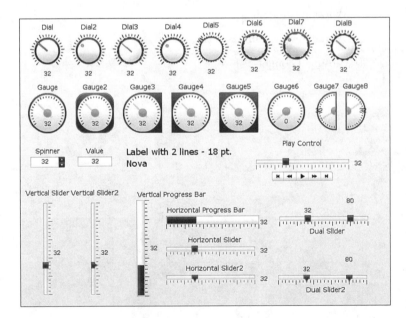

TABLE 6.1 SINGLE VALUE COMPONENTS FOR VARIOUS XCELSIUS THEMES

Theme	Dial	Dual Slider	Gauge	Horizontal Progress Bar	Horizontal Slider	Play Control	Spinner	Vertical Progress Bar	Value	Vertical Slider
Admiral	1	2	2	1	2	1	1	1	1	2
Aero	1	1	2	1	1	1	1	1	1	1
Aqua	4	2	6	2	2	1	2	2	2	2
Elan	1	1	2	1	1	1	1	1	1	1
Graphite	1	1	2	1	1	1	1	1	1	1
Halo	1	2	1	1	1	1	1	1	1	1
Nova	8	2	8	1	2	1	1	1	1	2
Windows Classic	1	1	2	1	1	1	2	1	1	1

CAUTION

When you switch themes, you need to pay close attention to whether the components translate correctly. As you switch themes, the components do not uniformly translate to similar counterparts in the respective theme. For instance, the Nova theme has eight distinct types of dials, and the Aqua theme has four. For example, if you render a dashboard with the Nova theme, using all eight types of dials, and then switch to the Aqua theme, your dials will translate to only four distinct types of dials.

The Single Value components category includes sliders, progress bars, dials, gauges, spinners, values, and play controls.

WORKING WITH SLIDERS AND PROGRESS BARS

The concept of a slider is really simple. You use it to adjust the value of a single data or input cell on the underlying spreadsheet. The data or input cell must be a numeric value and cannot contain a spreadsheet formula.

A slider is composed of a slider line, which may be decorated with tick marks, and a slider bead or marker. In addition, a slider can display a slider title, limits, and a value, which can be individually formatted and positioned.

When the user moves the bead on a slider or clicks the slider line, the value of the data cell is replaced with the slider value where the mouse button is released. In practice, sliders behave simply and intuitively.

SIMPLE SLIDERS

In essence, there are two types of sliders: horizontal and vertical. The primary difference between the two is the layout. Horizontal sliders allow the bead of a slider to move back and forth along a horizontal line. Vertical sliders allow movement of the bead up and down along a vertical column.

When thinking about sliders, progress bars, dials, and gauges, remember that multiple Single Value components can target a common data cell in the underlying spreadsheet. For example, you could have a horizontal slider setting the value of cell A1. Meanwhile, you could place a vertical slider that also sets the value of cell A1. If your dashboard user sets the value of the horizontal slider from 20 to 50, the bead on the corresponding slider automatically moves from 20 to 50. Visually, this is cool. However, if you are not careful, this can have some unexpected behavior. Say that your horizontal slider has limits set to the values of 0 and 100, and your vertical slider has lower and upper limits of 0 and 500. As long as the value of either slider stays between 0 and 100, everything behaves normally. What do you suppose will happen if you position the value of the vertical slider to 394? The vertical slider behaves normally, but the horizontal slider appears to hit a virtual wall when the slider value exceeds 100 (see Figure 6.2).

Figure 6.2
Problems can arise when two or more components target the same cell.

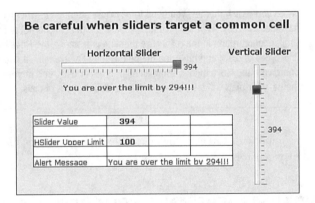

Although the cosmetic appearance of the dashboard is a bit askew, the behavior of the underlying spreadsheet is not in jeopardy. In this example, the vertical slider sets the value of cell B1 to 394. However, when the value of cell B1 exceeds 100, the horizontal slider isn't equipped to visually render this value, even if the value is 100.000000002. The significance of this issue could be an almost trivial issue. On the other hand, it could point to a critical flaw in the dashboard design.

Needless to say, you are not going to carelessly set up your dashboard if you can help it. Some dashboards can have many visual components and moving parts, which can make it difficult to see when something is out of alignment. For example, the value of cell A1, when set by a slider or another component, could be 100.02. You're going to have a problem on your hands if you have a formula in your spreadsheet like this:

```
=SQRT(100-A1)
```

The spreadsheet will not handle the square root of a negative number.

 There are a couple ways to guard against these kinds of problems. When you know for certain that some quantity should not exceed or fall below a threshold, you can build in some alerts. One way is to build an implicit, or "inline," alert within the slider component (see Figure 6.3).

Figure 6.3
Setting up a value-based alert within a visual component.

You can also set up an explicit alert through an independent computation. In this example, a message alert is computed with the following formula:

```
=IF(B1>B3,"You are over the limit by "&(B1-B3)&"!!!","")
```

In addition to building in alerts, you can proactively keep things in sync by linking the limits to spreadsheet cells. In this example, the upper limit for both the horizontal and vertical slider could be set to cell B3. This would prevent the sliders from being misaligned should the need arise to change the limit from 100 to some other value.

EXOTIC SLIDERS

On occasion, you may need to create what can be legitimately called an exotic slider—a slider that exhibits a more complex behavior than is normally expected of a generic slider. Let's look at the essential construction for negatively directed sliders and smart sliders.

6

NEGATIVELY DIRECTED SLIDERS

 The basic behavior of a slider is relatively straightforward. In a horizontal slider, the slider value increases as the marker bead moves from left to right. But what if you want the slider value to increase when the bead moves in the opposite direction? Although a generic slider cannot support this type of functionality, you can easily set up a negatively directed slider. Here's how you do it:

1. Place a horizontal (or vertical) slider on the canvas. In the Text subpanel of its Appearance tab, uncheck Values and Limits.

2. Map the slider data value to one of the spreadsheet cells (for example, cell A1).

    Type in the values for the lower limit and the upper limit in the spreadsheet cells of your choosing. In this example, I use the cells A2 and A3, respectively. Do not map the slider limits to these cells.

3. Shift the slider limits so that they start from the value 0 up through A3 minus A2. For convenience in this example, place the 0 in cell A4 and set the formula in cell A5 to this:
    =A3-A2

    In the slider properties, map the lower limit to cell A4 and the upper limit to cell A5. You could hardwire the value 0 to the lower limit, but it is better to map it to a spreadsheet cell so that you have the option of changing the slider limits through a computation later on, if needed.

4. In a cell of your choice (cell A6 in this example) type in the following formula:
    =A3-A1

    Place a Label component next to the horizontal slider where a slider value would be typically positioned, as shown in Figure 6.4, and map the label's text to cell A6.

Figure 6.4
Setup of a negatively directed slider.

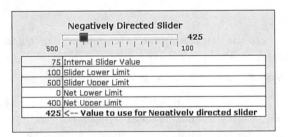

As the slider bead shown in Figure 6.4 is moved all the way to the right, the value slides down to 100.

SMART SLIDERS

 There's an interesting problem that is not easily handled in Excel but is almost trivial to set up in Xcelsius 2008. From time to time, you may have several quantities whose values are mutually interdependent on one another. Let's look at an example.

Say that you have four projects. You are expected to set up and allocate a budget for each of the projects so that the aggregate is $10 million—nothing over, nothing under. How do you set this up in a spreadsheet so that you are guaranteed not to exceed 100% of the available funds? Oh, and you have to do this without using macros, as Xcelsius 2008 doesn't support them.

Tackling this problem is not exactly simple. If you think about it for a moment, an "If over the budget then alert" strategy isn't going to be a terribly effective way to allocate a budget. The difficulty in Excel stems from the fact that there is no easy way to restrict how much is still available to spend. Managing user interaction with the underlying spreadsheet model is precisely what Xcelsius 2008 excels in (no pun intended).

Perhaps the simplest way to think of this is in terms of percentages. You have four projects, A, B, C, and D. The total available budget for the four cannot exceed 100%. If Project A is allocated 5%, B is 12%, C is 34%, and D is 17%, you have used up 68% of the budget. You still have another 32% to go. If you choose to put all this remaining amount into Project A, then you can have, at most, 37% (= 5% + 32%). If you choose to put all this remaining amount into Project B, then you can have at most 44% (= 12% + 32%). With Project C, it would be 66% (= 34% + 32%), and with D it would be 49% (= 17% + 32%).

If you translate this into sliders, Project A would be allowed to vary between 0 and 37%, Project B between 0 and 44%, and so forth (see Figure 6.5).

Figure 6.5
A smart sliders setup.

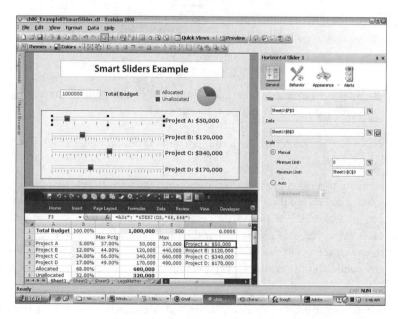

In the example shown in Figure 6.5, the sliders for Projects A through D vary between 0 and some value under 100%. For Project A, the maximum slider value is as follows:

```
=B3+$B$8
=PercentageForProjectA+TotalUnallocatedPercentage
```

For Project B, it is as follows:

```
=B4+$B$8
=PercentageForProjectB+TotalUnallocatedPercentage
```

The maximum slider values for Projects C and D follow a similar pattern.

Because the maximum slider values for each of the four projects are refreshed as any of the slider values are revised, there is never any chance that the values will fall out of sync. That is, as you allocate more for Project A, it dries up what is available for Projects B, C, and D.

Because the sliders in this example are pegged to percentages, the budget amount for each project is calculated separately and concatenated to the project name.

The whole idea behind smart sliders is that you can use them to make a bunch of components cooperate in satisfying simultaneous constraints.

Dual Sliders

Dual sliders are like horizontal sliders except that they can select two values over an interval. One of the nice features of a dual slider is that the values of the marker beads are displayed next to the markers and travel with them as they move along the slider. There is no vertical dual slider, only a horizontal one.

Spend a moment reflecting on the kinds of applications a dual slider could facilitate:

- A dual slider could be used as a kind of magnifying glass to examine data over an interval (see Figure 6.6 or open the ch06_DualSlider.xlf file)
- You might be projecting sales for two scenarios, one optimistic and the other conservative.
- You might have a pie chart of customer sales and want to characterize the top-tier, middle, and bottom-tier customers.

Notice in Figure 6.6 that the minimum and maximum values along the X-axis match the slider values.

In situations involving sliders and dials, you may want to run an animation over a range of values. You can use the Play Control component for this purpose. For example, the file ch06_PlayControl.xlf provides an example that targets the plot start cell B2 and "plays" values set within the General tab of the Play Control component. In this case, the values have been set to vary between 950 and 1010. Notice in Figure 6.7 that Play Time is set to 60 seconds. (Note that the Play Time setting controls the total animation time, not the time between increments.)

In you want to achieve a smooth animation between frames, you set Increment to a small value. In this example, Increment is set to 0.1. If you want your animation to feel more like a slide show, you set Increment to a larger value.

Figure 6.6
Using a dual slider as a data inspector.

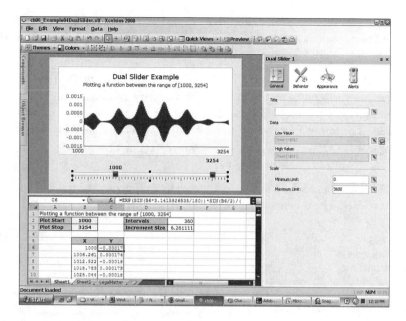

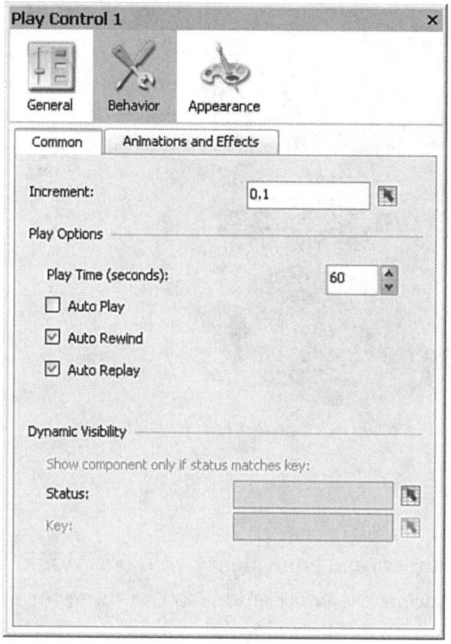

Figure 6.7
Setting the behavior in a Play Control component.

Before moving on to the next topic, let's look at one more example of how you can use a dual slider. Say you have sales information for 50 customers, sorted from highest to lowest. If you tried to place this information on a pie chart, it would appear a bit busy. It might be simpler to aggregate sales into three categories: top-tier customers, middle-tier customers, and bottom-tier customers. And what might you use to split sales into the three groups? A dual slider would be a natural for this.

You could set your dual slider to choose values from 2 to 49. (You wouldn't use 1 to 50 because you want to ensure that you always have a customer in the top tier and in the bottom tier.) You could use a SUMIF function to determine sales for the top and bottom tiers. The formula for the top-tier customers would be something like:

```
=SUMIF(ColumnOFSalesRank,"<"&SliderVal1,SalesData)
=SUMIF(A10:A59,"<"&E10,C10:C59)
```

The middle-tier sales would be computed by subtracting the top and bottom tiers from the total sales. These values could be presented in a pie chart, as shown in Figure 6.8.

Figure 6.8
Using a dual slider to aggregate customer sales based on sales rank.

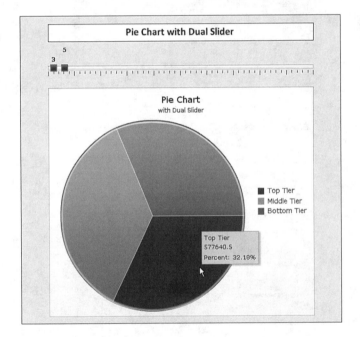

PROGRESS BARS

Progress bars are just about the functional equivalent of sliders. While you could use progress bars as a meter or thermometer, you could also use them for data entry because progress bars have a Data field, much as sliders do.

WORKING WITH DIALS

A dial is essentially a slider wrapped around a circle, with the marker converted into a needle or dial pointer. If you are planning on heavily using dials in your dashboards, you should spend a little time experimenting with the different dial appearances available in the dashboard themes. For example, the Nova theme has eight kinds of dials, and the Aqua theme has four. Because a dashboard bound to a spreadsheet can render only one theme at a time, it is not possible to mix and match visual components across themes.

Like a slider, a dial has a title, a value, lower and upper limits, and an increment size. There is no horizontal or vertical nature to dials; however, they do have something called mouse tracking. There are two types of tracking: vertical and radial. In vertical tracking, the dial responds to a straight up/down motion. In radial tracking, the dial responds as if you were physically rotating the dial knob. You should experiment with both types of settings to determine which kind is best for your dashboard. As a dashboard user turns a dial knob, a visual icon is displayed next to the mouse pointer, indicating whether the dial is set to radial or vertical tracking. In radial tracking, the dial needle always points toward the mouse, and the mouse pointer changes to a circular arc with an arrowhead (see Figure 6.9).

Figure 6.9
A dial with radial tracking enabled.

SCALING DIALS, GAUGES, AND SLIDERS

You may have noticed that the scaling options for your dials, gauges, and sliders are set to manual. You can set the dial minimum and maximum limits to numbers of your choosing. You can also have a dial read the limit directly from your spreadsheet. Having the ability to dynamically set the dial limits offers tremendous flexibility.

If the benefit is not immediately evident, consider the following. Your dial could be used to allocate funds you might invest in some financial venture. The amount of money you might invest would likely be capped based on liquid assets, your personal credit limit, your margin requirements, or some other factor. The point is, the maximum limit for the dial could be different for each person. It might require some complex computation based on a wide variety of factors that could change as the user enters information in the dashboard. (For example, if you start allocating funds for other ventures, the amount available for new ones would be diminished.) It is in precisely these kinds of situations that tapping into the rather hidden spreadsheet capabilities makes your dashboards and visualizations shine.

AUTO-SCALING

In addition to manual scaling, which really should be thought of as customizable scaling, you can use auto-scaling (see Figure 6.10).

6

Figure 6.10
Auto-scaling options
for dials, gauges, and
sliders.

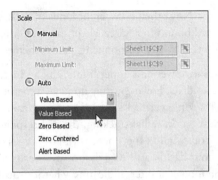

You want to use auto-scaling when you may have to vary a value with your dial or slider but
have not established a maximum or minimum limit. Auto-scaling computes limits so that
you can vary values of your dial or slider in a meaningful and useful fashion. The same holds
true of gauges, but the focus on gauges is on establishing the displayed minimum and maximum values.

Figure 6.11 gives you a sense of auto-scaling based on the same initialization value.

Figure 6.11
Comparison of how
different auto-scaling
options render.

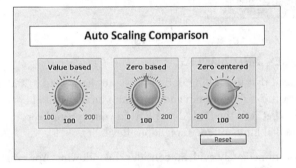

ENHANCING YOUR DIALS

The following sections outline a couple quick points about incorporating dials in your dashboards and then describe an important strategy that remedies a major criticism commonly
leveled against dials, gauges, and similar components.

GETTING A LITTLE MORE MILEAGE FROM YOUR DIALS

Notice that Figure 6.11 includes a reset button. A reset button is very handy as a development tool in calculator-type dashboards and simulation analysis. It gives you the ability to
return your dashboard to exactly the state it was in when it was first opened.

The visual appearance of a dial is enhanced when it is framed. In Figure 6.11, I placed
lightly shaded rectangles behind the dials. Having a heavily dark or black border for the
shaded rectangle can be distracting and turn attention away from the dial and dial values.
A discernable but not overwhelming gray, on the other hand, helps create a sleek and

professional appearance. In addition, the tick marks that surround the dial can sometimes lack sufficient contrast against its background. Don't be afraid to tweak the dial's appearance to achieve better visual clarity.

Dial Sharing: A Best Practice Strategy

There's no denying that dials and gauges, as pretty as they are, gobble up a significant amount of screen space. It would be difficult to prepare a serious dashboard if you attempted to display a dozen dials at one time. Problems like this are unsolvable unless you are willing to be a little imaginative.

If you have several dials on a dashboard or visualization, you are only going to turn the knobs of these dials one at a time. This means that while one of them is actively being turned, the others are sitting around waiting. In reality, you should only need one dial if it can be made to control more than one parameter. Basically, you need only a single dial to control a range of spreadsheet cells.

THE DETAILS BEHIND THE SHARED COMPONENT FRAMEWORK

This section provides an example of the Evolving Technologies Corporation (ETC) Shared Component Framework. This section is intended for those who want to understand the technical details of the framework. If you just want to apply the framework without the gory details, you can skip to the next section.

A Dial component (or any other component that is to be shared) wants to target or set the value in a single spreadsheet cell. In the example used here (and provided in the ch06_SharedDial.xlf file), the target or data cell is C3. The dial isn't concerned with what's going on in the rest of the dashboard or underlying spreadsheet. All it knows is C3's value and that, when you turn the knob, the value in that cell is going to be adjusted. The dial, of course, can read the contents of other spreadsheet cells to retrieve the dial's title, upper limit, lower limit, and increment. For now, you can focus on the dial's value in cell C3.

The key to using just one dial to set values across multiple cells lies in context switching. Because a dial operates on one cell, why not fetch data for a particular context, make note of it, and modify the original source? Figure 6.12 illustrates this setup. The input cells for the dial are all in column C. Columns E through H hold the bank of values waiting to be fetched for use by the dial.

When the user clicks one of the radio buttons below the dial, cell C1 is refreshed with the current radio button position.

If you click the first radio button (labeled North), the value 1 is placed in cell C1. If you click the second radio button, East, the value 2 is placed in cell C1. Clicking the third radio button places the value 3 in cell C1, and clicking the fourth radio button places the value 4 in cell C1.

This clicking triggers the fetching process. The fetch is accomplished using the following OFFSET formula:

```
=OFFSET(D3,0,$C$1)                                    formula for cell D3
```

6

Figure 6.12
Setup of the Shared Component Framework. (Printed with permission of Evolving Technologies Corporation.)

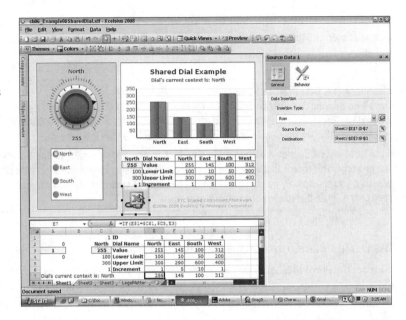

If the value of C1 is 1, then the data in the first column of E through H is pulled into column C. At this point, the dial is able to read and change the values in cells C2:C6.

Each of the cells in E7:H7 checks whether the current context number matches the value in row 1. This formula is in cell E7:

```
=IF(E$1=$C$1,$C3,E3)
```

Basically, the formula says "If my column is the same kind of data that the dial is working on, then retrieve the latest value set by the dial; otherwise, keep the data I already have."

Finally, the Source Data component copies the row data in cells E7:H7 and places it into E3:H3.

USING THE SHARED COMPONENT FRAMEWORK IN YOUR DASHBOARDS   There are basically four elements to the Shared Component Framework:

- **The context switcher**: The example shown in Figure 6.12 accomplishes context switching through the use of radio buttons. You can instead use other components, such as list boxes, menus, spinner controls, and even other dials.

- **The shared component**: The shared component does not need to be restricted to a dial or gauge. It could be a slider, an input field, or just about any selector or Single Value component.

- **The data bank**: This is the list of values that is retrieved when the context of the shared component is switched. It is important to have an identifiable ID or context number. In the example, this corresponds to cells E1:H1.

- **The updater facility**: This consists of a row of formulas that keeps the most up-to-date values around and uses the Source Data component to update the data held by the data bank.

Take a look at the example in file ch06_SharedDial.xlf to check all the individual settings.

The ETC Shared Component Framework provides a number of advantages:

- It can significantly reduce component redundancy, which simplifies the design, deployment, and maintenance phases for your dashboard. This also reduces the life cycle cost associated with dashboard production.

  Design and maintenance are simplified because you're not toiling with an overabundance of components. The reduction in the number of components on your dashboard canvas leads to a simpler, sleeker design. Updating the look and feel is simpler, as you need to make changes in only one place.

  Deployment of your dashboards should be simpler to manage. File size gets reduced as you can replace many dozens of components with a handful. Because the number of components could be drastically reduced, the dashboard computation speed could improve.

- The settings in each of the contexts have memory. That is, when the shared component switches from one context to another and back again, it doesn't forget the most recent settings.

- The construction of a shared component is relatively easy to do. It involves remarkably few formulas.

WORKING WITH GAUGES

Gauges are similar to dials, but they are essentially intended to be readout devices rather than input devices. Actually, gauges can also be used as input devices because you can "grab" an indicator needle of a gauge and move it, forcing the value in the underlying spreadsheet to be changed.

There's a new feature in Xcelsius 2008 that you won't find in its predecessors. If the data cell that's targeted by a gauge happens to have a formula in it, what do you suppose will happen if you grab and drag the indicator needle of the gauge? The value gets overwritten, but the formula in the spreadsheet cell is left intact. The very next moment, the formula computation is refreshed, and the result of the formula computation overwrites the previous data value. This is kind of an amazing feature. It allows for all sorts of imaginative dashboard designs.

USING GAUGES

Although you can apply a shared component framework with gauges, it may not be necessary to get so elaborate. Figure 6.13 and the file ch06_GaugeViewer.xlf shows how you can

6

punt information over to a single Gauge component. The dashboard user can click any month in the list box or select a row in the spreadsheet table. Based on the region selected from the radio buttons across the top, the gauge depicts the percentage increase or decrease of actual sales versus projected.

Figure 6.13
Gauge Viewer gets data for any chosen month and geographic region.

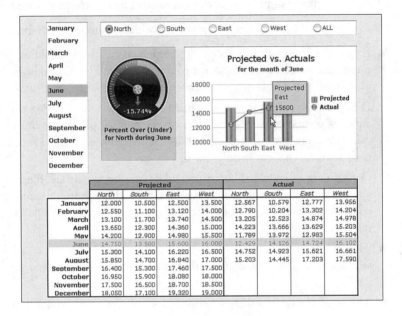

	Projected				Actual			
	North	South	East	West	North	South	East	West
January	12.000	10.500	12.500	13.500	12.567	10.579	12.777	13.956
February	12.550	11.100	13.120	14.000	12.790	10.204	13.302	14.204
March	13.100	11.700	13.740	14.500	13.205	12.523	14.874	14.978
April	13.650	12.300	14.360	15.000	14.223	13.666	13.629	15.203
May	14.200	12.900	14.980	15.500	11.789	13.972	12.983	15.504
June	14.750	13.500	15.600	16.000	12.429	14.126	14.724	16.102
July	15.300	14.100	16.220	16.500	14.752	14.923	15.621	16.661
August	15.850	14.700	16.840	17.000	15.203	14.445	17.203	17.590
September	16.400	15.300	17.460	17.500				
October	16.950	15.900	18.080	18.000				
November	17.500	16.500	18.700	18.500				
December	18.050	17.100	19.320	19.000				

There are some features you may want to harvest from this dashboard. For example, the gauge provides a conditional alert (see Figure 6.14).

In this case, the alert is based on a value. Notice that automatic colors are not enabled. The radio button High Values Are Good is selected, and the only alert location is the gauge background. You can change the marker (the gauge needle) as well as the value displayed in the gauge.

As an added touch, there is a Trend Icon component in an empty space on the gauge. The Trend Icon component conveys information using both color and arrow direction.

With this dashboard, you can click a row in the spreadsheet table and have the regional data for the corresponding month placed in both the combination chart and the gauge. The monthly data only begins in the third row of the spreadsheet table. The first two rows are headers. In the component's Behavior tab, you can tell the component to start selecting from the third row (see Figure 6.15).

There's a little wrinkle here. When you push the position of the selected row, the position starts with the value 3 for January! This is because the spreadsheet table has two header rows. You need to convert this to an offset. If the cell coordinates to which the position is pushed is A7, you can create a formula like this in a neighboring cell:

=A7-2

Figure 6.14
Setting a value-based alert for a gauge.

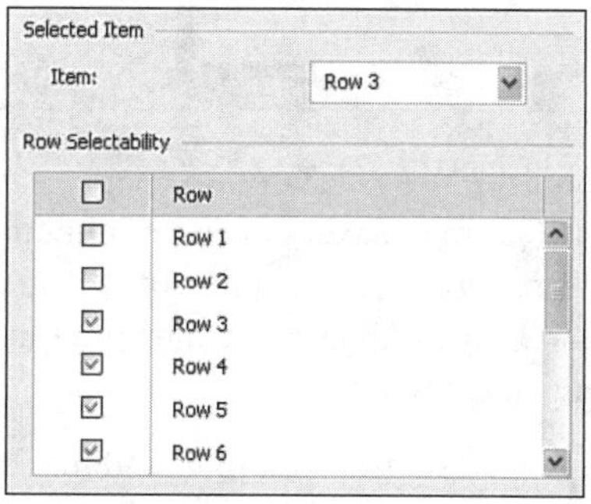

Figure 6.15
Setting a spreadsheet table to allow selection starting in the third row.

You can then use the Source Data component to punt this over to where it would be used by the chart and gauge. I leave you to explore the details in the ch06_GaugeViewer.xlf file.

NOTE

Let's talk a little about strategy. You could design a dashboard with the spreadsheet table pushing out a spreadsheet row instead of the select row position. Both of these approaches work. If you opt for the row contents, you are working directly on the table data. If you reference a position, you are using metadata. Because the source data is actually shown in the table, neither strategy is better than the other. If the data shown in the spreadsheet table is not laid out the way you need it for further analysis, or if you need to retrieve corroborating information not displayed in the spreadsheet table, then the metadata approach may better serve your needs.

CONSTRUCTING WRAPAROUND GAUGES

One of the perceived disadvantages of gauges is that you hit a barrier when you try to reach or exceed 360 degrees. But you actually can exceed 360 degrees, and it's not at all difficult (see Figure 6.16).

Figure 6.16
A wraparound gauge lets you break the 360-degree barrier.

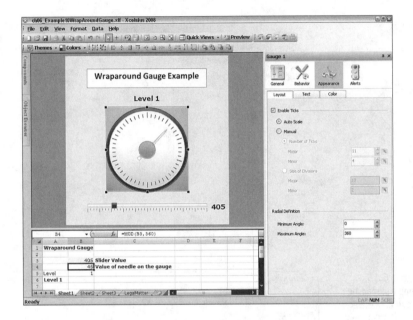

Here is the basic idea: Most gauges are set to a maximum and minimum angle of plus or minus 130 degrees. (And for dials, it is generally plus or minus 140 degrees.) You can find this setting in the Layout subtab of the gauge's Appearance tab. You can simply change the minimum angle to 0 and the maximum angle to 360.

In the Gauge component's General tab, you set the minimum and maximum limits to 0 and 359, respectively. Because you are starting from 0 and need to adjust your needle up by 360 positions, the maximum value winds up being 359. Don't worry about 360 being missing in this case; when you hit 360, the needle would be pointing to 0.

You need to map the data field of your gauge to a spreadsheet cell. In this example, it is set to cell B4. Cell B4 needs to take some value conceivably greater than 360 and map it to a 360-degree measure for the gauge. If the starting value is 405, you would have a formula like this:

=MOD(405,360)   returns 45

The needle on your gauge would be pointing at a 45-degree angle.

Of course, you don't want to hardwire the value 405 in the formula; you would set it to the value of another cell in your spreadsheet, perhaps B3. Now your formula looks like this:

```
=MOD(B3,360)
```

You can set the value of cell B3 by using any standard component, such as a slider. In this example, I have a slider that can change the value of cell B3 from 0 to 1800, a value well beyond 360.

That's all there is to creating the wraparound gauge. If you want a little more functionality, you can make use of dynamic visibility so you can see how many times you've gone around the gauge. You'll learn more about dynamic visibility in Chapter 7, "Using Multi-Layer Visibility in Your Dashboards and Visualizations."

You should be aware that although the wraparound gauge is fixated on a value between 0 and 359, the true value (cell B3 in the current value) is always available to the rest of the spreadsheet and dashboard.

WORKING WITH SPINNERS

Before leaving the topic of Single Value components, I want to show you a way to get a little more mileage out of a spinner. The technique is a hack and doesn't really constitute a best practice. But because it is elegant and it works, I include it.

If you read through Chapter 3, "Getting Familiar with Xcelsius 2008," you'll be familiar with date arithmetic. To quickly recap, Excel is able to calculate with dates by automatically converting them into numbers. If July 7, 2009, gets converted to the number 40001, then July 14, 2009, has a serialized day number of 40008. So if you want to advance your calendar by 7 days, you need only nudge the value 40001 by seven increments of 1.

Although it may be easy for a computer to work with numbers and date arithmetic, it is definitely not so easy for the majority of people. A Spinner component can increment a number such as 40001 and at the same time show a text representation of the day number in its title field. When you use a spinner in a dashboard to advance a date, the only one who needs to know the day number is the computer. You can hide the spinner's Value field by changing its font color to the same as its background, white. In the text properties of the spinner's Title field, you adjust the X- and Y-offset so that the spinner's title is positioned inside the control (see Figure 6.17).

When the dashboard is run, the spinner appears to be text based. Having the title positioned inside the Spinner doesn't prevent you from selecting the numeric value and changing it. You have to know that there is a number in the value field that can be selected and edited.

6

Figure 6.17
Setup of a text-based spinner.

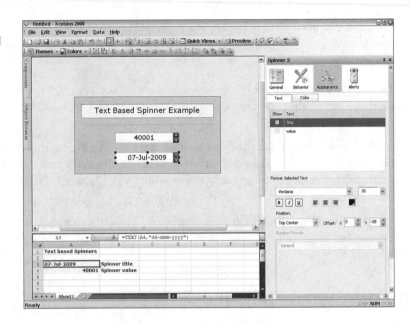

CLOSING THOUGHTS

This chapter covers a broad subcategory of components in Xcelsius 2008 called Single Value components, including sliders, progress bars, dials, gauges, spinners, values, and play controls.

Rather than trying to explain the full feature set, this chapter outlines key features you will likely need to know and then explores how to incorporate those components.

Because sliders, dials, and similar components are hooked into spreadsheets and dynamically changing data sources, not everything plays out in a fixed or restricted set of values. Unless you build some smarts into a slider, it is not going to know how to automatically adjust its limits so that, say, 100% of some budget or other quantity is never exceeded. This is where such design considerations are critical. It is here where the visual elegance of the dashboard and the analytical prowess of the spreadsheet engine come together. And this is where I make explicit the techniques, strategies, and best practices for building effective dashboards.

In particular, I provide an example of highly efficient component reuse: You can use a single dial or slider to set the values of many dozens of parameters in a dashboard or visualization. The technique lends itself to many situations and is not locked into sliders and dials.

Xcelsius 2008 gives you license to be creative with your dashboards and visualizations. The negatively directed slider is an excellent example of this. It is an almost trivial variation of a regular slider. In the horizontal version of this slider, increasing the value of the slider's data is done by moving the marker from right to left instead of left to right. For example, in a business setting you might be simulating two competitors vying for the customers' business.

For a fixed-size market, it's a tug of war between the two competitors who want to capture the market share. Having two sliders, one positively directed and the other negatively directed, sandwiching a finite and depletable customer pool or resource is a wonderful visual representation of this problem. Using two positively directed horizontal sliders is not nearly as exciting or intuitive in this situation.

The component construction techniques and practices outlined in this chapter and throughout the rest of this book are vehicles to help make your data, your analyses, their characterization, and conclusions crystal clear.

Chapter 7 deals with multi-layer visibility. You'll learn how to orchestrate the visibility of an ensemble of components with precision.

6

PART II

XCELSIUS 2008 BEST PRACTICES AND TECHNIQUES

CHAPTER

7

USING MULTI-LAYER VISIBILITY IN YOUR DASHBOARDS AND VISUALIZATIONS

In this chapter

Dashboards are tools for conveying and analyzing information visually. As a dashboard gets more sophisticated, there is an increasing tendency to wind up with more moving parts and more visual components to manage. Xcelsius 2008 compounds the picture by incorporating an underlying spreadsheet, and the components seem to have a mind of their own.

This chapter is all about handling complexity in dashboard design so that your dashboards and visualizations behave with simplicity. There are simple strategies for managing complexity. One approach involves containment through tab sets. Another is context switching. Xcelsius 2008 offers another feature that gives you great precision in your dashboard's behavior: dynamic visibility for each individual component. This fine-grained control is amazingly powerful. Unless you have a methodology for managing complex behavior, controlling visibility quickly becomes unwieldy. The framework outlined here is called multi-layer visibility.

TAMING COMPLEXITY AND USABILITY BY MAKING PRESENTATIONS COMPACT

At some point, you might want to beef up the complexity and capabilities of your dashboards, scorecards, and visualizations. Xcelsius 2008 allows you to add as many components to a dashboard as you like, and each can be performing a different task. Using more moving parts in your dashboards and visualizations enables greater capabilities, but you don't want it happening at the cost of needless clutter.

MANAGING COMPLEXITY THROUGH CONTAINMENT

The Tab Set component introduced in Chapter 3, "Getting Familiar with Xcelsius 2008," is one of the easiest-to-use facilities for helping manage complexity. It allows you to create multiple views in a footprint. Working with a Tab Set component requires very little skill: You simply place a Tab Set component onto the canvas, position and size it, and then drop visual components inside each of the tab views.

While working with a Tab Set component in the workspace, the component can be in one of two visual states: Its visual context can be set to the exterior visual rim or the interior contents of a selected tab. When you first place a Tab Set component onto the canvas, its focus is set to the exterior mode. The telltale sign is that you see a + and - pair of icons hovering just above the tabs (see Figure 7.1).

Initially, there is only one label, Tab 1. (Don't worry about changing its name right now; I'll show how to do that shortly.)

If you want to add more tabs, you just click the + icon, and you are prompted for a tab name. The tab label gets appended to the immediate right of whatever tab label currently has focus. When you become familiar with Tab Set components, you'll find that working with tabs is easy.

Figure 7.1
Clicking the outer edge of a Tab Set component allows you to add or remove tab views.

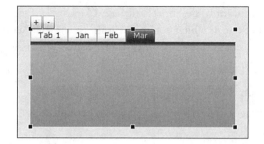

You can name tab labels as you add them. At first glance, it appears that the first tab label is hardwired to the name Tab 1, and it is not immediately evident that the name can be changed. To change the name, you just click the "interior" canvas of the first tab to open its properties panel. You can change the tab's Label field by typing in a name or by linking it to an underlying spreadsheet cell.

You can rearrange the tab order by reordering components within the Object Browser. Simply select the reference to the appropriate tab canvas in the Object Browser and use the + and - keys on your keyboard to rearrange the order of the tab within the Tab Set. Pressing the + key shifts the tab to the right and pressing the - key shifts it to the left.

The individual tabs can only be placed along the top of the Tab Set component, but they can all be left-, center-, or right-aligned. You can set the tabs so that they are in boldface, italics, or any other format you desire.

Creating all these tabs is wonderful, but what you want to do is place different content into each tabbed panel. To move a component into one of the tabbed panels, just click the tab label so that it has focus. Next, click or select the components you want to move into the Tab Set component and drag the selected components inside the Tab Set component.

Moving a component from one tab to another involves dragging the component inside the Tab Set component to some location on the "master" canvas that contains the Tab Set component. Click the tab label where the components are expected to go, so that it has focus. Next, click the component you want to move and drag it to the interior of the Tab Set component. All this may sound complicated, but if you're at all used to dragging and dropping components with any other software program, you should find this easy.

One of the nice benefits of working with tab sets both during the design stage and when the dashboard is exported to SWF or another format is that tab sets eliminate a lot of visual clutter.

NOTE

If you really want to, you can place a Tab Set component inside another Tab Set component.

7

Tab sets are useful when you want to do entirely different kinds of information inside each tab. Let's look at some situations in which you might want to use Tab Set components and some things you can do to prepare to use them. Consider using tab sets for the following:

- A welcome screen, possibly with some instructions
- Basic profile information
- Customer pricing packages and options that the user can select
- A summary of results

You may run into other situations in which supplied information is updated on a regularly recurring basis. For example, today the dashboard with a Tab Set component may have a March Sales label. Next month, "March" would need to be replaced with "April." It would not be very convenient if you had to hand edit the tab labels simply because you swap in new data. Fortunately, you can map a tab label to an underlying spreadsheet cell of your choosing. If the tab label is mapped to a cell containing the current month or other appropriate information, the tab label is automatically kept up to date.

Each of the interior panels in a tab set can have its own private canvas and can be set to a unique background. Using backgrounds of different colors can be helpful when you make different information visibly different; for example, you could subtly tint the panels associated with revenue production with green and those associated with expenses with red.

Remember that each of the panels in a tab set as well as the rest of the components used in a dashboard all map to the same underlying spreadsheet. Therefore, changes made to the spreadsheet from one of the panels can affect all the others. To see this in action, try setting up a tab set with two or more tabs. In the inside of the first panel, set up a horizontal slider and map its data field to cell A1. Copy this slider and then go to the second panel of the tab set and paste it there. Switch to Preview mode or export the dashboard and launch it. Your dashboard should have two horizontal sliders, one on each of the tabs. Move the slider on one of the tabs and make note of the slider value. Now click the alternate tab. Notice that the slider in the second tab has the same value as the slider in the first tab. The two always remain in sync, no matter what you do. Although the panels in a tab set can appear independent, the underlying data can be readily connected.

As you have seen, tab sets are good for constructing dashboards and visualizations with multiple views that are each fundamentally different.

Tab sets with replicated views but different datasets are not so easy to maintain. If you try setting up a tab set that displays monthly sales analysis for a whole year, you could have 12 tabs, all of which are nearly identical. That's a lot of setup work. Every time you make a change to the dashboard, you might have to make changes in 12 places and would need to validate each of those changes. Your interests could be better served if you made use of context switching to combine the context of 12 tabs into 1.

Using Context Switching to Contain Visualizations and Dashboards

When you set up a dashboard, you may go through a lot of effort to nail down your presentation so it does exactly what you want. You may have a chart that makes use of alerts or conditional formatting. The axes on your chart, the scaling, and the gridlines may be set in a very specific way.

The dashboard might fulfill your needs for monitoring and presenting your sales data during the month of March. On each subsequent month, you add a little nip and tuck to the chart, so that it keeps getting refined. By the time you reach December, your chart layout is exactly the way you want it.

There may be good reason to prepare a dashboard with the data for the whole year as well as month-by-month analysis. There are a couple ways you could go about this. One way is to create a tab set with a tab for each of the months (see Figure 7.2).

Figure 7.2
A visually appealing but not very effective way to utilize a tab set.

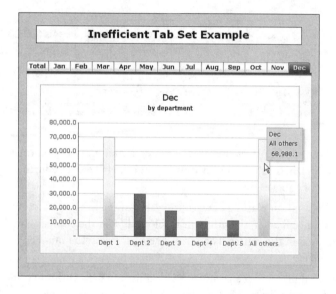

The tab views for the months of January through December are effectively identical. All that really changes is the data. There is really no need to keep a separate tab for each month if you can instead use just one and dynamically swap in the data for the desired month.

Dynamically swapping data in and out can be accomplished through a variety of mechanisms in Xcelsius 2008. You can choose interfaces such as label-based menus, radio buttons, list boxes, or tickers (see Figure 7.3).

The basic idea is that you allow the user to choose from a set of labels. The labels can either be a fixed list or can be read from the underlying spreadsheet. Based on whether the user chooses the first, second, third, or nth item from the set of labels, a corresponding response is placed in one or more destination cells. In the Insertion Type pull-down list, you can specify the kind of response you want (as shown in Figure 7.3). These are the available choices:

- **Position**: This option identifies the location of the item in the list of labels, starting from the value 1, for the first position. As you shall soon see, position and OFFSET become a potent combination for doing context switching.

Figure 7.3
You can use different component types to accomplish context switching.

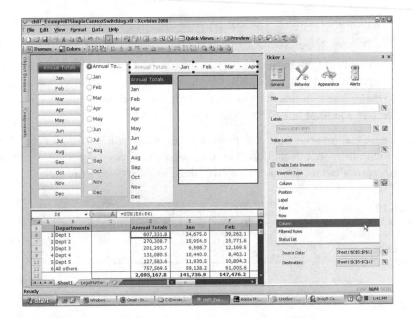

- **Label**: This option places the label of the chosen item in the destination cell. This is useful when labels can change at runtime and the labels carry further relevance, such as a subsequent data search.

- **Value**: This option places a copy of the value of the nth cell of a source data range into a destination cell when the nth item is selected from the component. The number of cells specified in the source data range needs to match the number of labels displayed in the component.

  You should think of Value as an association list of labels with their underlying values. You might have a list of labels such as "Sales for January," "Sales for February," and so forth. The values in cells E12 and F12 could be 141736.9 and 147476.2 for January and February, respectively. When you click Sales for February, the value 147476.2 is placed in the destination cell.

- **Row, Column, and Filtered Rows**: These options make use of a range of source data cells. When you specify Row, the contents of the nth row are placed into the destination cells. When you specify Column, the contents of the nth column are placed into the destination cells. Filtered Rows can grab multiple rows based on the selection you make.

- **Status List**: This option pushes a solid block of 0s across a range of destination cells, with the lone exception of a single cell in the range. Where that 1 is placed is dependent on which item you select in the list-based component.

The Position, Label, and Status List options only have destination cells and do not make use of source data cells.

NOTE

When you use these mechanisms, whether for context switching or simple menu-type selections, static values are written to the destination cells, and they do not change until the destination cells are subsequently overwritten.

In the example of Figure 7.3, Insertion Type is set to Column. This means that the content from a specific column is *copied* to the destination cells. If the underlying cells that are being "copied" happen to change, there is no automatic mechanism for reflecting this change without forcing a manual refresh. This poses an interesting challenge, and I have an interesting solution for it. The solution involves building a dynamically routed conduit. Instead of copying the actual value, you place in a destination cell a pointer that identifies which cells you want to retrieve. Then you use OFFSET to retrieve the contents of the cells you are interested in (see Figure 7.4).

Figure 7.4

Cells C5:C12 read the offset value in cell C4 to dynamically grab data from the appropriate column on the right.

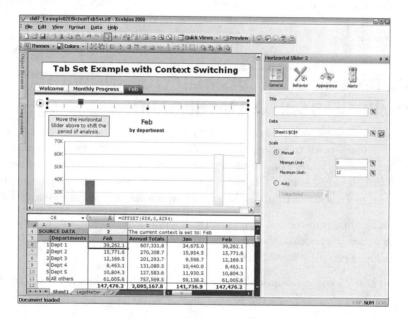

The advantage with this approach is that if the underlying cells change during the dashboard session, they will be automatically reflected here. If the data you are accessing is static data from a database and you do not imbue your dashboard with any intelligence, then there isn't much point of going though this exercise. But you are using Xcelsius, which is endowed with spreadsheet capabilities, so you can make use of these dynamic conduits to do things you couldn't attempt in other software.

In the example shown in Figure 7.4, I use a horizontal slider to allow the user to move across a timeline. The slider's value is mapped to cell C4. The OFFSET formulas below it use that value to retrieve data from the corresponding column on the right. This formula is in cell C6:

```
=OFFSET($D6,0,$C$4)
```

In addition to grabbing numeric data, you can also retrieve header information, such as the month label. Specifically, the tab label is reading the contents of cell C5, which also uses the same kind of OFFSET formula that is used to retrieve the values in cells C6 through C12. Consequently, as the slider value changes, so does the tab label. Also notice that I enable animation on the slider. This allows the user to run a little "movie" spanning the whole year.

Keep in mind that the values in this example are of historically recorded information, which is not going to change for any given month. Xcelsius 2008 allows you to retrieve values directly from spreadsheet formulas. Those retrieved values don't have to be static. They can change based on user interaction with a visual component or a real-time data feed.

When you use these conduits and the underlying values change, you get to see the impact of the changes. You can click the play button on the slider to see an animated sequence, much like a movie.

Controlling the Visibility of Individual Components in a Dashboard

Depending on your needs, your dashboards, scorecards, or other types of visualization can have many visual components. If you designate a specific location for each visual element in a dashboard, you are bound to run into design and layout challenges if you have too many visual elements. Even if you manage to arrange all the visual components, the last thing you want to do is distract the dashboard user with too many pieces of information.

One option is to create a dashboard with multiple screens. Many dashboard designers are reluctant to create dashboards with multiple screens because it goes against the grain of telling a complete story at a glance.

So how do you go about creating a dashboard with just the right blend of visual elements? You can individually control the visibility of components placed on the dashboard canvas.

Understanding Dynamic Visibility

Whenever a visual component is placed on the canvas, it is visible by default, unless, of course, if it is obscured by other visual components positioned in front of it.

You can customize a component to switch its visibility state on or off. Not surprisingly, this is accomplished by specifying spreadsheet cells that the component reads. You set the cells for dynamic visibility in the Behavior tab of the component's properties panel (see Figure 7.5). There are two elements for setting a component's visibility: one that watches a status cell on the spreadsheet and one that is a key.

7

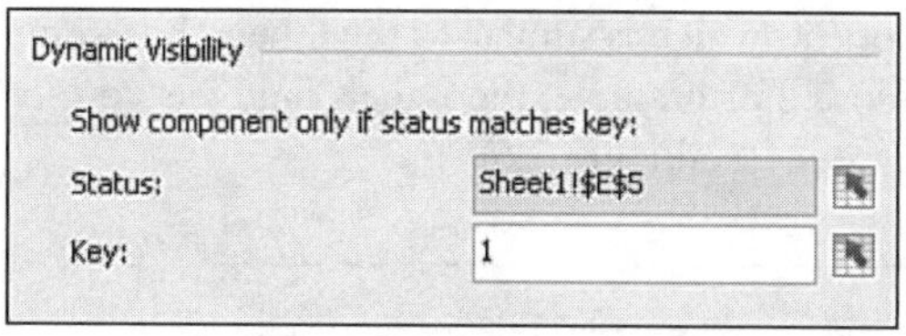

Figure 7.5
Dynamic visibility can
be specified for each
component.

Dynamic Visibility

Show component only if status matches key:

Status: Sheet1!$E$5

Key: 1

Both the visibility status and key fields can read spreadsheet cells. Unless you are looking to manage visibility in a very specialized way, it suffices to use a fixed value for the key field. In Figure 7.5, the visibility key is set to the value 1. The visibility status field is set to read the contents of cell E5. Whenever cell E5 of the underlying spreadsheet has the value 1, the component is made visible when the dashboard is running; otherwise, it is rendered invisible.

Pause a moment to contemplate the implications of what you've just learned: You have a dashboard with potentially many complicated spreadsheet formulas, possessing a high degree of interdependencies for computing the value of cell E1. Whenever this cell has the value 1, your component lights up like a Christmas tree. Your component could be a label with an important message. It could be a trend icon signaling a critical change in the financial viability of a business venture. It could be a URL button that allows you to forward information to a remote server after the user has answered the essential questions in a questionnaire. In all these situations and many more, you can use dynamic visibility to enable follow-on action. Don't limit yourself to only thinking about the mechanics of making things visible or invisible.

TOGGLING VISIBILITY

There are a wide variety of ways to manage visibility. One simple way is to toggle it. Conveniently, Xcelsius 2008 has both a Check Box component and a Toggle Button component for such purposes. These aren't the only components available, but they serve their purpose well.

A Check Box component has a single text field for a label. It also lets you specify source data cells and a destination cell. If you don't specify values for the source data cells, Xcelsius assumes that you want to use the values 0 and 1 for unchecked and checked states, respectively. When the check box is unchecked, the value 0 is placed in the destination cell; when the check box is checked, 1 is placed in the destination cell.

Within the Check Box component's Behavior tab you can set the initial state of the check box to be either unchecked or checked.

TIP

> The check box's title can either be a hand-typed entry that does not change, or it can be read from a spreadsheet cell. In the latter case, the spreadsheet cell can contain a formula that is context sensitive, and this allows you to adjust the text label of the check box, based on the user's actions.

7

The Toggle Button component, which is similar to the Check Box component, has some interesting features to explore. For example, the Labels field lets you specify two adjacent spreadsheet cells instead of one (see Figure 7.6)

Figure 7.6
For the Labels field of a Toggle Button component, you specify two spreadsheet cells—one for the "off" label and the other for the "on" label.

You also have the option of hand editing values by clicking the pencil icon next to the Labels field. If you have already specified cells but switch to hand-edited values, Xcelsius automatically lifts the values from spreadsheet cells previously specified (see Figure 7.7).

Figure 7.7
Setting up a check box and a toggle button for controlling visibility of other components.

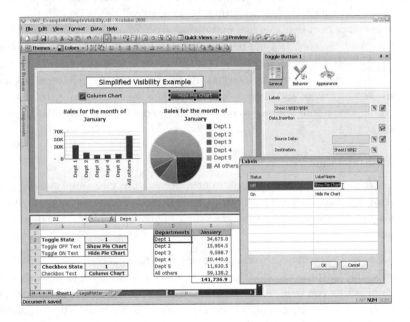

MUTUALLY EXCLUSIVE VISIBILITY

Figure 7.7 shows two charts. Each of these charts can be independently made visible or invisible. If you look carefully at this figure, you see that both the column chart and the pie chart represent the same data.

Chances are, when you're creating a real-world dashboard, you are not going to have the luxury of spacing out all your charts and leaving large voids when they are rendered invisible. You almost certainly wouldn't want to do this if the charts were different representations of the same data. A better strategy might be to show alternative views of the same data, one at a time. The Radio Button component is ideally suited for this situation (see Figure 7.8).

Figure 7.8
Using a Radio Button component to manage visibility of various charts, all mutually exclusive of one another.

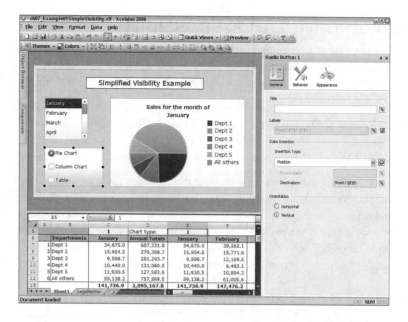

In this example, the Radio Button component places the value 1, 2, or 3 into cell E1. The Pie Chart, Column Chart, and Spreadsheet Table components set their visibility status to cell E1. The Pie Chart component has the visibility key set to the value 1. The Column Chart component has its visibility key set to the value 2, and the Spreadsheet Table component's visibility key is set to the value 3.

Although the three visual components—the pie chart, column chart, and spreadsheet table—are physically positioned in the same part of the dashboard, they never interfere with one another because no more than one of them is ever visible at any instant.

Notice in Figure 7.8 that you can retrieve data from any of a number of months through context switching and allow the user to switch viewing modes by controlling visibility through the use of the radio buttons.

TIP

> Sometimes you'll set up a visual component that is useful during the design of the dashboard but not for deployment. For example, I sometimes like to use a spreadsheet table to diagnose how computations in the underlying spreadsheet are handled. This is good for me, the dashboard designer, but the end user doesn't need it.
>
> It is not necessary to throw away such a component. If you want to save it for a rainy day, you can set the visibility key of the diagnostic component to some value that will never match the status cell. This renders the component invisible but allows you to save the component as part of the XLF file. When you export the dashboard, the component is embedded but invisible. When you need the component again, simply adjust the visibility key to allow the component to be visible while in Preview mode.

7

MANAGING MULTI-LAYER VISIBILITY

Getting multiple components to visually turn themselves on and off in unison is easy. You simply have them watch a single cell and use a common key value to set visibility. A simple example of this is a label-based menu that inserts the menu position in a single watched cell.

You could use a label-based menu with options such as Welcome, Instructions, Sales Performance, Operating Expenses, and Competitor Analysis. When the user clicks Welcome, the value of the destination cell (say, in this example, that it is cell E1) is set to the value 1. When the user clicks Instructions, it is set to the value 2, and so forth.

Aside from the label-based menu, your dashboard could have something like 25 or so other visual components. By using dynamic visibility, you can set related components to turn on and off in unison. For instance, the components related to operating expenses could be set to be visible only when the value of cell E1 is 4. The components related to competitor analysis could be visible only when the value of cell E1 is 5. To do this, you need a system to be manageable because you could easily construct a dashboard with 100 or more components.

DESIGNING A DASHBOARD WITH MULTIPLE SCREENS CONTROLLED BY A LABEL-BASED MENU

When you think about constructing a dashboard, there are some obvious challenges and some workarounds. Here's one challenge: You have a dashboard with five modes or states, corresponding to each of the five menu options. You may find it appropriate to have your corporate logo always visible, no matter which of the five menu options the user clicks.

There's a trivial response to this challenge. Because the logo is going to be present no matter what happens, you shouldn't bother trying to set its visibility. So far, so good. The situation could get a little more complex, however. It may be that you have two corporate logos. One of them is well suited for the Welcome screen and for when the user is presented with instructions. The other, smaller, logo is neatly tucked in the top-right corner of the screens related to sales, expenses, and competition.

There are a number of ways to handle this. One way is to apply brute force. You could have two copies of the larger logo and three copies of the smaller logo. Each one would make itself visible when the menu destination cell matches the key value assigned to each of the five logos. Obviously, this is not the way to design dashboards.

An alternative approach would be to have one copy of the large logo and one copy of the small logo. Instead of directly watching the cell E1, you could create more sophisticated visibility logic in, say, cell F1 with a formula like this:

```
=IF(E1<2,1,0)
```

The visibility status of your large logo could be set to cell F1, and its key field could be set to the value 1. Likewise, the visibility status of your smaller logo could also be set to cell F1, but its key field could be set to the value 0. The conditional logic is sure to work. You can be confident that visibility of all the components behaves correctly. There are no redundantly used components. But what's wrong with this picture? If the answer is not already evident, it will soon be clear that you are standing on a very dangerous and slippery slope.

7

Here is what is happening:

- To accommodate the two logos, it is necessary to create a secondary logic rule for visibility. If you decide at a later point in time to add a sixth or seventh item to the main menu, you are going to have to rewrite your logic rules. This creates extra work for you.

- Your rule for the secondary logic is not so robust. Suppose you want the big logo to appear with the first and third menu items and the small logo to appear with the second, fourth, and fifth menu items. How would you revise your formula for cell F1?

- Notice that your visibility criterion for the logos is based on a test for the values 0 and 1 in cell F1. For all the other components, the cells are looking at the value of cell E1 to determine whether it contains a value of 1, 2, 3, 4, or 5.

  In this situation, the burden is on you, the dashboard designer, to keep track of what cells are watched and what the numeric values signify in terms of visibility criteria. For instance, it would be nice in the case of the logos to use 0 for invisible and 1 for visible. This works for the large logo, but it's the exact opposite logic for the smaller one!

So far, this case involving the isolated use of corporate logos is a bit contrived. So let me inject an ounce of reality here to highlight how untenable a strategy of this kind is. If you truly want to take advantage of component reuse, you might find that through context switching, you could use a suitably set up pie chart for both the competitive analysis and the sales performance analysis. Component reuse comes at the cost of unwanted conditional logic to support dynamic visibility. You may have some components that would normally not appear together in some circumstances but appear together in others. With all the complicated rules for managing visibility, it would be quite a chore to maintain the dashboard design as it evolves.

THE LOGICAL APPROACH TO ORCHESTRATING MULTI-LAYER VISIBILITY

Think about how you would want to handle managing multi-layer visibility. To keep things simple, start with creating structure around a main menu.

To avoid getting academic or theoretical, I'll introduce the multi-layer visibility framework I developed a number of years ago. To help in outlining the framework, I use a dashboard application that contains some real data. The sample dashboard that is used incorporates some government data related to transportation. Keep in mind that the emphasis here is on managing visibility, so I don't spend much effort implementing a full-featured dashboard. I'm also keeping the dashboard barebones so that it will be easier for you to harvest for your own needs.

DESIGNING BY SPECIFICATION

It would be nice to specify your requirements in the form of a table or matrix. On the rows of such a table, you might want to identify all the visual *groups* that need to behave similarly. Consider the following:

- There may be some visual components that you want to always be displayed. You might want the same background for both the Welcome screen and any reports. Your main

7

menu should always be visible. You may have a copyright or confidentiality notice that needs to be displayed. Whatever your needs, you can call this a *background group* because such elements are always visible.

■ You may have a *Welcome* or *splash screen* that contains components that are visible when the dashboard is first launched or when the main menu item is set to the initial screen.

■ You may have some *branding visual elements* such as corporate logos that appear on some screens but not others.

■ You may have some dashboard components that you want to reuse for different data sets and for different screens.

■ You may have a slew of visual components to artfully present data visually.

■ You shouldn't forget about supplying some *documentation or instructions for the dashboard user*. I am sure there are critics who think that if a dashboard needs documentation, it's not correctly designed. Yes, dashboards should be intuitive, but users are always grateful when there's additional documentation. At the very least, the documentation portion of a dashboard could include notes on the data.

Each of these groups needs to have a defined behavior for any given menu state. In this example, there are five menu states that correspond to the five possible menu selections (see Figure 7.9).

Figure 7.9
Each selection from the menu constitutes a unique menu state.

The selected menu position is mapped to an underlying spreadsheet cell A8 (see Figure 7.10). This menu value or position *is* the menu state.

Figure 7.10
Menu options and the current menu value or position (cell A8).

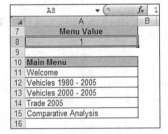

7

Now comes the first critical step: specifying the visibility logic through a switch map (see Figure 7.11).

Figure 7.11
Switch map specification.

Possible menu states-->	Switch Map				
	1	2	3	4	5
Group 0: Background	1	1	1	1	1
Group 1: Welcome	1				
Group 2: Big Logo	1				
Group 3: Small Logo			1		1
Group 4: Menus 2 & 3		1	1		
Group 5: Trade Visualization				1	
Group 6: Instructions		1	1	1	1
Group 7: Comparative Analysis					1
Group 8: Alt. Logo		1		1	
Group 9: [TBD]					

Take a little time to study this map. There are nine groups or classes of components plus one TBD, or to be determined, group. They more or less follow the sequence of the bullet points outlined a few paragraphs earlier.

NOTE

> There are 9 groups in this example, but there's no reason you couldn't specify a switch map with 99 groups. You just need to know what you're doing and keep track of things.

The switch map in this example has five columns, one for each menu state. If you later need to extend your main menu to seven items, you will need to add another two columns to the switch map.

To better appreciate how the switch map designates the visibility logic, it is worth looking at what happens for a couple of the menu states—menu states 1 and 4.

When the user starts the dashboard or clicks the Welcome button, the visual components associated with Group 0, Group 1, and Group 2 are all made visible. Group 0 includes the various "background" components, such as a shaded rectangle, a copyright notice, a spreadsheet table that is used to show the visibility logic in action while the dashboard is running, and the main menu. Group 1 consists of an input text area that serves as intro text. Group 2 consists of a large logo. Figure 7.12 shows how the dashboard appears when the menu is in state 1.

Only the elements in Group 0, Group 1, and Group 2 are visible. Also notice the spreadsheet table at the bottom of the dashboard. It lays out what is happening in the underlying spreadsheet while the dashboard is in menu state 1.

7

Everything else visible belongs to Group 0.

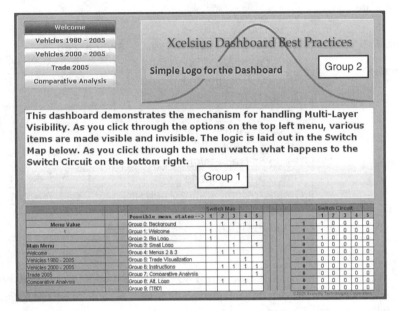

Figure 7.12
The dashboard menu in state 1.

When the dashboard is in menu state 4, the components associated with Group 0, Group 5, Group 6, and Group 8 are visible (see Figure 7.13).

Everything else visible belongs to Group 0.

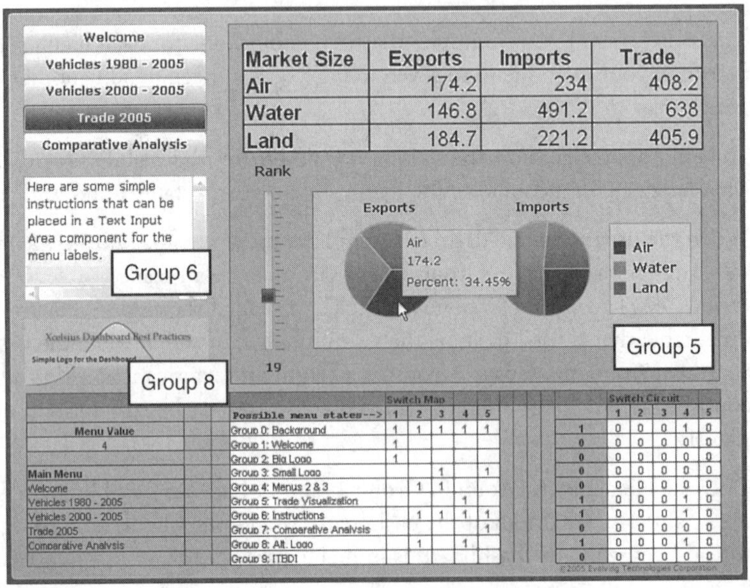

Figure 7.13
The dashboard in menu state 4.

In this figure, the fourth menu item is highlighted. All the visible items when the dashboard is in menu state 4 correspond to the 1s of the switch map in the column labeled 4. Also notice that the spreadsheet table at the bottom of the dashboard differs slightly from the way it appears in Figure 7.12. This is because the visibility states have been altered.

ACTIVATING VISIBILITY PATTERNS WITH THE SWITCH CIRCUIT

The switch map is a blueprint. If you look carefully in the ch07_MultiLayerVisibility.xlf file, you see that there is not a formula to be found anywhere inside the switch map (cells D5 though I16). Quite literally, it's a specification in the form of a static table; yet the dashboard follows the visibility logic laid out in this table. This happens because there is a switch circuit to the immediate right that watches the values on the switch map as well as the current menu state (see Figure 7.14).

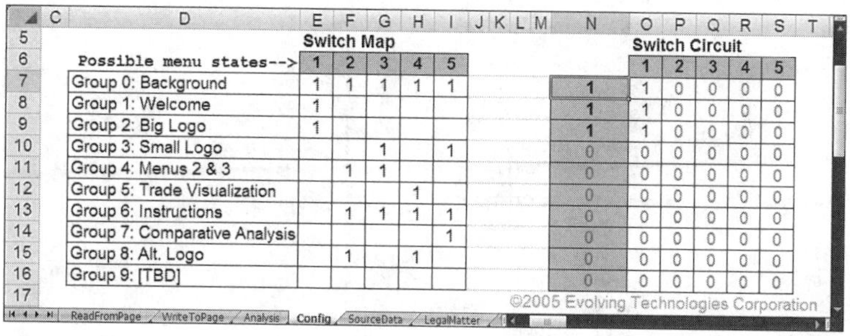

Figure 7.14
The switch map and switch circuit in menu state 1. (Printed with permission of Evolving Technologies Corporation.)

The basic idea of the switch circuit is that it lights up whenever the switch map elements and the current menu state match. Each of the cells in the interior of the switch circuit compares a switch map logic element with the menu state. For example, this formula is used in cell O7:

```
=IF(O$6=$A$8,1*E7,0)
```

Basically, this formula is saying "If the current menu state (in cell A8) matches the state ID in the column I belong to, then return 1 times whatever is in the matching column of the switch map; otherwise, return a 0." This formula is essentially the same in cells O7 through S16.

The left edge of the switch circuit (column N, highlighted in gray in Figure 7.14) aggregates all the cells across to the right. This formula is in cell N7:

```
=IF(SUM(O7:S7)>0,1,0)
```

Essentially, this formula says "If any match is found on my row, then send a signal to the dashboard components watching me that it's okay to light up, or become visible." So all the components associated with Group 0 are watching cell N7. The components associated with Group 1 are watching cell N8, and so forth.

7

GROUP MANAGEMENT

A dashboard can have many components floating on the canvas. How do you know which ones belong to which group? The Object Browser allows you to organize and name components (see Figure 7.15).

Figure 7.15
The Object Browser allows you to name and organize your components by group and position and adjust their depth.

Notice that I created and applied a naming convention. Each component is prepended with a group ID label followed by a text description. Although this labeling is purely cosmetic, it serves a number of purposes:

- At a glance, you can figure out how a component is expected to behave because you know what group number it belongs to (and the group behavior is spelled out in the switch map).

- It is easy to aggregate in the Object Browser components that have the same kind of visibility.

- This kind of naming makes it easier to work with many components in a dashboard.

Having built dashboards with several hundred components, I can personally attest to the value of adhering to a naming convention of this kind.

CONTROLLING GROUP BEHAVIOR

Just because all the items belonging to a group become invisible and visible in unison doesn't guarantee that they will be well behaved. There are many Group 5 items in this example. If they are not sequenced correctly in the Object Browser, some items, such as those in the background, could obscure items that should otherwise be in the foreground. If all the components belonging to a group appear in one place on the Object Browser, they will be easier to manage and arrange.

What exactly constitutes a group? The answer is simple: Any set of components that use a common watched cell to set the component's visibility status belong to the same group. In the example, the two pie charts along with the legend, labels appearing above the pie charts, the vertical slider, and a background rectangle all set their visibility status based on the contents of cell N12. All these components are grouped together because their visibility patterns are identical.

In case it is not obvious, you can achieve another kind of simplicity in your dashboard design. All the visual components of the dashboard can be uniformly keyed to the value 1 in the visibility status cell. This makes it possible to create a uniform criterion for setting visibility across *all* visual components in a dashboard. Having less to think about and less to go wrong, this approach helps keep potential errors at bay.

N O T E

> The managing of groups of components as discussed here applies to the controlling of behavior and visibility of components when your dashboard is deployed. This should not be confused with Xcelsius grouping functionality that allows you to group components and center them on the canvas.

WORKING WITH MULTI-LAYER VISIBILITY THE RIGHT WAY

Multi-layer visibility is not always the best solution for managing visibility. For one thing, this framework requires a certain level of abstraction. If you are designing a quick-and-dirty one-off dashboard, going though the level of effort required for basic visibility control may be overkill.

In the example presented, I outlined a simple scenario involving a menu with five options and a handful of components. But my experience shows that you'll likely end up specifying considerably more groups than menu items. Fortunately, adding more groups entails only having to add more rows to the switch map and switch circuit and mapping to the appropriate cells in the switch circuit.

As a practical matter, you will find yourself frequently creating new groups that are hybrids of existing groups. Creating the new groups is easy. The more difficult and tedious part is that you may need to change the names of some of the components in the Object Browser. Keeping the names in order requires a certain level of self-discipline. This helps to keep you from becoming embroiled micromanaging your dashboard design.

The good news about multi-layer visibility is that it is very scalable from both performance and organizational management perspectives.

7

THE PRACTICAL RATIONALE FOR MULTI-LAYER VISIBILITY

There are many good reasons for using multi-layer visibility, but there is one reason that trumps all the others. You can dynamically reroute the visibility characteristics and behaviors of armies of components by directly editing the values on a tiny table called a switch map.

There's no need to do surgery on components. All the handiwork and complex logic can be confined to the switch map. If you don't like the way the logic works, or if you want to experiment as you build your dashboard, you can simply mark up the table with 1s and 0s (or empty cells).

CLOSING THOUGHTS

As you've learned in this chapter, there are a variety of ways to tame dashboard complexity. Complexity takes many shapes and forms. Sometimes you need a way to visually "contain" dashboard content. Tab sets offer a way to create multiple views in a small footprint so that the dashboard user feels like he or she is looking at a single screen. The chief benefits of tab sets are that they are easy to set up and easy for the end user to use.

Another form of containment is context switching, which facilitates component reuse. Context switching allows you to direct different streams, or pipelines, of data into a chart or other graphical component. There are a number of distinct benefits to this approach. It reduces the file size of the dashboard because one component can be used for many data streams. In addition, you need to make a change to the visual component in only one place, and eliminating the need for multiple copies also eliminates a potential source of error.

There are a number of mechanisms for managing context switching. Some of them only pass static copies of data to the visual components. This chapter introduces a solution to this challenge, through the use of dynamic conduits.

Because the needs of users and dashboard capabilities have evolved over the years, there is a drive to keep pushing dashboards to more advanced uses. Xcelsius 2008, with its spreadsheet capabilities, extends this reach even further.

Even with containment and context switching, there comes a point at which a dashboard can become crowded with too many components. Xcelsius provides facilities for dynamic visibility of components on an individual component-by-component level. This chapter explores different ways to manage visibility, including toggling visibility and cycling though alternative views, one at a time.

Visibility is more than just flipping a switch to make a component invisible or visible. Dashboards can be designed to monitor data and automatically signal critical information or identify implications of some activity, and this may entail complex logic and formulas. You can harness dynamic visibility as a mechanism for enabling "gatekeeper" elements in a dashboard application. If you think creatively, you'll find all sorts of practical applications.

7

Dynamic visibility on a component-by-component basis is easy to handle. Simple, from-the–ground-up techniques do not scale particularly well when you need to mix and match views with multiple groups of components.

The multi-layer visibility framework is explained in detail in this chapter. This approach revolves around specifying a switch map as a simple table that can be read and used to instruct components on how to behave visually. Because with multi-layer visibility the mechanism for specifying behavior is centralized in a table external to the components, it is surprisingly easy to make significant changes to dashboard behavior. Another pleasant benefit is that the multi-layer visibility framework scales very well.

Chapter 8, "Managing Interactivity," shows you how to use some of the approaches introduced in this chapter to better manage interactivity.

CHAPTER **8**

MANAGING INTERACTIVITY

In this chapter

8

Every modern-day program involves some form of interaction. Xcelsius dashboards allow user interaction to play a prominent, if not central, role in dashboard design, so it should not be surprising that a chapter is devoted to this topic.

There are two approaches to consider. First, you can pay close attention to understanding and utilizing interaction at the component level. When you use your mouse to drill down to the details of a data element displayed in a chart, do you explicitly want the user to click the data point, or would you rather have the user pass the mouse over, like a magic wand?

Second, you might want to think about designing your dashboards and visualizations so that they behave more like full-fledged applications. They could have splash screens, provide context-sensitive help, and have different panels or screens for data entry and analysis. In other words, you can use them to provide some kind of navigational structure.

When a person interacts with components on a dashboard, there are two kinds of interactions happening. On one level, there is direct interaction with a component, such as a mouse click. On another level, there is the interaction of the component with other components, mediated through the underlying spreadsheet.

Xcelsius offers a wide array of visual components. Some of the noteworthy features are discussed in the following sections.

INTERACTING WITH CHART DATA

There are different ways of interacting with charts. A key point to recognize is that a great deal of chart behavior depends on the data that populates the chart. What is placed on a chart is not going to always be 100% under your control. You may, for example, scale some charts to display values between zero and $10 million for the cost of some initiative. You may feel that such a range is reasonable and hardwire the vertical axis of your chart to this range. After you produce the dashboard, there may be some extraordinary expenses that bring the project total beyond the $10 million mark. What should you do now? Consider the following three possibilities:

- Don't do anything at all. In this case, your chart will visually plateau at the hardwired limit you set. The underlying values can exceed the limits. Indeed, if you hover your mouse over the "maxed out" data point, you will see the correct values displayed in the hover text.

   With this scenario, there's no loss of data integrity. However, because there is no warning that the data value exceeds the chart limits, just looking at the chart can be misleading. If you are really maxing out a lot of data points, visualizing the plateau would be helpful in clueing the user that the visual representation requires further scrutiny.

- You can set the scale of a chart to be sensitive to the values displayed as the values change. (The topic of custom scaling is discussed at length in Chapter 5, "Using Charts and Graphs to Represent Data." There's a scaling lab dashboard in that chapter for you to explore.) Although this approach ultimately offers the greatest flexibility, it is also accompanied by some other features and obligations. When you choose custom scaling, you are responsible for managing *all* the scaling limits so that the dashboard or visualization behaves the way you expect it to, even though the underlying data varies.

■ You might want to provide the end user with the ability to custom scale at runtime but not get mired in the mechanics or mathematics of custom scaling. For such cases, Xcelsius gives you the ability to enable run-time tools (see Figure 8.1).

Results in additional controls on the chart

Figure 8.1
Selecting Enable Run-Time Tools in the Properties panel of a chart.

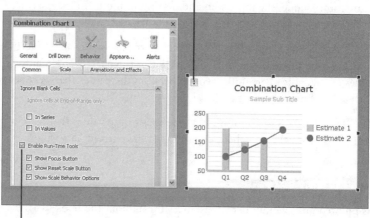

Selecting Enable Run-Time Tools

When you deploy the enabled run-time tools, clicking the control in the upper-left corner of the chart displays a number of additional options: Grow, Off, Auto, Focus Chart Data, and Reset Chart Scale (see Figure 8.2).

NOTE

The visual appearance of the five buttons for run-time tools (shown in Figure 8.2) varies, depending on the theme specified for the Xcelsius dashboard.

Figure 8.2
A variety of chart scaling options are available for dashboard users.

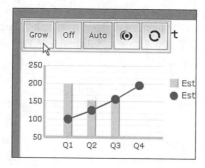

8

The Grow option is useful for situations in which the user is trying a number of different options that may push, or "grow," the scale limits and does not want to reset the scale.

The Off option sets the chart limits so that the chart hugs the outermost points of data. The minimum and maximum limits for the axes remain anchored at these values, regardless of how the data points change value.

The Auto option controls auto-scaling, which is the default scaling option on a chart. In auto-scaling mode, the minimum and maximum limits on the chart axes automatically scale or adjust up or down so that all data points are reasonably positioned in the chart.

The Focus Chart Data option forces the chart axes of a chart in Off mode to rescale so that all data in the first data series is displayed as if the chart were in auto-scaling mode. As data values change, the chart limits remain fixed on the values that were set when the Focus Chart Data button was pressed.

The Reset Chart Scale button resets the axes to the values that were in place when the dashboard was originally launched, regardless of the current data values.

DATA ANIMATION

As pointed out in a number of instances throughout the book, whenever you place a new chart onto the canvas, it is data animation enabled by default.

With data animation, data points smoothly transition from their old data values to their new ones rather than instantaneously jumping across the chart.

For some situations, having data animation enabled is wonderful. In other cases, it just simply doesn't help a dashboard or visualization. Fortunately you have the option of enabling or disabling this feature on any chart within the Animation and Effects tab of the chart's behavior properties.

CHART LABEL SIZE

In displaying values along the chart axes, you have the option of setting a constant width, using abbreviations for large quantities. Instead of displaying 125,000, you could instead show 125K. Instead of showing 125,000,000, you could display 125M. You can customize these abbreviations, as shown in Figure 8.3.

Figure 8.3
You can customize
label abbreviations
when Fixed Label Size
is enabled.

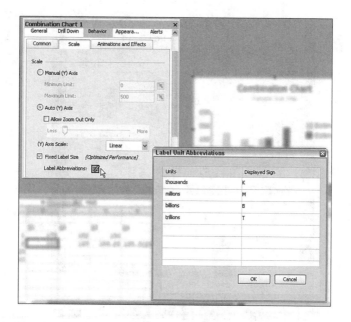

DRILL DOWN BEHAVIOR

With Xcelsius 2008, you can decide how you want drill down to work with your mouse
pointer. You have the option of explicitly clicking a data point on a chart to drill down to
underlying data. Alternatively, you can set the drill down mode to mouse over, in which case
you can use your mouse as a magic wand to reveal underlying information.

If all you want to do is quickly reveal some underlying or correlated information, then the
mouse over mode works well. If you need to analyze or scrutinize the drilled down data, the
mouse-click behavior works better.

Previous versions of Xcelsius (4.5 and earlier) did not permit the drill down of multiple data
series. Xcelsius 2008 now allows you to do this (see Figure 8.4).

 When you drill down with multiple data series, the destination cells for each of the data
series must be separately specified. So if you have three data series, as depicted in Figure 8.4,
you would wind up with three sets of destination cells, one for each series.

You need to be aware of an important subtlety. None of the destination cells are allowed to
overlap with the destination cells of another series. This makes it difficult to figure out
which series is being clicked or drilled into. Fortunately, you can tell Xcelsius to write the
name of the data series that's being drilled into (see Figure 8.5).

Figure 8.4
You can drill down to points on a data series on a chart.

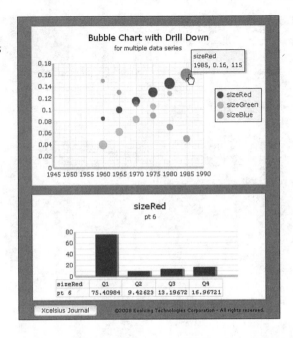

Figure 8.5
Setting up drill down for multiple data series.

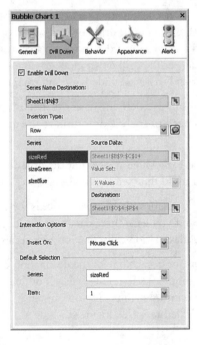

If you know the name of the data series that currently has focus, you can determine which destination data cells to use.

INTERACTING WITH SELECTORS

Many of the Xcelsius selector components are covered throughout the book, so I outline only a few characteristics and observations in the following sections.

THE ACCORDION MENU

The Accordion Menu interface provides support for drill down of multiple data series. The sample file `ch08ExampleAccordion.xlf` provides a sample of how it can be set up (see Figure 8.6).

Figure 8.6
Using the Accordion Menu component to drill down data.

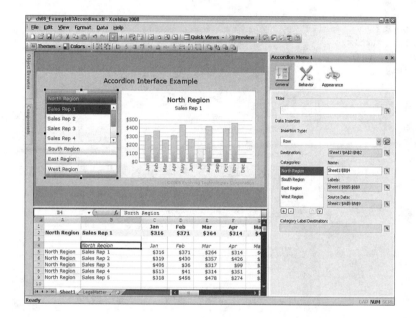

Notice in this example that as you choose a sales rep, you are retrieving a copy of the row of data that corresponds to that sales rep. Notice further that embedded in each of the rows is the name of the geographic region to which the sales rep belongs. Therefore, when the drilled down data is displayed in the column chart on the right, the geographic region is clearly identified.

THE CHECK BOX COMPONENT

You can easily customize the behavior of the Check Box component. In the sample file `ch08_ExampleCheckBox.xlf` you can customize the Check Box component to apply specific values to a destination cell. The values can be read from a spreadsheet or, as in the case illustrated here, hardwired to specific values, such as 0 and 1.

8

You can customize the text label next to the Check Box component, based on the checkmark state. You can place all the logic in a single cell, like this:

```
=IF(B3=0,"Click me to place a checkmark here","Click me to erase the checkmark")
```

In this example, cell B3 is the checkmark state.

Alternatively, you can place each of the messages in a separate cell (for example, B5 and B6) and then retrieve the appropriate message, based on the prevailing checkmark state, using a formula such as the following in cell B4 (see Figure 8.7):

```
=OFFSET(B5,B3,0)
```

Figure 8.7
Setup for customizing a Check Box component title.

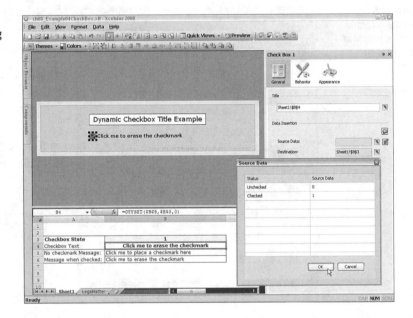

In this example, if the checkmark state in B3 is 0, the contents of B5 ("Click me to place a checkmark here") is displayed in cell B4. If the checkmark state in B3 is 1, the contents of B6 ("Click me to erase the checkmark") is displayed in cell B4.

NOTE

> Between these two approaches, I personally prefer the second. When you separate the alternative titles for the Check Box control, it becomes easy to update the labels and even add some context-sensitive information in them.

TRAFFIC LIGHT ALERTS IN COMBO BOXES AND LIST BOXES

 A Combo Box component is very similar to a List Box component. The main difference between the two is that a Combo Box component remains in a collapsed state until the user clicks it. A List Box component is always in an expanded state.

A Combo Box component is useful for situations in which the display screen real estate is precious or you want as few things as possible to visually distract the user.

New to Xcelsius 2008 is the ability to add traffic light–style alerts for Combo Box and List Box components (see Figure 8.8). The details of the alert features can be found in Chapter 12, "Smart Data and Alerts."

Figure 8.8
Comparison between List Box and Combo Box components (in unexpanded and expanded states).

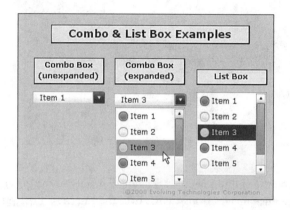

THE TICKER INTERFACE

Like the List Box and Combo Box components, Ticker components have traffic light–style alerts. They have another useful feature as well: the ability to display values for each of the ticker symbols as the symbols stream by. Figure 8.9 shows a comparison of the various ways a Ticker component can be set up.

Figure 8.9
Comparison of Ticker components with plain labels, value labels, alerts, and both value labels and alerts.

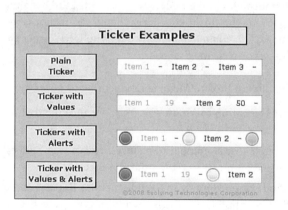

PICTURE MENUS

Both the Fisheye and Sliding Picture Menu components offer an easy way to select options in a menu (see Figure 8.10). As with many of the other selector components in Xcelsius, you have the option of specifying the menu position, label, value, row, column, or status list.

Figure 8.10
Fisheye and Sliding Picture Menu components.

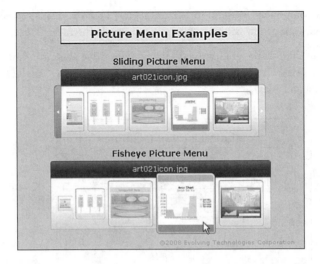

These menus give you the ability to embed thumbnail images in the generated SWFs (that is, Flash files) or reference images from a URL over the Internet. There are several advantages to retrieving images over the Internet:

- Not embedding the images helps prevent the dashboard from becoming bloated. If you have many dozens of images, your dashboard file size would quickly become large if the images were embedded.

- By using a URL reference instead of embedding images, you have the ability to update images without having to redesign the dashboard.

- You can construct formulas in the underlying spreadsheet to dynamically generate the URL reference. You might, for instance, have hundreds or thousands of images stored on a database server. You could dynamically build the URL string based on the user's ID or other values known by the dashboard.

You can fine-tune the Sliding Picture Menu component by using its interaction options:

- Setting the Insert On option to Mouse Over can enhance the dashboard's responsiveness.

- As you scroll through a large number of pictures, you can set Slider Amount to scroll forward one image at a time or a whole page at a time.

- The Slider Method option allows you to choose either Buttons or Mouse. You should experiment with these options to see what works best for your needs.

- The Fisheye Picture Menu option also allows for some tweaking. Again, the best way to determine which settings you want is to try them out for yourself.

TOGGLE BUTTON AND ICON COMPONENTS

 Toggle Button and Icon components are discussed throughout the book, so I won't delve into detail here. But I do want to mention something about Icon components. Frequently, it is helpful to overlay an Icon component over some "hotspot," such as over selected portions of an Image component. The file `ch08_ExampleHotspot.xlf` (see Figure 8.11) shows how to create such a hotspot map.

Figure 8.11

Setting up a hotspot map, using Icon components.

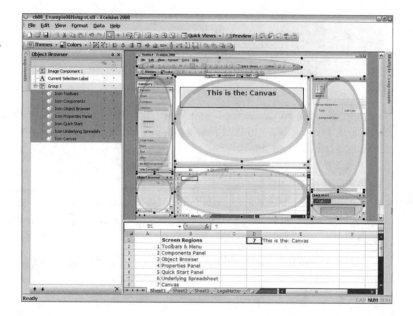

Basically, you position and size the Icon component over each hotspot. In Figure 8.11, there are seven such regions. Ultimately, you need to bring the transparency of each region to 0%. For the sake of illustration, I have left the transparency in Figure 8.11 at 25%. In this example, for region, a region number appears in a shared destination cell. In this example, they all update cell D1. The values in D1 will range from 1 to 7, depending on which hotspot was most recently activated. Cell E1 contains the following formula:

```
="This is the: "&"OFFSET(B1,D1,0)
```

Cells D2:D8 contain the appropriate label. When D1 is 7, the formula generates the following label for the seventh item:

```
This is the canvas
```

To make this work, you can set *both* the checked and unchecked parameters to the same value (see Figure 8.12).

8

Figure 8.12
Instead of using different values for checked and unchecked state, use the same amount.

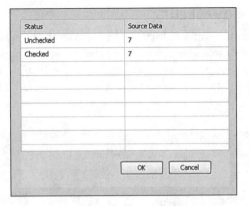

Normally, the Icon component allows for two different states. Because all you need to do is sense when a mouse is positioned over a hotspot, there is no need to track alternating checked and unchecked states.

FILTER COMPONENTS

Filter components allow users to take multiple combinations of large lists and identify a *specific unique* row that matches *all* the criteria (see Figure 8.13 or open the file ch08_ExampleFilter.xlf).

The essential item to understand with Xcelsius Filter components is that they must result in a single item. There is no provision to retrieve, say, multiple rows of data that satisfy the filter criteria.

Figure 8.13
Filtering multiple criteria to find a single item.

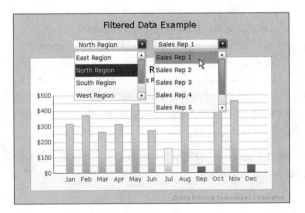

The setup involving Filter components is subtle, but when you understand the setup, it is rather straightforward. The first thing you need to do is to have your data (row 5 and below in Figure 8.14) flanked on the left by the Filter criteria. In this example, the first filter for geographic region is in column A, and the second (for the sales rep) is in column B. Notice in the Properties panel that the number of filters is set to 2. That accounts for columns A and B. The source data (cells A5:C81) spans three columns. Column C holds a lookup value, identifying which row matches the filter criteria. Notice that the destination cell (cell C2 in this example) is a single cell.

Figure 8.14
Setting up a Filter component.

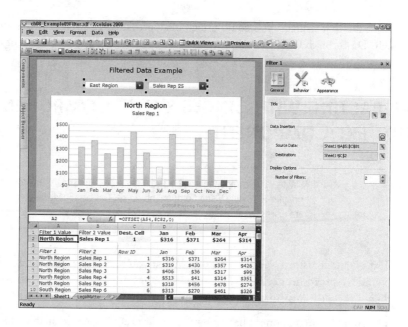

In this framework, each of the cells retrieved for the region, sales rep number, and sales for each of the 12 months can be accomplished using the following lookup formula in cell A2:

`=OFFSET(A$4,$C$2,0)`

This formula can be copied (from cell A2) and pasted to B2 and E2 through O2.

There is an alternative approach (found in the file `ch08_ExampleAlternateFilter.xlf`) that copies the whole row of monthly data. Instead of selecting 3 columns for the source data, you need to dredge up 15 columns, and the destination range is 13 columns (that is, 15 minus the 2 filters). While this works, there are some reasons to opt for the first of these two strategies:

- Although you can retrieve the monthly data for the sales rep, you need to identify the region and the sales rep name (columns A and B of the source data). You will still need to use a lookup formula with functions such as OFFSET, INDEX, and VLOOKUP. You're not going to altogether escape the use of a lookup mechanism unless you resort to some kludgey tactic.

- The second strategy involves copying the source data. If the individual column data changes between filter selections, you are not going to know about it because you are only retrieving frozen copies.

8

- There is no opportunity for context switching. In the sample data, you are selecting a region and the corresponding sales rep. The data you get back is the monthly sales data. While monthly sales data for sales rep number 25 (in the east region) is displayed, wouldn't it be nice if you could also reveal the number of new customers brought in each month for this rep?

With the first strategy, you could use context switching to swap in the appropriate data in cells D5 through O81. With the second strategy, doing this would be a lot more complicated.

INTERACTING WITH SINGLE VALUE COMPONENTS, MAPS, AND TEXT COMPONENTS

NOTE

> Single Value components, such as dials, gauges, and sliders, are covered at length in Chapter 6, "Single Value Components: Dials, Gauges, Speedometers, and the Like." Maps are discussed at length in Chapter 11, "Maps in Xcelsius."

Text components may seem innocuous. When you realize that text fields and labels can be bound to spreadsheet cells, and those cells change as you do things with your dashboard, then it is pretty clear that text components can play a significant role in your dashboards.

The Input Text component has a number of different options available. These relate to the "link to cell," the data insertion destination, and the Insert Data OnLoad feature.

Consider the following different scenarios:

- A text field can be static. In this situation, it is not linked to any underlying spreadsheet cell. That is, it can only get its value by someone hand-typing an entry into the text field and pressing the Enter or Tab key.

  Whatever is specified as the destination cell gets the value just entered into the text field. There's an interesting twist. Suppose the destination cell already has a formula in it. Then what happens? A couple things happen. The destination cell acquires the new value, but the formula is not wiped out. It's just dormant. If the formula needs to be recalculated, it is wiping out the value inserted by hand, and the formula reasserts its status of "owning" the destination cell. This "formula pushback" feature is unexpected but can turn out to be a handy feature.

- A text field can be linked to an underlying cell that also happens to be the same cell as the destination cell. If the underlying cell has no formula, everything is pretty conventional. You make a change by hand in the input text field, and the value is written to the destination cell.

In this scenario, only two things can possibly change the value. The first is hand-typing something new in the field. The second is some other part of your dashboard spontaneously deciding to overwrite the value in the destination cell. It could be, for example, that a Radio Button or List Box component targets that cell. The moment the cell is updated, the text in the input field is accordingly revised.

- A text field can be linked to an underlying cell that is different from the destination cell. At first, this may not seem very logical. Why would you want to read from one location but never write back to it? The reason actually turns out to be very practical. Imagine having one underlying source data cell (let's say it's cell A1) that holds a value between 0 and 10 (see Figure 8.15). That value could signify anything, such as the price at the pump for a gallon of gasoline (maybe I am being too conservative on the upper limit!). Cell A1 could be varied at the turn of a knob from the Dial component. Instead of one Text Input field, you now have three placed on the Canvas, and each of them uses cell A1 as its underlying cell or source data. The first of the three fields can write to cell B1, the second to B2, and the third to B3. You could now use the Dial component to set your price to, say, $5 per gallon.

Figure 8.15
A set of correlated input text fields that can be individually tweaked.

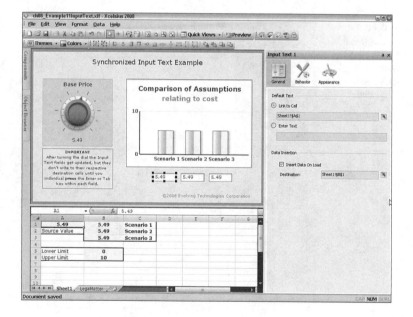

When you update your base price, you could individually adjust the value for each of the text fields. There's an important subtlety here. Just because the values in the text fields are updated by turning the Dial component doesn't mean that the destination fields are automatically updated. To push the values of the text fields to their destination cells, you actually have to press the Enter or Tab key within each field.

To overcome this obstacle and automatically push the values to their destination cells, you could enlist the aid of Source Data components. You would need one for each of

8

the input text fields. Alternatively, you could rearrange some of your formulas so that only one Source Data component needs to be used.

NOTE

> Note that with input text fields, you have the option of specifying the text field behavior. Specifically, you can enable password protection and limit the maximum number of characters allowed in the text entry.

LABELS AND INPUT TEXT AREAS

Labels and input text areas are powerful for two reasons:

- They can retrieve the text content computed from the spreadsheet at runtime.
- They support HTML editing.

This combination is incredibly potent, as illustrated in Figure 8.16.

Figure 8.16
A dynamic alert that changes with text size and color, changing continuously with underlying value.

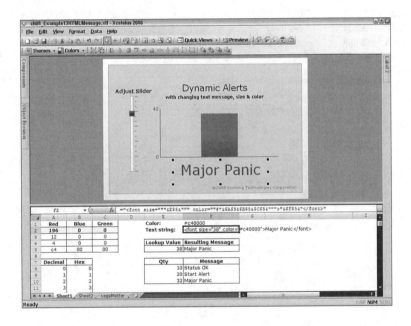

In this example (see the file ch08_ExampleHTMLMessage.xlf), you can adjust the vertical slider. In a real-world example, you won't be using a slider to adjust some underlying value. Instead, you would likely get real-time data feeds or retrieve information stored in a database, and you would use such values for presenting performance metrics.

As the slider value changes, the message under the data bar in the chart also changes. For one thing, the text message changes based on the values in a lookup chart from Status OK to Start Alert to Major Panic. This just uses VLOOKUP to retrieve the appropriate message from a table. There is nothing really new here.

 What is new, however, is that both the text font size and color *continuously* change with the underlying data value. The key to this is to enable HTML formatting in the text label's Behavior property. After you enable this property, it is just a matter providing some text with simple HTML coding.

You could hand-type the following static text in the Enter Text area of the text's Properties panel:

```
<font size="20">Hello World</font>
```

Alternatively you could link the text content to a spreadsheet cell, such as cell A1. Within cell A1, you could have a formula like this:

```
="<font size=""20"">Hello World</font>"
```

There wouldn't be much purpose if you hardwire the values in the formula. If your text size is in cell E5 and the message is in cell F5, then your formula would be as follows:

```
="<font size="""&E5&""">"&F5&"</font>"
```

Specifying color is a matter of converting three sets of decimal values into their hexadecimal equivalents for red, green, and blue.

Understanding Hexadecimal Numbers

Decimal counting uses 10 digits—0, 1, 2, 3, 4, 5, 6, 7, 8, and 9—for specifying numbers. When people first started counting, they probably chose 10 digits because that's how many fingers (and toes) we have.

For modern-day computers, the natural counting system is based on 16 digits, referred to as *hexadecimal*. (I guess if computers were given fingers, they would have 16 of them.)

A computer system needs 16 unique digits. The first 10 of them are the same as our regular decimals (0 through 9). To get the values 10 through 15, we can use the letters A through F. A would have the value 10, B would have the value 11, and so forth, up through the letter F.

It is commonplace to begin a hexadecimal number with a # symbol to signify that the digits that follow are hexadecimal. Here are some examples:

#0 is equivalent to the decimal number 0

#9 is equivalent to the decimal number 9

#A is equivalent to the decimal number 10

#E is equivalent to the decimal number 14

#F is equivalent to the decimal number 15

#10 is equivalent to the decimal number 16

#11 is equivalent to the decimal number 17

#20 is equivalent to the decimal number 32

#C4 is equivalent to the decimal number 196

#FF is equivalent to the decimal number 255

#FFFFFF is equivalent to the decimal number 16777215

Hexadecimal codes are generally case insensitive. For example, #C4 is treated the same as #c4.

8

When specifying color in HTML, you can use a hexadecimal representation. The format follows the pattern *#RRGGBB*. The first two hexadecimal digits, *RR*, specify the red component, ranging from 0 through FF. The second pair of hexadecimal digits, *GG*, does the equivalent for the green component. The third pair of hexadecimal digits, *BB*, corresponds to the blue component. For example, #C40000 has a red component of C4 (or, in decimal form, 196 on a scale of 0 through 255) and no blue or green component.

The file `ch08_ExampleHTMLMessage.xlf` (see the spreadsheet portion of Figure 8.16) converts the decimal numbers for the red, green, and blue components (cells A2, B2, C3) into their hexadecimal equivalent (cell F1).

Once you have generated a hexadecimal color (cell F1 in this example), you can use it directly in your HTML-formatted text:

```
="<font size="""&E5&""" color="""&F1&""">"&F5&"</font>"
```

If E5 is set to the value 38, the color in cell F1 is #c40000, and the message in cell F5 is "Major Panic," then the resulting text becomes this:

```
<font size="38" color="#c40000">Major Panic</font>
```

Three more things need to be said about HTML support:

- HTML formatting is supported for Input Text Area components.
- The supported HTML formatting applies to many kinds of codes, but not every type of encoding is supported.
- You can overlay Xcelsius formatting on top of HTML formatting. For example, notice that the HTML message displayed in Figure 8.16 is center-aligned, so it is directly underneath the vertical bar. This is set in the Properties panel for the Label component and is not encoded anywhere in the HTML text string.

ART & BACKGROUND COMPONENTS: USING THE IMAGE COMPONENT

There are three principal types of components in the Art & Backgrounds category:

- Rectangle, Ellipse, and Background components
- Image Component
- Horizontal Line and Vertical Line components

RECTANGLE, ELLIPSE, AND BACKGROUND COMPONENTS

Depending on the particular Xcelsius theme you apply to a dashboard, you may have a choice of between from two to six different types of textured backgrounds.

NOTE

If you are in need of graphical options, you should consider using an industrial-strength graphics program such as Photoshop to create your background and then import it through the Image Component.

The Rectangle component is a good component to use for a number of reasons:

- You can make it a border with a transparent interior or fill.
- You can make it a solid color of your choosing.
- You can specify a gradient fill that is linear or radial. If it is linear, you can rotate the angle of the gradient.
- Both linear and gradient fills can be multi-staged.
- A Rectangle component can be made fully opaque or partially transparent.

TIP

If you are preparing dashboards and visualizations for printed publications, you might want to consider using Rectangle components that are solid and avoid using gradient fills. If the printed document is published in black and white, be sure to achieve sufficient contrast between texts, chart contents, and their backgrounds.

Figure 8.17 illustrates various ways in which a rectangle component can be set up. To fully appreciate transparency in action, a visual block ranging from black to white is placed immediately behind various swatches.

Figure 8.17
Sampling of various backgrounds with differing transparencies and gradients.

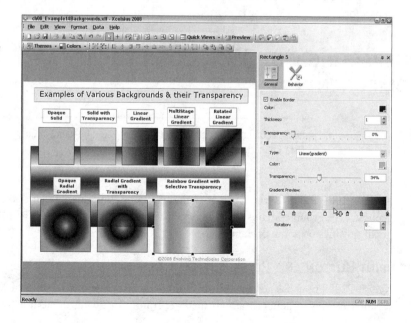

8

To layer additional gradients in a rectangle, you click inside the Gradient Preview block in the Properties panel. Xcelsius adds a new gradient handle point immediately underneath the point you click. You can adjust the color and transparency for each of the handle points. You can also click and drag the handle points to adjust the position on your Rectangle component.

THE IMAGE COMPONENT

You can use an Image Component to display an image in your dashboards and visualizations. There are several things you need to know:

- Xcelsius 2008 now supports various file formats, including JPG, SWF, PNG, GIF, and PNG. Previous versions of Xcelsius supported only JPG and SWF. This is a welcome and long-awaited addition.

- An Image Component embeds the file within the dashboard and increases the dashboard file size.

- SWF files are Flash files that can incorporate animation effects. When an SWF file is imported to your Xcelsius dashboard using the Image Component, it retains its interactive features.

- Like the other backgrounds, Image Components placed on the canvas can be made partially transparent.

HORIZONTAL LINE AND VERTICAL LINE COMPONENTS

You can use Horizontal Line and Vertical Line components as visual separators when displaying data and for constructing simple line diagrams. You can control their line thickness and color.

INTERACTING WITH WEB CONNECTIVITY AND OTHER COMPONENTS

NOTE

Information on web connectivity components can be found in Chapter 15, "XML and Data Connectivity."

Xcelsius 2008 has an "Other" category that contains components that don't belong in other groups. This group contains a rather eclectic bunch of components. The following sections detail specifics on some of them.

THE PRINT BUTTON AND RESET BUTTON COMPONENTS

Xcelsius 2008 now has a Print Button component. In previous versions of Xcelsius, there was no easy way to generate a high-quality printout by giving the user a "print" button embedded in the dashboard. This new feature is a welcomed addition. Another nice feature of the Print Button component is that the button itself doesn't show up in the printout.

The Reset Button component, another handy addition to Xcelsius 2008, restores the dashboard to the exact same state it was in the moment it was launched. This includes state information that is generally volatile, such as date and time, using the NOW spreadsheet function and forever-changing values such as the RAND function. If you are using such functions to set initialization values on load, you will be able to repeat initializing to the identical state. In certain situations, this could be useful. It could also pose a potential security concern.

NOTE

> Bear in mind that when these volatile functions are forced to recalculate, they take on new values, even though the initial state can be repeatedly restored.

 You can use the Reset Button component in Preview mode, when you are designing your dashboard. This way, you can return the dashboard to its original state and rerun it with new parameters and never have to leave the Preview mode of Xcelsius. When it comes time to deploy your dashboard, you can throw away the Reset Button component.

THE LOCAL SCENARIO BUTTON COMPONENT

The Local Scenario Button component saves the dashboard state to the Windows Registry. When you run the dashboard at a later time, you can access the earlier saved state.

NOTE

> Your visualization has to be exported for the Local Scenario Button component to work. It will not work while you are in Preview mode.

NOTE

> The Local Scenario Button component saves state information to the local machine on which it is running. Do not try to use the Local Scenario Button component to save the state of a dashboard or visualization on your office computer and then expect to retrieve it on your home computer.

THE CALENDAR COMPONENT

The Calendar component is discussed in Chapter 4, "Embedded Spreadsheets: The Secret Sauce of Xcelsius 2008." One of the improvements made to Xcelsius 2008 is better support for using the left, right, up, and down arrow keys to move from one selected date to another.

THE TREND ICON COMPONENT

A Trend Icon component is useful for displaying a particular performance metric. A Trend Icon component needs to be mapped to an underlying spreadsheet cell. If the cell value is positive, an up arrow icon is displayed. If it is negative, a down arrow icon is displayed. A - symbol is displayed if the value is zero. You can adjust the color and size of the Trend Icon component for each of the three states.

THE TREND ANALYZER

The Trend Analyzer, a new feature in Xcelsius 2008, is discussed in Chapter 9, "Xcelsius and Statistics."

GRID AND SPREADSHEET TABLE COMPONENTS

The Grid and Spreadsheet Table components are similar to one another in that they use rows and columns to present spreadsheet information in tabular form.

You can use the Spreadsheet Table component to display data and to click or select individual rows and have the component show a reference to the row. That reference could be the position or actual data from the selected row.

When working with the Spreadsheet Table component, it's important to understand that the formatting of the individual cells displayed is inherited from the underlying spreadsheet cells at design time. Suppose you want to display information like that shown in Figure 8.18 (or open the file ch08_ExampleSpreadsheetTableFormat.xlf).

Figure 8.18
Design-time formatting affects dashboard presentation.

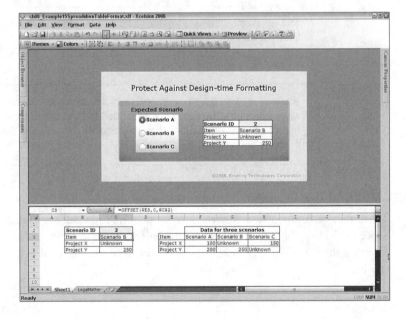

Notice that there is a Spreadsheet Table component on the right side of the dashboard canvas. Pay particular attention to the fact that the value for Project X is the word "Unknown," which is automatically left-aligned. Also, the value for Project Y is the number 250, and numbers are automatically right-aligned. When this dashboard is run in Preview mode or exported, the cells in the Spreadsheet Table component keep their left- or right-alignment, no matter how the values in the cells of the table change. That is, when the user clicks the various radio buttons for the different scenarios, the value for Project X is always left-aligned, and for Project Y, it is always right-aligned, even if both are numbers or both are text.

You can use two strategies to avoid this difficulty:

- Populate the cells with data before launching so that formatting behaves the way you want and expect it to.
- Format the cells in the underlying spreadsheet cells so that they lock in the behavior (that is, at the specific time you map the display data to the underlying spreadsheet cells). Any further formatting of cells read and displayed in the Spreadsheet Table component is not mimicked in the component until the component is rebounded to the cells.

TIP

> The second of these two strategies is more controllable and is the approach I advocate.

The Grid component is similar to the Spreadsheet Table component in that it displays data in tabular form. While it is not as pretty as the Spreadsheet Table component, it allows you to do two things:

- You can change the value of the underlying spreadsheet cells.
- You can make use of cell-by-cell colorized alerts.

The file ch08_ExampleGrid.xlf (see Figure 8.19) shows how you can set up a color grid dashboard that highlights manufacturing productivity for three product lines across four geographic regions. Notice that the colorized alerts are automatically based on the minimum and maximum data values. For more information on alerts, see Chapter 12.

Grid components normally have fixed upper and lower limits. You can remove these limits by changing Minimum and Maximum Limit in the Behavior tab from Fixed to Open. In addition, when you change values (by clicking a grid cell and dragging the mouse up or down), the jump occurs in fixed increments. You can also tweak these characteristics within the Grid component's Behavior tab.

8

Figure 8.19
Color grid alert.

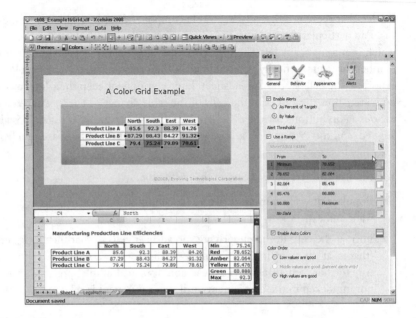

THE HISTORY COMPONENT

You can use the History component to "watch" designated spreadsheet cells and track their changes. The watching can occur at fixed time intervals or can be recorded whenever the watched cell changes values.

CLOSING THOUGHTS

Enhancing interaction is a key feature of dashboards. The better handle you have on some of the many kinds of available components, the more effective you can make your dashboards and visualizations. This chapter walks you through a range of components and features to think about.

A component really interacts with two entities—the underlying spreadsheet and the dashboard user. So components are really mediators between people and the underlying data and their business models.

There are many specific strategies and techniques for enhancing interactivity in your dashboard. Here are some key points to keep in mind:

■ To make a visualization appropriately interactive, you can enable or turn off data animation.

■ The use of label size in the chart axis can facilitate the readability of a chart.

8

- Xcelsius 2008 gives you the ability to drill down with greater ease and control. You now have better options for drill down when multiple data series are involved.

- Although charts play a central role, don't forget the importance of managing selectors. The Accordion view makes it easy to organize and sift through large swaths of information in order to get at the underlying details.

- Check boxes do not have to be static entities with fixed titles and only alternating 0 and 1 values. I show strategies for making Check Box components dynamic.

- One of the new features in Xcelsius is the ability to display traffic light alerts. I show how this can be done with Combo Box and List Box components. The Ticker interface has some of these options.

- Let's not ignore the ability to embed pictures in menus. Both the Fisheye and Sliding Picture Menu components offer interesting options. I outline some of the configuration options and strategies for these components.

- Toggle Button and Icon components are easy to set up and use. I point out some non-traditional ways to approach these components. In particular, I show how to create a hotspot map to provide users with instant help. The key feature to making this work is recognizing that you don't need to toggle alternating values.

- I outline how to set up filters to retrieve specific information. I compare and contrast two alternative ways to accomplish the equivalent task.

- Text components are surprisingly potent entities. Input Text Field components are surprisingly flexible. But the ability to combine HTML formatting with dynamically generated text (from spreadsheet formulas) is over the top. It gives Xcelsius unprecedented levels of agility in terms of text size, color, and messages that can quickly respond to every mouse move, click, or data value.

- Data and visualizations are greatly enhanced when a backdrop appropriately colors and frames the dashboard content. Xcelsius 2008 introduces some new and powerful features for both Rectangle components and Image Components. In the former, they relate to multistage gradient and transparency control. In the latter, they relate to new supported image formats.

- Xcelsius 2008 includes Print Button and Reset Button components, which make working with dashboards and visualization even easier than in previous editions of Xcelsius.

- In this chapter, I outline some features of the Grid and Spreadsheet Table components that will help you more productively use them.

Put simply, dashboards and visualization are a lot more effective when you manage interactivity with greater agility. This helps you learn more about components and how to work with them.

Chapter 9 walks through statistics from an Xcelsius-centric perspective. Viewing metrics and Key Performance Indicators (KPIs) is one thing, but analyzing them with the help of statistical tools is another.

CHAPTER

9

Xcelsius and Statistics

In this chapter

This chapter introduces statistics and statistical analysis from an Xcelsius-centric point of view. The overall goal is to have statistical tools at your disposal for the dashboards and visualizations you develop.

UNDERSTANDING STATISTICS

Statistics is a vast subject that encompasses a sizable chunk of mathematics. Although statistical analysis covers a tremendous amount of ground, the basic idea of statistical reasoning is rather easy to bottle, package, and consume.

Most people who work with dashboards are likely sitting on a mound (or perhaps a mountain) of data. How can you make heads or tails out of it? Data is complex, but decisions based on it are often simple. Has your company achieved better market penetration in the last quarter? Is the overall level of customer satisfaction acceptable? Questions like these need digital yes/no answers that can be tacked to a Trend Icon component or other visual components used to display key performance indicators (KPIs).

Although you need mountains of data, a single bit (0 or 1, or a yes/no response) can be very informative. The reality is that a binary KPI is revealing but not sufficient. You really need to characterize your response in a more suitable way. To arrive at the answer to a yes/no question, you have to quantify some information. You need to think of a way to measure the degree of market penetration. Customer satisfaction might be measured by how many customer service complaints were received for every 10,000 units sold from your high-definition TV product line.

Instead of single yes/no, you replace it with a quantitative measure (a number such as 0.003) and some decision criteria for how to interpret the metric (maybe any number less than 0.005 is good).

You can achieve a phenomenal level of data compression. Instead of wading though masses of data, you can aggregate information in a meaningful way so that the bulk of the data, without the details, can be reasonably characterized by a small group of numbers. Of course, the finer the level of granularity, the more numbers you will likely need. The mean value or average of some measure could be meaningful, but when accompanied with the standard deviation, it gets even more revealing.

The ability to achieve this extraordinary level of data compression is one of the most powerful features of statistics. Perhaps the term *data compression* sounds a bit austere. What statistics provides is a way to characterize large swaths of information so that the aggregate can be treated as if it is a single point or a few data points. If you can profile all your customers with just one or a few representative kinds of customers or measures, then your business analysis becomes vastly simplified. So not only are you compressing your data, you are simultaneously streamlining your decision analysis methodologies and criteria.

If you carefully examine *every* single piece of data to answer some question, you are bound to arrive at some conclusion related to the question. If you have a sure-fire way of arriving at the same answer without having to look at every iota of information, you achieve some real compression. This so-called compression could allow you to simplify your analysis because you need to deal with fewer variables. The ability to discern the important characteristics, to apply simple and verifiable analyses, is very closely aligned with what we think of as business intelligence.

WHAT MAKES STATISTICAL MEASURES SO SPECIAL?

You don't necessarily need statistical analysis to characterize some quantities. The total sales of a product line is a single number that characterizes your sales data. There's no statistical analysis going on.

Statistical analysis comes into play in situations in which you can treat the measure of some statistical variable as if it relates to a single item or transaction. If you divide the total revenue by the number of products sold or hours of servicing provided, you arrive at an estimate that characterizes a single transaction.

Analyzing a single transaction or a very small number of distinct kinds of transactions is easier than doing this for each and every data point. The key behind statistical analysis is that it helps you to find the right representation of an idealized transaction you can extrapolate to the population as a whole or some major segment of it.

Statistical analysis allows you to arrive at metrics to let you know how closely your estimate matches the other data points. Measures such as standard deviation and variance provide estimates of this kind. Aside from measures, you have an armory of methodologies for analyzing data, making decisions, and estimating your ability to rely on your conclusions.

ELEMENTARY STATISTICS CONCEPTS AND DASHBOARD TOOLS

A key concept of statistical analysis is the ability to characterize collected information. Even without measures such as mean and standard deviation, you characterize your data. A histogram provides a good example of this. The concept of histograms is straightforward: It allows you to visually display the distribution of values in a collection of data points (see Figure 9.1).

The setup shown in Figure 9.1 has a collection of data points (see the gray region of the underlying spreadsheet in Figure 9.1 or open the file ch09_Histogram.xlf).

You set up this histogram as follows:

1. Determine the minimum and maximum values of your data points. If you want to display the distributions of values, you need to know the minimum and maximum values. You can easily figure this out by using spreadsheet formulas. In this example, the minimum value is 20, and the maximum is 99.

2. Divide your data into distinct groups. One way to do this is to apply constant spacing between groups and then adjust it. If you start with the minimum value of 20 and use a spacing of 5, your first group begins with 20 and ends with 24. Your second group starts with 25 and ends with 29. This progression of groups continues until your maximum data value is included in your group.

9

Figure 9.1
Setup of a histogram with adjustable spacing.

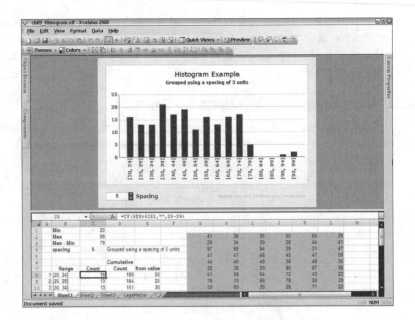

3. Count how many data points fall in the range of each group. There are two ways of approaching this. One way is to ask how many points that fall between are less than or equal to the upper limit of each group and are greater than or equal to the low limit of each group. Bundling this logic makes the computations more complicated than they need to be.

Another way to approach this is to look at only one side of each of the groups (such as the lower limit) and determine the difference between that value and the one derived for the neighboring group. Using the current example (with a minimum value of 20 and a spacing of 5), the lower limits for each of the groups are 20, 25, 30, 35, . . . 90, 95. If the total number of data points that are greater than or equal to 20 is 180 and the number of data points that are greater than or equal to 25 is 164, then the number of points in the interval [20, 24] must be 16 (= 180 – 164).

4. When you have computed how many data points fall into each of the groups, display the information using a Column Chart component or another appropriate visual component.

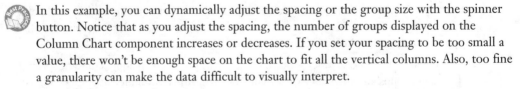

In this example, you can dynamically adjust the spacing or the group size with the spinner button. Notice that as you adjust the spacing, the number of groups displayed on the Column Chart component increases or decreases. If you set your spacing to be too small a value, there won't be enough space on the chart to fit all the vertical columns. Also, too fine a granularity can make the data difficult to visually interpret.

While fixed spacing is generally appropriate for histograms, you might want to have the freedom to pick and choose the boundaries of your groups. Figure 9.2 (or open file ch09_LowMidHighHistogram.xlf) shows how you can use a dual slider to reset the boundaries of a histogram.

Figure 9.2
This dual slider allows you to alter the boundaries used in a histogram.

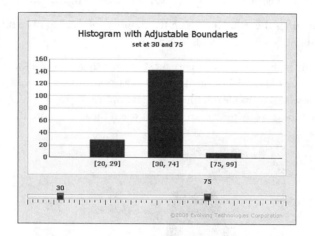

Altering the boundaries of a histogram with Dual Slider components and the like gives tremendous benefits to the dashboard user. Specifically, the user can classify data on-the-fly by setting what constitutes low, middle, and high and can then further determine the implications of the data, based on the classification criteria.

Your classification can have a tremendous impact on how your data gets interpreted. Let's look at an example. If you run a dashboard from the ch09_Histogram.xlf file and set the spacing to a value of 10, as in Figure 9.3, you will see that the most populous collection of data points occurs in the range [40, 49]. This point of highest frequency is often referred to as the *mode*. If you adjust the spacing to a finer level of granularity, say 5, you will find that the highest frequency (which is visible in Figure 9.1) in the histogram occurs in the range [35, 39]. These two sets of ranges don't even coincide!

Figure 9.3
When spacing size is set to 10, the highest frequency of data points occurs at [40, 49].

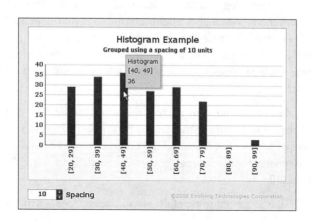

Histograms are great when you want to visually get a snapshot of data. But sometimes you might want to use more quantitative measures. The most prevalent of measures is the mean value, defined as the mathematical average value of a collection of points.

The median identifies the value for which the numbers of data points with higher values match the number of data points with lower values.

The mode identifies the value that occurs most frequently in a dataset. It is possible to have multiple modes (see Figure 9.4 or open the file ch09_Descriptive.xlf). In Figure 9.4, there are actually four values or modes. Rather than attempt to display every mode value, the dashboard signals how many modes are present when there are more than three modes.

Figure 9.4
Descriptive statistics example.

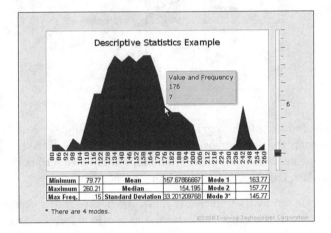

In this example, the data has a mean value of about 157. Visually, you can see the bulk of the data hovering around 151. The reason for the shift is a spike in the data that occurs on the right side of the chart. It skews the results of the average and of the standard deviation.

Understanding and interpreting anomalous data is an important part of statistical analysis and data analysis in general. Anomalies might indicate that your data has random noise in it. There are ways to discern such problems by using statistical methods. As a quick rule of thumb, random noise tends to degrade meaningful correlations and patterns in your data. Random noise will not likely conspire to aggregate all the anomalous values to the extreme right or extreme left.

You have to think about how you want to treat the data. One strategy could be to simply excise anomalous data. Look again at the data in Figure 9.4. There is a big empty space between the group of apparent outliers and the main sequence of data. It may be that the high values in the apparent spike are real, and you are actually missing data in the range of about 206 through 230.

The bottom line is that you need to carefully scrutinize and understand the nature of your data.

MEASURES OF DISPERSION AROUND A CENTRAL VALUE

It is easy to use an average or mean value when describing historical or future events. This is because the notion of an average value is intuitive. It is easier to use a single number to describe a collection of information than it is to present all the numbers at one time or to serially sift through them a chunk at a time.

Consider the following three collections of data points:

Scenario A	Scenario B	Scenario C
10,054	9,909	10,561
10,283	11,439	10,257
10,308	9,528	11,517
10,083	9,988	8,959
10,216	9,921	8,797
10,099	9,381	9,053
10,352	10,213	12,120
10,160	10,113	10,196
10,224	10,399	8,029
10,191	11,079	12,481

If you add up the numbers in Scenario C and divide it by the number of items, you find that the average is 10,197. The same goes for Scenario B and for Scenario A.

In all three scenarios, the numbers average 10,197. The numbers in Scenario A are closely coalesced around the number 10,197. On the other hand, the numbers in Scenario C are all over the place.

You can estimate how tight or loosely fit the numbers are relative to the average value by using the standard deviation. It turns out that there are two versions—one called the sample standard deviation (usually denoted by the letter s) and the other called the population standard deviation (usually denoted by the Greek letter sigma σ). Mathematically, they are defined as follows:

$$s = \text{SQRT}(\Sigma[(X[i] - X\_Avg)^2] / (n - 1))$$
$$\sigma = \text{SQRT}(\Sigma[(X[i] - X\_Avg)^2] / n)$$

In this definition, n is the number of items being counted, X_Avg is the mean value of data points 1 through n, $X[i]$ is the value of the ith data point, and the Greek symbol Σ is the sum of all the data points 1 through n of the expression enclosed in the square brackets.

Don't worry too much about the formal mathematical definitions for these standard deviations. You can use the STDEV spreadsheet function to carry out the calculation for the sample standard deviation (see Chapter 4, "Embedded Spreadsheets: The Secret Sauce of Xcelsius 2008," for more details on using STDEV). The population standard deviation is a slightly different story. In Excel, the population standard deviation is carried out by the STDEVP function. Unfortunately, STDEVP is not supported by Xcelsius. The good news is that there is an easy workaround. Here it is in mathematical form:

$$\sigma = s * \text{SQRT}((n - 1) / n)$$

If your data is contained in cells A1:A30 and B1 is as follows:

```
=COUNT(A1:A30)
```

then your population standard deviation (σ) would be computed using the following:

```
=STDEV(A1:A30)*SQRT(B1-1)/B1
```

NOTE

Of course, you can substitute whatever range of cells is appropriate in place of A1:A30 and B1.

The difference between the sample standard deviation and the population standard deviation is minor. As the number of sample points increases, the separation between these two measures narrows.

In this preceding example, the sample standard deviation of the values in Scenario A is 99.6. If you examine all the values in Scenario A, you will find that 6 of the 10 values fall within 10,097.6 (= 10,197 − 99.6) and 10,296.6 (= 10,197 + 99.6).

In Scenario B, the standard deviation is 640. Here, 6 of the 10 values fall between 9,557 (=10,197 − 640) and 10,837 (= 10,197 + 640).

The situation is almost the same in Scenario C, which has a standard deviation of 1,502. Here, 7 of the 10 values of the data points in Scenario C fall between 8,695 (= 10,197 − 1,502) and 11,699 (= 10,197 + 1,502).

There seems to be an interesting pattern here. Roughly two-thirds of the data points that make up the mean value fall within plus or minus one standard deviation of the mean. Because there are very few points in the sample (10 in this case), this relationship is approximate. As the number of points that make up the mean increases, the accuracy of this relationship improves. It turns out that 68.26% of the data points in a large sample fall within plus or minus one standard deviation, 95.44% fall within plus or minus two standard deviations, and 99.74% fall within plus or minus three standard deviations of the mean.

NOTE

For practical purposes, a "large" collection of data points is about 50 or more items.

Where do the numbers 68.26%, 95.44%, and 99.74% come from? This has something to do with the normal, or Gaussian, probability distribution, which is discussed a little later in the chapter. Before we get into probability distributions, it makes sense to say a few words about probability.

UNDERSTANDING PROBABILITIES

Probability and statistics are, figuratively speaking, two sides of the same coin. Statistics produces various measures, such as mean and standard deviation, about historical information. The mathematics of probability can help to assess possible outcomes and expectations.

Probability, $P(X)$, is defined as the number of outcomes having condition X divided by the total number of *all* possible outcomes. $P(X)$ varies between the values 0 and 1. A probability of 0 implies that X will not happen, and a probability of 1 implies that it is certain to happen. If you try computing a probability and find that the value is greater than 1 or is negative, then you can be sure that there is an error in the computation or that the assumptions the computations are premised on have to be revised.

SIMPLE RULES FOR COMBINING OUTCOMES

The example in this section illustrates how to account for various possible outcomes by using probabilistic reasoning.

A standard deck of playing cards consists of 52 cards. There are 13 distinct kinds of cards; 2, 3,...10, jack, queen, king, and ace. For each kind of card, there are four suits: clubs, diamonds, hearts, and spades. Each playing card has a unique kind and suit.

To better speak about probabilistic reasoning is this example, it helps to introduce a playing card alphabet. The 13 distinct kinds of cards can be represented by these symbols:

2, 3, 4, 5, 6, 7, 8, 9, 10, J, Q, K, A

The suits can be represented as follows:

C, D, H, S

You can juxtapose kinds and suits together to represent any playing card from the deck. For example, KD would represent a king of diamonds, and 4H would represent a 4 of hearts. We can use a mathematical set to represent the sample space of possible outcomes of cards matching some criteria that could be picked from the universe of possibilities. For instance, there are four possible members or outcomes if the card chosen is a king:

{KC, KD, KH, KS}

There are four members in the set. So the probability of randomly picking a king from a full deck on the first try is as follows:

$P(K) = 4 / 52 = 1 / 13$

Or approximately 0.0769

If the card turns out to be either a 9 or a king, the sample space of outcomes is as follows:

{9C, 9D, 9H, 9S, KC, KD, KH, KS}

and this is the probability:

$P(9 \text{ or } K) = 8 / 52 = 2 / 13$

or approximately 0.1538.

9

Retrieving a 9 or a king in a single trial is twice as likely compared to just picking a 9 (or just picking a king). This is because 9 and king are mutually exclusive. There is no card in a standard deck that is both a 9 and a king. Notice that probabilities of mutually exclusive outcomes are additive:

$$P(9 \text{ or } K) = P(9) + P(K)$$

Similarly, the probability of picking an ace, or a queen, or a 7 is as follows:

$$P(A \text{ or } Q \text{ or } 7) = P(A) + P(Q) + P(7) = 12 / 52 = 3 / 13$$

or approximately 0.2308. The combining or union of mutually exclusive events is additive.

Consider probabilities of satisfying two or more criteria in a single trial. The probability of selecting a card that is both a king and a diamond is as follows:

$$P(KD) = P(K \text{ and } D) = P(K) * P(D) = (4 / 52) * (13 / 52)$$

$$= 52 / 2704 = 1 / 52$$

or approximately 0.0769. So the intersection of independent outcomes is multiplicative.

Consider complementary outcomes. What would be the probability of picking a card that is *not* a king of diamonds? While it is possible to enumerate all the different card combinations, it is simpler to compute the compliment:

$$P(\text{not } DK) = 1 - P(KD) = 1 - 1 / 52 = 51 / 52$$

or approximately 0.981.

The rules presented so far for combining outcomes are relatively simple. What about combinations of outcomes that are not independent? Consider selecting a single card from a deck that can be either a king or a diamond. The sample space for this is as follows:

{KD, KC, KH, KS, 2D, 3D, 4D, 5D, 6D, 7D, 8D, 9D, 10D, JD, QD, AD}

Pictorially, this is represented in Figure 9.5 (also in the file ch09_PlayingCards.swf). The probability of randomly picking a card from a full deck that matches any of the cards shown here as face up is calculated and displayed at the top of the dashboard.

Figure 9.5
Sample space of cards that are either a king, or a diamond, or both.

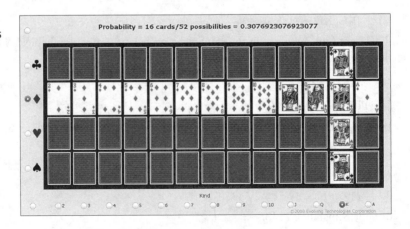

Obviously, the outcome of a card being a king or a diamond is more likely than only being a king (or only being a diamond). Adding up the probabilities of each $P(K) + P(D)$ could be used to compute $P(K$ or $D)$ if K and D are mutually exclusive of one another. However, they are not mutually exclusive. They occur independently of one another. A straightforward addition of probabilities would wind up in a double counting. The way out of this conundrum is to remove the double counting where K and D intersect. Here is how it is computed:

$$P(K \text{ or } D) = P(K) + P(D) - P(K \text{ and } D)$$
$$= P(K) + P(D) - P(K) * P(D)$$
$$= (4 / 52) + (13 / 52) - (4 / 52) * (13 / 52)$$
$$= (4 + 13 - 1) / 52 = 16 / 52$$

or approximately 0.308.

UNDERSTANDING CONDITIONAL PROBABILITY AND BAYES' THEOREM

 Conditional probability is something that is basically intuitive, but because it is so subtle, it is easy to overlook how its essential features can be put to use.

If you randomly select a month from the 12 months of the year, what are the odds that the month chosen is July? That's easy. There are 12 months in the year, each with an equal chance of being selected. The probability is therefore 1 / 12, or a little over 8%. Now, given that the month you select happens to be a summer month, what are the odds that the month chosen is July? Let's say the summer months consist of this set:

{June, July, August}

It should be reasonably evident that the correct answer is 1 / 3. This can be represented with the following notation:

$P(\text{July} \mid \text{Summer}) = 1 / 3$

The way this reads is "The probability that the month chosen *given* that the month is a summer month, is one-third."

The form $P(\text{Outcome} \mid \text{Condition})$ is what's commonly referred to as a conditional probability.

> **TIP**
> You can substitute the word *given* when you see the vertical bar in a conditional expression.

I'm about to throw several mental curve balls at you. I assure you it is not intended to confuse you. A conditional probability is defined as follows:

$P(A \mid B) = P(A \text{ and } B) / P(B)$

9

In the example of randomly picking July, given that the month is a summer month, you can apply the following:

P(July | Summer) = P(July and Summer) / P(Summer)

= (1 / 12) / (1 / 4) = 4 / 12 = 1 / 3

At first glance, it looks like everything is being needlessly complicated. You already know the answer is going to be one-third. In addition, there's P(July and Summer). How do you get that to be 1 / 12? It's simple:

P(July and Summer) = P(July and {June, July, August})

= P(July and June) + P(July and July) + P(July and August)

= 0 + P(July and July) + 0

= 0 + P(July) + 0 = 0 + (1 / 12) + 0 = 1 / 12

If you superimpose June over July, you will find that there is no common intersection. This is why P(July and June) is zero. The same goes for July and August. When you superimpose July over July, the intersection is just July. So P(July and July) is the same as P(July) and is calculated as 1 / 12.

Now for the second curve ball: A probability P(B) can be computed from other sets of mutually exclusive outcomes with the following formula:

P(B) = P(B | A) * P(A) + P(B | Not A) * P(Not A)

This is often referred to as the probability decomposition formula.

In keeping with this example, if you treat Summer as B and July as A, you have the following:

P(Summer) = P(Summer | July) * P(July) + P(Summer | Not July) * P(Not July)

The probability that the month is a summer month, given that it is July, is 1 (that is, 100%). P(July) is 1/12. This formula gets simplified to the following:

P(Summer) = 1 * (1 / 12) + P(Summer | Not July) * P(Not July)

Figuring out P(Summer | Not July) is rather subtle. If July is excluded from the outcome, you have only 2 possible outcomes for the summer months: June and August. If July is not a permitted outcome, you have only 11 months to choose from (January through June and August through December). So P(Summer | July) is 2 / 11.

P(Not July) is 11 / 12 because any month other than July is a possible outcome. P(Summer) can now be computed as follows:

P(Summer) = 1 * (1 / 12) + (2 / 11) * (11 / 12)

= (1 / 12) + (2 / 12) = 3 / 12 = 1 / 4 = 0.25

Because Summer is one of four seasons of equal duration, P(Summer) computes to 0.25.

The reason for going through the computation of P(Summer) using the probability decomposition formula is to help make it tangible. Notice that the denominator used in defining conditional probability is $P(B)$. Also notice that $P(B)$ is the expression computed using the probability decomposition formula. These two formulas can be combined into the following a single formula, a simplified form of Bayes' Theorem:

$$P(A \mid B) = P(A \text{ and } B) / (P(B \mid A) * P(A) + P(B \mid \text{Not } A) * P(\text{Not } A))$$

Bayes' Theorem, whether in its simplified form or more general form, is a very powerful analytical tool. This becomes evident when you look at some real-world applications. For example, say that you have three suppliers providing a 4GB memory module for a USB flash drive you distribute as a promotional giveaway.

You obtain 2,500 units from Supplier 1 at a price of $2 per unit. You obtain 8,000 units from Supplier 2 at a price of $2.25 per unit, and you obtain 4,000 units from Supplier 3 at a price of $2.10 per unit. In addition, you obtain 600 units of surplus stock at the bargain basement price of $0.75 per unit. The units are all warehoused in a single bin, as they are all supposedly identical. There is no easy way to tell which unit came from which supplier.

At some point down the road, you obtain additional information about the rate at which these units have defects. The defect rate of units from Supplier 1 is 3.8%. For Supplier 2, Supplier 3, and the surplus stock, the rates are 1.3%, 2.5%, and 21.5%, respectively. The incremental cost of replacing a flash drive after it is already delivered to the customer is $10 per unit.

The rates of defective units are a tad high, especially for the surplus stock (but at $0.75 per unit, is this really an issue?). If you could examine all this quantitatively, one of your first questions might be, given that unit delivered to the customer is defective, what is the likelihood that the unit originated from a specific supplier of interest? You might, for instance, be negotiating additional purchase from Supplier 2. It would help you to know the following:

   P(unit originated from Supplier 2 | unit is defective)

This is exactly the conditional probability that can be computed with Bayes' Theorem. As should be plainly evident, this problem is a little more detailed and involved than the earlier example involving months and seasons. It requires the use of a more general form of Bayes' Theorem. Rather than bore you with a complicated mathematical equation, I can provide you with a ready-made dashboard that works out all the details and makes it easy for you to insert in the numbers (see Figure 9.6 or open the file `ch09_Bayes.xlf`).

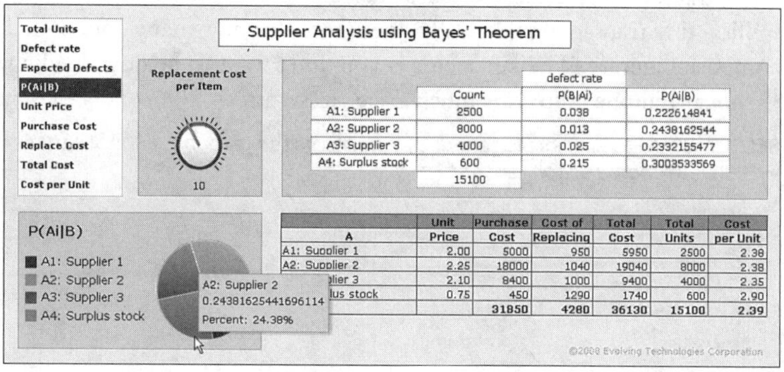

Figure 9.6
Bayesian analysis in a dashboard.

In this particular case, there's a 24.4% likelihood that that if a defective unit is found, it originated from Supplier 2. Although Supplier 2 provides units with the lowest rate of defects, the sheer volume of purchases contributes heavily to the overall number of defects encountered.

This is just one scenario with a specific set of assumptions. You would want to be able to tweak a lot of the parameters, and this dashboard provides the means to do so. This dashboard makes use of the Grid component to allow you to individually adjust the quantities of units for each supplier and also revise the defect rate. With the Grid component, you can use your mouse to click and drag each quantity you want to revise. You can adjust the replacement cost per item by using the dial.

Notice that the dashboard makes use of context switching, so that one Pie Chart component can be used to alternatively display by supply source the total units, defect rate, expected defects, conditional (Bayesian) probability of defect for each of the supply sources, unit price, purchase cost, replacement cost, total cost, and net cost per unit.

NOTE

> In the dashboard shown in Figure 9.6, I purposely keep the interface embellishments to a minimum so that we can concentrate on the spreadsheet structure and setup.

PROBABILITY DISTRIBUTIONS

A principal reason for using probability distributions is to characterize likely outcomes that have not transpired. This characterization takes the form of a probability distribution—a profile of likely outcomes. Probability distributions generally fall into two groups: discrete or continuous.

DISCRETE PROBABILITY DISTRIBUTIONS

Probability distributions provide succinct ways of characterizing and working with large quantities of information. This section briefly highlights why and how it can be beneficial to work with probability distributions rather than raw data.

In working with dashboards, you may be connecting to back-end data sources that contain a lot of transactional data. If you are analyzing sales, you might have something like a half million tiny transactions. It really doesn't matter how many data points are needed for a composite picture. The key factor is you don't want to be downloading all that data into a dashboard in one gulp. It is much easier to set up an SQL query like this:

```
SELECT COUNT(commission_amount), commission_amount FROM TransactionRegisterTable
➥GROUP BY commission_amount
```

This might return a result set like the following:

```
COUNT(commission_amount)   commission_amount
                62234                   0.02
               121139                   0.03
               186948                   0.04
               172556                   0.05
                49204                   0.06
                12112                   0.07
```

The raw data in this result set is composed of 605,393 data points. Obviously, it would not be feasible to throw this raw data into a spreadsheet and use STDEV to compute the standard deviation.

You can, however, use the definition for a standard deviation of a discrete probability distribution for this. The general form for mean and standard deviation is:

$$\mu = \Sigma[X * P(X)]$$

$$\text{Variance} = \sigma^2 = \Sigma[(X - \mu)^2 * P(X)]$$

The Greek symbol mu (μ) is the mean value of the population. The setup for calculating these quantities can be found in the ch09_DiscreteProbDist.xlf file (see Figure 9.7).

Figure 9.7
Basic setup for generating and displaying a generic discrete probability distribution.

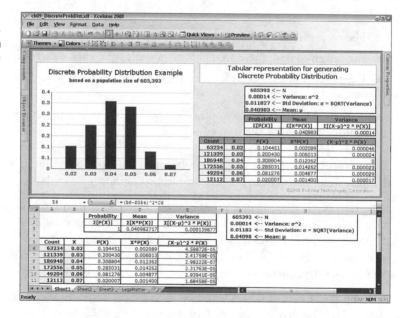

There are probably some critics who would say that you could do all the computations, such as computing the standard deviation, on the back-end server and just send the final results to be displayed on the dashboard. Although you could do this, it would mean forgoing some of the chief benefits of Xcelsius—primarily designing your own spreadsheet formulas to build whatever you want, the way you want. Let the database server do what it does best—warehouse and disburse the requested data as needed. Let the dashboard do what it does best—work out the computational formulas and place them onto an interactive presentation layer.

Keep in mind that in this example, the source data (cells A6 through B11) that drives the dashboard is static. (Chapter 15, "XML and Data Connectivity," describes interacting with remote data sources, so I don't embellish on connectivity issues here.)

A number of discrete probability distributions are frequently encountered and therefore worth mentioning here.

BINOMIAL DISTRIBUTION

Just about anywhere you go, you're bound to run into a binomial distribution without even knowing it. Pull a coin out of your pocket and toss it onto a table or flat surface. If your coin is a fair coin (that is, not unevenly balanced), there's a roughly 50% chance that it will land with heads facing up. Toss the coin again. There's a 50% chance that the coin will land with heads facing up again. If you go for a third try, the chances are still 50% that the coin will land with heads facing up. This hints at some fundamental properties of the binomial distribution:

- The outcomes of prior trials have no influence on future trials.
- For any given trial, there are only two possible outcomes: a success or a failure.
- The probability of success for each trial remains unchanged, as does the probability of failure.
- If the probability of success on a single trial is determined to have the value p, then the probability of failure has the value $1 - p$.

These properties make the binomial distribution easy to apply quantitatively. They come into play when you want to evaluate a collection of individual trials.

A business planner knows that her sales team typically makes a sale to one out of every five prospects. Let's assume that this success rate is pretty well established. An upcoming industry convention could result in 200 sales leads. While it can be reasonably guessed that 40 new customers (= 200 * 0.2) would result, there would be only a 26.5% percent chance that the planner's department would gain more than 43 new customers.

How can she be sure of this? The answer is based on the mathematics of the binomial distribution. The first step is to recognize the number of combinations that can make up a success and mesh this with the probability of success for an individual trial. In this example, each customer lead is considered an individual trial.

To keep things easy and intuitive, let's go with just six trials. Let N stand for the total number of trials (6 in this case) and x stand for the number of successes in gaining new customers. The values of x can be 0 for no new customers, 1 for one new customer out of the six sales leads, all the way up through 6.

The general formula for the binomial probability $P(x)$ is as follows:

$$P(x) = \text{COMBIN}(N,x) * p\wedge x * (1 - p)\wedge(N - x)$$

COMBIN is a spreadsheet function that computes the number of combinations of x successes in N trials. Let's now work through three examples. Each customer lead can result in a success, S, or a failure, F.

COMBIN(6,1) results in the value 6 as these are the possible outcomes:

{S, F, F, F, F, F}

{F, S, F, F, F, F}

{F, F, S, F, F, F}

{F, F, F, S, F, F}

{F, F, F, F, S, F}

{F, F, F, F, F, S}

COMBIN(6,2) results in the value 15 as these are the possible outcomes:

{S, S, F, F, F, F}	{F, S, S, F, F, F}	{F, F, S, S, F, F}
{F, F, F, S, S, F}	{F, F, F, F, S, S}	{S, F, S, F, F, F}
{F, S, F, S, F, F}	{F, F, S, F, S, F}	{F, F, F, S, F, S}
{S, F, F, S, F, F}	{F, S, F, F, S, F}	{F, F, S, F, F, S}
{S, F, F, F, S, F}	{F, S, F, F, F, S}	{S, F, F, F, F, S}

The number of combinations is just the first part. Remember, there are successes and failures, based on 20% and 80% likelihood, respectively:

$$P(2) = \text{COMBIN}(6,2) * 0.2\wedge 2 * (1 - 0.2)\wedge(6 - 2)$$

$$= 15 * 0.2\wedge 2 * 0.8\wedge 4$$

$$= 15 * 0.04 * 0.32768$$

$$= 0.39322$$

That is, there's a roughly 39% chance of succeeding with exactly two of the six customer leads.

Now that you're indoctrinated in the formulas and computations, take a look at Figure 9.8 (or open the file ch09_Binomial.xlf) to see how this is set up in a dashboard.

There are several key features to look at here:

- You can change the probability of success for a given trial and its complementary probability of failure by turning the dial.

- The value of the mean μ is computed as follows:

$$\mu = N * P(x)$$

9

Figure 9.8
Basic setup for generating and displaying the binomial probability distribution.

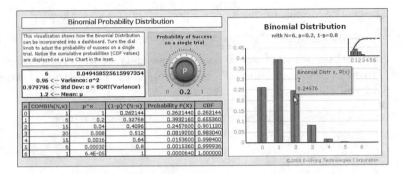

NOTE

$P(x)$ should not be confused with lowercase p.

- The variance is computed as follows:

Variance = $\mu * (1 - p)$

The lowercase p is used in this computation.

In addition to computing the probability of getting *exactly* x number of successes, you may also want to know the probability of getting *at least* x successes, or the probability of getting *no more* than x successes out of N trials. For this, you need to make use of the *cumulative distributions function* (CDF). The CDF is simply a running total of the individual probabilities. This is almost trivial to set up in the underlying spreadsheet of an Xcelsius dashboard. The notion of a CDF is generic to all probability distributions.

CONTINUOUS PROBABILITY DISTRIBUTIONS

One of the features of a discrete probability distribution is that the kinds of outcomes allowed to happen is finite. You could have a success or failure (two outcomes). As a real estate agent, you might sell 0, 1, 2, 3, or more properties in the next month. You are not going to close on 3.1179 properties.

In contrast, continuous probability distributions can take on any set of values. If you are a manufacturer that bottles soft drinks, you may be concerned with whether you are putting too much or too little liquid in the bottles. Your sample measurements are not going to be quantified into discrete units.

Continuous probability distributions overcome the limitation of a finite pool of outcomes. Continuous distributions such as the normal distribution offer interesting and useful ways to characterize datasets.

THE NORMAL DISTRIBUTION

 The normal distribution is well suited for situations in which there may be many measurements centered on some expected or average value. Basically, two parameters determine the size, shape, and position of a normal distribution. These are the mean value, μ, and the standard deviation, σ. You can open the file ch09_NormalCurves.xlf (see Figure 9.9) to try out different variations.

Figure 9.9
Comparison of standard normal distribution with second normal curve that you can tweak with the dials.

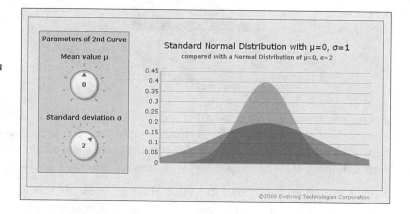

This dashboard contains two normal curves. One of them is called a standard normal distribution because its mean value is set to 0, and its standard deviation is set to 1. There is a second normal curve whose properties can be adjusted by turning the knobs on the dials for mean value and standard deviation. This gives you a tactile sense of how the normal distribution varies, based on the mean and standard deviation.

There are a few interesting properties associated with the normal distribution. No matter what the values are for the mean and standard deviation, the total area under the whole curve is equal to 1. Further, the area spanning any range of values of x is the probability that a measurement will fall in that range. A Dual Slider component is the perfect kind of component to use for setting these ranges. As you can see in Figure 9.10 (open the file ch09_Normal.xlf), 84% of the area under the curve lies to the left of the value 1.

Let's take a closer look at how this kind of a dashboard is set up.

To begin with, the kind of chart that's used to portray the normal distribution is an area chart. If you prefer, you could use a line chart in place of the area chart.

You compute the values for the probability density function (PDF). You will need to do this for each value of x that you want to display on the chart. So what range of values would you need? If you start with the mean value and extend your range by plus or minus three standard deviations, the curve will span 99.74% of the total visual area. This means that if the average is 100 and the standard deviation is 15, a chart with x ranging from 55 through 145 will capture 99.74% of the possible outcomes.

Figure 9.10
By using a Dual Slider component, you can determine the probability that *x* will fall within a specified range.

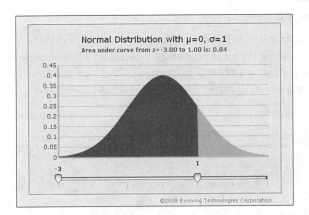

To keep things simple, I use a standard normal distribution, which by definition has a mean of 0 and a standard deviation of 1. You can transform your data to this standard normal form. Why deal with all the multiplicities of normal curves when there is a unique standard normal distribution? This simplifies a lot of statistical analysis.

It is not difficult to convert your data values that conform to the standard normal distribution. The operation involves subtracting the mean value from each of the data points and scaling it down by the standard deviation. Mathematically, this is done as follows:

$$z = (x - \mu) / \sigma$$

Whenever z is a positive value, without looking at anything else, you can be sure that the underlying x value has to be greater than the mean value. You can also be certain that the likelihood of achieving a value having z greater than 1 has to be 16% or less. When you convert your raw data to z values, the data is already partly statistically analyzed.

I want to recap where we are in the process: The goal is to generate some nice-looking normal distribution curves based on a mean and standard deviation. At a later point in the chapter, I walk you through automatically generating the curve from your raw data.

Right now, you need to pick all the z values to appear in the chart and their corresponding PDF values. I said before that selecting a range spanning from $\mu - 3\sigma$ to $\mu + 3\sigma$ would be adequate. For a standard normal curve, μ is 0, and σ is 1. So you only need to look at values from –3 to +3. Working with z values is already easier than dealing with the x value—you don't have to think about mean and standard deviation values!

To get the chart to appear smooth, you need to choose a sufficient number of points between –3 and +3. If you increment by 0.025, you will plot 241 points (241 = (6 / 0.025) +1).

For each of these points, you need to calculate the PDF value for the normal distribution. The spreadsheet function for this purpose is NORMDIST. It is used in the following manner:

=NORMDIST(X,μ,σ,*cumulative*)

The cumulative parameter tells the underlying spreadsheet whether you want to compute the PDF value (which is what you want in this case) or the CDF. Set the cumulative parameter to 0. Also, μ = 0 and σ = 1. If the first z value of –3 is placed in cell D2, your formula for cell E2 would be:

=NORMDIST(D2,0,1,0)

Assuming that all the subsequent z values in the sequence from –3 through +3 are immediately below, you can replicate your NORMDIST formula down. Now it's just a matter of plotting the PDF values on the area chart.

Area charts and line charts accommodate multiple data series. This means you can superimpose a second normal distribution curve. This second curve is identical to the first, except that you are going to nip off the left and right tails of the curve, based on whatever z values are set by your dual slider.

You set your dual slider to have a minimum and maximum value of –3 and +3, respectively. Then you link the low and upper data values of the dual slider to specific cells in your spreadsheet (see Figure 9.11).

Figure 9.11
Set the truncation point of the overlaid normal curve by linking the points from your dual slider.

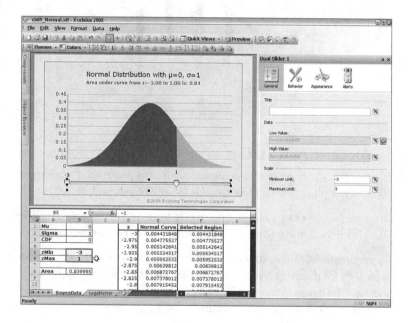

Assume for a moment that these points are cells B5 for the left truncation point and B6 for the right truncation point. Starting from cell F2, the formula for the normal curve with the truncation points would be as follows:

=IF(OR(D2<$B$5,D2>=$B$6),0,E2)

Basically, this formula says, "If the z value for the point about to be plotted is outside the data values set by the dual slider, then set the plot point to 0; otherwise, use the value that was already computed for the un-truncated normal curve."

If you overlay a normal distribution curve on top of a histogram, you can see how well the curve approximates the histogram bars (see Figure 9.12). ch09_NormalHistogram.xlf is a sample file for you to explore.

For the most part, I am not enthusiastic about overlaying separate charts. This approach is not terribly clean, as the position and alignment of chart axes is subject to change, depending on run-time data. Further, you are better off using the Trend Analyzer component, described later in this chapter.

Figure 9.12
Combining a histogram and a normal distribution.

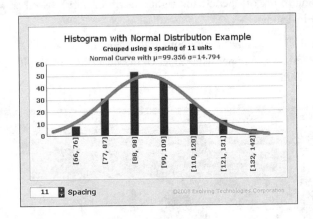

Histogram with Normal Distribution Example
Grouped using a spacing of 11 units
Normal Curve with μ=99.356 σ=14.794

[66, 76] [77, 87] [88, 98] [99, 109] [110, 120] [121, 131] [132, 142]

11 Spacing   ©2008 Evolving Technologies Corporation

EXTRAPOLATING FROM A SAMPLE TO THE POPULATION

To give you a true sense that statistical analysis is powerful, I want to briefly mention the topic of sampling. I would like to do it by way of an example.

Imagine that you run a bottling operation for a major soft drink supplier. One of the operations involves filling 64-ounce bottles with a carbonated beverage.

Approximately 8,000 bottles are filled in an eight-hour shift. Because the beverage fizzes, it is hard to fill precisely 64 ounces. Historically, the filled amounts vary with a 0.125-ounce standard deviation. Achieving this level of precision requires some machine calibration, taking into account temperature and atmospheric pressure.

If bottles are not filled with enough of the beverage, customers complain, and the company eventually loses business. If the bottles are overfilled, your company is spending more money than necessary. There are all sorts of incidental costs. The increased weight per bottle multiplied by some 8,000 bottles adds to the cost of purchased supplies and to the cost of transportation. These days, the costs of gasoline and diesel are factors that need to be reduced. In addition, overflowing bottles could interfere with production runs, and that could be expensive.

Before each production run, 15 bottles are tested to determine, among other things, whether the amount of fluid per bottle is accurate. The plant manager determines that the average of the sample is 64.78 ounces. Is recalibration necessary?

There are several issues to consider here:

- The only way to be certain about the average is to produce the bottles and measure them after the fact. Doing so would be prohibitively expensive.

- Increasing sample size (say, from 15 to 50 or 100 bottles) would improve the accuracy of sampling. The testing of larger samples requires additional time that cuts into the production run time.

- Fluid quantity is not the only test being run. The testing of each bottle is destructive, and it adds to the overall bottling costs.

If you can, you're going to make do with the information you already have (namely, the test results from the sample of 15 bottles).

There are two pieces of information I haven't supplied:

1. The plant manager wants to be 99% certain that bottles are not being underfilled. (The company management measures everything on dashboards—including unneeded testing and accurately filled bottles!)

2. The value of z on the normal curve needs to be adjusted from sample size to the population universe, using the following general formula:

$$z = (X\_Avg - \mu) * SQRT(n) / \sigma$$

The following values would be used:

$X\_Avg = 64.78$ ounces

$\mu = 64.0$ ounces

$n = 15$ bottles

$\sigma = 1.25$ ounces

When you insert these numbers, you get the following:

$$z = (64.78 - 64.0) * SQRT(15) / 1.25$$
$$= 0.78 * 3.873 / 1.25$$
$$= 2.4167$$

If you run your generated SWF file generated from the ch09_Normal.xlf dashboard and move the right pointer on the dual slider to 2.4, you see that over 99% of the curve is shaded. So the plant manager can be at least 99% certain that the bottles are not being underfilled.

Even with relatively small and incomplete information, you can make inferences that are not immediately evident. More importantly, you can attach levels of reliability to your decisions even when there is uncertainty in the information you have available. This underscores the power of statistical analysis.

THE TREND ANALYZER COMPONENT AND TREND ANALYSIS

Much of statistics deals with unstructured and unordered data. Sometimes the order in which data is read does matter. That is, the data exhibits a specific trend. You may be tracking a trend in growth of sales or monitoring the average temperature of a major city for the month of July over the course of a century.

There may be a trend that is linear, exponential, or logarithmic, or there may be one that follows some polynomial equation. If the data conforms to a linear pattern that can be quantitatively measured, then determining two numbers, the slope and the Y-intercept, quantifies the trend. You can then use this as a forecasting tool or simply interpolate values for a range of data your already have.

There are three types of trend analysis tools that I briefly outline here. One of them involves specific spreadsheet functions built into Xcelsius for forecasting. Another, the Trend Analyzer component, is new to Xcelsius 2008. Finally, if you want to veer off the smooth pavement and drive on a dirt road, you can use well-established regression techniques such as the method of least squares. Behind the scenes, the first two tools use regression techniques; they're just packaged differently.

EMBEDDING FORECAST AND INTERCEPT FUNCTIONS IN XCELSIUS SPREADSHEETS

As with Excel, Xcelsius 2008 provides two spreadsheet functions that take X and Y data and forecasts a Y value for a given X value, based on the assumption that the trend is linear. These are the two functions:

```
FORECAST(xValue,known_Y_values,known_X_values)
INTERCEPT(known_Y_values,known_X_values)
```

Figure 9.13 (see the file ch09_Forecast.xlf) shows how you can use these functions in conjunction with an XY Chart component and a slider.

The objective is to adjust the slider value (cell C3) and perform a forecast (cell B3) by using this formula:

```
=FORECAST(C3,B6:B14,C6:C14)
```

There are a couple things worth noting here:

- There can be breaks or holes in the data.
- Wherever data exists, the X and Y values need to be paired up.

THE TREND ANALYZER COMPONENT

The Trend Analyzer component is a new addition to the suite of analytical tools introduced with Xcelsius 2008. This handy little component works a little differently than the FORECAST function:

Figure 9.13
Forecasting on an XY Chart component.

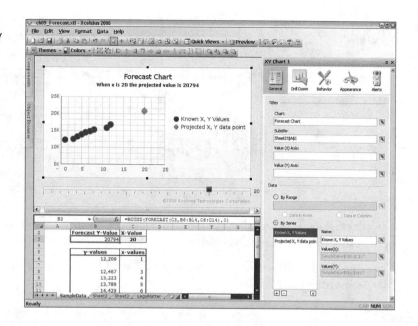

- It is not restricted to only linear trends. You can explicitly fit a curve for logarithmic, polynomial, power, and exponential trends.

- The Trend Analyzer component offers a "best fit" option, which automatically selects the curve type that best fits the data.

- Rather than project a single value for a single point at a time, the tool generates projected values over a range and places them into the spreadsheet cells that you designate.

- As your underlying spreadsheet values used for the projection change, so does the projected trend produced with the Trend Analyzer component. This makes the tool very interactive.

- The Trend Analyzer component can produce additional metrics, such as regression coefficients, on the reliability of a trend.

- The Trend Analyzer component is strictly one dimensional. That is, if you have a set of X and Y values, the Trend Analyzer component can only look at the progression of X values or the progression of Y values, but not the two taken together.

- The Trend Analyzer component works best with contiguous data.

The Trend Analyzer component lets you create charts like the one shown in Figure 9.14.

9

Figure 9.14
An exponential trend is generated.

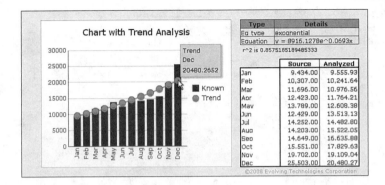

Notice that the mathematical equation and the numeric coefficients and statistical measure of correlation are automatically generated.

The setup of this is rather straightforward (see Figure 9.15 or open the file ch09_TrendAnalyzer.xlf):

Figure 9.15
Setup involving the Trend Analyzer component.

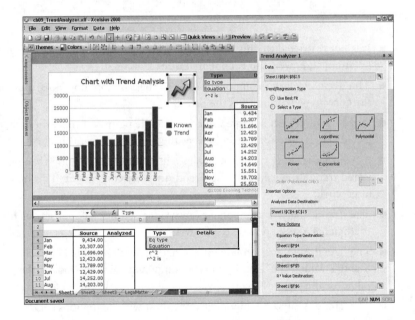

1. Identify the data you want to analyze. In this example, these are the cells B4:B15.
2. Choose the regression type. You can choose linear, logarithmic, polynomial, power, or exponential. If you are not certain what type to use, or your data may at times reflect different kinds of trends, choose Best Fit.
3. Identify the analyzed data cells. In this example, they are mapped to cells C4:C15.

Because your data for the column chart resides in cells B4:B15 and your data for the trend line resides in cells C4:C15, you can use a combination chart to display both the data series.

You can generate and display additional information about the projected trend, such as the equation type, the actual mathematical equation with the numeric coefficients, and statistical measures associated with things like correlation coefficient.

METHOD OF LEAST SQUARES

 If you want, you can unleash the full fury of mathematical tools for doing things like least squares curve fitting. The mathematics gets a little hairy. The slope of a "simple" linear curve, its Y intercept, and correlation coefficients are given as follows:

$$b = (n * \Sigma[XY] - \Sigma[X]\ \Sigma[Y]) / (n * \Sigma[X^2] - \Sigma[X]^2)$$

$$a = (\Sigma[Y]/n) - b * (\Sigma[X] / n)$$

$$r = n * (\Sigma[XY] - \Sigma[X]\ \Sigma[Y]) / SQRT((n* \Sigma[X^2] - \Sigma[X]^2) (n* \Sigma[Y^2] - \Sigma[Y]^2))$$

Is your head spinning already? If you have a degree in mathematics, you probably don't need me to explain all this. Otherwise, the previous two sections of trend analysis should be enough for you to get by.

CLOSING THOUGHTS

Probability and statistics span a very broad range of mathematics. This chapter gives you a flavor for probability and statistics as well as some information on how to apply statistical analysis with Xcelsius 2008.

The chief value of using statistical techniques and probabilistic reasoning is that doing so allows you to analyze your data and make decisions when the information is voluminous, possibly disorganized, or incomplete. The overwhelming abundance or paucity of data represents the two ends of the spectrum, and statistics gives you ways to systematically address both.

In practice, you'll find that using statistical methods will serve you well in two phases. In the first phase, you may be looking at a daunting amount of data and saying to yourself: "What is going on here? I have all this data, and I'm not sure what to make of it." In this phase, you can use statistical measures to characterize what is happening. The goal isn't to get all the answers; the goal is to understand your data.

In the second phase, you can use statistical techniques and tools to present your findings and allow users to critically and objectively address key decisions and walk away with answers that have reliability measures tethered to them. You may, for example, conclude that there is a loss of operating efficiency below a certain threshold, but with it, you know that you are 95% sure of your convictions. The ability to couple an estimate of reliability with the decision capacity is a pretty strong added value of dashboards.

Chapter 10, "Financial Analysis," introduces practical techniques for presenting financial information in a dashboard setting.

CHAPTER **10**

FINANCIAL ANALYSIS

In this chapter

There are few places where having a grasp on the numbers can count more than it does in financial analysis. It is incumbent on both a dashboard preparer and a dashboard user to have a firm understanding of the numbers and the dynamics behind the scenes of the interplay between the different kinds of financially reported information.

This chapter stitches together a broad array of topics. Some are of a conceptual nature (for example, the distinction between cash versus accrual-based accounting), and some are of a practical nature (such as applying Value at Risk [VaR] methodologies in a dashboard).

SOME BASIC IDEAS IN ACCOUNTING AND THEIR IMPORTANCE IN FINANCIAL ANALYSIS

Dashboards are frequently used to monitor trends of ongoing business operations. Sometimes you can focus on a specific isolated metric. For instance, you can ask "Is manufacturing production maintained at nominal levels?" The moment there is a drop signaled by a trend icon or another alert component, management can marshal their forces and take corrective action.

A dashboard used in this manner is easy to understand. It is very literal. Either production is running nominally, or it is not. Either server uptime in the company's network infrastructure exceeded 99.5%, or it did not.

Although this type of dashboard is easy to use, its usefulness is limited. The fact that the measure is isolated contributes to its limitation.

Financial analysis entails the interplay of a whole host of factors. Say that a company is seeking to expand operations by opening a plant in Asia and is looking for a bank loan. Is the company overextending itself? A look at the company's financial statements and doing analysis using financial ratios could quickly answer this question.

It may not even be necessary to delve deeply into financial statement analysis. A dashboard armed with a few sliders to adjust the timing and amounts in a financial projection could be very revealing. You could further couple the timing of events with probability distributions to address business risk.

VALUE AT RISK (VaR)

 Value at Risk, although a bit more specific in scope than the majority of topics covered in this chapter, drives home how interpretive analysis can play a role in historical patterns, future events over a time horizon, and financial risk.

VaR is a powerful technique for assessing risk and potential losses. Rather than giving a formal definition and getting into some heady math, I think it's better to just dive into a simple example that shows the essential concepts and the implementation. The example that follows focuses on a business operation. It does not use precise terminology.

Your company, a supermarket, is looking to establish a line of credit with a bank so that overdraft protection is in place to support its ongoing operations. There is a general expectation that your business in the future will be similar to your business in the past. Although the profit margin is slim, merchandise doesn't sit on the shelves too long. You don't have any reason to expect a sudden change in local demographics or buying patterns.

How much credit is really needed to keep operations afloat? It is in the interest of your company to not overshoot the amount needed, as you will have to set aside collateral.

Basically, you want a cash reserve capacity you can use if you need it at some point down the road. Logically speaking, there are three sets of numbers to quantify the problem:

- You might need to specify a duration for which your business operation could require additional capital reserves. In the next 30 days, you might not need a substantial spare reserve. Over the course of a full year, something unanticipated could easily happen, in which case you'd be happy you opted for a larger cash reserve.

- In deciding how much you might potentially need, you want to have a confidence level that you haven't understated your requirements. For instance, you might want to be 99% sure you won't be exceeding your line of credit.

- You will want to profile how things have changed and extrapolate how things could change.

Considering these factors allows you to project how much value is at risk, given a time horizon and level of certainty.

Here is the problem, specifically: You have daily cash inflows and outflows. For a 30-day period, cash is kept in an account from which payments are made. After this point, the money is moved to another account. For practical purposes, you can treat this as working capital. There's just one problem: There are times when the balance can be negative. One of several things must happen:

- Overdraft privileges will be needed.
- A cash reserve needs to be deposited.
- The period of time money is left in the account needs to be longer than 30 days.

If either of the first two options is pursued, how much reserve or overdraft privileges will be needed? This is the kind of question that a VaR methodology handles.

If you open the file ch10_VaR.xlf (see Figure 10.1), you will see data spanning 120 days (columns O and P). It doesn't matter how much comes in on a particular day or goes out on that day. All that matters is the running account balance (column Q in Figure 10.1). As you can see in the figure, there is a negative balance over several of the days. Actually, much earlier in the timeline, there is a much larger negative balance.

NOTE

The files identified in this and other chapters can be downloaded from the book website, www.XcelsiusBestPractices.com.

Figure 10.1
Historical data for establishing a statistical trend used for a VaR-inspired methodology.

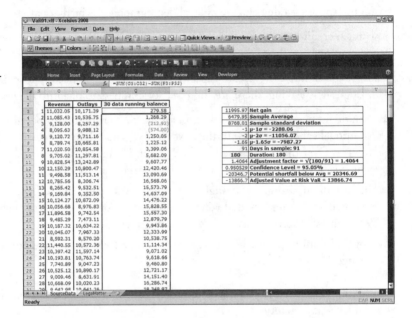

Assuming that the data reasonably follows a Normal distribution, you can quickly and easily determine the mean and sample standard deviation. (See Chapter 9, "Xcelsius and Statistics," to get the lowdown on statistical analysis.)

In this example, the average balance is about $6,500, and the standard deviation is $8,800 over a 91-day interval. Given that kind of a variation, it should not be surprising that the balance dips into the red rather frequently. How far it will go into the red is determined by a couple factors: the certainty you require and a time horizon. Let's take these two factors one at a time.

Because the pattern follows a Normal distribution, the yardsticks used for measuring uncertainty and variation are mean and standard deviation. There is a 95% chance that during any 90- or 91-day stretch, the dip will not go below μ-1.65*σ, which is approximately $8,000 into the red.

This calculation works well for a time horizon of 90 or 91 days. Is a reserve of $8,000 a good estimate for how much would be needed, say, over the course of a whole year? Intuitively, it should be evident that the longer you run your operation, the more likely you are to exceed the requirement of an $8,000 reserve.

There is a quantitative adjustment for the duration. It turns out that the standard deviation for a normally distributed sample grows in proportion to the square root of the time factor. The standard deviation of $8,800 is based on a sample of 91 days.

If you were to take a sample of similar data but stretching out over the course of a whole year, you would have about four times the amount of data. The standard deviation of this larger sample would increase by a factor of two (the square root of the fourfold increase in the time horizon), making the standard deviation approximately $17,600.

The reserve requirement for a whole year is now based on the larger standard deviation of $17,600. There is a 95% chance that during the course of a whole year, the dip will not go below μ-1.65*σ, which is approximately 6500-1.65*17600, or about $22,500 into the red.

Rather than go through these zany computations, you can just use the ch10_VaR.xlf dashboard shown in Figure 10.2, which does all the hard work for you.

Figure 10.2
A reserve requirements dashboard based on VaR methodology.

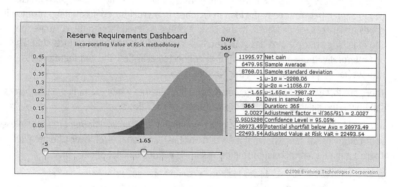

VaR is just one of many different methodologies for addressing financial analysis. This method, as just illustrated, gives you a flavor for how it can be applied.

BRINGING ACCOUNTING INTO THE DASHBOARD EQUATION

The use of dashboards and visualizations for presenting management and financial information reaches company management at all levels in the organization. Managers are likely to want to utilize financial statements such as income statements and balance sheets, but there is an important obstacle to their day-to-day use: Financial statements are largely historical. A balance sheet or an income statement for the prior fiscal year may not always be helpful in making decisions related to circumstances of the past 2 weeks or the past 48 hours.

Managers face yet another challenge with current financial information: Much of the information may not be stated in a form that is consistent with generally accepted accounting principles (GAAP). Sometimes there can be a real "gap" between raw, unaudited financial information and the audited financial statements that are produced in subsequent quarters or years.

You can take a few steps to bring the raw financial data in closer alignment with its eventual audited counterparts.

Accounting 099

Accounting has its own jargon, most of which is intuitive, but some fundamental concepts elude people. You may have heard terms such as *cash-basis accounting* and *accrual-based accounting*. With cash basis accounting, a sale is recorded when you are paid for the merchandise or item. In contrast, accrual-based accounting recognizes revenue when the product or service is delivered.

A cost is something incurred that does not result in making money. An expense is something incurred in the process of making money or earning a profit. The distinction between an expense and a cost is a subtle but critical one. The idea of coupling expenses with revenue so that they are appropriately correlated is called *matching*. In matching, you want to associate the money you spend in selling a product with revenue you gain from sales.

Matching is a central idea of accrual-based accounting. For example, say that you take a short-term loan or note to purchase goods for an order in July. The customer purchases the goods on credit in August and pays you in September. You repay the loan in October. In accrual-based accounting, revenue is recognized when the goods or services are delivered. In this case, it is August, even though the customer pays you in September. The matching principle also ties your purchases of products with the products sold. This allows you to think and interpret without a whole bunch of disconnected activities. You can therefore assess the full sales cycle without having pieces missing in the business cycle.

There are three main financial statements you'll run across when examining a company's financials: the income statement, the balance sheet, and the statement of cash flows.

A balance sheet provides a snapshot of a company at *a particular moment in time*. In essence, it shows what your company has (assets), what it owes (liabilities), and what is left over (the net worth, or owner's equity). There's a mathematical relationship between the various balance sheet items:

```
Total assets = Total liabilities + Owner's equity
```

An income statement measures profitability or income that is gained (or lost) *over a duration of time*. An income statement identifies revenue and their associated selling expenses to show gross profits. During this time, the company needs to stay afloat. It will incur various operating expenses, whether they be rent, salaries, insurance, or even unexpected losses or windfall gains. If you tally this up, you get income before taxes. Take away your tax expense, and you have net income.

A statement of cash flows shows where cash came from or went over a duration of time. There are three places cash can come from or go to: operating activities, investing activities, and financing activities.

If you own a chain of retail stores, the proceeds from the selling activities are associated with operating activities. To economize on your operations, you may use cash by setting up a central warehouse. Down the road, that warehouse will allow you to cut a major chunk out of your operating expenses. It is a capital investment in your business, so cash spent here is used in investing activities. If you are successful with your regional chain of stores, you may decide to expand your operations nationwide. To accelerate the expansion, you hit up your investors for funding; in this case, you are getting cash from financing activities.

ACCOUNTING FOR THE ELEMENT OF TIME IN A FINANCIAL ANALYSIS

We often get more data than can be easily handled at a glance. Call it a form of digital indigestion. Consider the transactional data (columns B and C) in Figure 10.3. There is no immediate discernable pattern or easy way to interpret the data just by looking at the data itself. Along with each transaction amount is a data. This data can be classified by month (column D). For cell D4, you use this formula:

```
=Month(C4)
```

From here, it's an easy process to tally the transaction amounts for each of the 12 months. In cell H5, you use this formula:

```
=SUMIF(D4:D203,F5,B4:B203)
```

Cells D4:D203 are the month numbers for each of the 200 data points. Cell F5 is the month number you are testing against, which can range from 1 to 12. If the month number of any data point in D4:D203 matches the value of cell F5, you need to tally up the corresponding receipt amount in column B.

Figure 10.3

Classifying and aggregating transactional data using SUMIF.

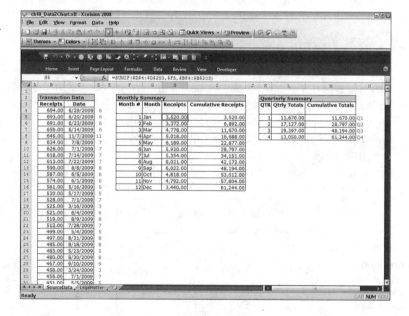

This process of tallying the amounts is very much like the preparation of a histogram. However, instead of counting frequencies, you are summing up the actual values.

Tabular data is useful, bit it's much easier to understand when it is turned into a visualization. The left side of the visualization shown in Figure 10.4 displays monthly totals and year-to-date totals by month. The right side of the visualization is the equivalent by calendar quarter. Even without further embellishments in the dashboard presentation, it is clear that you are looking at a seasonal business with peak activity in the second and third quarters.

Figure 10.4
Visualizing tabular data by month and by calendar quarter.

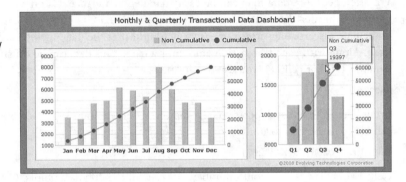

There's not much financial analysis going on here. The key take-away here is figuring out how to translate a mass of numbers (or, more appropriately, a "mess" of numbers) into a meaningful visualization. Classifying and totaling the dollar amounts by time is the key to simplifying the analysis of data.

PREPARING AN AGING REPORT

Plenty of accounting programs produce what's commonly referred to as an aging report—that is, a report that spreads out a schedule by, say, 30, 60, and 90 days. There's no sense in trying to re-create this functionality for the data you already get from your accounting applications. However, in many situations, you will be working with data that is not part of an accounting application and that will not be easy to shoehorn into a ready-made accounting application. Two such situations immediately come to mind: analyzing data about your company's competitors and projecting, in a what-if style, possible outcomes on the timing of receivables.

It would be nice to take data for an amount and a date and automatically place the amount into an appropriate column (see Figure 10.5).

Figure 10.5
Allocating values to the appropriate column(s) by month number.

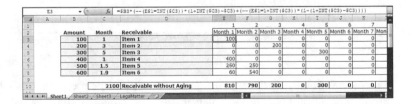

In this example, the $100 item shows up in the column labeled Month 1, the $200 item shows up in the column labeled Month 3. The month number next to the $500 item is 1.5, so half of the $500 falls in Month 1 and the other half in Month 2. Similarly, because the month number next to the $600 item is 1.9, 90% of it ($540) falls in Month 2, and 10% ($60) falls in Month 1. The allocation scheme follows whatever value happens to be the value next to the dollar amount.

This framework is very flexible and can be applied in a wide variety of circumstances that have nothing to do with this receivables aging example. You could, for instance, create a financial projection involving, say, individual projects or engagements you expect to get but for which the timing of contracts being awarded is subject to change.

In the context of receivables aging, you already have a schedule of payment due dates. The reality is that historically, maybe only 23% of all vendors pay immediately, 30% wait a month before paying, 23% wait two months, and 10% pay three months late. The remainder take 120 days or more to pay, and half of those are uncollectible. You can tweak your dashboard to reflect this reality by using sliders (see Figure 10.6).

Figure 10.6
Using sliders to "age" the scheduled receivables in 30, 60, 90, and 120 days and to provide for write-offs.

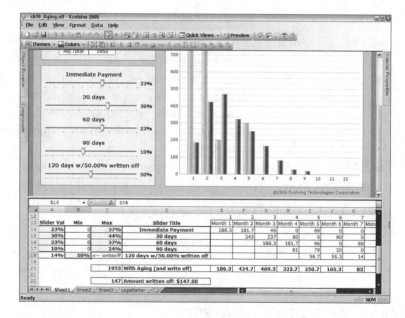

When you put this all together, you have a very flexible framework for projecting what the cash flow picture could look like (see Figure 10.7 or open the file ch10_Aging.xlf).

Figure 10.7
An interactive receivables aging dashboard.

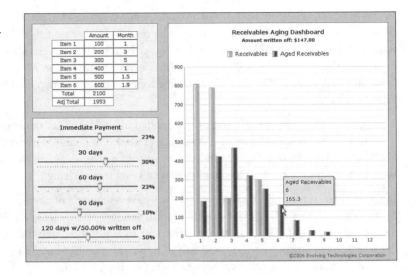

This dashboard is divided into three panels:

- The top-left panel has a Grid component that allows you, on a line-by-line basis, to adjust the dollar amounts and the timing by clicking and dragging the mouse.

- The five sliders in the bottom-left panel allow you to identify what proportion of receivables are paid immediately and what proportion are paid 30, 60, 90, and 120 days late. Notice that the collective sum of the percentages for the sliders never exceeds 100%. You can use the bottom slider to adjust the proportion that is written off for payment delays exceeding 120 days.

- The panel on the right contains a chart that shows both scheduled receivables and projected receivables, based on timing delays. As you adjust the values in the Grid component for amounts and month numbers and as you adjust the slider values, the chart values are instantly recalculated and displayed.

Because of the nature of its interactiveness, this dashboard gives a very real sense of how timing delays can play out.

FINANCIAL RATIO ANALYSIS

Financial ratios are great indicators of how a business is doing. Sometimes, it is important to know where the numbers are coming from. For example, the current ratio is defined as current assets divided by current liabilities. If your current assets are $700,000 and current liabilities are $300,000, then the current ratio is approximately 2.33. Retrieving numbers such as those for current assets and current liabilities could be straightforward, as this is the kind of information that is readily available from accounting applications. But what numbers make up the current assets? How much is in cash versus inventory or short-term receivables? Getting at the underlying information is not necessarily easy.

To assist in this kind of analysis, I provide a ratio analyzer dashboard that displays specific kinds of financial ratios and deconstructs how the numbers are derived (see Figure 10.8 or open ch10_RatioAnalyzer.xlf).

Figure 10.8
Deconstructing financial ratios.

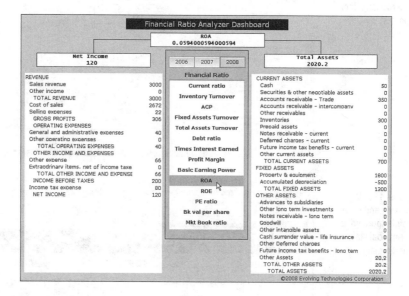

In this example, the dashboard starts with a list box that identifies various kinds of financial ratios. The one selected in Figure 10.8 is ROA (return on assets). When you click ROA, the ratio and its constituent components are displayed, along with the underlying calculations.

THE BUCK STARTS HERE

Constructing a dashboard like this requires a series of steps. Typically, data originating from some source—whether a database server, a connection over the Internet using Web Services, an XML file, or a spreadsheet—may not be in the specific accounting form you want. For instance, you might only have data that conforms to the chart of accounts. The calculations you may be interested in could involve having to combine information from various items. You might want to do all the mixing and matching using formulas in the underlying spreadsheet of your dashboard. In this case, you could start by designating a contiguous range of spreadsheet cells where you can place your raw data (see Figure 10.9).

In this example, there are 60 kinds of financial quantities—principally income statement and balance sheet data, sprinkled with supplementary financial data. With the exception of the initial retained earnings, there are three sets of data, one for each of three years.

The data elements shown in Figure 10.9 do not conform to a properly stated set of financial statements. There are many subtotals and totals missing. It is not difficult to pull the raw numbers into a prestructured financial statement template (see Figure 10.10).

Figure 10.9
Designating a starting location in your spreadsheet where raw accounting data originates.

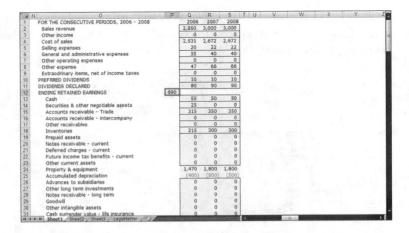

Figure 10.10
Retrieving and incorporating source data into financial statement templates.

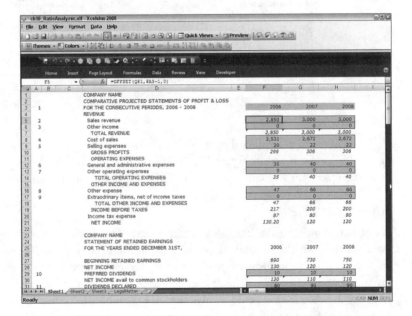

Notice that the data of Figure 10.9 populates the shaded cells of Figure 10.10. You could directly map each of the shaded cells to the source data with a simple "equals" formula. For example, the revenue figure $2,850 for the year 2006 could be directly mapped using this formula:

```
=Q2
```

I would advise against this kind of direct mapping because it is hardwired. Today, the source location of the revenue figure may reside in cell Q2. If your data is coming from a remote source, though, the data could easily be moved to a different cell coordinate. You don't want to have to manually perform surgery on each of the individual spreadsheet formulas.

In the underlying spreadsheet for this example, an OFFSET function reads a row number in column A. This tells the OFFSET function where to find the desired value. If the mapping changes, or if you discover that your row offset should be a different number, you can simply adjust the number, and you're done.

There are two benefits to converting your source data into financial statement format:

- You can incorporate ready-made financial statements at the presentation layer of your dashboard.

- Information presented in financial statement form may be easier to work with and analyze (for example, in calculating financial ratios).

The shaded cells in Figure 10.11 show a variety of financial ratio calculations.

Figure 10.11
Calculating financial ratios directly from the financial statements.

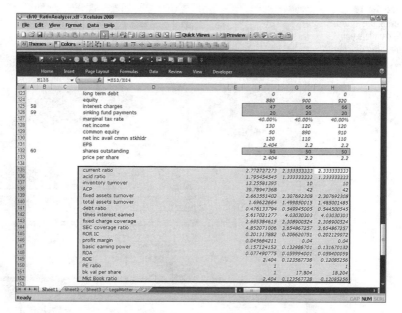

You could use a spreadsheet table component to display the ratios in tabular form on a dashboard. Such a table is a bit dense and is not easy to read. You could instead display one ratio at a time and show both the numerator and denominator directly in the spreadsheet (see Figure 10.12).

Figure 10.12
Spreadsheet cells can be used to depict the financial ratio and its constituent elements.

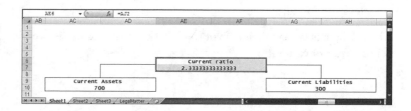

You could have individual diagrams like those shown in Figure 10.12 for each financial ratio, but that would be wasteful. A better strategy would be to apply context switching so you can swap in and out the appropriate financial ratio information.

Figure 10.13 shows a split view of an underlying spreadsheet and related components on the canvas. Column AJ (the leftmost column of the spreadsheet in Figure 10.13) lists the financial ratios. These are the same ratios that appear in the list box in the middle of Figure 10.13. To the immediate right of column AJ are the respective ratio values and their constituent elements. When the dashboard is deployed, clicking the various items on the list box has the effect of retrieving the appropriate values that are displayed in the organizational chart–style diagram near the top of Figure 10.13. Using the OFFSET or INDEX function lets you retrieve the selected ratio information.

Figure 10.13
Retrieving the appropriate data lets you populate the diagrammatic chart.

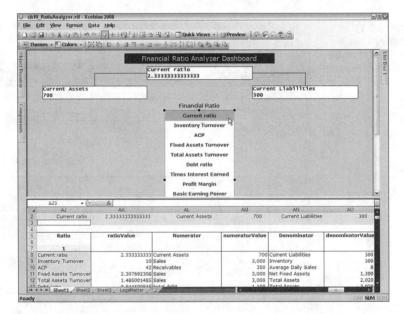

Having a diagrammatic representation of any of the financial ratios is nice, but having the ability to deconstruct the numerator and denominator from information in the income statement and balance sheet is much better. Figure 10.14 shows how this is done.

The numerator for the current ratio is Current Assets, which happens to live in rows 41 through 53 of the spreadsheet. By specifying the row numbers, you can actually retrieve the contents of those cells.

The key here is to map the range of rows that corresponds to the prevailing numerator and denominator of each ratio.

Figure 10.14
By identifying row numbers, you can retrieve the appropriate detailed information.

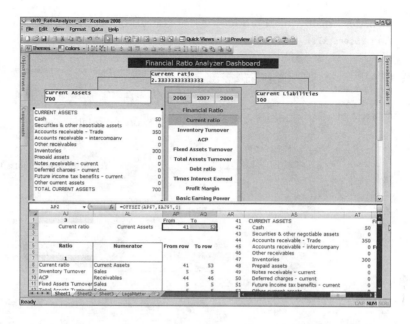

USING RATIOS AND METRICS TO JUDGE THE OVERALL HEALTH OF A BUSINESS

When you invest in a company, you are likely to be concerned about the safety of your investment. The marketplace is volatile. It would be nice to get assurances that your portfolio company isn't shooting itself in the foot. A company could be sitting on its inventory and not effectively moving its merchandise to generate revenue. A company could be dangerously overextending its obligations. Then again, a company may be doing all the right things it needs to keep its operations running smoothly.

It would be nice to have a metric to use for a dashboard that would be a reliable indicator of whether a company is likely to be in business or go belly-up a year from now. Such a metric exists. Actually, there are many such metrics. Among the better-known metrics and one that is well suited to dashboards and financial ratios is the Z score, pioneered by Ed Altman during the 1960s. The original formula, which is still in use today, is as follows:

```
Z = 1.2*WC/TA + 1.4*RE/TA + 3.3*EBIT/TA + 0.6*MKT/TL + 0.999*SALES/TA
TA is Total Assets
WC is Working Capital (Current Assets less Current Liabilities)
RE is Retained Earnings
EBIT is Earnings before interest and taxes
MKT is Market Value of Equity
TL is Book Value of Debt
SALES is just Sales
```

If a company's Z score is 1.8 or less, you shouldn't expect the company to be in business a year from now. If the score is 3 or higher, the company is likely healthy and not immediately headed on a collision course. Between the two ranges is a gray area where it is difficult to say if the company is on shaky ground. Obviously, the closer the Z score is to either of these thresholds, the more certain the outcome.

To better visualize this, I provide a Z score calculator (see Figure 10.15 or open the file `ch10_ZScore.xlf`).

Figure 10.15
This Z score calculator allows you to assess the health of companies.

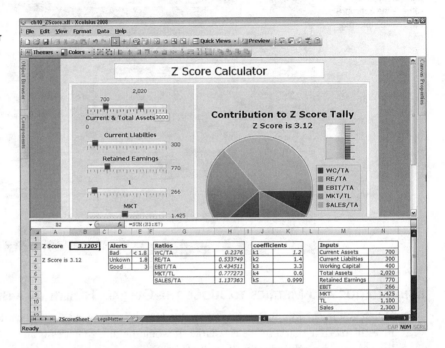

Notice that current and total assets are set using a dual slider and that the upper limit has been made adjustable. The pie chart shows the relative contributions from each of the ratios to the Z score. To give a better visual feel of how adjusting the sliders affects the Z score, the dashboard includes a vertical progress bar with color-coded alerts.

CLOSING THOUGHTS

Much of the focus of this chapter is on preparing dashboards used for financial analysis. These dashboards are quite different from metric-oriented "just show me the latest values" dashboards.

Financial analysis goes hand in hand with the need to make insightful judgments, often under uncertainty. Let's return to the example from earlier in the chapter: You need to determine how large a line of credit you *will* need. Of course, no one can precisely know how much they will need until the future becomes history. If hindsight has 20:20 vision, why not make use of historical patterns to project future requirements? While you're at it, why not take advantage of quantitative methodologies such as VaR?

Accountants go through a lot of effort to audit an organization's records and present the financials of the company in terms of GAAP. This involves establishing that accounting controls are in place and adequate. It also involves assessing materiality and having a reasonable assurance that information is not materially misstated. It involves careful judgments about how information is classified. An item being capitalized as a fixed asset when it should be expensed can dramatically alter the reported profitability shown on an income statement. Accountants expend considerable effort to consistently and objectively apply accounting principles to deal with these issues and document their assumptions. One of the first things I dive into after reading an auditor's opinion is the footnotes. After that, I proceed to the numbers.

Auditors have done the hard work of verifying the basis for relying on reported information. If you have audited financials and accounting data, you can incorporate that information into your dashboards and visualizations with a minimal amount of rework. In this chapter, I show how to use financial information in financial statement templates. Having information in a suitable form makes it easy to generate financial ratios, whether standard ratios such as a current ratio or ratios of your own concoction.

In this chapter, I also show how to deconstruct ratios—that is, how the numbers are calculated—by tracing them back to the source data.

What is all this ratio information good for? At the very least, you can answer obvious questions, such as "Will the business I am about to invest in likely go belly up in a year or two?" In this chapter, I provide a Z score calculator that lets you explore the dynamics of how various factors feed into the scoring process. Ratio analysis is not an exact science. However, if a metric such as a Z score indicated that a company is on shaky grounds, you owe it to yourself to investigate further. Regardless of any metric, you always need to be diligent. It is especially important to critically examine a company's financials and outlook when you spot potential trouble.

This chapter provides some food for thought in financial analysis. Even if you are a financial professional who knows analysis backward and forward, you can harvest a number of useful dashboard construction techniques from this chapter. Chapter 11, "Maps in Xcelsius," covers the topic of maps in Xcelsius, offering plenty of dashboard techniques.

10

MAPS IN XCELSIUS

In this chapter

Actively used business information is not only centered on what, how much, and when but is also concerned with where things take place. The geospatial significance of information and its role in dashboards is the focus of this chapter. Although geographic information systems and digital cartography are interesting, they are not the topic of this chapter. This chapter is about understanding and using Xcelsius Map components.

BASIC IDEAS ABOUT MAPS IN XCELSIUS

Trying to set up an Xcelsius Map component without any guidance can be a bit flummoxing. If you see a basic setup and get some explanation of some of its subtleties, using a Map component is rather easy.

A variety of different Map components are available. They all follow the same structure but differ in the geographic territory covered.

Xcelsius maps are divided into separate clickable geographic outlines (see Figure 11.1).

Figure 11.1
Xcelsius Map components let you select distinct clickable geographic regions.

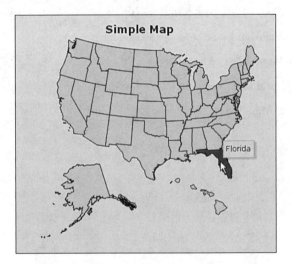

THE PARTS OF AN XCELSIUS MAP

To help you get familiar with Xcelsius Map components, the following sections discuss the various parts you need to know about, including regions and region keys, display data, and how data insertion is handled.

REGIONS AND REGION KEYS

All Xcelsius Map components come with prebuilt regions. If you're working with a map of the United States, the regions could be the various states. To be able to unambiguously retrieve the underlying spreadsheet data, you need to understand the following restrictions governing the behavior of regions:

- Your data for the various regions has to follow a specific order, which is generally alphabetical. You cannot switch the sequence of data. For example, with a map of the United States, you may receive data on an alphabetical state-by-state basis.

  If the data is listed in order of population, you could have California on the first row, Texas on the second, and New York on the third. Xcelsius will not take kindly to this order. It wants to see the data in terms of a strict alphabetic sequence. Xcelsius expects Alabama to appear first, Alaska second, Arizona third, all the way down to Wyoming as the last state listed. (Do not fret. I'll show you a workaround for this a little later in the chapter.)

- The region information cannot have missing or extra rows of data. As much as you or I might want, we cannot arbitrarily decide to throw in an additional region, such as Puerto Rico, into the Xcelsius United States Map component.

Fortunately, Xcelsius allows you to further customize regions for a map. To do so, you use a *region key*—a translation mechanism that tells Xcelsius to associate a name appearing in the data with a name it would not otherwise expect. While it is not likely, your data could be labeled with a state's nickname. Texas is often referred to as the Lone Star State. Your data for Texas might appear with the following label:

```
TX (aka Lone Star State)
```

You can provide Xcelsius with your own custom region keys (see Figure 11.2).

Figure 11.2
Custom region keys can be mapped to spreadsheet cells and then tweaked by hand.

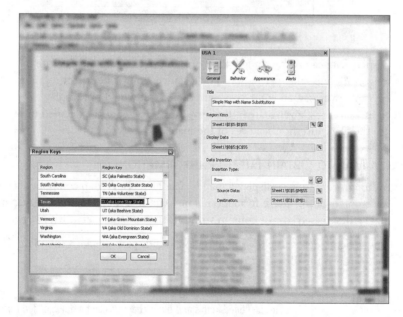

DISPLAY DATA

As you pass your mouse over a clickable region of an Xcelsius Map component, informative text can be displayed. You can define what is displayed in this hover text by filling in the Display Data setting in the Properties panel (refer to the right side of Figure 11.2).

In addition to displaying a label, you can also display a value associated with each map region (see Figure 11.3).

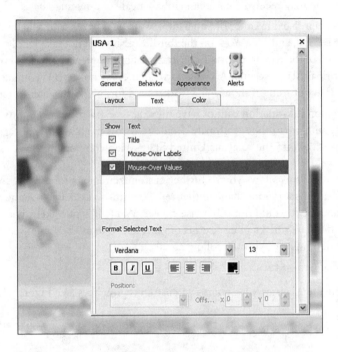

Figure 11.3
In addition to specifying labels, you can display data in a map.

Display data can represent any kind of value you care to incorporate in the hover text, as long as it's one value per region. For instance, your code might represent the total sales for any state over, say, an eight-year period, but you would not display the sales for each of the eight years for a given state in the hover text. To get at the detailed information, you would use the Data Insertion features of the map.

USING A MAP TO OBTAIN FURTHER INFORMATION

Although you can just display a map by itself, Xcelsius Map components tend to be used like selectors to get further information. The Data Insertion feature of a map allows you to populate a designated row or column with information associated with a specific map region.

The general idea is to click a map region and display the corresponding details (see Figure 11.4 or open the file ch11_SimpleMap.xlf).

NOTE

The files identified in this and other chapters can be downloaded from the book website, www.XcelsiusBestPractices.com.

Figure 11.4
Maps can be used to retrieve detailed information.

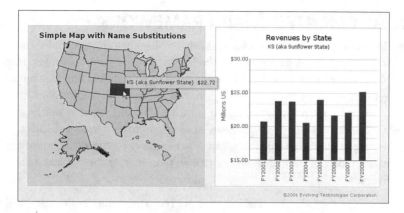

At the spreadsheet level, you identify a row (or, if you desire, a column) that you can populate with detailed data extracted from an Xcelsius Map component. This is your destination row (see the top spreadsheet row of Figure 11.5).

TIP

The destination row can be placed anywhere on your underlying spreadsheet. Typically, people creating dashboards place the destination row above or below the source data. I strongly suggest that you place the destination row *above* the source data and not below it because at some point down the road, you might need to add more rows to your data. Placing the destination data above potentially prevents your having to do significant spreadsheet redesign to accommodate your growing data.

11

Figure 11.5
Layout of spreadsheet data to accommodate Map and Column Chart components.

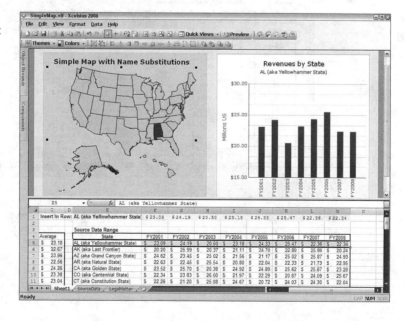

AN AUGMENTED MAP FRAMEWORK

The data you want to use with an Xcelsius Map component could come from a remote data source such as a database or over the Internet. In such situations, you might not have complete control over how the data is streamed to your dashboard. You might, for instance, not get data for every region. Then again, you might get data for regions that don't correspond to the map. Even if you manage to get this right, the data may not be arranged in the order Xcelsius expects. By itself, Xcelsius would figuratively throw its hands up in the air and deliver an empty, un-clickable map. You can easily fix this problem by using the Augmented Map Framework, which enables dynamic rearrangement of data and incorporates a data overpass.

Consider the following scenario. You are receiving demographic data, which may need some on-the-fly fixing to work with Xcelsius 2008. The data contains population statistics for all 50 states as well as the District of Columbia and Puerto Rico. The data appears in sequence of population size and not in alphabetical order. To complicate matters, the data uses a two-letter abbreviation in place of the state name (see Figure 11.6 or open the file ch11_AugmentedMap.xlf).

Figure 11.6
Layout of spreadsheet data that doesn't conform to an Xcelsius Map component.

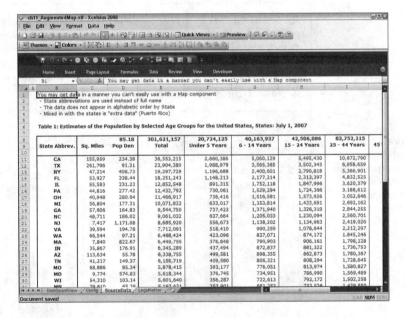

There are several things you need to do. The first is to map where everything is coming from and needs to go (see Figure 11.7). A simple VLOOKUP accomplishes this task. Notice that at the same time, the region key data is automatically switched from the two-letter designation to the full state name.

Figure 11.7
Finding where data is positioned.

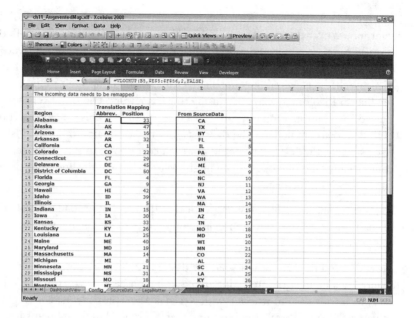

The next step is a little more complicated, as there are several moving parts working at one time. Before delving into those details, I want to explain how the augmented map dashboard works.

This dashboard is similar to the ch11_SimpleMap.xlf dashboard, as it displays specific detailed information on a state-by-state basis within a column chart (see Figure 11.8). There are, however, some important differences between this dashboard and ch11_SimpleMap.xlf. Specifically, we need to be able to represent the information for Puerto Rico. That information gets to piggyback with a state of our choosing.

Figure 11.8
Augmented map dashboard.

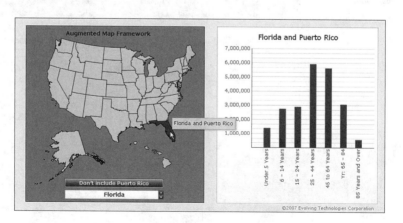

In Figure 11.8, the Puerto Rico data is combined with the figures for Florida. As you move your mouse over the various states, the only state that is paired up with Puerto Rico is Florida. Suppose you would rather pair it up with a different state—maybe Texas or New York. This is easy to do. You simply click the arrow keys on the spinner button to reassign the state that gets paired up with Puerto Rico. If you don't want to incorporate the figures for Puerto Rico or any extra data using this framework, you simply click the Don't Include Puerto Rico button. (You can turn it back on anytime.) This framework could be readily extended to accommodate The Bahamas, Bermuda, Jamaica, the Virgin Islands, or anyplace else. Actually, the "extra" data need not even correspond to a separate geographic region. It could be any kind of data that you might want to be able to allocate to any region of your choosing within the map.

Augmented maps are not very flashy. In fact, they are rather understated. The chief benefit of their use is derived from improving your ability to nimbly manage and control data to suit your needs.

Now that you have an idea of what the dashboard does, it's time to peek under the hood. There are a number of interesting things going on here, as you can see in Figure 11.9. If you are already used to working with Xcelsius Map components, you might think that a lot of data is missing. People tend to think that Xcelsius Map components have a ton of source data, and when a region is clicked, the whole row or column is populated with the corresponding data from the source. That is happening here. Rather than dredge and replicate all the data, you only need to get the reference to the data. So the source data (and destination cells) need only include columns D (the name of the region) and E (the location of the data).

Figure 11.9
The main worksheet for an augmented map dashboard.

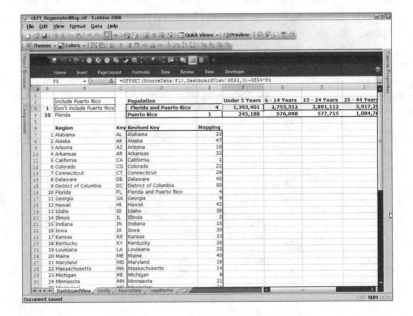

The destination cells are D3:E3. Cell E3 identifies the location of all the data that will make its way into the column chart. The data is retrieved using OFFSET.

There's another subtlety quietly at play. If you look carefully at the worksheet displayed in Figure 11.9 (or simply go to the DashboardView worksheet of ch11_AugmentedMap.xlf), you'll find that the extra data (that is, the population figures for Puerto Rico) is never combined with more than one region. (In Figure 11.9, it happens to be Florida.)

Cell A4 identifies which state in the list of regions would be paired up with the extra data. It has the value 10, and the 10th state in the list is Florida. If cell A4 were 11, the state to be paired up would be Georgia. If it were 12, it would be Hawaii. The Spinner Button for selecting the state is linked to cell A4.

The toggle button is linked to cell A3. It determines whether the state displayed in the spinner button gets paired with the supplementary data. The spinner button's visibility is determined by the toggle button's on/off state. Conveniently, when there is no need to incorporate the supplementary data, the spinner button is rendered invisible.

The spinner button is not the only element that makes use of the toggle button's state (in cell A3). All the data that is displayed in the column chart makes use of it, too. Don't worry too much about the details of the underlying formulas; you can just use them.

COLORIZING MAPS

 It's time to liven up maps a bit and enable them to convey additional information through the use of colors and shades.

If you take a look at the augmented map example, you will see that the only times any shading is applied to the map are when your mouse moves over a state and when you click the state. To colorize the data, you need to use the Display Data setting to associate a value with each region.

Open the file ch11_ColorMap.xlf. This file is very similar to the augmented map example (ch11_AugmentedMap.xlf). In fact, it is a direct modification of that file. (There's no sense in reinventing the wheel.)

If you look at the SourceData worksheet, you will find data on population density on a state-by-state basis. You can incorporate this date into the display data and use it for colorization.

The first step is to insert next to the region key the display data you want used for colorization. This data is highlighted in column E of Figure 11.10. The formula (for cell E7 in the DashboardView worksheet) that retrieves the population density, which resides immediately below cell D10 of the SourceData worksheet, is as follows:

```
=OFFSET(SourceData!$D$10,DashboardView!F7,0)
```

The value of cell F7 is 23: The population for Alabama can be found on the 23rd row below D10 in the SourceData worksheet. The formula for cell E7 can get replicated in column E for all 51 regions. To keep things easier to manage at the display level, it's a good idea to round the population density to two decimal places.

If you look at the population density estimates, you can see that it spans a broad range—from 1.2 people per square mile (Alaska) up to through 9,644 (District of Columbia). You need to think about an appropriate set of values to shade your map. As you can see in Figure 11.10, this is already done for you in cells I7:I16 on the DashboardView worksheet. Of course, you can change the scale values to numbers of your own choosing.

Figure 11.10
Spreadsheet setup for map colorization.

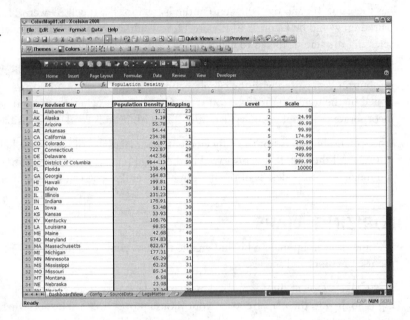

Make sure your display data encompasses the region keys and the data you want to use for the shading or colorization. In this example, it is cells D7:E57.

Next, you need to enable alerts by value for your map and then set a range that is mapped to cells I7:I16 of the DashboardView worksheet (see Figure 11.11).

Notice that Enable Auto Colors is checked. Most likely, you will want the option to adjust or create your own color schemes. If you do, click the rainbow icon to the right of the Enable Auto Colors check box. A panel pops up, allowing you to choose a color scheme or build one of your own (see Figure 11.12).

Figure 11.11
Initial dashboard setup for map colorization.

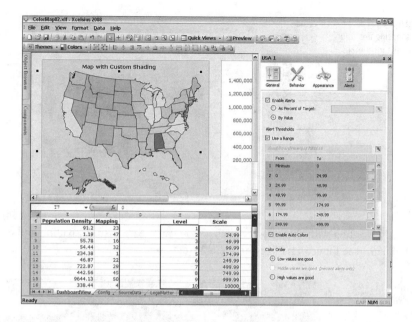

Figure 11.12
Custom color scheme selector.

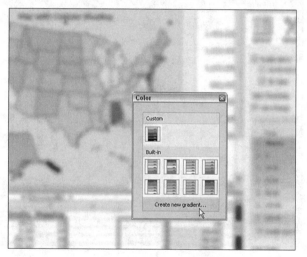

If you click the Create New Gradient option, you will get a Color panel like the one shown in Figure 11.13 that allows you to set the range or choose a color to indicate where there is no data. It's a good idea to use a significantly different color to signify no data (for example, a strong red). It's also a good idea to start with grayscales for the gradient when working with different values, such as population density. If you first concentrate on getting the scale thresholds correct, you can then play around with the colors.

Figure 11.13
Customizing the color gradients for a map.

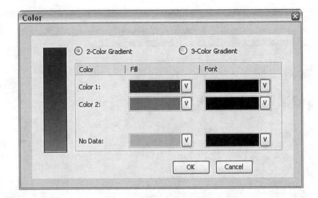

By working with the color gradients, you can create custom shading and colors for your maps (see Figure 11.14 or the file ch11_ColorMap.xlf).

Figure 11.14
Map with custom colors based on population density. (Darkest states have highest per capita population density.)

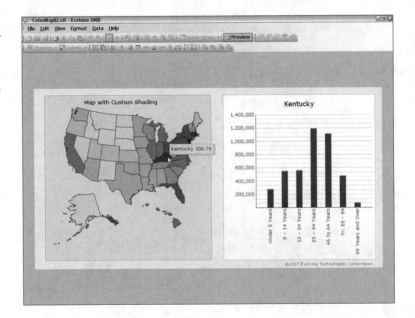

MULTIPLE-REGION MAP SELECTION AND TALLY MAPS

Generally, when you work with Xcelsius maps, clicking a region on a map selects data but doesn't affect its condition. It seems natural that if you click a region in a map, the map region should be "aware" that it was clicked, even after you go on to click other map regions. Unfortunately, there is no automatic provision for this kind of functionality. I therefore designed such a facility, called a multi-selection map, by using the ETC Shared Component Framework (described in Chapter 6, "Single Value Components: Dials, Gauges, Speedometers, and the Like").

MULTI-SELECTION MAPS

The basic premise of a multi-selection map is that as you click a region, the region needs to retain the fact that it has been clicked, even as you go on to click other regions on the map.

Say that you are doing some fundraising and want to tally pledges by state. As you click each state or region on a map, the region is selected, and a table is populated with pledged amounts. Each state has its own spot on the table (see Figure 11.15 or open the file ch11_MultiSelectionMap.xlf).

Figure 11.15
A multi-selection map that populates a table.

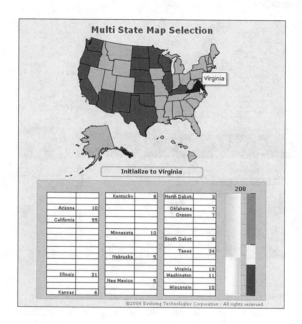

Notice there is also a vertical progress bar to the right of the table, showing the total pledges. The progress bar is color-coded so that when totals exceed a certain threshold, the color of the progress bar changes.

THE TECHNICAL DETAILS BEHIND A MULTI-SELECTION MAP

Creating a multi-selection map doesn't require much skill. All you really need to do is populate selected regions of such a map with the data values you want and rearrange the visual components to your liking.

To build a multi-selection map, you work through two steps:

1. Set Display Data so that color tracks the state of something being clicked (instead of using the Display Data to render, for example, population density).

2. Preserve the selection state so that it can be used in other spreadsheet computations.

The information that the map manages includes the region (for example, Alabama, Alaska), the old value of whether that region was selected, a row reference (to identify a region of interest), a new value for the selection state, and a corresponding data value (in this example, the specific pledge amounts that populate the table when a region is selected). Figure 11.16 shows how this is laid out at the spreadsheet level.

Figure 11.16
Spreadsheet layout for a multi-selection map.

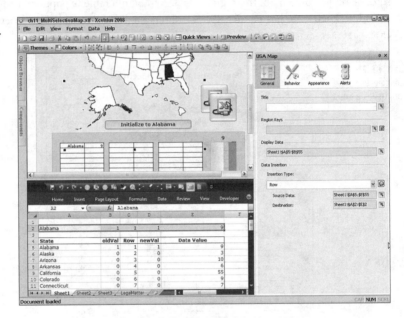

A Source Data component watches whenever you place a value on the destination cells A2:E2. When you click on a state (for example, Texas, New York), the cells A2:E2 get updated. This triggers the Source Data component to replicate the cells in the new value column onto the old value column. As you click various regions, the old values change from 0 to 1, and they stay there—until you click the Initialize to *State* button to reset the values.

TALLY MAPS

A tally map is very similar to a multi-selection map, but it goes further:

- Tally maps can assign more than one value to each region. In the simple multi-selection map, each region is either selected or not. In a tally map, you can do things like create a red state, a blue state, and a neutral state.

- You can easily switch the state of each region (and, hence, its color) by using components like spinner buttons.

Figure 11.17 shows a tally map (open the file ch11_TallyMap.swf). Notice that clicking the text-based spinner button sets the color of a highlighted state to red, neutral, or blue.

Figure 11.17
A tally map.

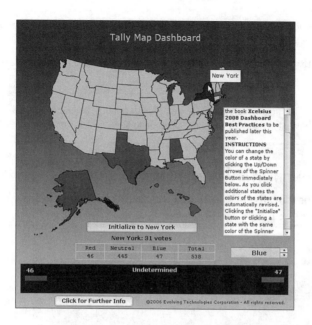

Near the bottom of the tally map are two colored bands—one on each side—with numeric scores. As each state is assigned a color, the respective band grows and inches toward the center. The first to get past the halfway point is announced the winner. Incidentally, the value associated with each state corresponds to the number of electoral votes.

From a design standpoint, the main difference between a tally map and a multi-selection map is that a tally map provides some extra structures for managing multiple color states. Instead of having only a 0 and 1 for unselected and selected, you have -1, 0, and 1 for the colors red, gray (or neutral), and blue, respectively. Of course, you can create tally maps with more than three color options.

INTERNATIONAL MAP TYPES

Xcelsius 2008 offers a broader array of maps than were available with earlier editions of Xcelsius. They are far too numerous to cover in detail, and they essentially work identically to those of the U.S. map examples already shown. The only real differences are the shapes and region names.

One of the great things you can do with Xcelsius 2008 Map components is connect two or more of them together. If you start with the World by Continent Map component and click, say, South America, it would be nice to have a South American map appear and to be able to get detailed data for Venezuela or Argentina.

Xcelsius 2008 comes with a spreadsheet file that contains a relatively comprehensive list of regions associated with the map components. If you have Service Pack 1 of Xcelsius 2008 (which contains some changes and enhancements to the original Xcelsius 2008 release), you will find the `MapRegions.xls` file in the following directory:

```
C:\Program Files\Business Objects\Xcelsius\assets\samples\User Guide Samples
```

NOTE

> The original release of Xcelsius 2008 does not contain the `MapRegion.xls` file. If you want access to it, you must upgrade to Service Pack 1 or later.

THE WORLD BY CONTINENT MAP COMPONENT

The base map or starting point for a world at your "clickertips" is the World by Continent Map component (see Figure 11.18).

Figure 11.18
The World by Continent Map component.

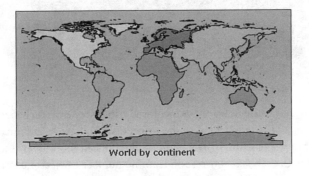

World by continent

The following regions of this Map component are clickable:

- Africa
- Antarctica
- Asia
- Australia
- Europe
- North America
- Oceania
- South America

For each of these "continents," Xcelsius provides one or more Map components. Creating a hierarchical multi-map visualization can pose some challenges. The best way to examine the design issues is to examine the Connected Maps reference implementation.

THE CONNECTED MAPS REFERENCE IMPLEMENTATION

 A reference implementation is a deliberately barebones design that exposes the essential logic, has enough features to be non-trivial, and allows room for enhancements and extensions.

This section walks you through the basic setup of a connected set of maps: a world map that links to two sub-maps—Europe and South America. The dataset used in this implementation tracks the number of cell phone subscribers worldwide over a 10-year period (see Figure 11.19).

Figure 11.19
Connected Maps reference implementation.

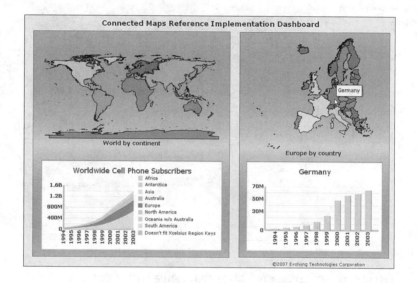

The basic capabilities of the Connected Maps reference implementation are as follows.

- The left panel of the dashboard contains a map of the world and an accompanying area chart that shows a count of cell phone subscribers, by continent, over a 10-year period. While an Area Chart component works well for visual display of the quantitative information, it does not support features such as drill down. You might want to use different charting components here. In any case, the drill down is really accomplished by clicking any of the continents in the world map.

- Each of the continents has a color based on the usage amounts as of the year 2003 (the last year of data appearing in the dashboard). This feature is implemented using alerts.

- When a dashboard user clicks one of the continents, the corresponding detailed map for that continent appears in the right panel of the dashboard. Again, this detailed sub-map is a colorized country or region based on the cell phone subscriber count as of the year 2003.

- Year-by-year information for any of the regions in the detailed map is only a click away. Simply click any of the colorized regions to reveal the details in the column chart below.

- Because this is a reference implementation, it is not populated with a vast storehouse of information. Detailed information by individual countries is provided only for Europe and South America. When you click one of the continents in the world map for which there is no detailed data, an appropriate message is displayed (see Figure 11.20).

Figure 11.20
Context-sensitive alert message.

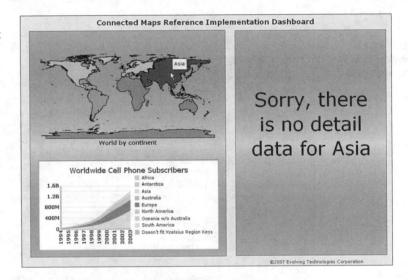

DETAILS OF THE CONNECTED MAPS REFERENCE IMPLEMENTATION

Multi-layer visibility is an important and integral part of the design of the Connected Maps reference implementation. When a person clicks a continent, the appropriate sub-map should be made visible and automatically render other components invisible if their presence is no longer relevant in the current context. For example, if you click the South America map (in the left panel) while the sub-map currently shown is Europe, then the map and data for Europe should disappear, and the relevant visual components, data, and context for South America should become visible. This is handled using the multi-layer visibility framework introduced in Chapter 7, "Using Multi-Layer Visibility in Your Dashboards and Visualizations" (see Figure 11.21 or open the file ch11_ConnectedMapsRefImplementation.xlf).

NOTE

Notice that an alert message, such as the one shown in Figure 11.20, is set to the "on" state whenever the sub-continent chart is turned off.

Figure 11.21
You set the visibility switching logic by entering values in a table in the embedded spreadsheet.

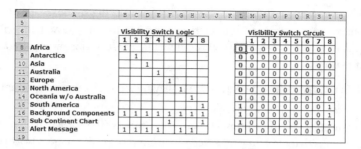

Figure 11.22 shows the guts of the spreadsheet design. Columns AD through AM hold the year-by-year data. Each row contains data for a specific country or region.

Figure 11.22
Principal data for the dashboard is swapped in and out using context switching.

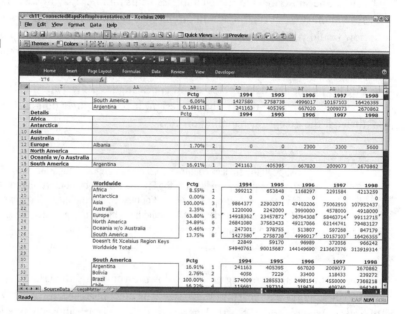

The data that makes its way onto the dashboard area chart and column chart is always in rows 5 and 6 of the spreadsheet, respectively. These two rows are constantly swapping data in and out, based on what the dashboard user clicks.

All the worldwide summary data (for each of the eight continents) is housed in rows 18 though 28. Notice that there's a category called Doesn't Fit Xcelsius Region Keys. This supplementary category contains data for countries that are generally regarded as Europe but are not specifically listed in the region key for the Europe by Country map component (for example, Romania).

To maintain the integrity of the worldwide totals and at the same time use the visual component that doesn't completely accommodate the standard countries, we need to create a supplementary category for the extra countries. Because the size of the data identified in the supplementary category may be comparatively small, the summary information, with or without the extra countries, is numerically very similar. As convenient as it might be to sweep details under the proverbial rug, I would advise against hiding information for a number of reasons:

- The need for adequate disclosure is playing an increasingly important role in business and finance.

- If you start chiseling a tiny bit here and a tiny bit there, so that things look nice, you lose objectivity in knowing exactly how good (or bad) the quality of your information is. In the long run, the loss of objectivity (in this case, the inability to estimate uncertainty) will cost you.

- The "extra little countries" are not so little. During 2003, there were some 7 million cell phone subscribers in these countries. This number may not seem large compared to 1.4 billion subscribers, but 7 million phone customers is nothing to sneeze at. Besides, how would you like to be figuratively and literally wiped off the map because of an inconvenience in data classification? The fallout of being politically incorrect because of an inconvenience is just not worth it.

- Finally, having the data disclosed and appearing (as a sliver) in the dashboard area chart does not complicate the dashboard design. It only requires diligence in thinking through the exception-handling process.

NOTE

> Although the smaller countries such as Romania are not listed in the Europe by Country component, they are listed in the Europe (Large) by Country, Europe (Large) by Country Mercator, and Europe (Small) by Country Map components. I could have used one of these three components. That would have been cutting corners by ignoring the problem of how to account for countries not listed in a component.

Starting in row 30 and working your way down through the worksheet, is all the detail on a country–by-country and year-by-year basis. The alert messages for when you click Africa, Antarctica, Asia, Australia, North America, and Oceania are all really one message, based on a single formula and adjusted for each region. You can find this formula in cell AA1:

```
=IF(L18=1,"Sorry, there is no detail for "&AA5)
```

Cell AA5 holds the name of the continent currently selected, and L18 is a cell that determines whether the message should be displayed.

CLOSING THOUGHTS

Without the use of Map components, the Xcelsius world of dashboards and visualizations would figuratively be two-dimensional. Dashboards generally provide information on how much (one of the pseudo-dimensions) and the element of time, or when (the other dimensions). Xcelsius Map components chime in with a third kind of dimensionality: where.

Interactive maps not only give a geospatial or regional awareness, they also alter the nature of interaction by providing visualizations. Maps are very effective communicators of information. Xcelsius Map components can reflect the "mood" of underlying data through the use of colorization and alert settings. Xcelsius Map components are also great for retrieving large amounts of underlying information and passing it off to their visual components, such as the wide variety of charts.

For all their expressive capabilities and expansive features, the setup and dashboard design process for incorporating Xcelsius Map components stands in stark contrast to their elegant look and feel. There's nothing fundamentally difficult or confusing about Xcelsius maps; to use them, you must follow certain ground rules, but when you understand how to work with them, you can turn them into dashboard workhorses, summoning data at the click of a mouse (as I like to say "Power at your clickertips").

The first goal of this chapter is to get you proficient in the mechanics of using maps. You need to understand them and some of their subtle features. First, you need to understand the standard features of Xcelsius Map components, such as display data, data insertion (the act of passing data elsewhere in the dashboard), and region keys (a cosmetic convenience to help bridge data, the way you have it, with predefined regions for a map). This chapter also shows how to deal with certain kinds of challenges in getting your data to mesh smoothly with an Xcelsius Map component. You can use the Augmented Map Framework to elegantly align your data with an Xcelsius Map component and at the same time give dashboard users flexibility in how the data is treated. This chapter also addresses the pragmatic issues of connecting maps so that clicking on one opens others, allowing you to effectively drill down several layers. This is most relevant in an international perspective. This chapter describes a reference implementation to help organize your data and addresses some challenges you are bound to encounter.

The second goal of this chapter is to introduce entirely new paradigms for Xcelsius Map components. There is no out-of-the-box provision for selecting a combination of regions in an Xcelsius map. But the need for such functionality is obvious. Wouldn't you want to spontaneously find the sales for Colorado, Illinois, Kentucky, Utah, and Washington just by clicking on those states in succession? This is a very powerful and alluring paradigm. Fortunately, the setup for multiple-region selection is not terribly difficult.

Some of the topics introduced in this chapter spill over to the next, which is all about smart data and alerts.

11

SMART DATA AND ALERTS

In this chapter

Prior to the advent of Xcelsius dashboards, some characterized dashboards as structured collections of reported information within a fixed-size footprint on the screen.

Of course, dashboards do more than just simply serve as an "at a glance" reporting and monitoring tool. Like many other dashboard systems, Xcelsius features colorized alerts, drill down, and information-on-demand capabilities.

Xcelsius 2008 enables you to use on-the-spot computations to manage the behavior of visual components, allowing you to take visual communication and interactivity to a new level. This ability is embodied in alerts and smart data and is the focus of this chapter.

Alerts are facilities for signaling information that may be out of the ordinary. Smart Data components typically have lots of tricks up their sleeves. They can position or colorize data, based on classification, and they can do things like dynamically adjust scaling, based on the settings of other components. There is a lot of overlap between alerts and smart data.

UNDERSTANDING ALERTS IN XCELSIUS

Xcelsius 2008 provides built-in alert facilities for many of the available components. The following section outlines which components have alerts and which do not.

THE HAVES AND HAVE-NOTS OF ALERTS

Although many Xcelsius 2008 components provide built-in alerts, a good many do not. To eliminate the guesswork, this section provides a list of the components that have and do not have built-in alerts. Interestingly enough, several of the related components do not uniformly support alerts. For instance, the RadarChart component supports alerts, but the FilledRadarChart component does not.

 The following Xcelsius 2008 components have built-in alerts:

- **Charts**: Bar Chart, Bubble Chart, Column Chart, Combo Chart, Line Chart, Radar Chart, Stacked Bar Chart, Stacked Column Chart, XY Chart
- **Selectors**: Combo Box, Icon, Label Menu, List Box, List Builder, Ticker
- **Single Value**: Dial, Dual Slider, Gauge, Horizontal Progress Bar, Horizontal Slider, Spinner, Value, Vertical Progress Bar, Vertical Slider
- **Maps**: All Map components
- **Other**: Grid

> **NOTE**
>
> Alerts are automatically disabled with *charts that display more than one data series*. There are workarounds for this. The technique involves splitting your data into multiple series that are pre-colored.
>
> This technique is applied in Chapter 5, "Using Charts and Graphs to Represent Data" (see the section entitled, "Extending Graphical Presentation with Bubble Charts"). Positive

values in a bubble chart populate one data series (colored green), and negative values populate a second data series (colored red). The technique is easily extended so you can have as many data series as you want, each with their own specific color.

The following Xcelsius 2008 components do not have built-in alerts:

- **Charts**: Area Chart, Candlestick Chart, Filled Radar Chart, OHLC Chart, Pie Chart, Stacked Area Chart, Tree Map

- **Containers**: Panel, Tab Set

- **Selectors**: Accordion Menu, Check Box, Filter, Horizontal Fisheye Menu, Horizontal Sliding Menu, List View, Play Selector, Radio Button, Spreadsheet Table, Toggle Button

- **Single Value**: Play Control

- **Text**: Input Text, Input Text Area, Label

- **Other**: Calendar, History, Local Scenario Button, Panel Set, Print Button, Reset Button, Source Data, Trend Analyzer, Trend Icon

- **Art and Backgrounds**: Background Component, Ellipse Component, Horizontal Line Component, Image Component, Rectangle Component, Vertical Line Component

- **Web Connectivity**: Connection Refresh Button, Reporting Services Button, Slide Show, URL Button

NOTE

Although the Label and Input Text Area components lack the built-in alert feature, they support HTML formatting. This is important. The HTML rendering, taken in conjunction with the ability to read the contents of the underlying spreadsheet, opens the door to creating very powerful alerts.

12

BASIC ALERT FEATURES IN XCELSIUS 2008

You can use conditional alerts to convey extra information within visualization. Consider the chart in Figure 12.1 (or open the file `ch12_AlertPctTargetValue.xlf`). It is a simple column chart that is colorized based on a set percentage of a target value, pegged at 30% and 70% of the value in cell C2.

NOTE

The files identified in this and other chapters can be downloaded from the book website, www.XcelsiusBestPractices.com.

Figure 12.1
Simple alert-based
column chart based
on a set percentage of
target value.

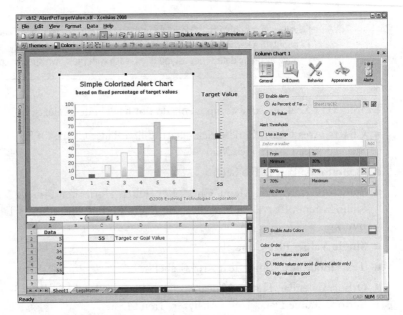

There are several things to notice here:

- When you enable alerts, you have the option of basing the alerts on either percentages of a value (which I often refer to as a "target value") or a range of threshold values.

- The target value can be hardwired into the dashboard or read from a spreadsheet cell. I recommend reading from the spreadsheet cell because the target value might be something you want to change down the road. In fact, you can set the target value by using a vertical slider.

- You have the option to auto-enable colors. This is useful when you want to show simple colorized alerts with colors such as red and green.

- When alerts are enabled in Xcelsius, certain colors are assigned to the high values (such as green) and others to the low values (such as red). Xcelsius lets you swap the assignment of colors associated with numeric value of the data. You can instruct Xcelsius to treat the low values as good or, alternatively, the high values as good. If you are using percentage-based alerts, you can also specify the midrange values as good.

- If you specify value-based alerts (instead of percentage-based alerts), you need to provide the range of threshold values from your spreadsheet (rather than a single target value). The number of threshold values you need is $n-1$. That is, if you intend to show three alert colors, you need to specify two threshold values to associate your data with three color ranges.

In the example shown in Figure 12.1, the Vertical Slider component for the target value is allowed to span a range between 0 and 100. In order to keep the column chart in visual parity, you can fix its scale to match the same range of 0 through 100.

WHY YOU SHOULD USE MULTIPLE DATA SERIES

Although Xcelsius provides built-in alerts for many components, the alert features are disabled when you attempt to place more than one data series on a chart. Say that you have data for multiple corporate divisions. You might want to compare product sales by division and by month. It would be nice to place them on a bubble chart so you can easily see how the different groups stack up against one another over time.

There are a number of ways to address this issue. The easiest is to incorporate what might be separate data series into a single, unified data series. Figure 12.2 (or open the file `ch12_BubbleAlert.xlf`) uses a bubble chart to show product sales (the bubble size) across three regions and six divisions.

Figure 12.2
Exploiting positional arrangement and alerts in a bubble chart.

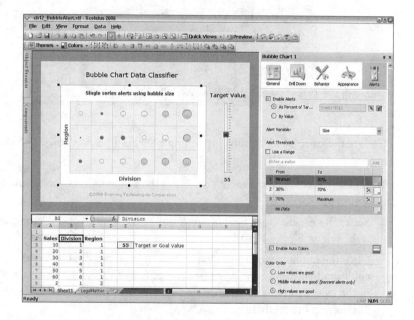

In this dashboard, the XY coordinates are used to uniformly spread out data by division and region. The sales or Key Performance Indicator (KPI) you want to present sets the bubble size. In addition, the bubble color can be used to classify the sales size into three categories. As in Figure 12.1, you have the ability to change the target value by adjusting the slider.

SHOWING MULTIPLE SHADES IN CHARTS BASED ON VALUES IN A CELL RANGE

 At some point, you will probably want to obtain a series of colorized alerts based on values designated in your spreadsheet (see the lower portion of Figure 12.3). The colors could span from red to green, or cyan to magenta, or they could be shades of gray.

Figure 12.3
Designating a
sequence of custom
alert shades.

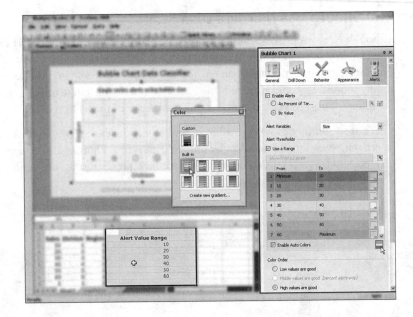

Here are the basic steps for showing multiple shades in charts based on values in a cell range:

1. Enable alerts for your chart by selecting the Enable Alerts check box at the top of the Properties panel.

2. Select the Enable Auto Colors check box at the bottom of the Properties panel (see the right side of Figure 12.3).

3. Click the rainbow icon to the immediate right of the Enable Auto Colors check box. A color gradient window appears (see the center of Figure 12.3). You can choose from one of the existing gradients or create a new gradient of your choosing (see Chapter 8, "Managing Interactivity").

UNCONVENTIONAL USES OF CONVENTIONAL COMPONENTS

Some Xcelsius 2008 components do not have an Alert icon in their Properties panel, yet they have some very powerful alert capabilities. The Label and Input Text Area components are examples of this.

USING SMART TEXT IN VISUALIZATIONS AND DASHBOARDS

New to Xcelsius 2008 is the ability to format text with HTML encoding (see Figure 12.4).

Figure 12.4
Embedding HTML tags in your text labels.

HTML Basics

As you undoubtedly already know, using Hypertext Markup Language (HTML) is the standard way of encoding text for most of the web pages you see on the Internet.

When you open a page in a web browser, you may notice that some text appears bold and other text is in italics. Some of the text is large, and some may have hyperlinks to other web pages. If you peek under the hood (by using your web browser's View Source or Page Source option), you will find that the text has a whole bunch of angle brackets (< >) and text codes surrounding pieces of text. Although the source code might appear too complicated to understand, a lot of it is comprehensible and actually easy to use. The following snippet of HTML code should give you a sense of how text content can be marked up:

```
<i>Xcelsius 2008</i> is <b>great!</b>
```

This HTML text is rendered as follows:

Xcelsius 2008 is **great!**

Notice that the text Xcelsius 2008 is surrounded by a pair of <i> tags. They tell a web browser (or Xcelsius software) to make the enclosed expression appear in italics. Your HTML-aware software knows that any text immediately following the <i> tag is to be rendered in italic-style text. The </i> tells your software to stop the italicized rendering. The <b> and </b> tags work the same way but instruct your software to apply boldface.

What if you want some of your text to appear in both boldface and italics? That's no problem. Here is an example:

```
<i>Xcelsius 2008 <b>is really great!</b></i>
```

This HTML text is rendered like this:

*Xcelsius 2008 **is really great!***

As long as your text is surrounded by the appropriate pairs of HTML tags, you can combine formatting. Although there's plenty more to HTML, you now have the basic gist of how it works.

Xcelsius 2008's Label and Input Text Area components are able to render many of the common HTML tags. If you can encode your text labels with HTML, Xcelsius 2008 can render it. That's a big *if*. The basic idea of HTML tagging is easy to understand, but encoding text by hand is difficult and error prone. That's why the HTML code for pages found on most websites is typically generated by computer and not by hand.

Xcelsius 2008 enables you to encode text labels by using HTML snippets. While you can write it out by hand, as shown in Figure 12.4, it's a lot easier and more purposeful to use your underlying spreadsheet to generate the HTML text.

Figure 12.4 plainly shows that Xcelsius 2008 is capable of rendering HTML. A magical thing happens when you combine HTML rendering with the ability to link the text content to a spreadsheet cell: You get smart text (see Figure 12.5 or open the file ch12_SmartText.xlf).

Figure 12.5
A Label component formatted based on a spreadsheet formula.

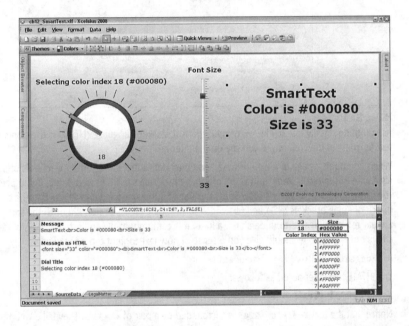

Both the label content and formatting are driven by the following spreadsheet formula in cell B5:

```
="<font size="""&$C1&""" color="""&$D2&"""><b>"&B2&"</b></font>"
```

NOTE

Normally, quotation marks don't appear in the middle of text strings within a spreadsheet formula. To get your spreadsheet to embed a quotation mark inside the text string, you need to use an extra quote mark. This is why these formulas appear with triple quote marks.

This formula generates the following HTML snippet:

```
<font size="33" color="#000080">
➥<b>SmartText<br>Color is #000080<br>Size is 33</b></font>
```

The formula is a little complicated. Cell C1 is the font size that is set by a Vertical Slider component. The text message (SmartText
Color is #000080
Size is 33) is retrieved from cell B2. The text message contains a little formula:

```
="SmartText<br>Color is "&D2&"<br>Size is "&$C1
```

The text message is rendered with HTML formatting enabled and retrieves the color from cell D2 using the formula:

```
=VLOOKUP(C2,C4:D67,2,FALSE)
```

The VLOOKUP formula gets hexadecimal color values from a table in cells C4:D67. You may notice that some of the color codes have redundant values. This is because this list is based on index colors established by Microsoft. The values 0 through 8 are provided for compatibility with legacy systems. You are, of course, free to choose any color combinations you want. The colors need to be specified in hexadecimal form, with a # followed by two hex digits for the red component, two hex digits for the green component, and two hex digits for the blue component. For instance, #ff0000 is a pure red. Hexadecimal notation is explained in detail in the sidebar "Understanding Hexadecimal Numbers" in Chapter 8 (p. 219).

NOTE

> If you only look at the formulas, you'll get lost—quickly. Instead, concentrate on what's happening in Figure 12.5. You have text content in cell C2 that you want displayed and formatted using HTML. You shroud it with some extra HTML tags in cell B5, and it's rendered with the proper HTML formatting in the Label component appearing on the right side of this dashboard example.

12

USING SPREADSHEET VALUES TO SET THE TEXT COLOR

You can adjust the dial to choose a color value that is used for the HTML-rendered text. You don't have to choose from 64 colors; you might need only 2 colors, such as black (#000000) for normal circumstances and red (#ff0000) when you want to alert the dashboard user to take action. For example, you might have a KPI value in cell A1. If the value dropped below 85, you might want to change the color. In this case, you would use the following formula:

```
=IF(A1<85,"#ff0000","#000000")
```

It's a better idea not to hardwire the threshold value in the formula. Instead, place the value in another cell, such as A2. In this case, you use the following formula:

```
=IF(A1<A2,"#ff0000","#000000")
```

Now if you really want to be clever, you could adjust the alert color incrementally by doing some hexadecimal computations, as shown in Figure 12.6 (or open the file `ch12_SmartText2.xlf`).

Figure 12.6
Setting text color by computing hex value from a spreadsheet formula.

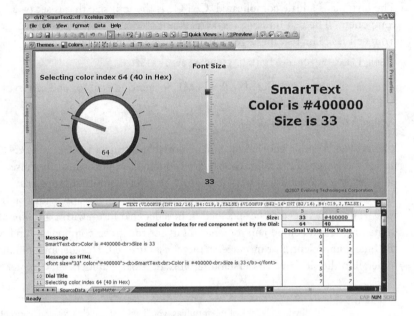

In this example, I adjust only the red component of the HTML-enabled label. If you are adventurous, you can do the same for the green and blue color elements in the label.

The formula for the hex value in cell C2 is as follows:

```
=TEXT(VLOOKUP(INT(B2/16),B4:C19,2,FALSE)&
➥VLOOKUP(B$2-16*INT(B2/16),B4:C19,2,FALSE),"00")
```

With this formula, you can use a Dial component or another component to set exactly how much red you want to appear in the text.

> **NOTE**
>
> Everything about HTML rendering that applies to Label components applies equally to Input Text Area components.

SMART TEXT SPINNERS

Xcelsius 2008 has a Spinner component for incrementing values on a spreadsheet. This is a great little facility for nudging the value of a spreadsheet cell. Other spreadsheet formulas can use a Spinner component to look up data or compute some numeric coefficient in a complicated formula. Whatever the case may be, using a Spinner component is simple:

- You map its value to a spreadsheet cell.
- You can set its title.
- You can also set the lower and upper limits of the spinner's value.

However, a Spinner component has some drawbacks:

- It consumes a lot of screen space. If you have a lot of spreadsheet cells you want to control using Spinner components, you'll quickly run out of screen space. (I have a solution for this, which is covered later in this chapter.)

- You may only want to use the up/down arrows and not want to display the numeric value in a Spinner component. You might, for instance, want to use a Spinner component to adjust a calendar date in one of the cells of your underlying spreadsheet. Calendar dates are represented using numeric values. You might see the value 39993 in a spinner. Most dashboard users would fail to associate this as the serialized date value for June 29, 2009. It would be much easier to display only the date represented and hide the numeric value, even though it is the numeric value that is being adjusted.

To tackle the second issue, you can create a text-based spinner (see Figure 12.7 or open the file ch12_TextSpinner.xlf).

Figure 12.7
Replacing the numeric value of a Spinner component with its text representation.

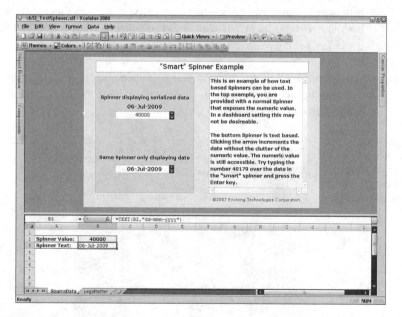

Here is the basic idea:

- Keep the numeric value set by the Spinner component, but shrink its font size down to zero.

- Reposition the Spinner component's title so that it sits where the Spinner component's numeric value would have appeared.
- Use the title to display some descriptive text that is directly associated with the Spinner component value or some follow-on computation based on it.

The example shown in Figure 12.7 uses the text representations of dates in place of their serialized values. You may recall from Chapter 3, "Getting Familiar with Xcelsius 2008," that calendar dates are kept in your spreadsheet as numeric values. This opens the door for date arithmetic: You can easily compute what day of the week it would be 30 days from today (refer to Chapter 3).

Converting a date to the serialized day number is great, but this numeric value is of little benefit to a CEO clicking a Spinner component to change the date for values retrieved from a database. Displaying the numeric value only creates visual clutter. By replacing a conventional spinner with a text-based spinner, you accomplish the following:

- You reduce the visual footprint of the spinner because the title is now inside the spinner button instead of hovering over it.
- You eliminate the visual display of information that would not be wanted or used.
- You lose no capability whatsoever. Just because the font size for the numeric value is zero doesn't mean you can't select it and type in a new value as you would with a regular Spinner component. (As with a regular Spinner component, you need to press the Enter key for the override value to take effect.)

If you think this is all there is to text-based spinners, you're mistaken. You can also make them smarter by adding alerts. Adding alerts is straightforward (see Figure 12.8 or open the file ch12_AlertBasedTextSpinner.xlf).

Figure 12.8
This text-based spinner can display appropriate colorized alerts based on the hidden value.

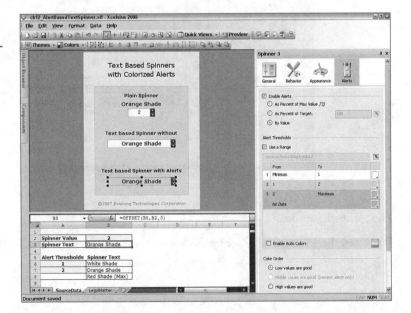

As in the previous example, the spinner value in Figure 12.8 is replaced with the spinner text. The spinner text for cell B3 uses the following OFFSET formula:

```
=OFFSET(B5,B2,0)
```

When the spinner value is set to 1, the text message White Shade is produced. When it is set to the value 2, the message Orange Shade appears. Otherwise, the text message Red Shade (Max) is produced.

LIST BOX AND OTHER INLINE ALERTS

 One of the new and interesting features of Xcelsius 2008 is the addition of embedded, or inline, alerts. With these alerts, a component can display an alert alongside the various clickable options within the component. The benefit of this should be obvious: Navigation components within a dashboard also double as conveyors of information. This helps to streamline the assimilation of information within an already high-density footprint.

Figure 12.9 shows the setup (see also the file ch12_InlinedAlerts.xlf). In this example, colorized alerts are adjacent to the List Box component options North, South, East, and West. The colors are based on the context. In this case, there are two possible contexts: Sales and Gross Profit.

Figure 12.9
You can set up inline alerts for components such as List Box components or Label Based Menu components.

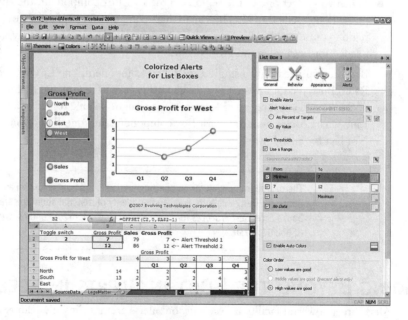

The idea here is to get two for the price of one. You have one List Box component that lets you select (in this example) a geographic region. The regions are going to be the same, regardless of whether you want to view sales revenue or gross profit. There is no reason to peg the colorization based on sales only or gross profit only.

To summarize, the dashboard design strategy is as follows:

- You have two or more datasets (in this case, quarterly sales and gross profit). Using the radio buttons, you can choose which dataset you want and retrieve it. In this example, the quarterly data for sales resides in cells I7:L10, and quarterly data for gross profit resides in N7:Q10. When you click the Sales or Gross Profit radio button, the respective data gets pulled into cells D7:G10.

- While you are pulling in the detailed dataset, you can also pull the specific threshold values from cells C2:D3 into cells B2:B3.

- The List Box component only knows about the regions mapped in cells A7:A10 (for North, South, East, and West). For the inline colorized alert, it is going to look at the values of the cells in B7:B10 and compare them to the threshold values in cells B2:B3. The List Box component doesn't know where or how the numbers in cells B7:B10 (and, for that matter, the cells B2:B3) originated. Frankly, it doesn't care. It just uses the numbers it has.

  Incidentally, the numbers in cells B7:B10 are computed using the sum of the quarterly data. For example, the formula for B7 is as follows:

  `=SUM(D7:G7)`

- When you select one of the regions in the List Box component, the appropriate data is pushed onto cells B5:G5. The Line Chart component simply plots the data for the region you select. Because context switching is being used here, only one chart is needed for both sales and gross profit.

  Because you need only a single Line Chart component, one List Box component, and a Radio Button component, your dashboard is easy to design and maintain. Later, if you decide to add another 4 or 14 datasets, you might be able to get away with just one Line Chart component, one List Box component, and one Radio Button component. Not bad for a day's work.

NOTE

> The overall framework for architecting this type of design is known as the Layered Approach Design Pattern. You can find plenty of material about this framework in my books *Excel Best Practices for Business* (ISBN: 076454120X) and *Escape from Excel Hell* (ISBN: 0741773182).

GOING BEYOND THE BUILT-IN ALERTS IN XCELSIUS

Alerts are a powerful facility in Xcelsius, but alerts are not the only feature that can make data appear smart. Chapter 6, "Single Value Components: Dials, Gauges, Speedometers, and the Like," describes the Shared Component Framework, and Chapter 7, "Using Multi-Layer Visibility in Your Dashboards and Visualizations," describes dynamic visibility.

While I cover some aspects of smart sliders in Chapter 6, I want to discuss some more aspects of these components here.

Smart sliders solve a very interesting problem, and they are easy to set up and accomplish with Xcelsius but considerably more difficult to use with Excel by itself. Let's look at an example of 3 companies that are competing for a fixed amount of business. It could be contracts awarded by a government agency, or it could be a projection regarding a fixed-size market. It doesn't need to be 3 companies; it could just as easily be 13 or 130 companies. To keep thing simple, though, let's stick with 3 companies (Company A, Company B, and Company C) and only address the issue of how to split up the pie.

If one company succeeds in getting a large portion of the business, what's up for grabs shrinks accordingly. How can you allocate the business among the three companies so that it is impossible for all three companies to collectively have more than 100% of the business market? Think a moment about how you would do this. Specifically, how could you do it without applying any kind of trial-and-error methodology? This is one of those problems where the answer is not obvious until you see the solution, and then the solution is very obvious.

Try reasoning out the problem by using numbers. Assume for the moment that Company A has 10% of the total business, Company B has 25%, and Company C has 12%. Collectively, between three companies, 47% (= 10% + 25% + 12%) is already allocated. This means that what's up for grabs is 53% (= 100% − 47%). Therefore, under the prevailing circumstances, the most that Company A can hope to achieve is the 10% it already has plus the 53% of what's up for grabs. So Company A can't go above 63%. Similarly, Company B only has the potential to get up to a 78% market share, as it can't push the market share more than 53% beyond the 25% share it already has. The most Company C can achieve is 65%.

As any of these companies gain in market share, the amount that's up for grabs diminishes. Figure 12.10 shows this within a dashboard (see also the file ch12_SmartSlider.xlf).

Figure 12.10
You can use smart sliders and progress bars to decide who ultimately controls the largest segment of the market.

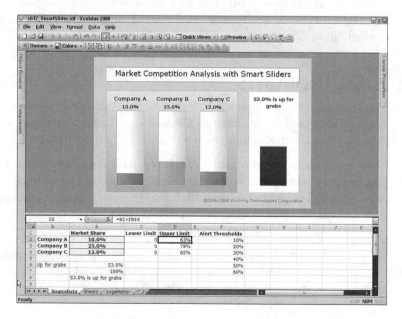

12

Here is the setup for this dashboard:

- The market share for each of the three companies can be found in three input cells—one each for Companies A, B, and C. They are located in cells B2 through B4. If you have more companies, you simply expand the number of input cells.

- Cell B6 calculates the unallocated portion:

  `=100%-SUM(B2:B4)`

- The upper limit for each of the smart sliders or progress bars is the sum of the current market share for the company plus the amount up for grabs (cell B6). For Company A, this is computed in cell D2, using the following formula:

  `=B2+B6`

- For each of the companies, there is a vertical progress bar. If you want, you can use a slider or dial.

- A column chart on the right side of the dashboard shows how much market share remains unallocated. In this chart I've stripped away the chart axes and labels for easier visualization.

When a dashboard user clicks and drags any of the progress bars, all the other bars and the column chart are automatically resized. A dashboard user can click and drag each of the company progress bars in both up and down directions.

Notice that each of the vertical progress bars is colorized based on the level of market share achieved. If 100% of market share is allocated approximately evenly among the three companies, they all get a yellow coloration or rating. If one of the companies winds up with a significantly smaller market share, then it gets tagged with a red color.

Because of the way these smart progress bars are used, they double as input devices (for adjusting market share of a specific company) and output devices (that is, their color automatically changes to reveal their status).

CLOSING THOUGHTS

Alerts can convey extra information that wouldn't necessarily be shown in an otherwise conventional dashboard or visualization. The basic premise is that alerts show themselves when they are needed, and when they are not needed, they get out of the way.

Alerts are handy in all sorts of situations. If you are doing fundraising or monitoring how your company's division economized on expenses, it would be nice to have an alert that signals when you have achieved your goal. It may be more important to signal that you are not achieving a critical goal or milestone on a timely basis.

It's important to draw a distinction between alerts that colorize already present components and ones that suddenly pop up onscreen. The latter category not only provides a visual cue but can also provide a new navigation pathway in your dashboard. You might, for instance, accompany an alert text message with a URL button.

This chapter explores both the basic functionality of visual alerts built into Xcelsius 2008 and creative uses of alerts. What constitutes an alert is relative. The threshold that a dashboard user might want to apply is something that can and should be tunable. This chapter shows how to set up sliders so that dashboard users can interactively "try on" different alert thresholds.

In addition to alerts, Xcelsius 2008 enables you to use smart text. Something magical happens when you combine a Label component capable of HTML rendering with text content that is dynamically generated from a spreadsheet formula. Instantly, you can have text that can change its size, color, and other attributes. This chameleon-like capability shifts the landscape of dashboard functionality, giving you sophisticated capabilities with inexpensive spreadsheet formulas.

Label and Input Text Area components are not the only components that are smart. You can also get creative with spinner buttons by, for example, making them text based.

There's a whole range of interesting new features to explore in Xcelsius 2008. For example, inline alerts are visible and adjacent to clickable options of a component, such as a List Box component or a Label Based Menu component. This chapter shows how to exploit these capabilities by combining them with context switching. This approach is premised on a framework known as the Layered Approach Design Pattern.

This chapter concludes by looking at the anatomy of smart sliders. Smart sliders are components that work with other components to create complex behavior within dashboards and visualizations. A simple and easy-to-follow example involves multiple agents vying for a limited resource. By using smart sliders, you can dynamically allocate resources with simplicity and elegance.

Enabling alerts in traditional input components such as sliders, progress bars, and dials allows them to serve as capable readout devices. The idea of dashboard components possessing both input and readout capabilities is likely to gain traction.

Chapter 13, "Working with Less-Than-Optimal Data," addresses the problems and issues of dealing with less–than-ideal data in your dashboards.

12

CHAPTER **13**

WORKING WITH LESS-THAN-OPTIMAL DATA

In this chapter

We all want dashboards to be stunning. The "wow" factor frequently overshadows the process of preparing underlying numbers for use with dashboard visualization. But a dashboard based on less-than-optimal data can suffer from a number of problems. Consider the following:

- In some cases, data is incomplete.
- You might at some point need to deftly disclose the fact that the numbers in your dashboard differ from those of accounting by $5 million.
- You may have two different sources of data that conflict on reported amounts.
- You might need to transform data that is not geared toward use within a dashboard.

The focus of this chapter is getting data in usable form and establishing the integrity of data and formulas. As you can tell, this chapter is spreadsheet centric. The reason should be clear: For all the sizzle and pizzazz that a dashboard can bring, it's the integrity of the underlying data and the way it's portrayed that brings value to a dashboard. If you don't get the numbers correct and work in a manner suited for the dashboard, the resulting dashboard may look pretty on the outside, but underneath it could be seriously limping or faltering. If you are going to tackle such problems, you need to trace them back to their roots—the digitization of data.

THE DIGITIZATION OF DATA

It is not out of the ordinary to be engulfed in a sea of data. During the twentieth century, there was a point in time when very little information was digitized. Today, it seems the tables have turned; there is relatively little that is not already digitized or digitizable.

The digitization of information can introduce errors. Errors and problems that plague your datasets have the potential to compromise your dashboards. For this reason, I briefly outline some of the vagaries related to the digitization of data.

There are three ways of digitizing data:

- **Category I digitization**: You can simply record data that is already digital. This type of digitization is typical of transaction processing and supply chain management systems, where the data that is created is generated by computer programs.
- **Category II digitization**: Non-digital data can be digitized automatically. An example of this might be the use of optical character recognition (OCR) in the scanning of text documents. If a document is being scanned, an OCR system could easily mistake the letter *o* for the number 0 or vice versa.
- **Category III digitization**: You can digitize data by directly entering it yourself.

Category I digitized data can be thought of as *data that is born digital*. Category II digitized data goes through a structured or automated conversion. Category III digitized data entails a more manual conversion process, where the primary driver of quality of the digitized data is the human doing the data entry. From a pragmatic standpoint, the real distinction between the last two categories is that the process and results of converting information tends to be repeatable for Category II digitized data. If, for instance, you scan a document and then scan it a second time with the same equipment and software, the result should be identical or nearly identical.

Each of these three categories has unique classes of errors and methodologies for dealing with them.

DEALING WITH CATEGORY I DIGITIZATION ERRORS

With Category I digitization, the big bugaboo is atomicity of transactions. When you have thousands or millions of transactions, or even billions of transactions, there's bound to be a hiccup somewhere at some point in time. Given the speed and sheer volume of transactions, errors can quickly compound and are hard to eradicate.

One of the ways to prevent errors from creeping in is to make transactions *atomic*. That is, ensure that there is no such thing as a half-complete transaction. If the system of processing involves journal entries in an accounting system, a journal entry where the total debits don't match the total credits could not be considered atomic. If the recorded transaction is not atomic, the transaction is rejected and rolled back to its state just before the transaction was attempted.

In transaction processing, it is better to have some missing information or complete information that takes slightly longer to process than it is to have a snappy system whose validity lacks integrity. This is the way of life for large database systems.

DEALING WITH CATEGORY II DIGITIZATION ERRORS

With Category II, automated digitization of inherently non-digital data can be plagued by two kinds of issues—systematic and random errors.

Systematic errors are the easy ones to fix. If you scan a 100-page printed document, you may find that the same mistake is consistently repeated. You could clean up the document using global search and replace. By the time you fix all the errors in the first 15 or so pages of a 100-page document, there may be very few uncaught errors in the remaining 85 pages.

You might think issues such as scanning are not so significant because most important documents are already in digital form, but this is not always the case. There are times when there is a need to digitize documents. For example, a business may come across a printed document from a competitor and want to prove copyright infringement. As another example, say that new economic data is printed, and you need to incorporate those numbers in your analyses and projections.

Scanning is not the only form for automating the digitization of non-digital data, but it is a common mechanism, and it is easy to understand. Other forms involve screen scraping and graphical data digitizers.

13

DEALING WITH CATEGORY III DIGITIZATION ERRORS

Category III involves challenges associated with the creation of digital data. There are many kinds of issues that arise because of human error. Here are some examples you may be able to guard against:

- Transposition of digits
- Removal of extraneous spaces in a list of names
- Rounding and truncation errors
- Poorly positioned data on a worksheet

FIXING PROBLEMATIC SPREADSHEETS

Many problems can get in between your data and a superlative dashboard. Often, it's the tiny little gotchas that are problematic. The key is to know how to deal with them. This section walks you through a bunch of them.

DETECTING THE PRESENCE OF TRANSPOSED DIGITS

Every now and then, someone may supply you with detailed data that's basically correct, but something is wrong with it. Say that you are given a list of 100 numbers that have been hand entered into a spreadsheet. The total of all your numbers is 1691472. It should be 1628472 (see the spreadsheet file ch13_TransposedDigitsTest.xls). If you have such a discrepancy, you either need to go to the source to chase down the differences or explain why or how they are different. It would help if you could limit the initial scope of your search. In this particular example, your discrepancy is exactly 63000. None of the other numbers in your dataset have such nicely rounded digits. They're all numbers like 23023 and 27051.

It's a good guess that the error resides in the data you already have and is not based on a missing entry. If you're an accountant or a bookkeeper, you would likely surmise that a pair of digits may have accidentally been transposed. It is generally common knowledge within the accounting community that if you have two sets of totals that should be the same and differ by an exact multiple of 9, chances are that a pair of digits within the sub-elements of the total have been transposed. The number 63,000 happens to be an exact multiple of 9.

If you rummage through the list of numbers in Figure 13.1 (or open the file ch13_TransposedDigitsTest.xls), you will quickly see that the size of this discrepancy is larger than any of the detailed numbers, save one. Within the list there is an entry in the amount of 81347. It is much larger than the other entries; all the others are under 38000. This spreadsheet not only includes a tool that determines whether there is a possible transposition of digits, it deftly flags which of the numbers may have been transposed.

Figure 13.1
Spreadsheet tool for testing and detecting digit transposition.

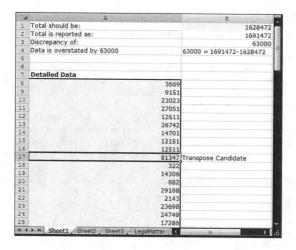

	A	B
1	Total should be:	1628472
2	Total is reported as:	1691472
3	Discrepancy of:	63000
4	Data is overstated by 63000	63000 = 1691472-1628472
5		
6		
7	**Detailed Data**	
8	3669	
9	9151	
10	23023	
11	27051	
12	12611	
13	26742	
14	14701	
15	12151	
16	12511	
17	81347	Transpose Candidate
18	322	
19	14306	
20	682	
21	29168	
22	2143	
23	23698	
24	24749	
25	17286	

Sheet1 / Sheet2 / Sheet3 / LegalMatter

NOTE

There are several limitations of this tool. Numbers must be whole numbers in the range of 0 through 99999. In addition, the tool can only handle a transposition of an adjacent pair of digits in a single entry.

DEALING WITH RAW DATA

 I would like to draw a distinction between raw and unclean data, even though the treatment of the two types of data can be dealt with using similar techniques. Raw data is data that may be valid but may require some kind of processing before it takes a useful form.

For example, you might download some economic or demographic information from a government agency. You can't count on government agencies always providing direct file compatibility with Excel or, for that matter, any of your other favorite software products. Frequently, however, these agencies provide files that are generic and transparent enough that they can be made to work with Excel.

The following snippet of text is typical of data you might get from a government agency:

```
AL35004    6998    2815     49387881     259146    19.068768    0.100057
AL3500     8985    3690     92158183      14126    35.582475    0.005454
AL35006    3109    1488    339241043    1012342   130.981705    0.390867
AL35007   20157    7762    128235102     752940    49.511852    0.290712
AL35010   21732   10033    616923491    1904553   238.195502    0.735352
AL35014    4480    1725    245144985    1878618    94.651012    0.725338
```

Although the text is human readable, it does not lend itself to analysis. Each line of text is a continuous stream of characters, and there is no hard segmenting of data into individual

13

columns. You might get this data in a text file and need to separate the data into individual columns. You might be given a specification like this:

```
Columns 1-2: United States Postal Service State Abbreviation
Columns 3-4: State Federal Information Processing Standard (FIPS) code
Columns 5-7: FIPS county code
Columns 9-15: Total Population (2000)
Columns 17-24: Total Housing Units (2000)
Columns 26-38: Land Area (square meters) - Created for statistical purposes only.
Columns 40-52: Water Area(square meters) - Created for statistical purposes only.
Columns 54-64: Land Area (square miles) - Created for statistical purposes only.
Columns 66-77: Water Area (square miles) - Created for statistical purposes only.
```

You can use a couple strategies to get a dataset of this kind into a usable form. One of them is to have Excel convert the data for you (see Figure 13.2).

Figure 13.2
Using an Excel wizard to import and convert text.

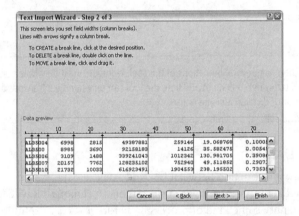

If you need to import data, using an Excel wizard to convert text to columns is expedient and reliable. In certain situations, you might want to repeatedly tweak the processing of your source data to match different kinds of criteria. In such cases, a splitter tool like the one shown in Figure 13.3 might work for you.

DEALING WITH UNCLEAN DATA

When you first receive data from a third-party source, it may contain irregularities that are purely cosmetic. These could be problematic in your dashboard. For instance, having two spaces between the first and last names in a list of names could cause your lookups to work improperly.

A data scrubber can help make your data conform to a uniform structure by helping with the following:

- You might want to remove extra spaces between names.

- Occasionally, you might see some unusual symbols appearing in a spreadsheet cell. Excel may render them as hollow rectangular boxes.

Figure 13.3
Spreadsheet formulas can read parsing criteria from a table and extract column data.

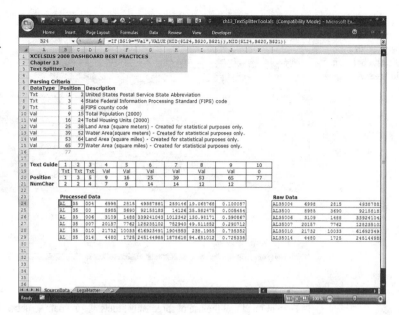

- It may be important to ensure that all names in a list are properly and uniformly capitalized. For example, "Loren Abdulezer" is the same person as "LOREN ABDULEZER".

- Inconsistent use of periods with middle initial can cause problems. I think you would agree that "John Q Adams" and "John Q. Adams" refer to the same person.

- Depending on your needs, you might want to flag the names in your list for redundancies.

The spreadsheet file ch13_DataScrubberToolset.xls (see Figure 13.4) shows how you can use a data scrubber to fix such problems. The basic approach is to start with a list of names in the left column; zap or clean the gremlins; trim the excess spaces; convert to upper, proper, or lowercase form; and eliminate period symbols. The spreadsheet performs each of these steps in succession. You can, of course, modify the spreadsheet to add your own housekeeping tasks.

There are several things to note here:

- When working with lists and names, I recommend using a monospace font, such as Courier or Courier New, to view your data. That way, every letter takes up the same amount of horizontal space, and it's easier to see discrepancies.

- You want to scrub your data *before* it reaches Xcelsius 2008. One reason for this is that you can make use of spreadsheet functions that are not supported by Xcelsius 2008. For instance, the Excel functions CLEAN and PROPER help you clean up data, but they are not supported in Xcelsius 2008.

Figure 13.4
Data scrubbing tools can help you fix problematic data before it gets to Xcelsius.

	A	B	C	D	E	F
1	XCELSIUS 2008 DASHBOARD BEST PRACTICES					
2	Chapter 13 - Data Scrubber Toolset					
3	Cleaning up of a list of names					
4						
5					Subst '.' with ' '	Highlight
6	Original List	Cleaned	Trimmed	Proper		Possible Problems
7	Jane ☐Doe	Jane Doe	Jane Doe	UPPER	ne Doe	Jane Doe
8	Mary Smith	Mary Smith	Mary Smith	Proper	ry Smith	Mary Smith
9	Jane P. Doe	Jane P. Doe	Jane P. Doe	lower Jane P. Doe	Jane P Doe	Jane P Doe
10	John Adams	John Adams	John Adams	John Adams	John Adams	John Adams
11	Jane P Doe	Jane P Doe	Jane P Doe	Jane P Doe	Jane P Doe	Jane P Doe
12	Jane C Doe	Jane C Doe	Jane C Doe	Jane C Doe	Jane C Doe	Jane C Doe
13	John Doe	John Doe	John Doe	John Doe	John Doe	John Doe
14	Jane P Doe	Jane P Doe	Jane P Doe	Jane P Doe	Jane P Doe	Jane P Doe
15	J Doe	J Doe	J Doe	J Doe	J Doe	J Doe
16	jane P Doe	jane P Doe	jane P Doe	Jane P Doe	Jane P Doe	Jane P Doe
17	J. Adams	J. Adams	J. Adams	J. Adams	J Adams	J Adams
18	john smith	john smith	john smith	John Smith	John Smith	John Smith
19	L. Abdulezer	L. Abdulezer	L. Abdulezer	L. Abdulezer	L Abdulezer	L Abdulezer
20	jon a smith	jon a smith	jon a smith	Jon A Smith	Jon A Smith	Jon A Smith
21	john B. sMith	john B. sMith	john B. sMith	John B. Smith	John B Smith	John B Smith
22	John Q.Adams	John Q.Adams	John Q.Adams	John Q.Adams	John Q.Adams	John Q.Adams
23	Jane☐Doe	JaneDoe	JaneDoe	Janedoe	Janedoe	Janedoe
24	Jane P.☐Doe	Jane P.Doe	Jane P.Doe	Jane P.Doe	Jane P.Doe	Jane P.Doe
25						
26						
27						
28						
29						
30						
31						
32						

NameCleanup / Config / LegalMatter

NOTE

Keep in mind that the use of spreadsheet tools like the data scrubber in this example is for the purpose of preparing data that will eventually be used by Xcelsius. When you import data to Xcelsius, you only need to import the finalized data. There is no need to import all the complicated formulas used to clean the data.

When you have your final list of names all squeaky clean and pristine, you can copy it and use Paste Special, Values to paste it onto a new workbook that Xcelsius can use. Because it is all text, there is no lingering memory of the exotic formulas used to prepare the data.

NOTE

When using the PROPER function, be aware that it capitalizes the first letter of every word in a phrase. For example, SOUTH CAROLINA is converted to South Carolina, and DISTRICT OF COLUMBIA is converted to District Of Columbia. If you want the latter phrase to appear as District of Columbia, you need to be prepared to do some additional processing or hand editing.

DEALING WITH ROUNDING AND TRUNCATION ERRORS

It can be very frustrating trying to get rounded numbers and their totals to work the way you want. The main challenge occurs when you try rounding numbers that then need to be added together. Figure 13.5 (or open the file ch13_rounding.xls) shows a set of 15 numbers that add up to 56,175,478.88. You tell your boss that the revenue for this quarter is

$56,175,000. If you round the 15 numbers to the nearest thousand and then add them together, they total $56,174,000. I know it sounds strange that a list of numbers *above* 56 million 175 thousand gets rounded *down* to 56 million 174 thousand. These things can and do frequently happen.

Figure 13.5
Discrepancies can arise when you round numbers.

	Data	Original Values	Adjustment	Revised Values	Rounded Value	Difference
			Precision	-3	Nearest value within 1000	
5	Item 1	9,501,482.33		9,501,482.33	9,501,000.00	482.33
6	Item 2	3,365,488.28		3,365,488.28	3,365,000.00	488.28
7	Item 3	4,987,948.87		4,987,948.87	4,988,000.00	-51.13
8	Item 4	278,936.81		278,936.81	279,000.00	-63.19
9	Item 5	7,005,496.67		7,005,496.67	7,005,000.00	496.67
10	Item 6	9,314,469.79		9,314,469.79	9,314,000.00	469.79
11	Item 7	3,057,940.99		3,057,940.99	3,058,000.00	-59.01
12	Item 8	3,612,914.67		3,612,914.67	3,613,000.00	-85.33
13	Item 9	2,060,995.46		2,060,995.46	2,061,000.00	-4.54
14	Item 10	8,408,055.59		8,408,055.59	8,408,000.00	55.59
15	Item 11	7,051,693.60		7,051,693.60	7,052,000.00	-306.40
16	Item 12	4,004,146.82		4,004,146.82	4,004,000.00	146.82
17	Item 13	-1,407,287.40		-1,407,287.40	-1,407,000.00	-287.40
18	Item 14	-4,427,803.05		-4,427,803.05	-4,428,000.00	196.95
19	Item 15	-639,000.55		-639,000.55	-639,000.00	-0.55
20	Total	56,175,478.88	0.00	56,175,478.88	56,174,000.00	1,478.88

AdjustingWorksheet / LegalMatter

TIP

Incidentally, the tool shown in Figure 13.5 allows you to set the number of decimal digits used for rounding (the colorized cell D2). If you want the numbers rounded to the nearest penny, you set the precision to 2 (for two decimal places). If you want the numbers rounded to the nearest dollar, you set the precision to 0 (for zero decimal places). To round to the nearest hundred, you set the precision to -2, and for rounding to the nearest thousand, you set it to -3.

With a minimal amount of adjusting to the raw numbers, you can tweak the rounded totals. An adjustment of $3.33 in cell C9 is enough to get the numbers rounded so that they total $56,175,000 (see Figure 13.6). The value of 7,005,496.67 gets bumped up to 7,005,500. When rounded to the nearest thousand it is 7,006,000.

Figure 13.6
Adding a tiny adjustment of $3.33 bumps up the rounding so that the total is 1,000 higher.

	Data	Original Values	Adjustment	Revised Values	Rounded Value	Difference
			Precision	-3	Nearest value within 1000	
5	Item 1	9,501,482.33		9,501,482.33	9,501,000.00	482.33
6	Item 2	3,365,488.28		3,365,488.28	3,365,000.00	488.28
7	Item 3	4,987,948.87		4,987,948.87	4,988,000.00	-51.13
8	Item 4	278,936.81		278,936.81	279,000.00	-63.19
9	Item 5	7,005,496.67	3.33	7,005,500.00	7,006,000.00	-500.00
10	Item 6	9,314,469.79		9,314,469.79	9,314,000.00	469.79
11	Item 7	3,057,940.99		3,057,940.99	3,058,000.00	-59.01
12	Item 8	3,612,914.67		3,612,914.67	3,613,000.00	-85.33
13	Item 9	2,060,995.46		2,060,995.46	2,061,000.00	-4.54
14	Item 10	8,408,055.59		8,408,055.59	8,408,000.00	55.59
15	Item 11	7,051,693.60		7,051,693.60	7,052,000.00	-306.40
16	Item 12	4,004,146.82		4,004,146.82	4,004,000.00	146.82
17	Item 13	-1,407,287.40		-1,407,287.40	-1,407,000.00	-287.40
18	Item 14	-4,427,803.05		-4,427,803.05	-4,428,000.00	196.95
19	Item 15	-639,000.55		-639,000.55	-639,000.00	-0.55
20	Total	56,175,478.88	3.33	56,175,482.21	56,175,000.00	482.21

AdjustingWorksheet / LegalMatter

13

You can fix the apparent discrepancy by adjusting numbers very close to the borderline for rounding up or down. It suffices to add $3.33 to the fifth item in the list of numbers to increase the totals of the rounded numbers to $56,175,000.

CAUTION

It is very easy to go overboard with tweaking numbers that get rounded. In this example, an adjustment of $62.93 ($17.67, $11.72, $3.33, and $30.21 for items 1, 2, 5, and 6, respectively) drives the total to $56,178,000. Getting creative and adjusting numbers to suit your needs is misleading and will most surely come back to haunt you. Whenever you make adjustments for rounding purposes, be sure to properly disclose the adjustments you are making and why you are making them.

POORLY POSITIONED DATA ON A WORKSHEET

In the following example (see Figure 13.7 or open the file ch13_PoorSpreadsheetLayout.xlf), the List Box component pushes the row of data for the selected product onto cells B10:F10. This dashboard is well behaved but can wreak havoc when you expand the number of products.

Figure 13.7
The layout of this spreadsheet cramps future spreadsheet changes.

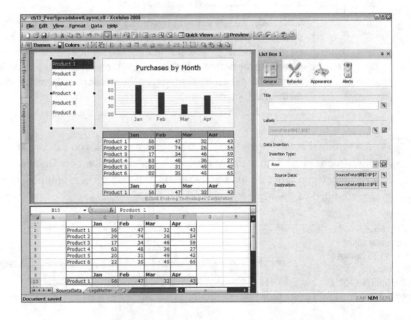

This sample dashboard is a classic example of poor spreadsheet layout. It is almost literally set to fall on its own sword. When spreadsheets and dashboards are as simple as this example, they are easy to fix. Instead of having the destination cells (the highlighted yellow cells, B10:F10) immediately below the source data (cells B2:F8), you should position the destination cells above the source data. Doing so gives the source data freedom to grow, in case you need to select from more than six products.

When your dashboards and visualizations become large and complex, with many moving parts, making such changes can be problematic.

DETECTING AND FIXING FORMULA PROBLEMS

Small spreadsheets are easy to handle, validate, and, where necessary, fix. When dashboards and underlying spreadsheets become large and complex, the once-easy-to-fix problems are suddenly not so simple to deal with. The key is to eliminate spreadsheet formula problems as you go along. Two problems commonly get people into hot water:

- Embedded hardwired values within spreadsheet formulas
- Absolute, relative, and hybrid cell references

ISSUES WITH HARDWIRED VALUES AND WHAT TO DO WITH THEM

 Spreadsheets are plagued with small and easy-to-correct spreadsheet formula errors and deficiencies. If these annoyances are not weeded out early, they can blossom into big problems. One important type of problem to tackle is hardwired values embedded in spreadsheet formulas. You might have a formula like this:

```
=A2*1.025^B1
```

In this example, cell A2 is the principal, the interest rate is 2.5%, and the time period is in cell B1. It's a simple enough calculation. On the face of it, nothing really looks wrong. But hardwiring the interest rate with the formula is a ticking time bomb. Today, you have this one formula that's a cinch to validate and modify. What's going to happen when you have a spreadsheet with 200 formulas? Let me revise that a bit. In Excel and most any spreadsheet, it is exceedingly easy to replicate formulas, so maybe there could be a couple thousand formulas floating around, some on different worksheets. Many of them may be easy, like this simple formula involving interest. Or a spreadsheet could have a half dozen complicated formulas. It is easy to see how an innocuous formula (such as `=A2*1.025^B1`) could get lost in the shuffle.

The basic solution for embedded hardwired values is to quarantine them. By this, I mean place the hardwired value in an isolated cell and have *all* formulas that previously embedded that value reference the quarantined cell. Then, if you need to make a change to the value, you only need to do the following:

- Make that change in just one place, without worrying about updating multiple formulas.
- Because that isolated value is just a value and not a formula, use Xcelsius to change the value directly from the dashboard. To do so, you might be able to use a slider or similar component.

In this example, you could alter the formula in either of two ways. First, you could place the value 1.025 in an isolated cell, such as cell A1, and use a formula like this:

```
=A2*A1^B1
```

Alternatively, you could place the rate 0.025 in a cell such as A1 and use the following formula:

```
=A2*(1+A1)^B1
```

I know the value 1 in this formula is hardwired. This kind of hardwiring is definitional in nature; it is not going to change. Similarly, the number of months in a year won't change, so it is fair to use the factor 12 to convert months to years and vice versa.

Either of these two approaches to handling the hardwired value is equally valid. The choice depends on your personal preference.

USING ABSOLUTE, RELATIVE, AND HYBRID CELL REFERENCES IN FORMULAS

The section "Spreadsheet Cell References" in Chapter 4, "Embedded Spreadsheets: The Secret Sauce of Xcelsius 2008," explains how absolute, relative, and hybrid cell references work in spreadsheet formulas. To quickly recap, the dollar sign before the column letter or row number keeps the respective column or row reference constant when the cell is replicated.

The following sections provide some guidelines for deciding when to use each kind of referencing in your formulas.

SETTING UP CELL REFERENCES IN A VLOOKUP FORMULA   Say that you need to perform a lookup on three of your customers whose names appear in cells A1, A2, and A3. The information is looked up against a comprehensive table of data in cells T1 through Z300. This table has seven columns. The customer names are in column T, and the credit rating you are interested in appears in the seventh column, Z.

To look up the rating for the customer in cell A1, you could use a formula like this:

```
=VLOOKUP(A1,T1:Z300,7,FALSE)
```

This formula is okay, but if you replicate the formula to the next cell down so it looks up the value for cell A2, you might have this:

```
=VLOOKUP(A2,T2:Z301,7,FALSE)
```

This is not what you want. The lookup table should still be set to T1:Z300 and not T2:Z301. If the value of A2 doesn't appear in the very first row of your lookup table, the problem in your formula may go unnoticed. You can guard against problems of this kind by appropriately inserting dollar signs in the cell references. Here is one such formula:

```
=VLOOKUP(A1,$T$1:$Z$300,7,FALSE)
```

When you replicate this formula down to the two cells below, these are the formulas:

```
=VLOOKUP(A2,$T$1:$Z$300,7,FALSE)
=VLOOKUP(A3,$T$1:$Z$300,7,FALSE)
```

This is basically what you want, but it can be improved. Notice that in these three formulas, the lookup value is always in column A, and this doesn't change. You might want to keep the lookup column so that it is always set to column A. If so, you can use the following formula:

```
=VLOOKUP($A1,$T$1:$Z$300,7,FALSE)
```

When you replicate the formula using copy and paste, it should behave in the expected manner.

It shouldn't be surprising that I have yet another improvement to the formula. You may have noticed that this formula contains a hardwired value—the number 7 for the seventh column in the lookup table. Today you are interested in how much business you did with the customer during the previous sales cycle, which might reside in column Y (or the sixth column) of your lookup table. But it would be best to place the hardwired number 7 (or 6, if you are interested in column Y) in an isolated cell such as C1. Your lookup formula then becomes the following:

```
=VLOOKUP($A1,$T$1:$Z$300,$C$1,FALSE)
```

Admittedly, this formula looks more complicated than the original, but it doesn't fall apart when you copy and paste it to other cells.

SETTING UP CELL REFERENCES IN A MULTIPLICATION TABLE   At one point or another, we've all worked with some kind of multiplication table, where numbers across a top row and down a column, are multiplied. Creating such a table in a spreadsheet is straightforward. Here is how you do it if your top row is in row 1, starting with cell B1, and the left column is in column A, starting with cell A2. In cell B2, place the following formula:

```
=$A2*B$1
```

You can replicate this cell down and across to populate the cells in your multiplication table. Of course, you can make a more complicated table. The key here is to know how to apply the cell references, as described in the following section.

SETTING UP CELL REFERENCES IN A MORE COMPLICATED TABLE   Using the earlier example of the interest rate calculation, you could set up a table to calculate interest with various values for the principle and period and varying the interest rate by tweaking an isolated cell from a dashboard slider.

Let's assume that you have five different principal amounts in cells A2 through A6 (these could be the values 100, 200, 300, 400, and 500, for example). The time period could be in cells B1 through E1 (these could be the values 1, 2, 3, and 4, for example). The interest rate 0.025 could reside in cell A1. You can apply the following formula to cell B2:

```
=$A2*(1+$A$1)^B$1
```

You can then copy and paste this formula to all the cells in B2 through E6. Rather than copy and paste one cell at a time, you could instead use the fill-down and fill-across features of Excel (see Figure 13.8 or open the file ch13_FormulaReplication.xlf).

13

Figure 13.8
Basic setup of calculated values within a table.

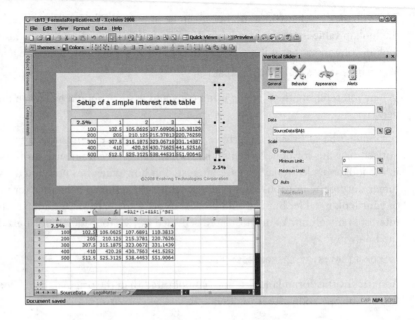

DEALING WITH SCALING ISSUES

It is very easy to get in over your head with more data than you can handle. Spreadsheets make it especially easy to drown in data. Some simple guidelines and strategies can help prevent the sheer volume of data from growing out of control:

- Eliminate redundancies in the data.

- Freeze-dry cells that are not going to change and, where necessary, retain seed formula.

- Avoid throwing in the kitchen sink, especially if the data doesn't get used.

- Use formulas where the options are combinatorially explosive.

The more formulas you have in an underlying spreadsheet, the more computational resources are going to be required to run the dashboard. Consider the multiplication table and interest rate table examples introduced earlier in the chapter. If such a table were 100 columns by 200 rows, it would have 20,000 formulas. Any dashboard relying on such a large table is bound to have problems. Of course, you can forgo creating a table altogether, replace it with a single formula, and allow the dashboard user to vary the inputs.

The key point here is that you can reduce spreadsheet overhead by eliminating formulas or freezing the computed values that don't change. To "freeze-dry" cells, you can copy the spreadsheet cells and paste their values (using Paste Special, Values) onto the same cells. Here's a trivial example that shows what happens. Place the value 0 in cell A1. In cell A2, enter the following formula:

```
=A1+10
```

Replicate the formula in cell A2 down the column—say, some 500 rows. You will get a sequence of numbers like 0, 10, 20, 30 . . . to some number such as 5,000, depending on how many rows you replicate to. If all you need is the sequence 0, 10, 20, 30, and so on, then you can safely dispose of all the formulas and simply copy and paste the values back onto themselves to erase the formulas.

Although erasing the formulas is a good idea, you might want to keep a "seed formula" around so you can regenerate a new set of computed values. In the preceding example, you can freeze-dry cells A3 and below and leave the formula =A1+10 intact in cell A2. This way, you can always generate a new set of values. Keeping one formula around involves a lot less computational overhead than having 500 cascading formulas.

NOTE

> A business associate asked me to enhance a dashboard and gave me an XLF file containing a bunch of data, most of which was not needed. Although it was nice to have the extra data, most of it could be safely eliminated. Removing it cut down the file size by over 80%.

REPURPOSING EXISTING SPREADSHEETS

 The use of spreadsheets and the ability to make them do just about anything you want is a double-edged sword. You have the freedom to make your spreadsheets as complex and elaborate as you need them to be. If you are less than diligent, no one will automatically warn you that you may be improperly applying your spreadsheet design.

One of the best favors you can do for yourself is to make your spreadsheets modular and artifact free. By modular, I mean organize your spreadsheet design so that all the source data is cleanly isolated and structured. This makes it easy to swap out the old data and replace it with a new set, even if the new data is something entirely different from what was previously used.

Similarly, you can take all your heavy-duty computations and have them work only on the data that is needed for the dashboard at the moment. You can use functions such as VLOOKUP and OFFSET to retrieve only the pieces of data you need for the values specified in the dashboard. The advantage of separating your computations is that it becomes a lot easier to repurpose them. Today, you might be monitoring the average daily customer support cost for the past week. After some major incident, company management may decide to closely monitor the peak cost on any day during the week. Having a modular design in your spreadsheet gives you the ability to make such changes with minimal effort.

If you have a whole year's worth of sales and customer support data and you are monitoring metrics for the month of March, there is no need for your spreadsheet to work out the equivalent computations for January and February. You can let VLOOKUP and other similar functions bring in the data for the month at hand.

13

It pays to isolate the portions of a spreadsheet that are used for mapping and configuration purposes or are driven by inputs from the dashboard user. To help make this concrete, I provide a simplified reference implementation of the Layered Approach Design Pattern demonstration dashboard (see Figure 13.9 or open ch13_LayeredApproachTemplate.xlf).

Figure 13.9
Simplified setup for the Layered Approach Design Pattern demonstration dashboard.

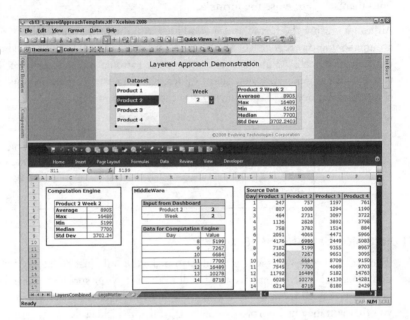

For the sake of clarity and illustration, I combine all the layers into a single worksheet. In a real-world and full-featured application, the Source Data, MiddleWare, and Computation Engine information would likely reside on separate worksheets.

Notice that the Source Data section is just plain data. There is not a single formula in this section. There are 364 rows of data, but there could just as easily be 3,640 rows of data. Of course, having more rows of data bloats the file size, and when you jump into Preview mode or generate the SWF file, it will take longer to generate. Once the SWF file is generated, it performs very smoothly. This is largely because there are 21 formulas in the whole spreadsheet. Two of them are used for cosmetic purposes to aid in readability of the spreadsheet and dashboard. The Computation Engine section is kept lean. It uses just five formulas (cells D5:D9). Seven formulas (cells I10:I16) in the MiddleWare portion, one for each day of the week, are used to retrieve the appropriate portions of data from the Source Data region. There are seven helper formulas (cells H10:H16) that identify which rows in the datasets should be retrieved.

If at some point you invent your own kind of metric, you can just write your new formula in the Computation Engine section. There is no need to worry about how it affects your source data; it doesn't. Likewise, if you want to change your source data so that you can examine 14 products instead of 4, you can. Your MiddleWare portion formulas don't need to be revised; neither do the Computation Engine section formulas.

So how do the life cycle costs and maintenance effort in managing this kind of dashboard stack up against a monolithic design? I'll let you be the judge of that.

DEALING WITH IMPROPERLY STRUCTURED DATA

 Often there is the need to convert digital data that's not quite structured the way you want it to a form suitable for use in Xcelsius. In such a situation, challenges can occur on multiple levels.

One of the dashboards used in Chapter 11, "Maps in Xcelsius" (ch11_AugmentedMap.xlf), uses a spreadsheet whose original form is not at all suited for a dashboard. Figure 13.10 shows a spreadsheet that contains state-by-state population data for various age groups:

- Total (all age groups combined)
- Under 5 years
- 5 to 13 years
- 14 to 17 years
- 18 to 24 years
- 16 years and over
- 18 years and over
- 15 to 44 years
- 45 to 64 years
- 65 years and over
- 85 years and over

There is nothing wrong with this data, but it may not be organized in a way that is useful for your needs. In a histogram, it is not very meaningful to show a side-by-side comparison of the number of people 16 years and over with those who are 18 to 24 years and the number of people ages 14 to 17 years. This data, published by the U.S. Census Bureau, may provide data useful for specific age groups, but it is difficult to use for other purposes.

The spreadsheet as it now stands is not well suited for a uniform range of ages. But all is not lost. You can back into certain numbers. For instance, it would be nice to compare the tally of people in the following age ranges:

- 45 to 64 years
- 65 to 84 years
- 85 to 104 years

These are precise 20-year intervals. The number of people who are 85 and over is virtually identical to the number of people who are 85 to 104 years.

13

Figure 13.10
Population statistics broken out by non-uniform categories.

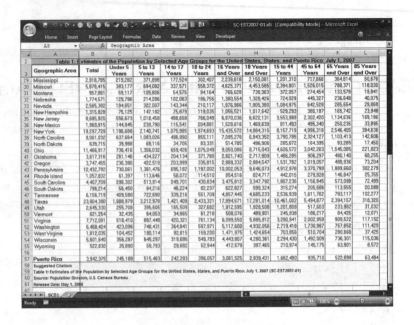

Table 1: Estimates of the Population by Selected Age Groups for the United States, States, and Puerto Rico: July 1, 2007

Geographic Area	Total	Under 5 Years	5 to 13 Years	14 to 17 Years	18 to 24 Years	15 Years and Over	18 Years and Over	15 to 44 Years	45 to 64 Years	65 Years and Over	85 Years and Over
Mississippi	2,918,785	219,282	371,898	177,524	302,407	2,239,618	2,150,061	1,201,310	717,666	364,614	50,676
Missouri	5,878,415	393,177	694,082	337,571	558,372	4,625,371	4,453,585	2,394,801	1,526,015	798,371	118,030
Montana	957,861	59,117	105,806	54,575	94,164	766,628	738,363	372,057	274,454	133,578	19,841
Nebraska	1,774,571	129,796	214,286	102,063	186,756	1,380,554	1,328,426	724,029	445,327	236,648	40,075
Nevada	2,565,382	194,651	322,007	143,344	210,117	1,976,966	1,905,380	1,084,975	642,528	285,654	29,868
New Hampshire	1,315,828	75,125	147,182	75,879	119,035	1,056,521	1,017,642	529,293	380,187	165,742	23,948
New Jersey	8,685,920	556,673	1,018,458	488,658	766,049	6,870,036	6,622,131	3,553,989	2,302,420	1,134,636	169,186
New Mexico	1,969,915	144,945	239,790	115,541	204,881	1,528,616	1,469,639	811,493	495,340	250,235	33,895
New York	19,297,729	1,196,680	2,140,741	1,075,985	1,974,693	15,435,572	14,884,315	8,157,719	4,996,316	2,546,405	384,636
North Carolina	9,061,032	637,664	1,083,026	496,990	855,111	7,095,276	6,843,352	3,790,795	2,324,127	1,103,413	142,606
North Dakota	639,715	39,988	68,116	34,705	83,331	514,785	496,906	265,672	164,395	93,285	17,450
Ohio	11,466,917	736,416	1,356,032	659,426	1,075,049	9,050,086	8,715,043	4,626,572	3,042,263	1,545,085	221,823
Oklahoma	3,617,316	261,146	434,227	204,134	371,780	2,821,740	2,717,809	1,486,285	906,297	480,140	68,255
Oregon	3,747,455	236,390	422,519	203,999	335,815	2,988,332	2,884,547	1,631,782	1,019,057	488,936	73,204
Pennsylvania	12,432,792	730,061	1,361,476	695,182	1,197,002	10,002,053	9,646,073	4,912,976	3,370,799	1,889,660	302,279
Rhode Island	1,057,832	61,397	113,646	58,072	114,510	854,516	824,717	442,015	279,928	146,847	25,355
South Carolina	4,407,709	296,302	513,914	249,701	430,834	3,475,812	3,347,792	1,807,236	1,156,945	573,098	72,499
South Dakota	796,214	56,450	94,216	46,224	82,237	622,827	599,324	315,274	205,566	113,555	20,088
Tennessee	6,156,719	409,580	722,690	339,216	551,709	4,857,445	4,685,233	2,536,939	1,611,762	793,117	102,277
Texas	23,904,380	1,986,979	3,212,978	1,421,409	2,433,321	17,994,671	17,281,014	10,461,002	5,494,877	2,394,157	318,320
Utah	2,645,330	255,708	395,605	165,509	327,682	1,912,595	1,828,508	1,201,809	517,603	233,982	31,032
Vermont	621,254	32,435	64,053	34,865	61,218	508,076	489,901	245,936	186,217	84,425	12,071
Virginia	7,712,091	518,410	887,448	420,321	761,134	6,099,550	5,885,912	3,290,941	2,002,959	909,532	117,152
Washington	6,468,424	423,096	748,431	364,841	597,971	5,117,600	4,932,056	2,719,410	1,730,987	757,852	111,429
West Virginia	1,812,035	104,452	190,114	92,815	159,200	1,471,975	1,424,654	703,956	510,704	280,668	37,425
Wisconsin	5,601,640	356,287	645,297	319,695	549,793	4,443,807	4,280,361	2,294,430	1,492,009	736,301	115,036
Wyoming	522,830	35,890	59,793	29,682	52,944	412,679	397,465	210,974	145,175	63,901	8,572
Puerto Rico	3,942,375	245,168	515,463	242,293	396,057	3,061,525	2,939,431	1,662,480	935,710	522,899	63,484

Suggested Citation:
Table 1: Estimates of the Population by Selected Age Groups for the United States, States, and Puerto Rico: July 1, 2007 (SC-EST2007-01)
Source: Population Division, U.S. Census Bureau
Release Date: May 1, 2008

NOTE

According to a government study conducted in 1990 and issued in 1999, the nationwide total number of people in the United States who were 105 years and over was about 6,350. Today the counts are more likely double or triple this figure, and the number is growing. For the purposes of a simple histogram-based dashboard, the differences between counts for 85 years and over and 85 to 104 years are virtually indistinguishable.

The source data in the Census Bureau spreadsheet (see the file SC-EST2007-01.xls) does not contain data for 65 to 84 years, but it does contain data for 65 years and over and 85 years and over. If you subtract the counts for 85 years and over from the counts for 65 years and over, you will arrive at accurate counts for 65 to 84 years (see Figure 13.11).

Extracting the data for ages 65 to 84 years was easy. Getting the age group 25 to 44 years represents more of a challenge. Basically, you start with the total population among all age categories and chip away the ages you don't need. That is, you remove the population counts for ages 24 and lower as well as 45 and higher:

```
= Total population for all ages
  - (Under 5 years + 5 to 13 years + 14 to 17 years
    + 18 to 24 years + 45 to 64 years + 65 and over)
```

For example, for the state of Alabama, the number of people between 25 and 44 years is calculated as follows:

```
= 4627851 - (308234 + 552768 + 262535 + 446948 + 1195948 + 625756)
= 1235662
```

Figure 13.11
Three of the age groups are now comparable to one another.

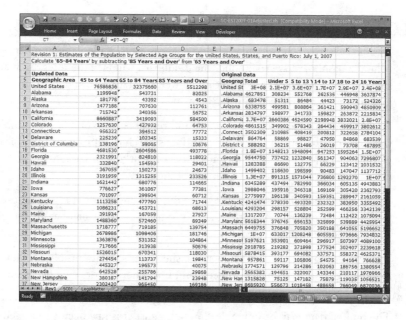

Of course, this is tedious to do by hand, but with spreadsheets, it's a straightforward formula that can be applied to all 50 states and any other geographic region, such as the District of Columbia or Puerto Rico.

At this point, you already have data for 15 to 44 years. What you need is data for 25 to 44 years. There are a number of ways to get at this number. Probably the simplest is to find out how many people are over age 24 and subtract from that number the people who are over age 44.

You calculate the number of people who are 45 or older as follows:

```
45 to 64 years + 65 to 84 years + 85 years and over
```

You calculate the number of people who are 25 years and over as follows:

```
= Total population for all ages - Population under 25 years
= Total population for all ages
➥    - (Under 5 years + 5 to 13 years + 14 to 17 years + 18 to 24 years)
```

The total number of people in the 25 to 44 years range is as follows:

```
= Total population for all ages
➥    - (Under 5 years + 5 to 13 years + 14 to 17 years
➥    + 18 to 24 years + 45 to 64 years + 65 and over)
```

13

CLOSING THOUGHTS

Dashboards are great presentation and analysis tools. Unless the numbers (and formulas) behind a dashboard are rock solid, the dashboard will lack the integrity it aims to portray. A silly thing like an extra space inserted between a first name and last name could mess up lookups or counts associated with the name.

It makes no sense to pour your energy and resources into building an exquisite dashboard that's essentially correct but is deficient in a small but critical area. This chapter is about getting data and spreadsheet formulas in good working order so that the flashy sizzle in a dashboard is accompanied by spreadsheet integrity.

The longer faulty data is used, the more difficult and costly it is to eradicate. If faulty data makes its way into a dashboard, it may lead to lost business and easily outweigh the cost of fixing clerical errors.

It is interesting to note that while spreadsheets can contain problems, they can also be used as effective tools to identify problems and find where errors may occur. An example of this is the spreadsheet tool described in this chapter that detects the presence of transposed digits.

The bulk of data may be unusable simply because it is raw or not packaged in a usable form. Fortunately, Excel provides some basic wizards to process raw data.

Things get a little trickier when data is unclean. Say that you have two names in a list, "Julius A Caesar" and "Julius A. Caesar." It is evident to you and me that the two names should most likely be treated as the same name. Computers have a commonsense blind spot. Unless you tell them to be specifically on the lookout for middle initials with and without periods, they may treat the two names as distinct names, and this may go unnoticed—until a costly mistake occurs.

The good news related to dealing with unclean data is that it can be systematically treated and scrubbed. There's a simple spreadsheet in this chapter for weeding out commonly recurring problems. When cleaning and fixing data, there is no need to do it inside Xcelsius. For that matter, there is no need to restrict yourself to Excel. You can use other tools, ranging from UNIX shell scripts to Java, Action Script, SAS, C++, Python, Ruby, Visual Basic, and even DOS batch scripts, to clean up your data. When your data is in good form, you can bring into Xcelsius 2008.

Unfortunately, good form doesn't take care of everything. Numbers that are accurate may not be well behaved. You can have a list of numbers that, when rounded, don't quite add up the way you might expect, and miniscule tweaking can create comparatively wild swings in the total.

Even when you get numeric data values the way they need to be, your spreadsheet formulas could be problematic. Two common problems arise from hardwired values embedded inside spreadsheet formulas and faulty cell referencing. The latter problem tends to crop up when you're replicating spreadsheet formulas.

When you get past these pitfalls, you have to start taking control. The underlying spreadsheet for a dashboard may contain excess computations that are not needed or could be streamlined. One approach to taming this beast is to architect your spreadsheet into logically distinct layers. This greatly facilitates the ability of the dashboard to harness the heavy-duty processing capabilities of the underlying spreadsheet, and that is very much the goal of Xcelsius as a dashboard or visualization technology.

In the Chapter 14, "Other Dashboard Techniques and Practices," I address the flip side of the spreadsheet/dashboard problems and tackle commonly encountered interface design issues.

13

CHAPTER **14**

OTHER DASHBOARD TECHNIQUES AND PRACTICES

In this chapter

This chapter outlines a variety of techniques and practices that are helpful in building Xcelsius dashboards. There is no one particular theme; this is just a collection of techniques and approaches you may find useful. There is, however, one undercurrent that runs throughout many of the chapter's examples: Rather than say that something cannot or should not be done, I describe workarounds.

AN IMPORTANT PRELIMINARY ISSUE

When you deploy a dashboard, a scorecard, or any other kind of visualization, you can give the end user a lot or very little control over his or her environment. It is a judgment call you need to make, and it behooves you to decide on this as early possible in the dashboard design process.

The process of managing control is complicated by the fact that Xcelsius exerts some control over a dashboard's behavior. For example, if you have a chart that displays percentages, Xcelsius will take your data and automatically set the upper and lower limits on the vertical, or Y scale.

 If you have value that varies between the range of 0% and 100%, you might find that Xcelsius sets the scale limits between say, 0% and 120%. This may or may not be what you want. If you know that you will never have a percentage that exceeds 100%, then a significant portion of your screen space would be consumed but never utilized. More importantly, your dashboard users may not be thrilled about a chart scaling beyond 100% when, by definition, certain things should never exceed 100%.

If you need, you can wrestle control of this away from Xcelsius, but then you have to take ownership over the process. This means you may have to competently handle exceptions, such as these:

- If your limits are set to 100%, what do you do if one or more of the values on the chart actually exceed 100%?
- What do you do about negative percentages?
- How would you want information rendered on the chart?

There are plenty of other ways to handle this. Here is one solution that may prove useful. In the chart's Properties panel, you can set the Y-axis scale to manual and point the lower and upper limits to spreadsheet cells that contain formulas for computing the limits.

If your chart data resides in cells A1:A10, you could use a spreadsheet formula like the following as the upper limit:

```
=MAX(100%,A1:A10)
```

Similarly, the lower limit on the chart could be mapped to a cell containing a formula like this:

```
=MIN(0,A1:A10)
```

In this manner, you can tell the chart limits to stay between the fixed bounds of 0% and 100%, unless some of the data misbehaves. The ch14_CustomScaling.xlf file shows this implemented (see Figure 14.1). In this dashboard example, there is a vertical slider that lets you adjust one of the data points to values that are negative or greater than 100%. The purpose and effect of this slider is to show how the chart scaling behaves when your data falls outside the expected data bounds of 0 and 1 (or 100%).

Figure 14.1
A chart with elastic limits.

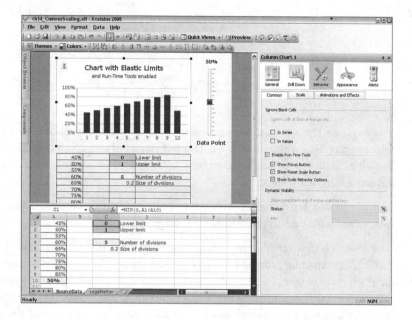

You can give the dashboard user additional control by enabling run-time tools (see the panel on the right side of Figure 14.1).

SIMPLE FIXES IN VISUALIZING DATA

Sometimes the data that appears in a chart is hard to view. This problem has nothing to do with dashboard design; it is simply related to an unfortunate set of values that makes viewing the data difficult because it is hard to distinguish or interpret. In certain types of charts, such as area charts, important data can be obscured.

The following sections outline a few strategies that address such challenges.

CHARTING MULTIPLE DATA SERIES THAT HAVE SIMILAR VALUES

It frequently happens that dashboards are used to compare two or more data series whose values may be similar to one another. If you have allocated a budget, the expectation is that actual recorded values may closely match the budgeted estimates. You can easily display such data on a chart. There's just one problem: The values may match so closely that it might be challenging to discern one dataset from the other (see Figure 14.2).

14

Figure 14.2
Chart values in multiple data series may be difficult to tell apart.

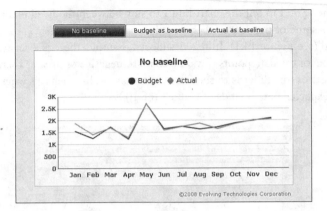

You can use a couple strategies for dealing with this. One approach is to use a Combination Chart component with one of the data series rendered as a column chart and the other as a line chart. This works well up to a point, but if the values are relatively close, it is hard to discern which one is larger.

Another approach may better serve your needs. It involves setting one of the data series as a *baseline* and adjusting all the others accordingly.

The ch14_Baseline.xlf file provides a working example of how a baseline dashboard is set up. In this sample file, shown in Figure 14.3, there are two data series represented on a line chart (in this example, budget values and actual values). This dashboard provides three viewing modes: one for comparing the literal values of budget and actual recorded data, one that sets the budget as a zero-based baseline, and one that sets the actual as the zero-based baseline.

Figure 14.3
You can choose which of your data series is treated as a baseline.

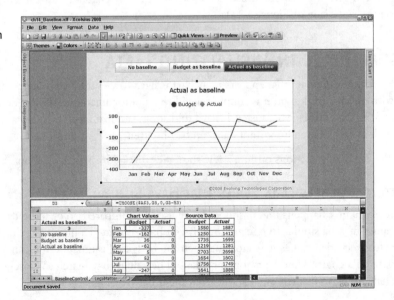

14

The overall design for this kind of dashboard is as follows:

1. Place your source data (in this example, budget and actual values) in columns G and H.

2. Set up a mechanism for selecting how you want to view the data. In this example, I use a Label Based Menu component. The labels are read from cells A4:A6, and the component inserts the position of the selected menu item in cell A3. This menu position is used to choose among three different ways of viewing the data (no baseline, budget as baseline, and actual as baseline).

3. Pull the data the way you want it to be displayed in the chart in columns D and E. For example, cell D3 (the first value in the first data series appearing in the chart) should retrieve the value in cell G3 (the budget value) if the menu position is 1 (that is, No baseline is selected). Cell D3 should be set to 0 if the menu position is 2 (Budget as baseline is selected). Cell D3 should be set to G3-H3 if the menu position is set to 3 (Actual as baseline is selected). You therefore use the following formula:
   ```
   =CHOOSE($A$3,G3,0,G3-H3)
   ```

4. Similarly, you use the following formula for cell E3:
   ```
   =CHOOSE($A$3,H3,H3-G3,0)
   ```

The strategy here is to put into the hands of the dashboard user the choice of how to view the chart data and to empower him or her by not restricting the options.

Step back a moment and look at what is happening here. The data that appears in the Source Data section may be data retrieved from a remote repository such as a database. Rather than accessing the repository every time the data needs to be viewed differently, you can just get the data once; it's not going to change each time it is viewed differently. Then you can use the spreadsheet formulas and calculation capabilities to choose how you want the data to be viewed. This underscores one of the reasons Xcelsius paradigm is so compelling.

FILLED RADAR CHARTS WITH ALERTS

 In working with Xcelsius 2008, you may have noticed that Filled Radar Chart components do not support alerts. Interestingly, plain radar charts do support alerts. You can have the best of both worlds by overlaying two charts. You place in the foreground a standard radar chart that supports alerts. Directly underneath it, you place a filled radar chart (see Figure 14.4 or open the file ch14_FilledRadarwithAlerts.xlf).

Here are some things to keep in mind when setting up this type of dashboard:

- The chart is really a compound chart that overlays a radar chart in the foreground over a filled radar chart in the background.

- The foreground and background layers are identically sized and read the same data cells for the chart values and category labels.

14

Figure 14.4
A filled radar chart with alerts can be easy to read and interpret.

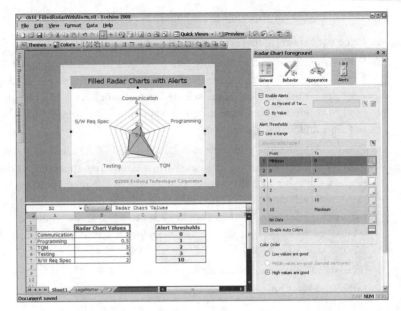

- Avoid using a chart title inside the Radar Chart component or the Filled Radar Chart component. This maximizes the size of the chart content. Instead, you position a Label component directly above the chart, and it serves as the chart title.

- The marker size in the Radar Chart component is sized to be easily visible but not overwhelming.

- In the Radar Chart component, you enable alerts and have the alert thresholds read directly from the spreadsheet cells (in this example, they are located in cells D3:D7). Reading from the spreadsheet lets you easily revise your criteria for colorizing the points on the radar chart.

This technique is more of a magician's sleight of hand than a best practice. When you need to get the job done, however, you do what works.

AVOIDING OCCLUSION WITH AREA CHARTS

 In some data visualization programs, you may encounter a situation in which some of the data in an area chart is hidden (see Figure 14.5).

One way around this problem is to avoid using solid colors in your area charts. Xcelsius 2008 gives you the option to set the level of transparency (see Figure 14.6).

NOTE

> Note that by default Xcelsius 2008 area charts use translucent shading and not solid colors. Also, minor and major gridlines are shown by default. You can tweak these to suit your comfort level.

Figure 14.5
Some of your data can be obscured when using an area chart with solid colors.

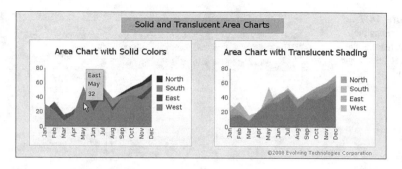

Figure 14.6
You can adjust the transparency of your chart data.

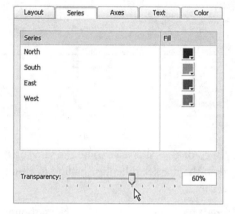

Even with translucent shading, it may be difficult to view the data. In such instances, you may be better off using a line chart instead of an area chart.

VIEWING LINE CHART DATA

 You can improve the readability of a chart by adjusting the appearance of the data series:

- You can change marker size and fill color for the data series markers. You should be aware that the marker size you set applies to all the data series displayed in the line chart. The fill color applies to each individually selected data series.

- You can adjust marker transparency. Like the marker size, the transparency value applies to all the data series. It cannot be independently set for each individual data series.

- You can independently set line thickness for each of the data series.

- You can select the marker shape for each of the data series (see Figure 14.7).

14

Figure 14.7
Customizing the appearance of the data series in a line chart.

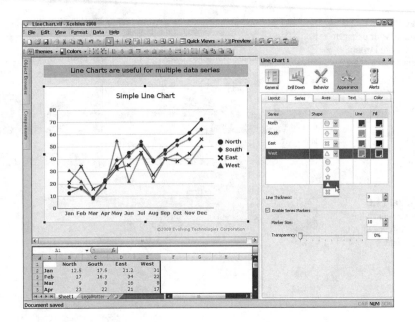

Keep in mind that the marker fill color does not have to be the same as the line color. You might, for instance, want to darken the marker fill color shading to emphasize the data points instead of using large markers.

If you want to streamline the appearance of a line chart, especially if only one data series is displayed, you can remove the appearance of markers altogether. You can do this by setting the transparency to 0% or by shrinking the marker size to 0.

In the example shown in Figure 14.7, there are 4 data series (North, South, East, and West) and 12 data points for each of the series. As you display additional data series and more data points, your chart quickly becomes saturated. You can avoid needless clutter by using the List Builder component (which is covered in Chapter 5, "Using Charts and Graphs to Represent Data").

CONSTRUCTING ABC (ACTUAL BUDGET COMPARISON) CHARTS

 An ABC chart is a very simple dashboard that flows selected data from two independent charts to a merged chart (see Figure 14.8 or open the file ch14_ABC_Chart.xlf).

The setup of an ABC-style charting dashboard involves the following:

1. Start with a set of data that conform to a certain structure, such as actual expenses by geographic region, perhaps for a given quarter. You can call the *actual* data the A component. This data is displayed in the top-left chart in Figure 14.8.

2. Add a corresponding dataset that matches the structure of the A component. You might chose to display *budget* estimates for the same set of geographic regions and accounting period. You can call this the B component. This data is displayed in the top-right portion of Figure 14.8.

Although it is easy to see the A and B portions and understand that they are related, it is difficult to *compare* the actual and budget for the same region (that is, actual to budget for just the North, just the South, and so on). For this, you need to create a comparison chart, or a C component. In Figure 14.8, this is the bottom chart.

When the dashboard user moves the mouse over any of the geographic regions in the top two charts, a drill down mechanism automatically pushes the corresponding data onto the comparison chart.

3. To let you know what data is being moved to the comparison chart, a set of flow lines automatically highlights the path the data takes. Underneath the hood, this is handled through dynamically controlling the visibility of horizontal and vertical lines.

Notice that all the charts are equivalently scaled so that visual proportions can be objectively interpreted.

In addition to drill down, the dashboard user can choose the desired accounting period or quarter from the list box.

Figure 14.8
An ABC-style dashboard lets you merge two data sources and compare corresponding points one at a time.

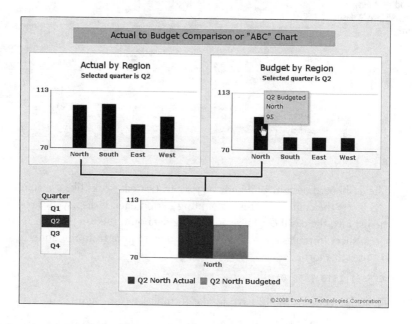

Keep in mind that there is no restriction on the kind of data used in an ABC-style dashboard. You might, for instance, compare revenue and expense items or degree of risk and frequency of occurrence. This kind of dashboard offers one more way to view data.

Now that you have an idea how the visual part of the dashboard is handled, let's spend a few moments examining the spreadsheet setup:

- The underlying spreadsheet is divided into three colorized sections: one for the A component, one for the B component, and one for the C component (see Figure 14.9).

- The source data for each of the three colorized sections resides in rows 19 through 22. The position of the selected item in the list box shown in Figure 14.8 is mapped to cell A2. In this case, the position is 2. This pulls the Q2 data into row 12, and this data is displayed in the top two column charts in Figure 14.8.

- The top two column charts in Figure 14.8 have drill down enabled. For both of these charts, the drill down destination cell is A3. The selected data value position is written to that cell. Figure 14.8 shows the mouse hovering over the North region, which is the first position, so the value 1 is placed in cell A3. This moves the data values for the North region from the A and B components into cells O12 and P12.

- There are four groups of vertical and horizontal line segments; in effect, there is one for each region. Each group watches the value of cell A3 and uses that value as a switch to make the line segments visible or invisible.

Figure 14.9
Spreadsheet design
for an ABC-style dash-
board.

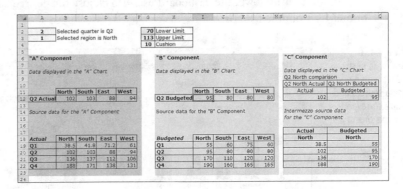

The dashboard design, while not very sophisticated, works like a machine. The list box, which sets the context for the accounting period data, is displayed. From the standpoint of the list box, the dashboard user is pushing data onto the top two charts. Internally, the spreadsheet formulas are pulling the data they require from the underlying source data. Cell I12 uses this formula:

```
=OFFSET(I$18,$A$2,0)
```

The other cells in row 12 have similar formulas.

Similarly, as a dashboard user hovers the mouse over any of the vertical bars in the top two column charts, the position value is pushed onto cell A3. Cells O12 and P12 watch the value in A3 and use it to pull data from cells B12:E12 and I12:L12, respectively. This kind of push-pull technique is a very powerful framework.

USING A CANDLESTICK COMPONENT AS A BOX PLOT

Candlestick components, dual sliders, and percentile calculations can be combined to provide a dashboard user with a lot of data visualization dexterity. An example of this is shown in Figure 14.10 (or open the file ch14_BoxPlotCandleStick.xlf). Simply adjusting a dual slider allows the dashboard user to visually characterize and classify data.

Figure 14.10
A Candlestick component is adapted to work like a box plot.

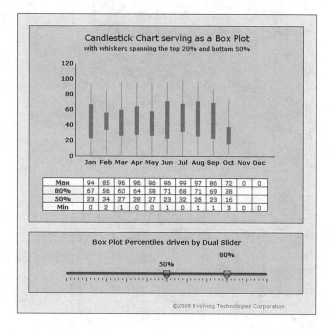

Candlestick Chart serving as a Box Plot
with whiskers spanning the top 20% and bottom 50%

	Jan	Feb	Mar	Apr	May	Jun	Jul	Aug	Sep	Oct	Nov	Dec
Max	94	85	96	96	96	96	99	97	86	72	0	0
80%	67	56	60	64	58	71	68	71	69	38		
50%	23	34	27	28	27	23	32	26	23	16		
Min	0	2	1	0	0	1	0	1	1	3	0	0

Box Plot Percentiles driven by Dual Slider
80%
50%

©2008 Evolving Technologies Corporation

The Candlestick component is a particular kind of charting component in Xcelsius 2008. Like the OHLC component, the Candlestick component follows an Open-High-Low-Closing convention (see Figure 14.11). That is, there are four separate data series for open, high, low, and closing values. This naming convention makes sense for the stock market and investment management. But candlestick charts do not have to be restricted to Wall Street–type applications.

By using a dual slider and some percentile applications, you can set up a basic box plot in Xcelsius 2008. To illustrate how this is done, let's use the dynamically ranged sums spreadsheet data from Chapter 4, "Embedded Spreadsheets: The Secret Sauce of Xcelsius 2008."

Data is captured daily over a period of months (see Figure 14.12). Each column represents a separate month, and the rows correspond to the values recorded for the days of the month. In this example, recorded data extends up to October 8.

14

Figure 14.11
A Candlestick component uses four data series that correspond to open, high, low, and closing sets of values.

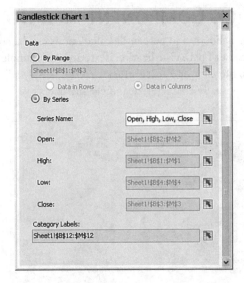

Figure 14.12
Daily data captured over the better part of a year that needs to be analyzed.

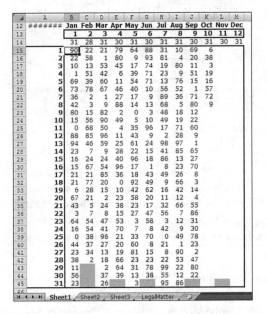

	Jan	Feb	Mar	Apr	May	Jun	Jul	Aug	Sep	Oct	Nov	Dec
	1	2	3	4	5	6	7	8	9	10	11	12
	31	28	31	30	31	30	31	31	30	31	30	31
1	90	22	21	79	64	88	31	10	69	6		
2	22	58	1	80	9	93	81	4	20	38		
3	10	13	53	45	17	74	19	80	11	3		
4	1	51	42	6	39	71	23	9	51	19		
5	69	39	60	11	54	71	13	76	15	16		
6	73	78	67	46	40	10	56	52	1	57		
7	36	2	1	27	17	9	89	36	71	72		
8	42	3	9	88	14	13	68	5	80	9		
9	80	15	82	2	0	3	48	18	12			
10	15	56	90	49	5	10	49	19	22			
11	0	68	50	4	35	96	17	71	60			
12	88	85	96	11	43	9	2	28	9			
13	94	46	59	25	61	24	98	97	1			
14	23	7	9	28	22	15	41	85	65			
15	16	24	24	40	96	18	86	13	27			
16	15	67	54	96	17	1	8	23	70			
17	21	21	85	36	18	43	49	26	8			
18	21	77	20	0	92	49	9	66	3			
19	6	28	15	10	42	62	16	42	14			
20	67	21	2	23	58	20	11	12	4			
21	43	5	24	38	23	17	32	66	55			
22	3	7	8	15	27	47	56	7	86			
23	64	54	47	53	3	58	3	12	31			
24	16	54	41	70	7	8	42	9	30			
25	0	38	96	21	33	70	0	49	78			
26	44	37	27	20	60	8	21	1	23			
27	23	34	13	19	81	15	8	90	2			
28	38	2	18	66	23	23	22	53	47			
29	11		2	64	31	78	99	22	80			
30	56		37	39	13	38	55	12	22			
31	23		26		3		95	86				

Sheet1 / Sheet2 / Sheet3 / LegalMatter

During any month, you can see that recorded amounts vary between a low number and a high number. The majority of values fall within some in-between range. Is this starting to sound familiar? It pretty much follows a candlestick or OHLC structure.

The data shown in Figure 14.12 is not quite set up to feed into the Candlestick component. You need to add some processing to convert the data:

- You need to retrieve the high and low values for each of the months. This means calculating maximum and minimum values.

- In place of the open and close values that the Candlestick component or OHLC component expects, you could supply percentile thresholds.

- As a precursor to calculating percentiles or rank, you may need to know the count of values in each of the columns.

Figure 14.13 shows how this is set up:

- The counts in row 7 are needed to determine what rank corresponds to a specific percentile.

- If there is a count of 31, then the 25 lowest values will be under the 80% mark. For example, this is the formula for cell B8:

  =ROUND(B7*A8,0)

  In this example, the result is 25 (=ROUND(80%*31,0)).

- When you can determine where the split occurs, you can find the value that corresponds to that threshold. In keeping with this example, the value 67 in cell B2 (=SMALL(B16:B46,B8)) corresponds to the 80th percentile.

Figure 14.13
Counts, percentile thresholds, and corresponding values need to be calculated for the Candlestick component.

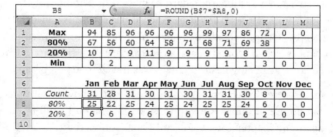

	A	B	C	D	E	F	G	H	I	J	K	L	M
1	Max	94	85	96	96	96	96	99	97	86	72	0	0
2	80%	67	56	60	64	58	71	68	71	69	38		
3	20%	10	7	9	11	9	9	9	9	8	6		
4	Min	0	2	1	0	0	1	0	1	1	3	0	0
5													
6		Jan	Feb	Mar	Apr	May	Jun	Jul	Aug	Sep	Oct	Nov	Dec
7	Count	31	28	31	30	31	30	31	31	30	8	0	0
8	80%	25	22	25	24	25	24	25	25	24	6	0	0
9	20%	6	6	6	6	6	6	6	6	6	2	0	0
10													

B8 f_x =ROUND(B$7*$A8,0)

If you look at the formulas in rows 2 and 3, you will see that they have a slightly more complicated form. For instance, cell B2 has this formula:

=IF(ISERROR(SMALL(B$16:B$46,B8)),"", SMALL(B$16:B$46,B8))

There is a good reason for this formula logic: Some of the columns have no data. The following formula will return a #NUM! error if there is no data:

=SMALL(B$16:B$46,B8)

Normally, Xcelsius 2008 doesn't complain about such errors when it charts data. However, such errors are displayed as errors in the Spreadsheet Table component. Visually, it is cleaner to force the errant cell to appear as blank. The IF ISERROR formula handles this.

14

Finally, to allow a dashboard user to drive the data analysis visualization, you can include a Dual Slider component that the user can use to set the values in cells A2 and A3.

CLOSING THOUGHTS

One of the lessons I have learned over the years is to, where possible, empower dashboard users as much as possible but avoid giving them license to be dangerous. It is very easy to create a dashboard with sliders that can tweak a wide variety of variables. If you are not careful, your dashboard users could figuratively slide off a data cliff.

Setting limits in your visual components is only one kind of safety measure. You have to forever be on guard that your formulas are calculating valid results. Some empty data can inadvertently create a visual eyesore. A subtraction of two numbers that should exactly equal 0 may turn out to be -0.00000001. If you attempt to take the square root or logarithm of such a number, you will introduce errors in your calculations.

It is indeed challenging to empower users of dashboards and at the same time incorporate features that make it safe to push dashboards to the limits.

A chief reason I wrote this chapter is to address situations that are too often brought in as afterthoughts or addressed without seeking resolution. Deciding how much empowerment your dashboard users should get is one such item. Another is that dashboard designers frequently try to accomplish something, encounter some obstacle, and then give up too easily. Sometimes data within a dashboard is hard to view. This should not come as a surprise. Data is very fluid, so it can be difficult to tame. But Xcelsius is a visual data analysis tool, and it's designed to rework data after the fact. You saw in this chapter how this was accomplished with data values in separate data series that are very close to one another. The technique involved converting any desired data series to a zero-based baseline at will.

Another reason I wrote this chapter is to outline in detail how to set up cleanly designed dashboards that do useful things. One of these involves a push-pull framework. You will see this at work again in Chapter 15, "XML and Data Connectivity."

ADVANCED FEATURES

CHAPTER 15

XML AND DATA CONNECTIVITY

15

Most of the features of Xcelsius 2008 do not require a connection to remote data sources in order to work. Let's face it: A dashboard with interactivity and sophisticated spreadsheet formulas but without connectivity is a fixed snapshot of some dataset. A key feature that distinguishes Xcelsius 2008 Engage from its earlier equivalent (Crystal Xcelsius Professional) is the ability to make *connected presentations*. My goal in this chapter is to get you thinking about extending your dashboards so that they can tap into external sources of information.

NOTE

> While the product Xcelsius 2008 Present provides a great many of the features found in Xcelsius 2008 Engage and Engage Server, it does not come with built-in support for connecting to remote data sources.
>
> This chapter is really targeted to those who have the Engage or Engage Server products. In the remainder of this chapter, when I refer to Xcelsius 2008, I am *not* including Xcelsius 2008 Present.
>
> If you are using Present and want to experiment with the remote connectivity features of Xcelsius, you can download and install the trial version of Xcelsius Engage.

STRATEGIES FOR PACKAGING DASHBOARD INFORMATION

Dashboards can be packaged in a number of different ways. One approach is to have everything already contained the day the dashboard is deployed. The advantage of this approach is that when the dashboard is created, it needs no further upkeep. You can email the dashboard to a colleague, who saves the file to her laptop computer. She won't need a connection to the Internet to open the dashboard file and use it.

If connectivity is so significant, why not introduce it earlier in the book, rather than wait until near the end of the book to introduce the topic? There are several good reasons:

- The principles and practices associated with dashboard design and preparation (including the use of spreadsheet formulas, managing dynamic visibility, setting attributes of visual components, and the like) do not require connectivity to remote data sources.

- The moment you bring connectivity into a dashboard, you need to take into account the infrastructure used to deploy the dashboard. Each company, organization, or individual who deploys a connected presentation is bound to have a unique set of requirements and network environments.

  Illustrating dashboard features in the context of a connected presentation introduces excess baggage that is largely unrelated to the dashboard feature. For example, you don't need an Internet connection to illustrate the basic features of dynamic visibility of a component.

- Designing dashboards that are connected requires a network infrastructure be in place. Not every reader will have at his or her disposal convenient access to a full-fledged network infrastructure.

OPEN-ENDED DASHBOARDS

A dashboard that connects to a remote data source is referred to as *open ended*. This means that the dashboard can continuously be refreshed with new and changing information. There are really two kinds of open-ended dashboards:

- **Dashboards that rely on passive feeds**: This kind of dashboard is used to monitor trends or key performance indicators (KPIs). As necessary, computations can be performed on the incoming data. Anything can be done to the data, including calculating relevant statistical measures such as mean, standard deviation, minimum, maximum, or moving averages. Also, data can be reclassified or numerically revised.

- **Dashboards that allow people or computations to dictate where the next piece of information is going to come from or what it needs to be**: This kind of dashboard allows people or computations to dictate where the next parcel of information comes from or what it needs to be.

THE XCELSIUS DATA MANAGER

The WorkGroup version of Crystal Xcelsius (the high-end version of the older generation of Xcelsius) supported various ways to connect to remote data, but it was not centralized. All versions of Xcelsius 2008 except Xcelsius 2008 Present support remote connectivity and include the Data Manager, which places all the connectivity options under one roof.

The idea of the Xcelsius Data Manager is simple. To add connectivity to a remote data source, you add a connection and specify the type of connection you want. The following connection types are available:

- Query as a Web Service (QaaWS)
- Web Services Connection
- XML Data
- Flash Variables
- Portal Data
- Crystal Report Data Consumer
- FS Command
- LCDS Connections
- External Interface Connection
- Excel XML Maps
- Live Office Connections

The connectivity options in Xcelsius 2008 span a broad range. Rather than attempt a cursory across-the-board discussion, this chapter outlines from a hands-on perspective pragmatic issues and techniques for accessing XML data, particularly Excel XML maps.

XML: The Rosetta Stone of Machine- (and Human-) Readable Content

Every computer system and every software application has its own way of representing information. Unless these systems agree in advance to use a predefined structure common to all of them, they are going to have a hard time exchanging information or talking to one another.

XML was created as a platform-neutral way for computers (and people) to exchange information by using plain text. At its core, XML is very simple. It simply packages text content with tags. These tags create a structure that makes it easy to interpret information. Consider the following snippet of XML:

```
<invoice>
<invoice_number>15926</invoice_number>
<invoice_date>September 27, 2009</invoice_date>
<transactions>
    <transaction>
        <model_number>Model 100</model_number>
        <unit_price>49.95</unit_price>
        <units>89</units>
    </transaction>
    <transaction>
        <model_number>Model 300</model_number>
        <unit_price>89.25</unit_price>
        <units>67</units>
    </transaction>
</transactions>
</invoice>
```

Without really knowing anything about XML, you can interpret and extract meaningful information. In this example, invoice number 15926, with an invoice date of September 27, 2009, has two transactions. One of these is for 89 units of Model 100, at a price of 49.95, and the other is for 67 units of Model 300, at a price of 89.25.

One of the liberating features of XML is that it does not limit you to a fixed vocabulary of tags to identify your content. You can create tags of your own choosing. This makes it easy to package and exchange meaningful information for easy consumption by other computer systems.

What if the computer system receiving your custom-designed invoice is not familiar with the structure of your invoice? That's no problem. You can create a dictionary that defines how the XML is to be structured. This is generally referred to as a *schema*, and you can incorporate the schema inside the XML content.

If the XML content is small, or if you are going to send a large number of XML documents that conform to the same structure, packaging the schema definition inside each and every XML file would be wasteful. It would be simpler to have the schema reside in a known location and use a link to that location in its place.

All this is very practical, but another challenge looms: In the earlier example, I defined a very specific type of structure for the `invoice` tag. That might work for me, but you may have a different notion of how invoices should be structured, and it may not be consistent with my precepts. XML avoids this naming collision by using *namespaces*.

TIP

> There are plenty of online resources and tutorials about XML. A simple search (such as www.google.com/search?q=XML+online+tutorials) provides a wealth of resources.

ADDING XML MAPS TO XCELSIUS 2008

Xcelsius 2008 provides support for the Microsoft XML maps facility. Tapping into this capability may require some setup. You can forgo setting this up in your Xcelsius workspace and define all your XML maps in Excel, save the spreadsheet, and then import it into Xcelsius. This approach defeats the benefits of a tightly integrated Xcelsius/Excel design environment. I heartily recommend that you go through the steps of integrating XML support in Excel so that the features can be tapped directly from the Xcelsius workspace.

15

> **NOTE**
>
> The Home and Student Editions of Excel and Microsoft Office do not support certain XML features, such as XML maps. Make sure you are using the Professional Edition of Excel 2003 or Excel 2007. In the remainder of this chapter, any reference to Excel assumes the use of the Professional Edition and not the Home or Student Editions of Excel.

SETTING UP XML FOR XCELSIUS WHEN YOU ARE USING EXCEL 2007

Although Excel is directly integrated in the Xcelsius 2008 workspace, it does not make available 100% of the features you get when you work with Excel as a standalone application. By default, the Excel 2007 Ribbon displays Home, Insert, Page Layout, Formulas, Data, Review, and View. The XML features of Excel 2007 live in another Ribbon tab called Developer, which you need to add to your Ribbon. Here are the steps to do so:

1. If you have Xcelsius 2008 running, close it. If you have Excel 2007 running, close it as well. To make sure there are no instances of either program, view the processes in the Windows Task Manager. There should be nothing named Xcelsius or Excel in the list of running processes.

2. Launch Excel 2007 so that it is the *only instance* of Excel running.

3. In the main application menu of Excel 2007, click the Excel Options button.

4. Under the Popular options, make sure there is a checkmark next to the Show Developer tab in the Ribbon. Click the OK button, and close Excel. The next time you start up Xcelsius 2008, the Developer tab should be present in the Ribbon.

> **NOTE**
>
> Depending on how you lay out the various elements of your Xcelsius workspace, the Excel 2007 Ribbon may be hidden. You can either resize the spreadsheet portion of your workspace or select Show Spreadsheet Only in the Quick Views menu to reveal the Ribbon.

SETTING UP XML FOR XCELSIUS WHEN YOU ARE USING EXCEL 2003

To make use of the XML features of Excel 2003 within Xcelsius 2008, you need to have these features visible in the Excel toolbar. Here are the basic steps to set this up:

1. If you have Xcelsius 2008 running, close it. If you have Excel 2003 running, close it as well. To make sure there are no instances of either program running, view the processes in the Windows Task Manager. There should be nothing named Xcelsius or Excel in the list of running processes.

2. Launch Excel 2003 so that it is the *only instance* of Excel running.

3. In Excel, select Tools, Customize to open the Customize dialog box.

4. Add some toolbar icons. (Although you could add the icons to an existing toolbar, I recommend that you create a new one for the XML features you will be enabling in the Xcelsius workspace.) Within the Toolbars tab of the Customize panel, click the New button and give the toolbar an appropriate name, such as XML Toolbar, and then click OK. This produces an empty floating toolbar that needs to be populated with the XML toolbar icons.

5. In the Customize dialog box, click the Commands tab. Within the list of categories, select Data. To the right of the list, you see a set of toolbar icons that is appropriate to the selected category. Scroll down this list until you see XML Source, Import XML Data, and XML Map Properties. Drag these icons to the floating toolbar you created in step 4 (see Figure 15.1).

Figure 15.1
Locating the XML toolbar icons you will need.

If you accidentally add a toolbar icon you don't want, you can just drag it off the toolbar.

TIP

If there are other toolbar icons you want to enable in the Xcelsius workspace, you can add them here. Keep in mind that as you add toolbar icons, your screen quickly gets crowded.

6. When you are done adding icons, drag the floating toolbar and park it along the other Excel toolbars at the top of your application window. Close Excel. The next time you start up Xcelsius 2008, the new toolbars should be visible.

> **NOTE**
> Before proceeding to the next section, make sure you have completed the setup instructions for your version of Excel.

SETTING UP EXCEL XML MAPS

Excel supports XML maps, which can be used to translate XML content from a remote data source to the rows and columns of a spreadsheet.

Creating an XML map and mapping elements to spreadsheet cells involves getting the XML schema definition file or a representative sample of the XML. There are three ways to build an Excel XML map:

- Read in XML content that references a schema definition file. In this case, Excel will build the XML map based on the schema definition.

- Read in XML content that doesn't reference any kind of schema definition. In this case, the XML map is constructed using the sample file as the blueprint. If you rely on this strategy, you need to make sure your sample file has all the bells and whistles built into it.

- Instead of depending on a physical file on your hard drive, connect to the remote data source via a URL.

Let's look more closely at the third approach. Follow these steps:

1. Set up a test harness so that you can sample data or a schema definition from which to build your XML map. For purposes of illustration, try using a URL such as the following (but one that points to your own data) to fetch some XML content:

   http://www.evolvingtech.com:8080/ExcelDB/GetSpotExchRateServlet?
   currency=RAND&date=2000-2-1&duration=7&country=SOUTH%20AFRICA

   The query might return content like:
   ```
   <?xml version="1.0" encoding="UTF-8"?>
   <tables>
   <tab>
   <EXCH_DATE>2000-02-01</EXCH_DATE>
   <EXCH_RATE>6.2800</EXCH_RATE>
   </tab>
   <tab>
   <EXCH_DATE>2000-02-02</EXCH_DATE>
   <EXCH_RATE>6.2825</EXCH_RATE>
   </tab>
   <tab>
   ```

```
<EXCH_DATE>2000-02-03</EXCH_DATE>
<EXCH_RATE>6.2575</EXCH_RATE>
</tab>
<tab>
<EXCH_DATE>2000-02-04</EXCH_DATE>
<EXCH_RATE>6.2860</EXCH_RATE>
</tab>
<tab>
<EXCH_DATE>2000-02-07</EXCH_DATE>
<EXCH_RATE>6.2905</EXCH_RATE>
</tab>
</tables>
```

NOTE

The URLs and the sample files used here are intended for illustration purposes. The URLs and data values shown in this chapter should work as is but are subject to change. As URLs change, I will place notices at www.XcelsiusBestPractices.com.

2. Create the XML map. If you have Excel 2007 integrated into your Xcelsius workspace, click the Developer tab of your Excel Ribbon and then click the Import button. If you have Excel 2003 integrated into your Xcelsius workspace, click the Import XML Data icon on the XML toolbar created during the setup.

At this stage (regardless of whether you have Excel 2007 or Excel 2003 integrated into your workspace), you will be presented with a dialog box to point to the XML content (see Figure 15.2).

Figure 15.2
Instead of supplying a file, you can supply a URL that retrieves XML content.

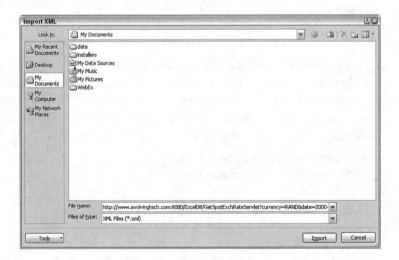

The XML content can be a file on your hard drive. It can, as shown in Figure 15.2, be a URL reference. In the File Name field of the Import XML window, type your URL reference and then click the Open button. In the current example, the URL reference that would be typed would be:

```
http://www.evolvingtech.com:8080/ExcelDB/GetSpotExchRateServlet?
➥currency=RAND&date=2000-2-1&duration=7&country=SOUTH%20AFRICA
```

NOTE

> It may seem unintuitive to type a URL when Excel is looking for a file, but it does work.

If the XML content you get back doesn't incorporate a schema definition or refer to such a definition, you will be prompted with a message like the one shown in Figure 15.3.

Figure 15.3
Your XML map can be constructed from the raw XML even if no schema exists.

Click the OK button. You will be further prompted to identify where to put the XML table (see Figure 15.4). For this example, designate cell A4 and click the OK button. If all goes well, you'll see a table populated with data.

Figure 15.4
Your XML map elements need to be associated with spreadsheet cells that you designate.

3. Embed the URL that will be used to fetch your data in the underlying spreadsheet. Enter the following static query in cell A1:

```
http://www.evolvingtech.com:8080/ExcelDB/GetSpotExchRateServlet?
➥currency=RAND&date=2000-2-1&duration=7&country=SOUTH%20AFRICA
```

This is the same URL you used in step 1.

4. Convert this static query into an interactive query by turning it into a formula that reads values located in other spreadsheet cells. First, create input cells in your spreadsheet to set the duration and day number. In cell E2 type Duration. In cell E3 type 7. In cell D2 type Day. In cell D3 type 5.

Modify cell A1 so that it reads the day and duration values from cells D3 and E3, respectively. Cell A1 should have a formula that looks like this:

```
="http://www.evolvingtech.com:8080/ExcelDB/GetSpotExchRateServlet?
➥currency=RAND&date=2000-2-"&D3&"&duration="&E3&"&country=SOUTH%20AFRICA"
```

15

5. Add two Spinner components to the canvas. Map one of them to the day number (cell D3) and the other to the duration (cell E3). Add a Spreadsheet Table component and map the Display Data field to cells A1:E9. This way, you will be able to see what is happening to the underlying spreadsheet as you adjust the spinner controls.

6. Create a connection from the mapped XML cells to the URL in cell A1. Click anywhere on the canvas and press Ctrl+M (alternatively, you can select Data, Connections in Xcelsius). A Data Manager window appears. Click the Add button and select Excel XML Maps (see Figure 15.5).

Figure 15.5
Select the type of data connection you want Xcelsius to create.

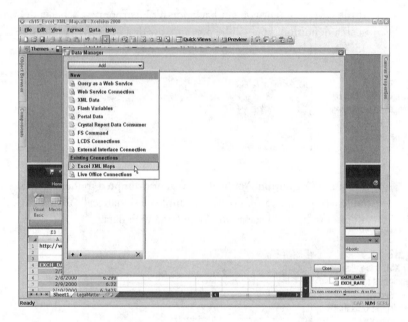

In the Definition tab, there are two fields—Name and XML Data URL. The Name field is mapped to `tables_Map` that was created in step 2. Instead of getting the XML data URL from the sample file, map it to cell A1 so it can dynamically pick up values from the spreadsheet (see Figure 15.6).

7. You need to get the dashboard to retrieve data from the remote data source any time either of the spinner buttons is clicked. The key to doing this is to identify a single trigger cell to force such an action. Cell A1, the cell that is used to set the URL, is perfect for this purpose.

In the Data Manager window, click the Usage tab. Map the trigger cell to A1. The radio button options When Value Changes and When Value Becomes are enabled. Select the When Value Changes radio button.

Select the Refresh on Load check box and click the Close button (see Figure 15.7).

Figure 15.6
Be sure to link the XML data URL to the spreadsheet formula in cell A1.

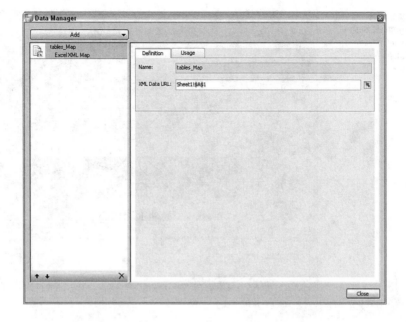

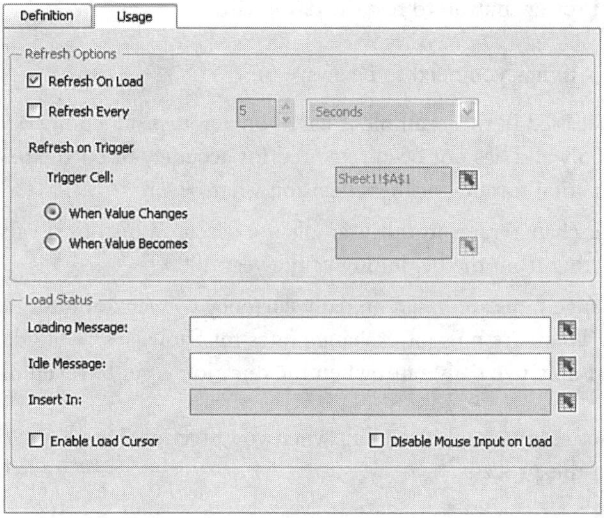

Figure 15.7
Set your refresh options so that the dashboard updates automatically.

If you haven't already done so, save your file. It should look something like Figure 15.8 (see the file ch15_Excel_XML_Map.xlf). Notice the XML map that appears in the lower-right corner.

15

Figure 15.8
The complete dashboard file, based on an XML map.

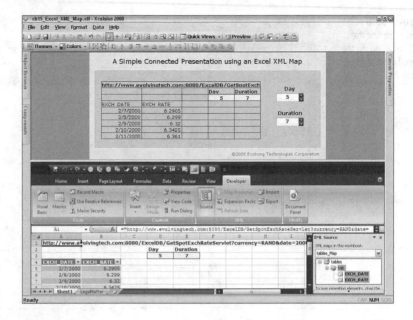

8. Click the Preview button to test the dashboard.

There are a few things you need to be aware of:

- The dataset used in this example is based on a non-production system for illustrative purposes only and has not been reviewed for accuracy or correctness. Do not rely on this information for any business decision whatsoever.

- The spot exchange rates in this example are based on historical values over a six-month period starting from the beginning of the year 2000.

- Spot exchange rates are based on daily currency conversion rates occurring during business days. There are no spot exchange rates for Saturdays or Sundays. This is why you see at most only five daily rates when the duration is set to seven days.

These steps may seem complicated, but when you practice them a few times, you'll quickly get the hang of this process.

CONNECTING YOUR DASHBOARDS TO WEB SERVICES

XML provides a way to transfer complex and structured information. XML is concerned only with the message content. If you want a sure-fire way of properly asking for the information, you need to turn to Web Services.

15

UNDERSTANDING WEB SERVICES

Web Services is a communications framework for exchanging information that uses XML content as the transport medium. The general idea is that you want to retrieve information from a remote server. Do you know in advance what kinds of questions or services it is prepared to answer? It would be nice if you could just ask it and it would tell you what you want to know. That's a tall order, but it is what actually happens with Web Services.

The server you need to connect to can publish a special type of XML file called a WSDL (Web Services Definition Language) file that tells all about what the server is willing to do.

You can retrieve a WSDL file from a server just as you would pick up any web pages. You can even read the contents of a WSDL file in your web browser. Although the information may not be easy for you or me to read, it will make perfect sense to Xcelsius 2008. Basically, this file identifies the following:

- The list of methods or requests it will answer
- What information it wants you to supply for a given method, including the data type for each parameter that is needed
- For each method, what exactly it will return to you (including the data type of each kind of returned value)

If you are having trouble getting a handle on WSDL files, think about the following analogy. When you go to a restaurant, you may not know all the different kinds of foods and beverages served, their prices, or even whether the restaurant accepts credit cards. All this information can be obtained at a glance if you look at a menu. A WSDL file for Web Services is the electronic equivalent of a menu for a restaurant.

USING WEB SERVICES IN XCELSIUS 2008

The Xcelsius 2008 Data Manager facilitates the process of asking for and receiving XML data using a Web Services connection. The example that follows illustrates how to capture some weather information that is available from a government agency using Web Services.

NOTE

Like any other data source on the Internet, the URL references and available datasets used here are subject to change. This should not cause a problem, as you should be able to apply the same steps for your URL references and corresponding datasets.

Here are the basic steps involved:

1. Set the URL of the WSDL file. In your dashboard, open the Data Manager and add a Web Services connection. In this example, you are requesting some wind data from a server at the National Oceanic and Atmospheric Administration. In the WSDL URL field, add the following and then click the Import button:

   `http://opendap.co-ops.nos.noaa.gov/axis/services/Wind?wsdl`

15

In a few moments, the Input Values and Output Values boxes will be populated for a method called getWind (see Figure 15.9).

Figure 15.9
Setup of a Web Services connection.

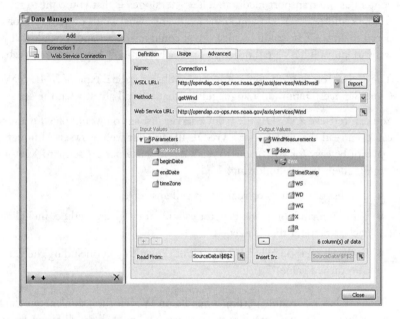

If there is more than one method available, you will be able to select among them by using a pull-down list in the Method field. For this WSDL, getWind happens to be the only method the service provides.

2. Map the input values and output values of the getWind method to spreadsheet cells in your dashboard. The input values needed for getWind are stationId, beginDate, endDate, and timeZone. Map this to cells of your choosing. Here is how to map them: Select stationId in the Input Values pane. When this is selected, the Read From field becomes enabled. In this example, I map it to cell B3. Map beginDate, endDate, and timeZone to cells B4, B5, and B6, respectively.

3. Make sure you have suitable input values in the spreadsheet. Now that you know that cells B3, B4, B5, and B6 are going to be used to supply data for your request, you have to populate them with input values. You can temporarily close the Data Manager window. Enter the values 8454000, 20080910, 20080910, and 0 into cells B3, B4, B5, and B6, respectively. In cells A3, A4, A5, and A6, enter appropriate labels, such as Station ID, Begin date, End date, and Time zone, respectively. It also helps to place identifying headers for this table of input values. In cell A1, type Input name, and in B1, type Value.

4. Create a trigger cell to automatically signal when to make a request. In cell B1, place the following spreadsheet formula:

```
=B3&B4&B5&B6
```

Also type an identifying label, such as Trigger, in cell A1.

5. Map the output values of getWind to your spreadsheet. The results returned by getWind are timeStamp, WS, WD, WG, X, and R. These are the date and time of the data, wind speed in meters per second, wind direction in degrees, wind gust in meters per second, and flags to indicate when maximum wind speed and rate of change tolerance limit are exceeded.

   You can individually map each of these results, or you can do it in a single step. Click the enclosing folder (called item) in the Output Values pane. Notice that when you do this, the message "6 column(s) of data" appears, and the Insert In field becomes enabled. Map the results to spreadsheet cells of your choosing. Of course, you will need to specify six columns for the six return parameters. The number of rows you will need is dependent on your begin and end dates, as well as the number of values recorded each day. If you are getting measurements every 6 minutes, you will need 10 rows per hour, or 240 rows per day. For now, specify a grid of 240 rows by 6 columns.

6. In the Usage tab of your data connection, set Refresh Options to Refresh on Load and refresh every time the trigger cell (B1 in this example) changes. The setup is virtually identical to Figure 15.7 except that the trigger cell is B1 instead of A1.

7. You might want to place some input fields on the canvas so that you can interactively change values. I've created a sample file (ch15_WebServiceExample.xlf) that you can examine and extend.

8. Test your connection.

9. Close the Data Manager window and populate your canvas with components such as Grid or Spreadsheet Table to view values returned. Click the Preview button. If all goes well, you should see something like what is shown in Figure 15.10.

NOTE

For the sake of simplicity, Figure 15.10 displays only the first few rows of the data that is returned. As a further simplification, I set the end date to always match the value of the begin date. This is why you do not see an end date input text field in the dashboard.

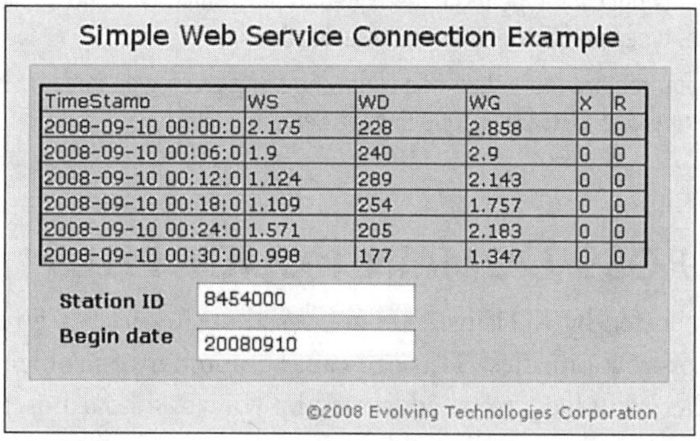

Figure 15.10
A simple Web Services connection dashboard.

Simple Web Service Connection Example

TimeStamp	WS	WD	WG	X	R
2008-09-10 00:00:0	2.175	228	2.858	0	0
2008-09-10 00:06:0	1.9	240	2.9	0	0
2008-09-10 00:12:0	1.124	289	2.143	0	0
2008-09-10 00:18:0	1.109	254	1.757	0	0
2008-09-10 00:24:0	1.571	205	2.183	0	0
2008-09-10 00:30:0	0.998	177	1.347	0	0

Station ID   8454000

Begin date   20080910

©2008 Evolving Technologies Corporation

15

It is possible that you may get an error message, which is generally displayed as an alert message with an error number. An error number 2032 means that something failed, and the nature of the error is not determined. Perhaps you are supplying an invalid input value, the URL for your Web Services query is incorrect, or something else equally innocuous is going on. Check and recheck your setup for something you may have done incorrectly.

> **TIP**
>
> In the Usage tab of your data connection, you can have Xcelsius 2008 write the load status of your query to spreadsheet cells. You can do this to alert the dashboard user when a web query is being made and when it is completed.

When you can successfully connect to remote data sources, there are steps you can take to improve the dashboard. Here are some ideas to think about:

- You can make input easier. In the sample file for the Web Services connection, the begin date requires a hand-entered value. Why not use a Calendar component instead?

- The website for this example (http://opendap.co-ops.nos.noaa.gov) has data for several hundred weather stations. You need only pop in a different station ID to get data for other locations. A simple list box will suffice for this purpose.

- Depending on the duration of data, you could easily get back hundreds of rows of data with each request. This data is just begging to be graphed on some kind of chart.

- Be sure to place some safety covers on your web application. There is no sense trying to retrieve data for nonexistent stations or invalid dates.

> **NOTE**
>
> Xcelsius Engage supports multiple connections in a single visualization, but only one connection of each type of data connection. For instance, a visualization could have one "Web Service" connection, one "XML Data" connection, and one "FS Command"; once that connection type has been added to the visualization, no additional connections of that type can be added to that visualization.
>
> If you require more than one connection of a given type in your visualizations, you need to upgrade to Xcelsius 2008 Engage Server.

SETTING UP CROSS-DOMAIN POLICY FILES

Dashboard files generated by Xcelsius 2008 are based on Adobe Flash technology and are subject its security protection rules. This can cause a number of problems. Some of them you can fix, and others will have to be addressed by your dashboard users.

Consider the following scenario. You design a connected presentation dashboard in your development environment. It is your first dashboard that connects to data on a back-end server. It works like a charm. You place this dashboard on the web for your colleagues.

Using their web browsers, they locate the dashboard. It looks beautiful. The moment the dashboard attempts to connect to your remote data source, your dashboard users get security violation errors.

 This problem can occur if the dashboard is served from one server at a specific domain and the data resides on another domain. To enable connectivity across domains, you must place a cross-domain policy file called `crossdomain.xml` at the root of your server that serves up the data.

To open up connectivity, you create a file like the following:

```
<!DOCTYPE cross-domain-policy SYSTEM
"http://www.macromedia.com/xml/dtds/cross-domain-policy.dtd">
<cross-domain-policy>
<allow-http-request-headers-from domain="*" headers="*" secure="false" />
<allow-access-from domain="*" secure="false" />
</cross-domain-policy>
```

This `crossdomain.xml` file would be placed on the root directory of the application server that serves up the content. You might, for instance, have a Tomcat servlet engine serving up content for `data_repository.example.com`. If the root directory for this server is the following:

```
C:\Program Files\Business Objects\Tomcat\webapps\ROOT
```

this is where you would place the cross-domain file.

CLOSING THOUGHTS

The purpose of this chapter and Chapter 16, "Creating Custom Components for Fun and Profit," is to give you the means to figuratively drive across unpaved roads. In this chapter, the focus is on data connectivity. In Chapter 16, it is on building custom components.

Rather than attempt a whirlwind tour of all the Xcelsius 2008 connectivity features, this chapter presents two hands-on examples. One of them relates to the XML map features of Excel and the other to Web Services. You can use both of these features out of the box. Because connectivity is centrally handled through the Xcelsius Data Manager, there is a high degree of commonality among the various connection options. For instance, quite a few of the connectivity options in the Data Manager let you specify data refresh options. You can therefore apply your experiences here to other types of connection options.

Now that you can tap into remote data sources, you might find that your approach to designing dashboards may be different. If you don't access data remotely, you may be tempted to "swallow" data in large gulps. When you have access to data as you need it, you will find that it suffices to "sip" data. This is bound to have a significant impact on your design approach. The good news is that everything you've learned in the earlier chapters about things like constructing spreadsheet formulas, dynamic visibility, managing interactivity, and charting and graphing techniques, carries over into the connected realm.

Chapter 16 introduces the software development kit (SDK) and the design of custom-built components that you can incorporate into dashboards.

CREATING CUSTOM COMPONENTS FOR FUN AND PROFIT

In this chapter

Xcelsius has a wealth of components to choose from. It should be clear from the previous 15 chapters that you can be endlessly inventive with Xcelsius components. As good as the components in Xcelsius 2008 are, though, you might want to do things that simply cannot be done with the built-in components. If you are willing to really roll up your sleeves, you can construct your own components and incorporate them into your Xcelsius dashboards. That's what this chapter is about.

There are several things to keep in mind as you read this chapter:

- Building custom components requires the use of third-party commercial software, such as Adobe Flex Builder.

- Creating custom components is a technically intense process and requires that you have under your belt a substantial level of knowledge of the Flex Builder development environment, as well as ActionScript programming.

- The technology and framework for designing, building, and testing/deploying custom components is continually and rapidly evolving.

The goal of this chapter is to introduce you to custom components in Xcelsius and get you started producing custom components. This chapter walks you through the basic setup and introduces you to various components.

CAUTION

Building custom components is not for the faint of heart.

UNDERSTANDING CUSTOM COMPONENTS

In contrast to creating custom components, the process of installing them is comparatively trivial. If someone supplies you with a custom component, you can just load it into Xcelsius 2008.

NOTE

Custom components are not limited to Xcelsius 2008 Engage. They can be used in all the editions of Xcelsius 2008 Service Pack 1 (SP1), spanning all the way from the Enterprise version down to Xcelsius 2008 Present.

INSTALLING CUSTOM COMPONENTS

One of the things you may have noticed in Xcelsius 2008 that didn't exist in its predecessors is a new option in the File menu called Manage Add-Ons.

NOTE

Make sure you are running the SP1 version of Xcelsius 2008 and not any of the earlier versions. To check this, in Xcelsius 2008, select Help, About Xcelsius. The build number should be something like 12,1,0,247. If the last set of digits is lower than 247, you are not using SP1.

The process of installing custom components with the Add-On Manager is very easy. Simply click the Install Add-On button, locate the desired component, and click the Open button. Immediately after you install or remove components, you are prompted to restart Xcelsius.

Custom components are first-class citizens. After you install a component, it remains in your Xcelsius workspace. You can then use the custom component just as you would any other Xcelsius component. Custom components work in your dashboards just the same way as any of your other components.

CUSTOM COMPONENT CONSTRUCTION WORKFLOW

The process of building custom components is a little involved. The overall steps are as follows:

1. Build a component using Flex Builder.

2. For the component, set up a property sheet so that the custom component's attributes can be specified. When your custom component is added to Xcelsius, those attributes can be set from the component's property sheet.

NOTE

When you build the property sheet, you will be able to endow your custom component with all sorts of capabilities. You could, for instance, allow the component to bind its title attribute to a spreadsheet cell.

3. Package your component so that that it can be loaded from Xcelsius 2008.

4. Load your custom component with the Xcelsius Add-On Manager and test the component.

PROGRAMMING WITH FLEX BUILDER

Flex Builder is a high-level development environment that generates Flash content (see Figure 16.1). It is built on top of an Integrated Development Environment called Eclipse. This development environment is full of features and supports all sorts of program development facilities using plug-ins. Flex Builder is actually a plug-in that runs on top of Eclipse. You can find out more about Eclipse at www.eclipse.org.

Figure 16.1
The Flex Builder environment.

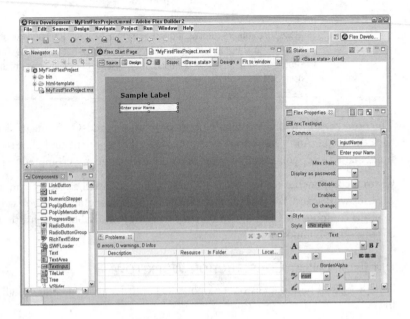

The paradigm for programming with Flex Builder is innovative and unconventional. Flex Builder lets you program in three modes:

- You can program visually by dragging components onto a Flex Builder Design canvas (see Figure 16.1). As you select the Flex Builder components on the canvas, you can adjust the properties of the selected components. In some ways, this is reminiscent of the Xcelsius workspace.

- You can change the viewing mode from Design to Source and reveal the graphical representation of your visual layout in XML. The XML code that is generated might look something like this:

```
<?xml version="1.0" encoding="utf-8"?>
<mx:Application xmlns:mx="http://www.adobe.com/2006/mxml" layout="absolute">
    <mx:Text x="40" y="36" text="Sample Label" fontSize="18"
➥fontWeight="bold"/>
    <mx:TextInput x="40" y="72" text="Enter your Name" id="inputName"/>
</mx:Application>
```

This way of representing the visual elements on the Flex Builder canvas is called MXML. MXML is actually a programming language. If you look at it for a moment, you will see that all the programming statements in this sample code, and indeed in all of MXML, are written as XML content.

One of the nice features of Flex Builder is that you can tweak the MXML, and the visual presentation on the canvas is instantly changed. You can jump back and forth between the Design and Source modes and make changes. Flex Builder automatically keeps those changes in sync.

- You can embed ActionScript code directly inside the MXML content. ActionScript, the programming language used for creating Flash content, is an object-oriented programming language. If you are already familiar with, say, the Java programming language, you should have little trouble transitioning to writing programs using ActionScript. Because Flex Builder provides support for things like code auto-complete, refactoring, and debugging support, you can quickly and easily construct ActionScript code.

A great deal of the time you spend developing custom components for Xcelsius involves working with ActionScript code. Fortunately, much of it is tweaking rather than writing code from scratch.

You now have an overview of what Flex Builder is like. The process of building custom components involves a rather steep learning curve.

GETTING READY TO BUILD CUSTOM COMPONENTS

Before you begin building custom components, you need to procure specific software and do some initial setup. In addition to Xcelsius 2008, you need the Xcelsius 2008 Component SDK and Flex Builder. As part of the installation process, you need to configure your environment and map library files.

SOFTWARE YOU WILL NEED FOR CONSTRUCTING CUSTOM COMPONENTS

To build custom components, you need to have the following in place:

- Xcelsius 2008 SP1 (or later).
- Xcelsius 2008 Component SDK SP1 or later (available from https://boc.sdn.sap.com/xcelsius/sdk). The SDK (software development kit) is not bundled with Xcelsius and is a separate (but free) download.

    When you download the SDK, you get two sets of files. One of them is a set of documents that includes technical guides, tutorials, and API documents you can peruse from your web browser. The other is an installer application that installs the Add-On Packager application on your system. This application allows you to finalize your custom components for deployment. With the SDK, you also get a special set of files you need for building custom components. Assuming that Xcelsius 2008 is installed on the C drive in the default directory, you can find these files in the following path:
    `C:\Program Files\Business Objects\Xcelsius\SDK\bin`

- Flex Builder. Flex Builder is a commercial product of Adobe Systems, Incorporated. If you do not yet have Flex Builder, you can download a trial version from www.adobe.com.

16

NOTE

> The version of Flex Builder that is required for building custom components with Xcelsius 2008 SP1 is Flex Builder SDK 2.0.1 Hotfix 3. This is because Xcelsius 2008 is built using Flex Builder 2 SDK. If you want to use a later Flex Builder version, such as Flex Builder 3, you can, but you will have to tell Flex Builder to compile projects using the Flex Builder 2.0.1 SDK Hotfix 3 SDK.

Flex Builder is available in two different forms: as a full featured standalone application and as a plug-in that you can load onto the Eclipse development environment.

Flex Builder makes use of the features built into Eclipse. The standalone version of Flex Builder has Eclipse built into it. If you are already running Eclipse, there is no need to download the standalone version of Flex Builder. Just get the Flex Builder plug-in and install it in your Eclipse environment.

TIP

> The Flex Builder environment is a rather heavyweight piece of software. Be sure you have a lot of RAM (think in terms of multiple gigabytes), disk space, and processor speed at your disposal. In addition, having a large screen will help you work more productively. A workstation class computer should fit the bill.

INITIAL SOFTWARE SETUP

Before you can go to work on building components, you need to install the Xcelsius SDK and then install and configure Flex Builder.

INSTALLING THE XCELSIUS SDK

Download the Xcelsius SDK (from https://boc.sdn.sap.com/irj/boc/xcelsius-sdk) and run the installer named `Xcelsius_ComponentSDK_Installer_XXXX.exe` (where the *XXXX* identifies the version of the SDK, such as `2.0.640`). This installer does two things:

- It installs the Add-On Packager application on your system.
- It creates an SDK directory in the Xcelsius application path and inserts a bunch of files there. Typically, these files are installed in `C:\Program Files\Business Objects\Xcelsius\ SDK`. For the moment, make note of the location.

NOTE

> The instructions here are specific to SP1 of Xcelsius 2008. Be sure that Xcelsius and Microsoft .NET Framework 2.0 are already installed before you install the Xcelsius SDK.

INSTALLING AND SETTING UP FLEX BUILDER

Before you can develop custom Xcelsius components for Xcelsius 2008 SP1, you need to download and install Flex Builder SDK 2.0.1 Hotfix 3. At some point down the road, you will be able to make full use of later versions of Flex Builder to create custom Xcelsius components. Whether you use the standalone version of Flex Builder or the Flex Builder plug-in and install it on top of Eclipse is entirely up to you.

TIP

> If you don't spend 75% of your professional life developing code and have no other reason to work with Eclipse, you will probably find it easier to install the standalone version of Flex Builder than to use the plug-in.

Place a copy of the file `xcelsiusframework.swc` in the library path of Flex Builder. Normally, the `xcelsiusframework.swc` file can be found here:

```
C:\Program Files\Business Objects\Xcelsius\SDK\bin
```

The library path of Flex Builder 2 is generally found here:

```
C:\Program Files\Adobe\Flex Builder 2\Flex SDK 2\frameworks\libs
```

For Flex Builder 3, this is the path:

```
C:\Program Files\Adobe\Flex Builder 3\sdks\2.0.1\frameworks\libs
```

NOTE

> There is an optional step of installing Apache Ant for Flex Builder. For further information, refer to the `Xcelsius2008_componentsdk_install_guide.pdf` file supplied with the Xcelsius SDK.

When you launch Flex Builder for the first time, you are prompted to select a directory where you want to place your Flex Builder project files. This directory is referred to as the Workspace.

TIP

> Don't confuse the Flex Builder Workspace with the Xcelsius workspace discussed in earlier chapters. Flex Builder also uses the terms *components* and *canvas*, but they are not exactly the same as the ones used in Xcelsius.

The examples in this chapter are all based on using `C:\FlexBuilderFiles` as the directory for the Flex Builder workspace. You can map your Flex Builder workspace to a different directory by selecting Switch Workspace from the Flex Builder application menu.

16

BUILDING CUSTOM COMPONENTS

The process of building custom components is multifaceted. Let's begin by a simple example. This "Hello, World"–style example involves a rudimentary horizontal slider. It's not a sophisticated example, but it shows the elements you need to address when building components and how to go about building components. It should give you a fair idea of how things fit together.

This example isn't terribly complex, but it's also not plain vanilla. There are two more things you'll do with this example:

- Enhance some of the features of the rudimentary dashboard
- Think about other kinds of components you can construct and deploy

CONSTRUCTING A BASIC SLIDER COMPONENT

Xcelsius provides a set of sample files for building custom components that are automatically installed when the Add-On Packager is installed. You should carefully examine these files, which are located in the following directory:

`C:\Program Files\Business Objects\Xcelsius\SDK\samples`

At first glance, it may not be evident how the various pieces of code fit together. Very briefly, there are two sides to constructing a custom component:

- There is the construction of the component itself. In effect, you need to create the source of what is needed to make a component.
- The flip side is the property sheet, a mapping that glues together the elements of a custom component to the Xcelsius component's property sheet so that values can be defined.

After you define these two sides, they can be fused or packaged together to create an installable component.

The following sections walk through the task of building a custom component and outline some tips.

BUILDING A COMPONENT'S SOURCE

You need to begin by creating a Flex Builder project. You can give the project a name like `MyComponentSource`. In Flex Builder, select File, New, Flex Builder Project. You are prompted to select Basic, Cold Fusion Flash Remoting Serving, or Flex Data Services. Choose Basic and click the Next button.

For the project name, enter `MyComponentSource`. Flex Builder automatically sets the location where the project is saved. If you have been adhering to the settings in this chapter, this location is `C:\FlexBuilderFiles\MyComponentSource`. (You are free to change it to a different location, but this chapter assumes that you are following the settings listed in this chapter.) Click the Next button.

Before finishing the Flex Builder Create Project task, you need to hook in the xcelsius-framework.swc file. Hopefully, you already copied this file to the libs directory, as outlined in the setup steps earlier in the chapter. In Flex Builder 3, files placed in the frameworks\libs folder are automatically available for use.

If you are using Flex Builder 2, you have to explicitly associate the xcelsiusframework.swc file with the project's library path. Click the Library Path tab, and you see a set of entries in the Build Path Libraries box (see Figure 16.2). Check whether the file xcelsiusframework.swc is present. If it is not present, you need to add it by clicking the Add SWC button and navigating to where the xcelsiusframework.swc file is located.

TIP

You can type ${FRAMEWORKS}\libs\xcelsiusframework.swc instead of manually navigating to locate the file. Flex Builder 3 automatically knows to include files in the libs directory as part of the library path.

Figure 16.2
The xcelsius-framework.swc file needs to be included in your project's library path.

After the xcelsiusframework.swc file is added to your project's library path, click the Finish button to complete the project creation.

Next, you need to adjust the project properties (see Figure 16.3). With your source project selected in the Flex Compiler navigation pane, open the project properties from the Flex Builder File menu (alternatively, you can press the Alt+Enter or right-click with the mouse) to open a properties window. On the left panel, select Flex Complier. In the Additional Compiler Arguments field, change `-locale en_US` to:

```
-locale en_US -keep-as3-metadata+=Inspectable,Style,CxInspectableList
```

Figure 16.3
Setting compiler options.

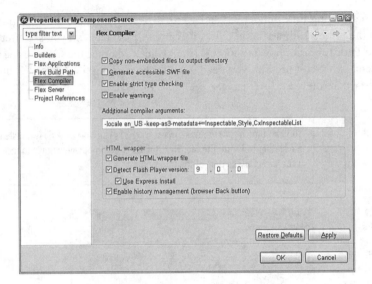

This setting tells the Flex Builder compiler that it is okay to access specified properties and styles in the custom component and make them available in the Xcelsius Properties panel.

With this setup in place, you are ready to do some coding. At this point, you are looking at an empty Flex Builder project with the following MXML code:

```
<?xml version="1.0" encoding="utf-8"?>
<mx:Application xmlns:mx="http://www.adobe.com/2006/mxml" layout="absolute">
</mx:Application>
```

To this barebones source component you need to add some ActionScript code for a custom component. In this example, the component is a basic horizontal slider. Indeed, the name of the ActionScript class you will create is going to be `BasicHorizontalSlider`.

An interesting issue looms here. Just as you might elect to use the name `BasicHorizontalSlider`, so might an army of other independent developers. What would happen if a dashboard practitioner were to load your slider component as well as a similarly named component from another independent developer? There would be a naming collision.

To avoid such difficulties, you can "package" your ActionScript class by using a unique classpath. The practice that professional programmers use for naming a classpath is to base it on the company's or organization's network domain and tack on to the path appropriate subcategories. For example, for Business Objects, whose domain is `businessobjects.com`, a suitable classpath for code used in the Xcelsius SDK sample files might look like this:

```
com.businessobjects.xcelsius.sdk.samples
```

NOTE

By convention, classpaths in ActionScript (and in Java) are generally lowercase.

Go ahead and create an ActionScript class called BasicHorizontalSlider with the appropriate classpath. In Flex Builder, select File, New, ActionScript Class. Supply the appropriate package name and the name of the class and then click the Finish button (see Figure 16.4).

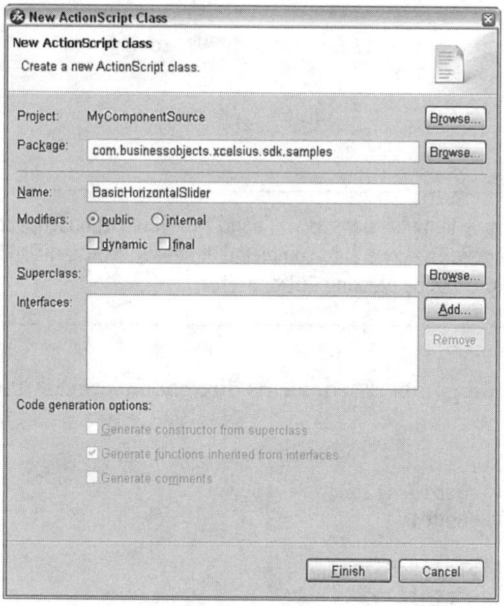

Figure 16.4
Package your files based on your company's network domain and logical organization.

A new editor window appears, and it contains the following code:

```
package com.businessobjects.xcelsius.sdk.samples
{
    public class BasicHorizontalSlider
    {
    }
}
```

At this point, the code is really a placeholder. The first thing you want to do is incorporate code already developed and built into Flex Builder. There is a built-in class called HSlider that has features you might want to use in your custom component. There is no need to reinvent the wheel.

To incorporate the code, you can declare the class you just created, BasicHorizontalSlider, to be a subclass of HSlider so that it inherits all the HSlider's properties and behavior. (BasicHorizontalSlider *extends* the HSlider class.) In your subclass, you can add additional properties and define new kinds of behaviors. You can also override the properties and behaviors inherited from the superclass (in this example, HSlider).

HSlider lives in a package called mx.controls. So you have to *import* a reference to where the HSlider class is defined. An import statement does not physically import a file; rather, it just tells the ActionScript compiler that when it sees HSlider, it should automatically associate it with the HSlider that resides in the mx.controls package.

To reflect all this, your ActionScript code should look something like the following:

```
package com.businessobjects.xcelsius.sdk.samples
{
    import mx.controls.HSlider;

    public class BasicHorizontalSlider extends HSlider
    {
    }
}
```

> **TIP**
>
> An interesting thing happens as you hand type your ActionScript code in the Flex Builder editor window: The code auto-completed. If needed, you can also kick-start the auto-complete process by pressing Ctrl+spacebar.

You need to add the following import statements directly underneath the import statement for the HSlider:

```
import mx.controls.Label;
import mx.styles.CSSStyleDeclaration;
import mx.styles.StyleManager;

import flash.text.TextFieldAutoSize;
import flash.text.TextFormatAlign;
```

When you create an ActionScript class, you can endow it with properties and have it run through an initialization process every time you create a new instance of the class. To understand what is meant by *instance*, think of your custom components as classes and every custom component that is dropped onto the Xcelsius canvas as an instance. The properties could include the following:

```
//-----------------------------------
// Properties
//-----------------------------------

    private var _title:Label;
    private var _titlesChanged:Boolean = true;
    private var _titleText:String = "Title";

    private var _showTitle:Boolean = true;
```

When you construct instances of a class, you use a *constructor*. Constructors tell a class to perform certain tasks before creating instances of that class. In many cases, it may not be necessary to include a constructor if you don't need to do any special initialization each time an instance of a class is created. But what if the class you are inheriting from performs some specialized task for initialization? In that case, it would be prudent to perform the same initialization task for the inherited subclass. Because `BasicHorizontalSlider` inherits from `HSlider`, it would be nice for each instance of `BasicHorizontalSlider` to say "Yeah, I'll do whatever my superclass does when its instances are initialized. You know what? Don't even bother telling me the gory programming details. I'll just do it."

You accomplish all this by embedding a `super()` construct within the constructor:

```
//----------------------------------
//  Constructor
//----------------------------------

    public function BasicHorizontalSlider()
    {
        super();
    }
```

The next step is to make properties of the custom component available within the Xcelsius Properties panel. To do this, you need to do the following:

- Provide getter and/or setter methods. This allows the custom component to programmatically respond to some sort of request.
- Explicitly identify that the feature or attribute is `Inspectable`.
- Control when the inspectable features or attributes will be shown in the property sheet.

 Immediately following the import statements, but before the class definition for the `BasicHorizontalSlider`, you need to enter the following line:

```
[CxInspectableList ("title", "showTitle")]
```

This lets the property sheet know that there will be entries for the slider's `title` and `showTitle` attributes. If you don't include this line, every setting is exposed. The meaning of `title` is obvious. `showTitle` lets you control whether a title should appear on the custom slider component.

The next step is to create setter and getter methods so that the component knows how to respond to requests, and the methods expose these attributes. After the constructor, add code for this set of methods:

```
//----------------------------------
//  titleText Property
//----------------------------------

    [Inspectable(defaultValue="Title", type="String")]
    public function get title():String
    {
        return _titleText;
    }

    public function set title(value:String):void
    {
        if (value == null)  value = "";
        if (_titleText != value)
        {
            _titlesChanged = true;
```

```
        _titleText = value;
        invalidateProperties();
    }
}
```

The code for showTitle is fairly equivalent to the code for title.

When a custom component is installed in Xcelsius, it becomes draggable onto the canvas. When it is dragged onto the canvas, a new instance of the component (in this case, the custom slider) is created. Every time a new instance of the custom component installed in Xcelsius is dragged onto the canvas, the createChildren function is called. The super.createChildren function runs createChildren as it is defined in the superclass (in this example, HSlider) and then does all these other things, as spelled out in the following code:

```
override protected function createChildren():void
{
    super.createChildren();

    // Allow the user to make this component very small.
    this.minWidth = 0;
    this.minHeight = 0;

    //set snapInternal
    this.snapInterval = 0.01;

    // Title.
    _title = new Label();
    _title.setActualSize(152, 20);
    _title.y = _title.y - 20;
    _title.setStyle("textAlign", TextFormatAlign.LEFT);
    _title.minWidth = 0;
    _title.minHeight = 0;
    _title.selectable = false;
    _title.truncateToFit = true;
    _title.percentWidth = 100;
    this.addChild(_title);
}
```

When a property is changed on the component, invalidateProperties should be called. For efficiency reasons, the changes are not handled as the property is changing but later, in commitProperties, which is called by the Flex Builder framework to process the property changes. These housekeeping tasks are handled by the following code:

```
override protected function commitProperties():void
{
    super.commitProperties();

    // Check if we need to update the title.
    if (this._titlesChanged)
    {
        _title.text = _titleText;
        _title.includeInLayout = true;
        invalidateDisplayList();  // invalidate in case the titles
                                  // require more or less room.
        _titlesChanged = false;
```

```
    }

    // Update title's visibility
    _title.visible = _showTitle;
}

override protected function updateDisplayList(unscaledWidth:Number,
➥unscaledHeight:Number):void
{
    super.updateDisplayList(unscaledWidth, unscaledHeight);
    // give the title Label more room based on the text width
    _title.setActualSize(unscaledWidth, 20);
}
```

CONNECTING YOUR ACTIONSCRIPT AND MXML CODE

Now that you have created ActionScript code for the BasicHorizontalSlider, you need to find a way to tie it into the Flex Builder MXML application. Replace the MXML code with the following:

```
<?xml version="1.0" encoding="utf-8"?>
<mx:Application xmlns:mx="http://www.adobe.com/2006/mxml" layout="absolute"
        xmlns:ns="com.businessobjects.xcelsius.sdk.samples.*">
    <ns:BasicHorizontalSlider width="100%" height="100%"/>
    </mx:Application>
```

There are two significant changes here:

- There's a reference to the BasicHorizontalSlider calls, along with some initialization information concerning width and height.

- There's a namespace reference to the com.businessobjects.xcelsius.sdk.samples package.

GENERATING THE SWF FILE FOR YOUR CUSTOM COMPONENT

Before you generate the file that you will use for the custom component, you need to tell the Flex Builder compiler that it needs to retain certain information about the component. At the root level of your project, create a file that has the name of your project immediately followed with -config.xml. In this example, select File, New, File in Flex Builder. Set the file name to MyComponentSource-config.xml. In this file, place the following content:

```
<?xml version="1.0"?>
<flex-config xmlns="http://www.adobe.com/2006/flex-config">
    <compiler>

<!-- Add the Xcelsius 2008 Component SDK framework
    to the Adobe Flex classpath.
  -->
        <library-path append="true">
            <path-element>
                ${flexlib}\libs\xcelsiusframework.swc
            </path-element>
        </library-path>
```

```
<!-- Keep additional metadata needed for use with
     the Xcelsius 2008 Default Property Sheet.
-->
        <keep-as3-metadata>
            <name>Inspectable</name>
            <name>Style</name>
            <name>CxInspectableList</name>
        </keep-as3-metadata>
    </compiler>
</flex-config>
```

This tells the Flex command-line compiler to retain the metadata for the tags in your code that relate to `Inspectable`, `Style`, and `CxInspectableList`.

It is time to generate the SWF file that will be packaged in your custom component. This entails invoking the Flex SDK directly from the command line. This is called `mxmlc.exe` and is bundled with Flex Builder. The file might be located in `C:\Program Files\Adobe\Flex Builder 2\Flex SDK 2\bin`.

From a command prompt (in Windows XP, run the `cmd.exe` file), you set the directory to the project:

`cd C:\FlexBuilderFiles\MyComponentSource`

Then you compile the file:

```
"C:\Program Files\Adobe\Flex Builder 2\Flex SDK 2\bin\mxmlc.exe"
➥MyComponentSource.mxml -output BasicHorizontalSlider.swf
```

NOTE

> If you have spaces in your path or file name, you must enclose the full path and file name in quotes.

The Flex compiler generates a file called `BasicHorizontalSlider.swf`, which is placed in the root directory of your Flex Builder project (in this example, the directory would be `C:\FlexBuilderFiles\MyComponentSource`).

THE RELATIONSHIP BETWEEN A CUSTOM COMPONENT AND A PROPERTY SHEET

One of the guiding principles behind the architectural design of the Xcelsius SDK is modularity. In particular, the designer of a custom component shouldn't have to know much of anything about Xcelsius. In an ideal world, you would want the custom component to say "When a custom component is dragged onto the Xcelsius canvas, I only want certain features to be `Inspectable`." Likewise, the Properties panel in the Xcelsius workspace doesn't really care about the inner workings of your custom components. All it wants to know is what attributes and values of the custom components are readable and changeable.

This separation of responsibilities, much like the layered approach design pattern strategy outlined earlier in the book, is very liberating. It allows you to build custom components without having to worry about how everything works inside Xcelsius. The only things you need to concern yourself with are the features you want to expose to Xcelsius.

With a custom component making itself accessible, you need to address how to tap into those features within Xcelsius 2008. This is the role of the property sheet.

In an ideal world, it would be nice to have Xcelsius inspect a custom component and automatically assemble the various attributes within the Properties panel of the Xcelsius workspace. The good news is that it can do this. The Xcelsius SDK has a ready-made file called `PropertyInspector.swf`, located in the following directory:

```
C:\Program Files\Business Objects\Xcelsius\SDK\bin
```

All you need to do is reference this file when packaging your component, and you're done. It's simple.

NOTE

> Of course, if you want more control and capabilities within the Properties panel for your custom component, you need to create a custom property sheet, and that does entail coding.

PACKAGING AND DEPLOYING YOUR CUSTOM COMPONENTS

Packaging and deploying custom components involves the following steps:

1. Create and build a packaging project file, using the Xcelsius Add-On Packager application.
2. Export the packaged component to an `.xlx` file and distribute the file to users running Xcelsius 2008.
3. From the Xcelsius 2008 application, access the Add-On Manager from the File menu, locate the `.xlx` file, and install it.
4. Close and restart Xcelsius 2008.

PACKAGING YOUR CUSTOM COMPONENT

As indicated by its name, the Add-On Packager allows you to package add-on components for Xcelsius 2008. Basically, you define a packaging project, including information about your components, and build a loadable add-on for use with Xcelsius, which gets saved as a `.xlx` file. A nice feature of the Add-On Packager is that it enables you to bundle multiple custom components in a single build.

16

The Xcelsius Add-On Packager application (see Figure 16.5) contains a number of tabs:

- **Details**: This is the basic tab that appears when a component is selected in the Xcelsius Add-On Manager.

- **Visual Components**: This tab tells the packager where the custom component and property sheets are located. You can also specify the version number of the component and upload bitmap icons for your custom components.

- **Connections**: This tab is similar to the Visual Components tab except that the components in this section target the Xcelsius 2008 Data Manager.

- **Functions**: This tab allows you to identify the function name, SWF files, and version numbers for simulated Excel functions that are not currently supported in Xcelsius 2008.

- **Build**: Building is a very simple process: You save an `.xlx` file, and you're done with packaging.

The following sections quickly step though the process of packaging a custom component. To help keep things concrete, we'll principally stay with the `BasicHorizontalSlider` example.

DETAILS TAB VIEW

The information in the Details tab includes the name, publisher, website, publish date, version, description, and license agreement (see Figure 16.5). All the fields except License Agreement (EULA) are fill-ins. The license agreement is a text file that you can create separately and incorporate into your component.

Figure 16.5
Add-On Packager.

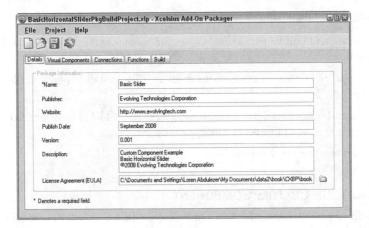

TAB VIEWS FOR ASSEMBLING SPECIFIC INFORMATION ABOUT YOUR COMPONENTS

The Xcelsius 2008 Component SDK supports three different kinds of custom components. Depending on the kind of component, you select one of the following three tab views:

- Visual Components
- Connections
- Functions

Each tab view lists the collections of components for that type (see Figure 16.6) and displays relevant information about each component. In each view, you can add additional components and edit or remove components.

Figure 16.6
Tab view showing existing components with ability to add, remove, or edit components.

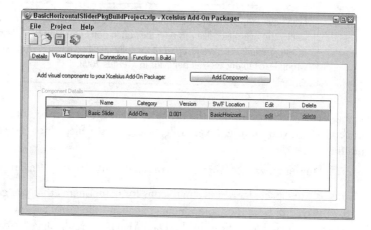

When you click the Add Component button or the edit link, you are prompted to supply information about the component (see Figure 16.7).

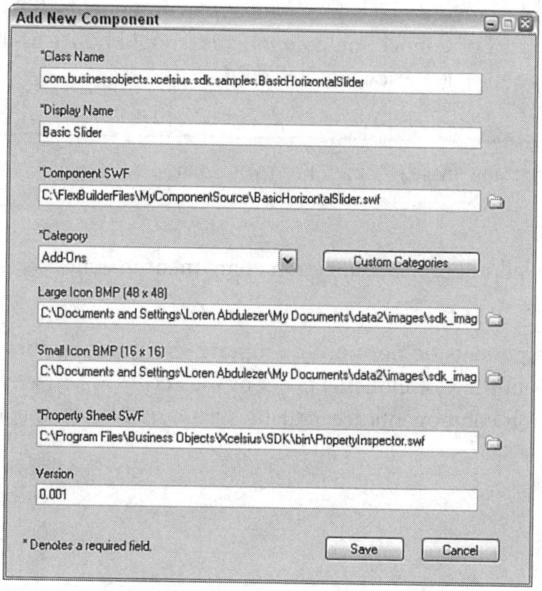

Figure 16.7
When adding or editing a component, you are prompted to supply specific information about the component.

The class name needs to be the fully qualified name with the classpath. In this example, it would look like this:

```
com.businessobjects.xcelsius.sdk.samples.BasicHorizontalSlider
```

The location of the component's SWF file needs to be identified. In this example it is as follows:

```
C:\FlexBuilderFiles\MyComponentSource\BasicHorizontalSlider.swf
```

CAUTION

> I can't overemphasize the importance of getting all the parameters correct. People constantly trip over fields like this one; they often don't enter the right class name, have missing periods, or have just part of the fully qualified name. Getting such information wrong leads to unexpected behavior in Xcelsius 2008.

You need to provide the location of the property sheet file. If you do not need to use a custom property sheet, you can use the `PropertyInspector.swf` file, which has the following full path and file name:

```
C:\Program Files\Business Objects\Xcelsius\SDK\bin\PropertyInspector.swf
```

In the Xcelsius workspace, large and small icons for components that you can drag onto the canvas are displayed in both the Components panel and the Object Browser. Similarly, icons for the various kinds of connections in the Data Manager are displayed as you add connections.

You can create your own icons by using bitmap images and incorporate them into your custom visual and connection components. Your large icons should be 48-by-48 pixels for visual components and 32-by-32 pixels for connection components. Small icons, regardless of whether they are visual or connection components, should be 16-by-16 pixels. If you don't supply any image files, generic icons are used.

NOTE

> Be sure your image files use 24-bit color depth.

The information needed to build a connection component matches the structure shown in Figures 16.6 and 16.7.

Custom function components do not need a property sheet, nor do they need image icons, as they do not appear in the Components panel or Object Browser (see Figure 16.8). In this regard, custom function components are actually a little simpler than components built using custom property sheets.

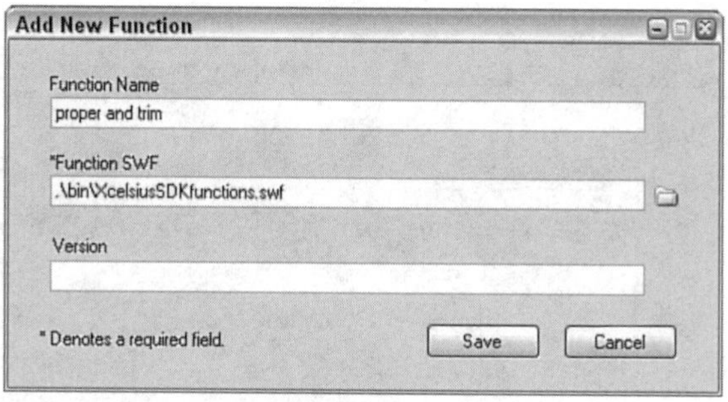

Figure 16.8
Function components require comparatively less information than their visual and connection component counterparts.

COMPONENT PROJECT AND BUILD FILES

The Add-On Packager conveniently allows you to save/load all your settings so that it is not necessary to re-enter all the information used to generate the custom components. Package project files have the `.xlp` extension.

The Add-On Packager generates a loadable custom component that has an `.xlx` extension. To generate the file, you follow these steps:

1. Select the Build tab in the Add-On Packager.

2. Click the Build Package button. You are prompted to give the generated file a name and specify a drive location. For this example, save the generated file as `BasicSlider.xlx`. If the build is successful, a notification is displayed in the Build tab.

3. When the file is generated, load it into Xcelsius 2008.

NOTE

You can bundle more than one custom component in an XLX file.

LOADING, TESTING, AND ENHANCING COMPONENTS

Now it is time to start getting some gratification for all your hard work. The following sections walk you through the steps of loading and removing components, giving your components a test run, and enhancing your components.

LOADING AND TESTING COMPONENTS

Imagine that you are an Xcelsius dashboard practitioner who just got a new custom component and is about to install it in Xcelsius 2008. For this example, you'll use the `BasicSlider.xlx` file.

Launch Xcelsius 2008 and select File, Add-On Manager. The Xcelsius Add-On Manager window appears (see Figure 16.9).

Figure 16.9
Installing custom components with the Xcelsius Add-On Manager.

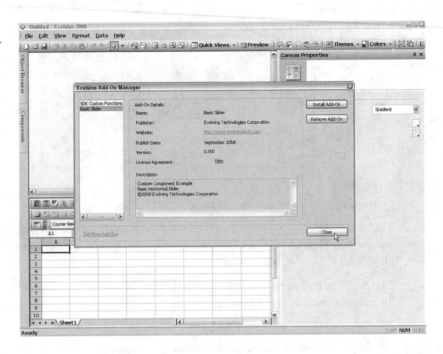

The panel on the left side of the Add-On Manager window displays a list of component sets that are loaded in the Xcelsius workspace. When you click one of these sets, the information from the Details tab becomes visible. If a license agreement was packaged with the build, there will be a link you can click.

To remove a loaded set of custom components, you select the set and click the Remove Add-On button. If you want to remove more than one add-on, you just repeat the process. When you're done, you click the Close button.

NOTE

If you removed or installed any add-on components, Xcelsius will force you to quit the application, as it is forced to register the component changes.

As you remove or install each component, you are forced to quit and restart Xcelsius so the program can register the component changes. This is a little cumbersome. But because it's essentially a one time process, it's not worth fretting over.

TIP

To save time and avoid needless quitting and restarting, you can remove a set of add-ons and then install your add-on. You can also use the command-line version of the Add-On Manager. This is especially helpful when you're testing a component.

The Xcelsius 2008 Component SDK provides a fair amount of documentation related to debugging and tracing. If you are the program developer type, you should read it.

NOTE

> For Flex Builder 2, debug SWFs are separate from the production SWF. For Flex Builder 3, the production SWF contains debug information as well.
>
> Also, when testing, you can use the Flash debug player to see runtime ActionScript errors, if any.

Another kind of testing can and should be done, and it doesn't require any programming. Simply take your custom component and put it through its paces:

- Test to see that the component initializes to correct values when placed on the canvas in Designer mode and then actually run it in Preview mode.

- Don't just settle for testing in Preview mode; export the dashboard with the custom component as an SWF and run it outside Xcelsius.

- When running the dashboard, try to see if you (or really, dashboard users) can break it by putting in invalid or inappropriate values.

- Drag a custom component onto the canvas. Bind the properties or attributes to some spreadsheet cells. Copy and paste the components so that you have effectively cloned a component on the dashboard. When the dashboard is run, does it behave as expected? Does anything else go awry?

- Test the interactions of your component with Xcelsius components on the canvas and in Preview mode.

If you are going to distribute dashboards with custom components, you need to ensure that your components have been tested.

ENHANCING YOUR COMPONENTS

One of the things you'll find when you create custom components is that the process of building them is cyclical: You design, build, test, repeat. You find out what is wrong or determine how you want to improve something, and then you go back and tweak your design.

If you followed along with the basic slider example earlier in this chapter, you created a slider that works, but it isn't very useful. You can move the slider, but the slider value can't be mapped to an underlying spreadsheet cell.

In the code, the BasicHorizontalSlider class is declared as a subclass of HSlider, a standard component that is built into Flex Builder. It needs to support accessing values. You only need to figure out how to unlock the desired features of the component so they will show up in the Xcelsius Properties panel. To make it accessible, here are the steps you follow:

1. Change the line of code in the `BasicHorizontalSlider.as` file from this:

   ```
   [CxInspectableList ("title", "showTitle")]
   ```

   to this:

   ```
   [CxInspectableList ("title", "showTitle", "value")]
   ```

   Then save the file.

2. Using the Flex Builder SDK command-line compiler, regenerate the SWF component:

   ```
   "C:\Program Files\Adobe\Flex Builder 2\Flex SDK 2\bin\mxmlc.exe"
   ➥MyComponentSource.mxml -output BasicHorizontalSlider.swf
   ```

3. Rebuild your XLX file, using the Add-On Packager.

4. Remove the old component and install the new one, using the Add-On Manager.

When you follow these steps, you may notice that the title of the slider can be mapped to a spreadsheet cell. You can even map it to the slider value. Therefore, the title that appears with the slider is dynamic.

Notice that changing the slider value updates the title, but only after you release the mouse button. The slider is not as interactive as you might like. You can quickly remedy this. In the same ActionScript file you used earlier, add the line that appears in boldface in the code snippet shown here:

```
//set snapInternal
this.snapInterval = 0.01;
this.liveDragging = true;
```

Now repeat steps 2 through 4. This time, you will find that the title that was mapped to the slider value changes continually as you move the slider marker.

WHERE TO GO FROM HERE

I would be remiss if I didn't touch on two topics of importance in this chapter. One of them relates to additional features of the SDK, some of which are new since SP1 of Xcelsius 2008 was introduced. The other is a brief list of potential landmines to avoid when constructing custom components.

ADDITIONAL FEATURES IN THE SDK

There are four items worth mentioning here: custom property sheets, connection components, function components, and visual components centered around Flex MXML.

PROPERTY SHEETS

The property sheet portion permits fine-grained control in setting the Properties panel. The documentation set comes with a set of tutorial files. Tutorial 4 deals exclusively with custom property sheets. It is worth spending some time going through this.

CONNECTION COMPONENTS

Connection components are a new feature of the Xcelsius 2008 Component SDK. They are designed to work through the Xcelsius Data Manager (see Chapter 15, "XML and Data Connectivity"). To build a connection component, you absolutely must use a custom property sheet, which is why I suggested that you spend some time going through Tutorial 4.

FUNCTION COMPONENTS

Another class of components that you can construct is called *function components*. Here's the deal: Out of the box, Xcelsius 2008 supports approximately 160 Excel functions. While you are in Designer mode, building dashboards, Xcelsius 2008 is actually running Excel, and you have full command of the Excel environment, which includes some 340 functions. When a dashboard is exported into an SWF file, it runs a program that simulates your Excel spreadsheet.

Xcelsius does a pretty good job of mimicking your spreadsheet's behavior in Excel. But it only really handles it for some 160 Excel functions. One day, Xcelsius may be able to support all of Excel's functions, but that day is not here yet. So if there is a "must have" Excel function that cannot wait until Business Objects makes it a standard part of Xcelsius, you can write your own code to mimic the specific Excel function. The code that you write has to be written in ActionScript.

One of the sample files provided with the Xcelsius 2008 Component SDK is an example of how to construct such function components (illustrated using code examples based on Excel's TRIM and PROPER functions).

MXML-BASED COMPONENTS

When you use Flex Builder–based components, the traditional process has been to use the top-level MXML to rope in ActionScript code, which basically winds up taking over the show.

There's nothing wrong with tapping into raw ActionScript, but doing so glosses over one of the chief benefits of working with Flex Builder—the ability to design components visually and then tweak the visual layout and behavior at the XML coding level or graphically.

New to the Xcelsius 2008 Component SDK is the ability to blend MXML and ActionScript. The SDK comes with a sample MXML slider. Keep in mind that this technology is rapidly evolving and morphing.

AVOIDING POTENTIAL LANDMINES

In working with custom components, there are several things you need to keep in mind. The technology is brand spanking new, so some of the wrinkles are being ironed out. Gaps are being filled, and new features are being added.

16

Keep in mind the following as you develop components:

- Add-on components do not work with the Local Scenario or Reset buttons. The Local Scenario and Reset buttons work with regular components on a dashboard, but they may not correctly save and restore the state of custom components.

- When you create Flex Builder projects, be sure to utilize the correct Flex SDK version. At the time of this writing, it is the Flex Builder 2.0.1 SDK Hotfix 3. It won't be long before everything moves to a Flex 3 SDK or later. The expectation is that even when it does, there could be some changes to the setup and configuration involved in building custom components, but the overall techniques outlined here should still be valid.

- If you are trying to create a component based on mixing ActionScript 2 and ActionScript 3, forget about it. Everything you do related to building custom components is ActionScript 3 based.

- When you build custom Xcelsius components, be sure to create unique classpaths to avoid naming collisions if Xcelsius users install similarly named classes from components created by another developer.

  If everyone who reads this chapter develops and posts a sample slider with a fully qualified name like this:

  `com.businessobjects.xcelsius.sdk.samples.BasicHorizontalSlider`

  a lot of potential name collisions could occur. The moment two XLX files are installed on an Xcelsius user's system, it's going to wreak havoc.

  Do yourself a favor and follow the Java naming convention for classpaths: premise it on your own network domain instead of the one listed in the examples. Or take it a step further by trying to create unique class names.

- Avoid the having two or more components with the same class name in an add-on package.

- The Add-On Packager creates XLP and XLX files. Do not copy an XLP file, change its name, open the copied file, possibly tweak it, generate a new XLX, and install that new XLX when you already have the original XLX file installed in Xcelsius.

- If you are building a connection component, be sure to create the custom property sheet. It will not suffice to use the generic `PropertyInspector.swf` file normally found here:

  `C:\Program Files\Business Objects\Xcelsius\SDK\bin`

- At present, the Xcelsius 2008 Component SDK (SP1) is currently in English only.

These reminders may help keep you out of hot water. Hopefully, by the time you read this, many of them will be obsolete.

CLOSING THOUGHTS

One of the basic goals of this book is to empower you to do more with Xcelsius 2008. You can do more if you learn about the wealth of components and features of the product. You can do more by applying best practices. You can do more by getting a real handle on the data that makes its way into your dashboards.

Ultimately, there is a limit to what you can do if the building blocks of your dashboard (namely, the components) are taken from a fixed selection of components. This chapter changes all of that by showing you how to build components to your specification from the ground up.

16

APPENDICES

SUPPORTED SPREADSHEET FUNCTIONS IN XCELSIUS 2008

In this appendix

Xcelsius 2008 supports a wide variety of spreadsheet functions. This appendix provides a comprehensive list of supported functions, their arguments, and a brief description.

SUPPORTED SPREADSHEET FUNCTIONS IN XCELSIUS 2008

The functions in this section are organized into the following distinct groups for easy reference: date and time functions (Table A.1), financial functions (Table A.2), logical functions (Table A.3), math functions (Table A.4), reference functions (Table A.5), statistical functions (Table A.6), and text-related functions (Table A.7). This section also provides a brief description of the various operators used in spreadsheet formulas.

The use of square brackets in a spreadsheet function denotes optional arguments. For instance, the following example:

```
SUMIF(range, criteria[, sum_range])
```

is the same as both of the following:

```
SUMIF(range, criteria)
SUMIF(range, criteria, sum_range)
```

TABLE A.1 DATE AND TIME SPREADSHEET FUNCTIONS IN XCELSIUS 2008

Spreadsheet Function	Description
DATE(year, month, day)	Returns the sequential Excel date/time serial number that represents a particular date.
DATEVALUE(date_text)	Converts a date text form to an Excel date/time serial number.
DAVERAGE(database, field, criteria)	Returns the average of selected list or database entries based on specified criteria.
DAY(serial_number)	Converts an Excel date/time serial number to the day of a month.
DAYS360(start_date, end_date, method)	Calculates the number of days between two dates, using a specified 30-day month/360-day year method.
EDATE(start_date, months)	Returns the Excel date/time serial number of the date that is the indicated number of months before or after the start_date.
EOMONTH(start_date, months)	Returns the Excel date/time serial number of the last day of the month before or after a specified number of months from start_date.
HOUR(serial_number)	Converts an Excel date/time serial number to an hour.
MINUTE(serial_number)	Converts an Excel date/time serial number to a minute.

Spreadsheet Function	Description
MONTH(*serial_number*)	Converts an Excel date/time serial number to a month number.
NETWORKDAYS(*start_date, end_date, holidays*)	Returns the number of whole working days between two dates, excluding specified holidays.
NOW()	Returns the Excel date/time serial number of the current date and time. Volatile.
SECOND(*serial_number*)	Converts an Excel date/time serial number to a second.
TIME(*hour, minute, second*)	Returns the decimal portion of an Excel date/time serial number for a particular time.
TIMEVALUE(*time_text*)	Converts the time in an acceptable form of text enclosed in quotation marks to the decimal portion of an Excel date/time serial number.
TODAY()	Returns the Excel date/time serial number of today's date. Volatile.
WEEKDAY(*serial_number, return_type*)	Converts an Excel date/time serial number to the number of the day of the week, based on the counting system *return_type*.
WEEKNUM(*serial_num, return_type*)	Returns the week number in the year. The first week starts January 1; the second week starts the following Sunday (*return_type* = 1) or Monday (*return_type* = 2).
WORKDAY(*start_date, days, holidays*)	Returns the Excel date/time serial number of the date before or after a specified number of workdays, excluding holidays.
YEAR(*serial_number*)	Converts an Excel date/time serial number to a year.
YEARFRAC(*start_date, end_date, basis*)	Returns the difference between start_date and end_date, expressed as a number of years, including the decimal fraction of a year.

TABLE A.2 FINANCIAL SPREADSHEET FUNCTIONS IN XCELSIUS 2008

Spreadsheet Function	Description
DB(*cost, salvage, life, period, month*)	Returns the depreciation of an asset for a specified period, using the fixed declining balance method.
DDB(*cost, salvage, life, period, factor*)	Returns the depreciation of an asset for a specified period, using the double-declining balance method or some other method that is specified.

continues

TABLE A.2   CONTINUED

Spreadsheet Function	Description
FV(*rate, nper, pmt, pv, type*)	Returns the future value of an investment.
IPMT(*rate, per, nper, pv, fv, type*)	Returns the amount of the interest element in a payment for an investment for a given period.
IRR(*values, guess*)	Returns the internal rate of return for a series of cash flows.
MIRR(*values, finance_rate, reinvest_rate*)	Returns the modified internal rate of return, based on different finance and reinvestment rates for negative and positive cash flows.
NPER(*rate, pmt, pv, fv, type*)	Returns the number of periods for an investment.
NPV(*rate, value1, value2, ...*)	Returns the net present value of an investment, based on a series of periodic cash flows and a discount rate, where the first cash flow is received at the end of the first period.
PMT(*rate, nper, pv, fv, type*)	Returns the periodic payment for an annuity.
PPMT(*rate, per, nper, pv, fv, type*)	Returns the amount of principal element in a payment for an investment for a given period.
PV(*rate, nper, pmt, fv, type*)	Returns the present value of an investment.
RATE(*nper, pmt, pv, fv, type, guess*)	Returns the interest rate per period of an annuity.
SLN(*cost, salvage, life*)	Returns the straight-line depreciation of an asset for one period.
SYD(*cost, salvage, life, per*)	Returns the sum of years' digits depreciation of an asset for a specified period.
VDB(*cost, salvage, life, start_period, end_period, factor, no_switch*)	Returns the depreciation of an asset for a specified or partial period, using a variable declining balance method.

TABLE A.3   LOGIC SPREADSHEET FUNCTIONS IN XCELSIUS 2008

Spreadsheet Function	Description
AND(*logical1, logical2, ...*)	Returns TRUE if all its arguments are TRUE.
IF(*logical_test, value_if_true, value_if_false*) IF(*logical_test, value_if_true*)	Returns *logical_test* if *value_if_true* evaluates to TRUE. If *logical_test* evaluates to FALSE, IF returns *value_if_false*, and if *value_if_false* is not supplied, it simply returns FALSE.
ISBLANK(*value*)	Returns TRUE if *value* is blank.
ISERR(*value*)	Returns TRUE if evaluating *value* returns an error other than the #N/A error.

Spreadsheet Function	Description
ISERROR(value)	Returns TRUE if evaluating value returns any kind of error including #N/A, #VALUE!, #REF!, #DIV/0!, #NUM!, #NAME?, or #NULL!.
ISEVEN(value)	Returns TRUE if value is a whole number divisible by 2 having no remainders.
ISLOGICAL(value)	Returns TRUE if value is a TRUE or FALSE value.
ISNA(value)	Returns TRUE if value is the #N/A error value.
ISNONTEXT(value)	Returns TRUE if value is any item that is not text. ISNONTEXT returns TRUE when a cell is blank, but if a cell equates to an empty string, it returns FALSE.
ISODD(value)	Returns FALSE if value is a whole number divisible by 2 having no remainders.
ISNUMBER(value)	Returns TRUE if value is a number.
ISTEXT(value)	Returns TRUE if the value is in the form of text.
NOT(logical)	Reverses the logic of the argument.
OR(logical1, logical2, ...)	Returns TRUE if any argument is TRUE.

TABLE A.4   MATH SPREADSHEET FUNCTIONS IN XCELSIUS 2008

Spreadsheet Function	Description
ABS(number)	Returns the absolute value of a number.
ACOS(number)	Returns the arccosine of a number, in radians.
ACOSH(number)	Returns the inverse hyperbolic cosine of a number.
ASIN(number)	Returns the arcsine of a number, in radians.
ASINH(number)	Returns the inverse hyperbolic sine of a number.
ATAN(number)	Returns the arctangent of a number, in radians.
ATAN2(x_num, y_num)	Returns the arctangent from X and Y coordinates, in radians.
ATANH(number)	Returns the inverse hyperbolic tangent of a number.
CEILING(number, significance)	Rounds a number away from zero, to the nearest multiple of significance.
COS(number)	Returns the cosine of a given angle, given in radians.
COSH(number)	Returns the hyperbolic cosine of a number.
DEGREES(angle)	Converts radians to degrees.

continues

TABLE A.4 CONTINUED

Spreadsheet Function	Description
DOLLAR(*number, decimals*)	Converts a number to text, using currency format.
DPRODUCT(*database, field, criteria*)	Multiplies the values in a particular field of records that match the specified criteria in a database.
EVEN(*number*)	Rounds a number away from zero, to the nearest even integer.
EXP(*number*)	Returns e (= 2.71828182845904) raised to the power of a given number.
FIXED(*number, decimals, no_commas*)	Formats a number as text, with a fixed number of decimals.
FLOOR(*number, significance*)	Rounds a number down toward zero, to the nearest multiple of significance.
FORECAST(*x, known_y's, known_x's*)	Calculates a predicted value of y for a given x value based on known values for x and y.
INT(*number*)	Rounds a number to the left on a number line. (Positive rounds toward zero. Negative rounds away from zero.).
INTERCEPT(*known_y's, known_x's*)	Calculates from given x and y values the point at which a line will intersect the Y-axis.
LN(*number*)	Returns the natural logarithm (base e = 2.71828182845904) of a number.
LOG(*number, base*)	Returns the logarithm of a number to a specified base.
LOG10(*number*)	Returns the base-10 logarithm of a number.
MOD(*number, divisor*)	Returns the remainder from division, with the result having the same sign as the divisor.
N(*value*)	Returns a value converted to a number.
PI()	Returns the number 3.14159265358979, the mathematical constant pi, accurate to 15 digits.
POWER(*number, power*)	Returns the result of a number raised to a power.
PRODUCT(*number1, number2, ...*)	Multiplies together 1–30 numbers.
QUOTIENT(*numerator, denominator*)	Returns the integer portion of a division.
RADIANS(*angle*)	Converts degrees to radians.
ROUND(*number, num_digits*)	Rounds a number to a specified number of digits to the left (-) or right (+) of the decimal point. The midway digit 5 is rounded away from zero.

Spreadsheet Function	Description
ROUNDDOWN(*number, num_digits*)	Rounds a number down toward zero, to a specified number of digits to the left (-) or right (+) of the decimal point.
ROUNDUP(*number, num_digits*)	Round a number up away from zero, to a specified number of digits to the left (-) or right (+) of the decimal point.
SIGN(*number*)	Returns 1 for positive numbers, 0 if the number is zero, and -1 if the number is negative.
SIN(*number*)	Returns the sine of a given angle, in radians.
SINH(*number*)	Returns the hyperbolic sine of a given angle.
SQRT(*number*)	Returns a positive square root.
TAN(*number*)	Returns the tangent of a given angle, in radians.
TANH(*number*)	Returns the hyperbolic tangent of a number.
TRUNC(*number, num_digits*)	Truncates a number to an integer or to specified precision by removing the fractional part of the number. (Serves to round down toward zero.)
VALUE(*text*)	Converts a text argument to a number.

TABLE A.5 REFERENCE SPREADSHEET FUNCTIONS IN XCELSIUS 2008

Spreadsheet Function	Description
CHOOSE(*index_num, value1, value2, ...*)	Uses a specified index number to select an index from up to 29 specified values.
DGET(*database, field, criteria*)	Extracts from a specified database a single value that matches specified criteria.
HLOOKUP(*lookup_value, table_array, row_index_num, range_lookup*)	Looks in the top row of a table or array and returns the value of the indicated cell. Note that HLOOKUP uses only the initial values of *table_array*. That is, HLOOKUP ignores changes to the cells associated with *table_array* anytime after loading.
INDEX(*array, row_num, column_num*) INDEX(*reference, row_num, column_num, area_num*)	Alternative forms. The *array* form returns a value or an array of values. The *reference* form returns a reference. Volatile pre-Excel 97.

continues

TABLE A.5 CONTINUED

Spreadsheet Function	Description
LOOKUP(`lookup_value, lookup_vector, result_vector`) LOOKUP(`lookup_value, array`)	Alternative forms. The vector form looks up values in a one-row or one-column range and returns a value in a second one-row or one-column range. The array form looks in the first row or column of an array for the specified value and returns a value from the same position in the last row or column of the array.
MATCH(`lookup_value, lookup_array, match_type`)	Returns the relative position of an item in an array that matches a specified value in a specified order.
OFFSET(`reference, rows, cols, height, width`)	Returns a reference to a range that is a specified number of rows and columns from a cell or range of cells. Volatile.
TYPE(`value`)	Returns a numeric value that corresponds to the data type of `value`. (1 if it is a number, 2 if it is text, 4 if it is a logical value, 16 if it is an error value, and 64 if it is an array.)
VLOOKUP(`lookup_value, table_array, col_index_num, range_lookup`)	Locates a specified value in the leftmost column of a specified table and returns the value in the same row from a specified column in the table. Note that VLOOKUP uses only the initial values of `table_array`. That is, VLOOKUP ignores changes to the cells associated with `table_array` anytime after loading.

TABLE A.6 STATISTICAL SPREADSHEET FUNCTIONS IN XCELSIUS 2008

Spreadsheet Function	Description
AVEDEV(`number1, number2, …`)	Returns the average of the absolute deviations of data points from their mean.
AVERAGE(`number1, number2, …`)	Returns the average (arithmetic mean) of up to 30 numeric arguments.
AVERAGEA(`value1, value2, …`)	Returns the average (arithmetic mean) of its arguments and includes evaluation of text and logical arguments.
BETADIST(`x, alpha, beta, A, B`)	Returns the cumulative beta probability density function.
COMBIN(`number, number_chosen`)	Returns the number of combinations for a given number of objects.

Spreadsheet Function	Description
COUNT(*value1, value2, ...*)	Counts the number of cells that contain numbers and also numbers within the list of arguments.
COUNTA(*value1, value2, ...*)	Counts how many values are in the list of arguments.
COUNTIF(*range, criteria*)	Counts the number of cells that meet the criteria specified in the argument.
DCOUNT(*database, field, criteria*)	Counts the cells containing numbers from a specified database that match specified criteria.
DCOUNTA(*database, field, criteria*)	Counts non-blank cells from a specified database that match specified criteria.
DEVSQ(*number1, number2, ...*)	Returns the sum of the squares of the deviations from the sample mean.
DMAX(*database, field, criteria*)	Extracts the maximum number in a column of a list or database that matches specified conditions.
DMIN(*database, field, criteria*)	Extracts the minimum number in a column of a list or database that matches specified conditions.
DSTDEV(*database, field, criteria*)	Estimates standard deviation of a population, based on a sample, using numbers in a column of a list or database that match specified conditions.
DSTDEVP(*database, field, criteria*)	Calculates the standard deviation based on the entire population, using numbers in a column of a list or database that match specified conditions.
DSUM(*database, field, criteria*)	Adds the numbers in the field column of records in the database that match the specified criteria.
DVAR(*database, field, criteria*)	Estimates the variance of a population, based on a sample, by using the numbers in a column of a list or database that match specified criteria.
DVARP(*database, field, criteria*)	Calculates the variance of a population, based on the entire population, by using the numbers in a column of a list or database that match specified criteria.
EXPONDIST(*x, lambda, cumulative*)	Returns the exponential distribution.
FACT(*Number*)	Returns the factorial of a number.
FISHER(*x*)	Returns the Fisher transformation at x.
FISHERINV(*y*)	Returns the inverse of the Fisher transformation.
GEOMEAN(*number1, number2, ...*)	Returns the geometric mean of an array or a range of positive data.
HARMEAN(*number1, number2, ...*)	Returns the harmonic mean of a dataset by calculating the reciprocal of the arithmetic mean of reciprocals.

continues

TABLE A.6 CONTINUED

Spreadsheet Function	Description
KURT(*number1*, *number2*, ...)	Returns the kurtosis of a dataset, a measure that compares the relative peakedness or flatness of a distribution compared with the normal distribution.
LARGE(*array*, *k*)	Returns the *k*th largest value in a dataset.
MAX(*number1*, *number2*, ...)	Returns the maximum value in a list of arguments, ignoring logical values and text.
MEDIAN(*number1*, *number2*, ...)	Returns the median of the given numbers.
MIN(*number1*, *number2*, ...)	Returns the minimum value in a list of arguments, ignoring logical values and text.
MODE(*number1*, *number2*, ...)	Returns the most common value in a dataset.
NORMDIST(*x*, *mean*, *standard_dev*, *cumulative*)	Returns the cumulative distribution function or probability mass function for the value x, with specified mean and standard deviation.
NORMINV(*probability*, *mean*, *standard_dev*)	Returns the inverse of the normal cumulative distribution for the specified probability, mean, and standard deviation.
NORMSINV(*probability*)	Returns the inverse of the standard normal cumulative distribution.
RAND()	Returns an evenly distributed random number greater than or equal to 0 and less than 1. RAND is a volatile function; which means it cannot be used to generate the same sequence of values as the function is repeatedly calculated.
RANK(*number*, *ref*, *order*)	Returns the rank of a number in a list of numbers.
SMALL(*array*, *k*)	Returns the *k*th smallest value in a dataset.
STANDARDIZE(*x*, *mean*, *standard_dev*)	Returns a normalized value from a distribution with known *mean* and *standard_dev*.
STDEV(*number1*, *number2*, ...)	Estimates standard distribution based on a sample, ignoring text and logical values.
SUM(*number1*, *number2*, ...)	Adds its arguments. Note that in contrast to Excel, the SUM function in Xcelsius 2008 treats TRUE and FALSE values as if they are zero. In addition, text values that appear as numbers are treated as if they are zero.
SUMIF(*range*, *criteria*[, *sum_range*])	Adds the cells specified by the given criteria.

Spreadsheet Function	Description
SUMPRODUCT(array1, array2, array3, ...)	Returns the sum of the products of corresponding array components.
SUMSQ(number1, number2, ...)	Returns the sum of the squares of 1–30 numbers.
SUMX2MY2(array_x, array_y)	Returns the sum of the difference of squares of corresponding values in two arrays.
SUMX2PY2(array_x, array_y)	Returns the sum of the sum of squares of corresponding values in two arrays.
SUMXMY2(array_x, array_y)	Returns the sum of squares of differences of corresponding values in two array.
VAR(number1, number2, ...)	Estimates variance based on a sample, ignoring logical values and text.

TABLE A.7 TEXT-RELATED SPREADSHEET FUNCTIONS IN XCELSIUS 2008

Spreadsheet Function	Description
CONCATENATE(text1, text2, ...)	Joins several text items into one text item.
EXACT(text1, text2)	Checks whether two text values are identical.
FIND(find_text, within_text [, start_num])	Finds one text value within another (case-sensitive).
LEFT(text, num_chars)	Returns the leftmost characters from a text value.
LEN(text)	Returns the number of characters in a text string.
LOWER(text)	Converts text to lowercase.
MID(text, start_num, num_chars)	Returns a specific number of characters from a string, starting at a specified position.
REPLACE(old_text, start_num, num_chars, new_text)	Replaces characters within text.
REPT(text, number_times)	Repeats text a given number of times.
RIGHT(text, num_chars)	Returns the rightmost characters from a text value.
TEXT(value, format_text)	Formats a number and converts it to text.
UPPER(text)	Converts text to uppercase.

LOGICAL VALUES AND SPREADSHEET OPERATORS IN XCELSIUS 2008

The use of operators in a spreadsheet is so fundamental and ingrained in our thinking that we almost take operators for granted. It is helpful to enumerate them explicitly (see Tables A.8 and A.9).

TABLE A.8   LOGICAL VALUES IN XCELSIUS 2008

Logical Value	Description

TRUE	TRUE is a Boolean literal value used to signify when some condition is satisfied. For instance, the following two spreadsheet formulas return identical results:
	`=IF(99>58,"Test passes","Test fails")`
	`=IF(TRUE,"Test passes","Test fails")`
	Both formulas return Test passes.
	Note that when TRUE or an expression that evaluates to TRUE is coerced into a numeric value in the underlying spreadsheet of an Xcelsius dashboard, it is treated as 0 and not as 1.
	For example:
	`=10*(1+TRUE) returns 10`
	`=10*(1+(3>2) returns 10`
	In Excel, the value that would be returned for both of these formulas would be 20.

FALSE	FALSE is a Boolean literal value used to signify when some condition is not satisfied. For instance, the following two spreadsheet formulas return identical results:
	`=IF(43>58,"Test passes","Test fails")`
	`=IF(TRUE,"Test passes","Test fails")`
	Both formulas return Test fails.

TABLE A.9   SPREADSHEET OPERATORS IN XCELSIUS 2008

Spreadsheet Operator	Description
= (assignment operator)	The assignment operator is used to identify a spreadsheet formula with a cell. In this context, the = symbol must be the very first character to appear in the spreadsheet formula. For example, `=2+3` returns the value 5.
= (logical equality operator)	The logical equality operator returns a Boolean TRUE or FALSE, depending on whether two expressions evaluate to the same value. For example, `=IF(2=3,"2 equals 3","2 doesn't equal 3")` returns 2 doesn't equal 3.
/ (division operator)	The division operator returns the numeric ratio of two expressions. For example, `=6/2` returns 3.

Spreadsheet Operator	Description
' (comment operator)	The comment operator (signified by an apostrophe symbol appearing as the very first character of the spreadsheet cell contents) signifies that the remainder of the expression is to be treated as literal text and cannot be evaluated as a conventional spreadsheet formula. For example, `'=2*3` returns =2*3.
^ (exponentiation operator)	The exponentiation operator raises an expression to a given power. For example, `=2^3` returns 8.
>= (greater-than-or-equal-to operator)	The >= operator tests whether the first expression is greater than or equal to the second expression. For example, `=3>=3` returns TRUE.
> (greater-than operator)	The > operator tests whether the first expression is strictly greater than the second expression. For example, `=3>3` returns FALSE.
<= (less-than-or-equal-to operator)	The <= operator tests whether the first expression is less than or equal to the second expression. For example, `=2<=3` returns TRUE.
< (less-than operator)	The < operator tests whether the first expression is strictly less than the second expression. For example, `=-30<5` returns TRUE.
- (minus operator)	The minus operator reverses the sign of an expression from positive to negative and vice versa. The minus operator requires only one input. It also has a higher precedence than the subtraction operation (see Chapter 4, "The Spreadsheet: The Secret Sauce of Xcelsius 2008," for details). For example, `=-(3+5)` returns -8.

continues

TABLE A.9 CONTINUED

Spreadsheet Operator	Description
- (subtraction operator)	The subtraction operator requires two inputs. It multiplies the second input by a negative 1 and then adds it to the first operator. For example, `=17-5` returns 12.
+ (addition operator)	The addition operator returns the numeric sum of its two inputs. For example, `=13+5` returns 18.
* (multiplication operator)	The multiplication operator returns the numeric product of its two inputs. For example, `=13*5` returns 65.
& (concatenation operator)	The concatenation operator joins two text values. For example, `="4th"&"of July"` returns 4th of July.
<> (not-equal operator)	The <> operator returns TRUE if two expressions do not evaluate to the same value; otherwise, it returns FALSE. For example, `=3<>2+1` returns FALSE.
: (range operator)	The RANGE_COLON operator specifies a contiguous range of cells between and including two cell references. The RANGE_COLON operator is always used in conjunction with other spreadsheet functions, such as SUM, AVERAGE, MIN, or MAX. For example, `=SUM(A1:A3)` returns the values computed by adding the cell values of A1, A2, and A3.

Xcelsius Product Family Comparison

In this appendix

Xcelsius 2008 encompasses a broad range of products, including Present, Engage, Engage Server, and Enterprise editions. This book is largely centered on Xcelsius 2008 Engage. Although most of the features described and the book examples pertaining to Xcelsius 2008 Engage apply equally well to the other Xcelsius editions, there are some differences between the different editions.

Many of the components and functionality features of Xcelsius are covered in detail throughout the book, so I do not embellish on them here. My chief aim here is to highlight what is similar and different among the various Xcelsius editions.

To help you sort out these similarities and differences, this appendix includes tables that list the various Xcelsius features and whether each feature is supported in the various Xcelsius editions. A "Y" indicates that a feature is available, and an "N" means it is not.

The tables are organized in two broad categories: general functionality within Xcelsius and specific components.

XCELSIUS FUNCTIONALITY

The general functionality in Xcelsius includes features that do the following:

- Are typically pervasive (such as scaling and drill down)
- Are relevant to getting started
- Are important for font support
- Indicate available data update options
- Indicate available export and snapshot options
- Show the supported themes and styles.

Tables B.1 through B.8 provide information on the functionality of the various Xcelsius editions.

TABLE B.1 GENERAL XCELSIUS FUNCTIONALITY

Feature	Present	Engage	Engage Server	Enterprise
Drill down charts	Y	Y	Y	Y
Logarithmic scale for charts	Y	Y	Y	Y
Dynamic chart scale	Y	Y	Y	Y
Dynamic data sources	Y	Y	Y	Y
Dynamic minimum and maximum limits (charts and single values)	Y	Y	Y	Y
Add-on Manager	Y	Y	Y	Y
Animation (charts)	Y	Y	Y	Y
Alerts in selectors	Y	Y	Y	Y

Feature	Present	Engage	Engage Server	Enterprise
Insert filtered range	Y	Y	Y	Y
Dynamic selected item	Y	Y	Y	Y
Print from SWF	Y	Y	Y	Y
Secondary axis (charts)	Y	Y	Y	Y
Value-based alerts	Y	Y	Y	Y

TABLE B.2   EFFICIENCY FEATURES

Feature	Present	Engage	Engage Server	Enterprise
Templates	Y	Y	Y	Y
Samples	Y	Y	Y	Y
Quick Start pane	Y	Y	Y	Y

TABLE B.3   FONT SUPPORT OPTIONS

Facility	Present	Engage	Engage Server	Enterprise
Support for non-embedded fonts	Y	Y	Y	Y
Support for Unicode	Y	Y	Y	Y

TABLE B.4   DATA UPDATE OPTIONS

Option	Present	Engage	Engage Server	Enterprise
Data Manager	N	Y	Y	Y
Use another Excel file	Y	Y	Y	Y
Use Web Services (via SOAP; new)	N	Y	Y	Y
Use Flash variables	N	Y	Y	Y
Enable collaboration	N	Y	Y	Y
Export model (to Excel)	Y	Y	Y	Y
Ignore end blanks	Y	Y	Y	Y
XML map options (Excel 2003)	N	Y	Y	Y
Live Office	N	N	N	Y
Query as a Web Service (QaaWS)	N	N	N	Y
Connection Manager	N	Y	Y	Y
FSCommand	N	Y	Y	Y

TABLE B.5   EXPORT OPTIONS

Deployment Format	Present	Engage	Engage Server	Enterprise
Macromedia Flash	N	Y	Y	Y
HTML	N	Y	Y	Y
Power Point	Y	Y	Y	Y
Outlook	N	Y	Y	Y
PDF	Y	Y	Y	Y
Word	Y	Y	Y	Y
Portal	N	N	Y	Y
Business Objects Enterprise	N	N	N	Y
Crystal Report	N	Y	Y	Y
AIR	N	Y	Y	Y
Acrobat 9	Y	Y	Y	Y

TABLE B.6   SNAPSHOT OPTIONS

Format or Environment	Present	Engage	Engage Server	Enterprise
Macromedia Flash	N	Y	Y	Y
HTML	N	Y	Y	Y
PowerPoint	Y	Y	Y	Y
Outlook	N	Y	Y	Y
Export to Excel	Y	Y	Y	Y
PDF	Y	Y	Y	Y
AIR	N	Y	Y	Y
Acrobat 9	Y	Y	Y	Y

TABLE B.7   ART AIDS

Theme or Style	Present	Engage	Engage Server	Enterprise
Color schemes (global styles)	Y	Y	Y	Y
Élan skin	Y	Y	Y	Y
Aqua skin	Y	Y	Y	Y
Aero skin	Y	Y	Y	Y
Graphite skin	Y	Y	Y	Y
Halo skin	Y	Y	Y	Y

Theme or Style	Present	Engage	Engage Server	Enterprise
Windows Classic	Y	Y	Y	Y
Admiral	Y	Y	Y	Y
iTheme	Y	Y	Y	Y
Nova	Y	Y	Y	Y

TABLE B.8   SERVER PIECES

Backend Support	Present	Engage	Engage Server	Enterprise
SharePoint	N	N	Y	Y
WebSphere	N	N	Y	Y
Flynet	N	N	Y	N
Reporting Services	N	N	Y	Y

XCELSIUS COMPONENTS

Xcelsius components are organized into the following categories: Charts, Containers, Single-Value Components, Selectors, Maps, Art & Backgrounds, Text, Web Connectivity, and Other Components. These categories correspond to matching categories found on the Components Panel of the Xcelsius Designer. Tables B.9 through B.17 identify which components are available in the various Xcelsius editions.

TABLE B.9   CHART COMPONENTS

Component	Present	Engage	Engage Server	Enterprise
Line Chart	Y	Y	Y	Y
Pie Chart	Y	Y	Y	Y
OHLC Chart	Y	Y	Y	Y
Candlestick Chart	Y	Y	Y	Y
Column Chart	Y	Y	Y	Y
Stacked Column Chart	Y	Y	Y	Y
Bar Chart	Y	Y	Y	Y
Stacked Bar Chart	Y	Y	Y	Y
Combination Chart	Y	Y	Y	Y
Bubble Chart	Y	Y	Y	Y

continues

TABLE B.9 CONTINUED

Component	Present	Engage	Engage Server	Enterprise
XY Chart	Y	Y	Y	Y
Area Chart	Y	Y	Y	Y
Stacked Area Chart	Y	Y	Y	Y
Radar Chart	Y	Y	Y	Y
Filled Radar Chart	Y	Y	Y	Y
Tree Map	Y	Y	Y	Y

TABLE B.10 CONTAINER COMPONENTS

Component	Present	Engage	Engage Server	Enterprise
Panel	Y	Y	Y	Y
Tab Set	Y	Y	Y	Y

TABLE B.11 SINGLE-VALUE COMPONENTS

Component	Present	Engage	Engage Server	Enterprise
Play Button	N	Y	Y	Y
Gauge	Y	Y	Y	Y
Half Gauge	Y	Y	Y	Y
Dial	Y	Y	Y	Y
Horizontal Slider	Y	Y	Y	Y
Vertical Slider	Y	Y	Y	Y
Horizontal Progress Bar	Y	Y	Y	Y
Vertical Progress Bar	Y	Y	Y	Y
Value	Y	Y	Y	Y
Dual Slider	Y	Y	Y	Y
Spinner	Y	Y	Y	Y

TABLE B.12 SELECTOR COMPONENTS

Component	Present	Engage	Engage Server	Enterprise
Radio Button	Y	Y	Y	Y
List Box	Y	Y	Y	Y

Component	Present	Engage	Engage Server	Enterprise
Check Box	Y	Y	Y	Y
Label Based Menu	Y	Y	Y	Y
Table	Y	Y	Y	Y
Play Selector	N	Y	Y	Y
Combo Box	Y	Y	Y	Y
Filter	Y	Y	Y	Y
Toggle Button	Y	Y	Y	Y
Icon	Y	Y	Y	Y
List Builder	Y	Y	Y	Y
Source Data Component	N	Y	Y	Y
Ticker	Y	Y	Y	Y
Accordion Menu	N	Y	Y	Y
Sliding Picture Menu	Y	Y	Y	Y
Fish-Eye Picture Menu	Y	Y	Y	Y
List View	Y	Y	Y	Y

TABLE B.13   MAP COMPONENTS

Component by Geographic Region	Present	Engage	Engage Server	Enterprise
United States by State	Y	Y	Y	Y
Europe Map by Country	Y	Y	Y	Y
World Map by Continent	Y	Y	Y	Y
Asia Map by Country	Y	Y	Y	Y
California Map by County	Y	Y	Y	Y
Africa Map by Country	Y	Y	Y	Y
North America Map by Country	Y	Y	Y	Y
Central America Map by Country	Y	Y	Y	Y
South America Map by Country	Y	Y	Y	Y
USA (50 states)	Y	Y	Y	Y
Europe Maps	Y	Y	Y	Y
Asia-Pacific Maps	Y	Y	Y	Y
Canada by Province	Y	Y	Y	Y

TABLE B.14   ART AND BACKGROUND COMPONENTS

Component	Present	Engage	Engage Server	Enterprise
Horizontal Line	Y	Y	Y	Y
Vertical Line	Y	Y	Y	Y
Background	Y	Y	Y	Y
Rectangle	Y	Y	Y	Y
Ellipse	Y	Y	Y	Y
Image Component	Y	Y	Y	Y

TABLE B.15   TEXT COMPONENTS

Component	Present	Engage	Engage Server	Enterprise
Label	Y	Y	Y	Y
Input Text	Y	Y	Y	Y
Input Text Area	Y	Y	Y	Y

TABLE B.16   WEB CONNECTIVITY COMPONENTS

Component	Present	Engage	Engage Server	Enterprise
XML Data Button	N	Y	Y	Y
XML Map Refresh	N	Y	Y	Y
Web Service Connector	N	Y	Y	Y
URL Link Button	Y	Y	Y	Y
External Slide Show	N	Y	Y	Y
Reporting Services Button	N	N	Y	Y
Portal Consumer	N	N	Y	Y
Portal Provider	N	N	Y	Y
Portal Param	N	N	Y	Y
Connection Refresh Button	N	Y	Y	Y

TABLE B.17   OTHER COMPONENTS

Component	Present	Engage	Engage Server	Enterprise
Interactive Calendar	N	Y	Y	Y
Trend Icon	Y	Y	Y	Y

Component	Present	Engage	Engage Server	Enterprise
Local Scenario Buttons	Y	Y	Y	Y
Grid	Y	Y	Y	Y
Panel Set	N	Y	Y	Y
History Component	N	Y	Y	Y
Trend Analyzer	N	Y	Y	Y
Print Button	Y	Y	Y	Y
Reset Button	Y	Y	Y	Y

APPENDIX C

XCELSIUS BEST PRACTICE TECHNIQUES AND HIP POCKET TIPS

This book is loaded with all sorts of valuable information. To make this information more conveniently accessible, I've listed more than 100 of this book's best practice techniques and tips in this appendix. They are arranged by technique, chapter, and section. Within the chapter text, a corresponding "Best Practice Tip" icon identifies each tip.

Best Practice	Chapter Number—Section Title (Page Number)
1. ABC charts and merging data	Chapter 14—"Constructing ABC (Actual Budget Comparison) Charts" (page 344)
2. Adding features and interactivity to your custom components	Chapter 16—"Enhancing Your Components" (page 393)
3. Adjusting for headers when clicking rows	Chapter 6—"Using Gauges" (page 172)
4. Aging a dashboard report	Chapter 10—"Preparing an Aging Report" (page 264)
5. Alerts in input devices such as sliders	Chapter 6—"Simple Sliders" (page 161)
6. Avoiding using hardwired values in spreadsheet formulas	Chapter 13—"Issues with Hardwired Values and What to Do with Them" (page 325)
7. Avoiding potential pitfalls in designing custom components	Chapter 16—"Avoiding Potential Landmines" (page 396)
8. Baselining specific data series	Chapter 14—"Charting Multiple Data Series That Have Similar Values" (page 339)
9. Battlefield testing of a custom component	Chapter 16—"Loading and Testing Components" (page 393)
10. Benefits of statistics—data compression	Chapter 9—"Understanding Statistics" (page 230)
11. Candlestick box plot design	Chapter 14—"Using a Candlestick Component as a Box Plot" (page 347)
12. Caption display technique	Chapter 5—"Displaying Values of Individual Data Points" (page 147)

Best Practice	Chapter Number—Section Title (Page Number)
53. HTML coding for labels and input text area components	Chapter 8—"Labels and Input Text Areas" (page 219)
54. HTML encoding in dashboard text	Chapter 12—"Using Smart Text in Visualizations and Dashboards" (page 302)
55. HTML labels embedded in a dashboard	Chapter 3—"Text-Based Components" (page 54)
56. Inline traffic light alerts	Chapter 8—"Traffic Light Alerts in Combo Boxes and List Boxes" (page 210)
57. Inline alerts	Chapter 12—"List Box and Other Inline Alerts" (page 309)
58. Inputs and outputs explicitly stated in the underlying spreadsheet	Chapter 1—"Xcelsius: The Whole Is Greater Than the Sum of Its Parts" (page 22)
59. Intelligently detecting transposed digits	Chapter 13—"Detecting the Presence of Transposed Digits" (page 318)
60. Layered approach design pattern	Chapter 13—"Repurposing Existing Spreadsheets" (page 329)
61. Layered design approach	Chapter 12—"List Box and Other Inline Alerts" (page 310)
62. Linking a text label to a spreadsheet cell that contains a formula	Chapter 3—"Text-Based Components" (page 53)
63. List Builder—general construction technique	Chapter 5—"Avoiding Needless Data Series Congestion" (page 137)
64. Logarithmic scaling	Chapter 5—"Dealing with Vastly Different Values on the Same Chart" (page 152)
65. Mathematics of the least-squares method	Chapter 9—"Method of Least Squares" (page 255)
66. Matrix style calculator	Chapter 2—"Embedding Spreadsheet Smarts in a Dashboard" (page 34)
67. Multi-criteria filters	Chapter 8—"Filter Components" (page 214)
68. Multi-selection maps	Chapter 11—"The Technical Details Behind a Multi-Selection Map" (page 287)
69. Negative values in bubble charts	Chapter 5—"Extending Graphical Presentation with Bubble Charts" (page 146)
70. Negatively directed sliders	Chapter 6—"Negatively Directed Sliders" (page 162)
71. Overcoming design-time formatting challenges	Chapter 8—"Grid and Spreadsheet Table Components" (page 225)
72. Parsing data into columns	Chapter 13—"Dealing with Raw Data" (page 319)

Best Practice	Chapter Number—Section Title (Page Number)
73. Placing destination cells above spreadsheet data	Chapter 11—"Using a Map to Obtain Further Information" (page 279)
74. Pointer-based approach to filters	Chapter 8—"Filter Components" (page 215)
75. Positioning destination cells above the source data	Chapter 13—"Poorly Positioned Data on a Worksheet" (page 324)
76. Properly setting up cell references in VLOOKUP formulas	Chapter 13—"Setting Up Cell References in a VLOOKUP Formula" (page 326)
77. Pushing with pointers versus pushing with content	Chapter 6—"Using Gauges" (page 173)
78. Recommended practices for line charts	Chapter 14—"Viewing Line Chart Data" (page 343)
79. Reconstructing data	Chapter 13—"Dealing with Improperly Structured Data" (page 331)
80. Retrieving a range of cells with offset	Chapter 4—"Retrieving a Range of Cells with OFFSET" (page 120)
81. Retrieving a single cell with offset	Chapter 4—"Retrieving a Single Cell with OFFSET" (page 119)
82. Setting up a continuous distribution	Chapter 9—"The Normal Distribution" (page 247)
83. Setting up a Web Services connection	Chapter 15—"Using Web Services in Xcelsius 2008" (page 365)
84. Setting up matrix-style calculators	Chapter 13—"Setting Up Cell References in a Multiplication Table" (page 327)
85. Setup of the Trend Analyzer component	Chapter 9—"The Trend Analyzer Component" (page 252)
86. Shared Component Framework	Chapter 6—"Dial Sharing: A Best Practice Strategy" (page 169)
87. Simulating RANDBETWEEN	Chapter 4—"RAND, NORMINV, and NORMDIST" (page 92)
88. Smart sliders—general setup	Chapter 6—"Smart Sliders" (page 162)
89. Smart sliders—interface design	Chapter 12—"Going Beyond the Built-in Alerts in Xcelsius" (page 311)
90. Smart triggers—using a single formula with multiple criteria	Chapter 15—"Using Web Services in Xcelsius 2008" (page 366)
91. Spreadsheet formulas: recommended techniques for constructing formulas	Chapter 4—"Building on Simple Formulas" (page 71)
92. Statistical sampling with Xcelsius	Chapter 9—"Extrapolating from a Sample to the Population" (page 250)

INDEX

Bayes' Theorem, 241-242

Behavior tab (Properties panel), 24

BETADIST function, 408

binding attributes to underlying spreadsheet, 24-26

binomial distributions, 244-246

branding visual elements, 194

bubble charts, 145-146

budgets, ABC (Actual Budget Comparison) charts, 344-346

built-in alerts, 298-299

buttons, toggle buttons, 190

C

calendar arithmetic
at dashboard level, 114-115
setting up on spreadsheets, 113-114

Calendar component, 223

Candlestick components, 347-350

canvas
adding components to, 19-21
definition of, 46
resizing, 48

capabilities of Xcelsius, 16-17

caret (^), 413

cash, statement of, 262

cash-basis accounting, 262

Category I digitization errors, 317

Category II digitization errors, 317

Category III digitization errors, 318

CDF (cumulative distributions function), 246

CEILING function, 100, 405

cells
evaluating, 79-80
formatting in Spreadsheet Table component, 224-225
named ranges, 77-79
references, 73
absolute references, 73-74
in complex tables, 327
example, 75-76
hybrid cell references, 74-75
isolating hardwired values, 76-77
in multiplication tables, 327
percentage symbols in, 76
relative references, 74
in VLOOKUP formula, 326-327

chaining formulas, 72

charts
ABC (Actual Budget Comparison) charts, 344-346
avoiding occlusion, 342-343
bubble charts, 145-146
Candlestick components, 347-350
charting multiple data series with similar values, 339-341
choosing for dashboards, 128-131
column charts, 56-57, 129-131
combination charts, 132-134
dynamic data grouping, 137-138
filled radar charts, 341-342
interface design, 154
label abbreviations, 206-207
line charts, 343-344
pie charts, 54-56, 139-140
scaling, 204-206
auto-scaling, 150
logarithmic scaling, 152-153
scaling laboratory dashboard, 150-152
stacked charts, 135-136
tree maps, 148-149
Xcelsius product family comparison, 419
XY charts, 141-145

Check Box component, 189, 209-210

CHOOSE function, 123, 407

G

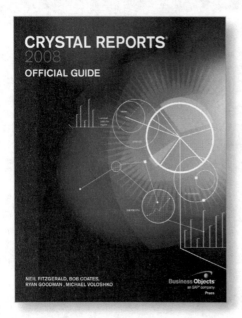

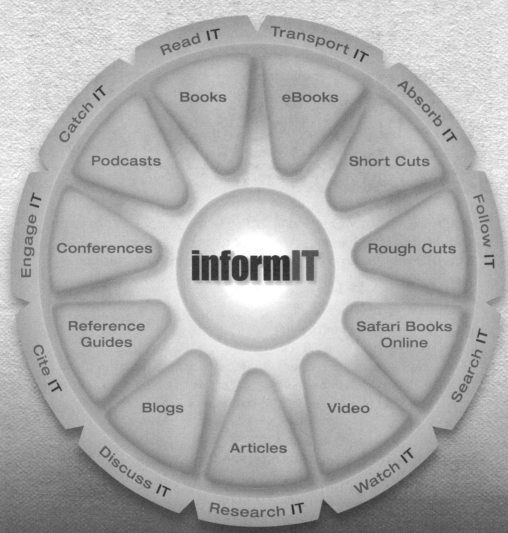

FREE Online Edition

Your purchase of **Xcelsius 2008 Dashboard Best Practices** includes access to a free online edition for 45 days through the Safari Books Online subscription service. Nearly every Sams book is available online through Safari Books Online, along with more than 5,000 other technical books and videos from publishers such as Addison-Wesley Professional, Cisco Press, Exam Cram, IBM Press, O'Reilly, Prentice Hall, and Que.

SAFARI BOOKS ONLINE allows you to search for a specific answer, cut and paste code, download chapters, and stay current with emerging technologies.

Activate your FREE Online Edition at
www.informit.com/sa

> **STEP 1:** Enter the coupon

> **STEP 2:** New Safari users .... jistration form.
> Safari subscribe

If you have difficulty registering on Safari or accessing the online edition, please e-mail customer-service@safaribooksonline.com